THE MEN'S SHED MOVEMENT

The Company of Men

Edited by
Barry Golding

THE MEN'S SHED MOVEMENT

The Company of Men

Edited by
Barry Golding

COMMON GROUND PUBLISHING 2015

First published in 2015 in Champaign, Illinois, USA
by Common Ground Publishing LLC
as part of Aging in Society books

Library of Congress Cataloging-in-Publication Data

The men's shed movement : the company of men / edited by Barry Golding.
    pages cm
 Includes bibliographical references and index.
 ISBN 978-1-61229-787-3 (pbk : alk. paper) -- ISBN 978-1-61229-788-0 (pdf)
 1. Men--Social aspects. 2. Social movements. 3. Community development. 4. Makerspaces. I. Golding, Barry.

 HQ1090.M4736 2015
 305.31--dc23

                          2015013998

Cover Photo Credit: Phillip Kalantzis-Cope

Table of Contents

Part III: Men's Shed Innovation and Diversity

Part IV: Conclusions after Two Decades of Men's Sheds

ACKNOWLEDGEMENTS

I acknowledge and sincerely thank the many inspirational and generous people in Men's Sheds organisations who have 'done the hard yards', typically in the face of considerable scepticism, difficulties and resistance, to carefully take a good Australian innovation and turn it into an active and growing international Movement in four countries to 2015.

From early beginnings less than two decades ago, Men's Sheds now have Movement status in Australia and New Zealand on one side of the globe, and the Island of Ireland[1] and the UK[2] on the other. I acknowledge the thousands of people who have been working selflessly to develop and sustain their Men's Shed organisations (often simply described as 'Sheds' in this book) for the greater good of other men, their families, the community and the Men's Shed Movement. Hundreds of these people and Men's Shed organisations have also generously shared their information, histories and stories. Those individuals who have generously assisted in some way during the researching, writing and editing of this book are sincerely thanked and acknowledged by name in Appendix 1 'Individual Acknowledgments'. My sincere thanks and apologies to those who contributed and are not named.

My particular thanks go to the Men's Shed peak bodies in Australia (AMSA), Ireland (IMSA), the UK (UKMSA) and New Zealand (MENZSHED NZ) who gave encouragement and support by generously opening up their files and providing invaluable advice and Men's Shed contacts. Specifically, I gratefully acknowledge the support and advice of David Helmers (CEO, AMSA) and Ted Donnelly (former AMSA President); John Evoy (CEO, IMSA) and George Kelly (President, IMSA); Mike Jenn (President, UKMSA); Ray Hall (President), Roger Bowman (Secretary) and Peter Blackler (Treasurer) of MENZSHEDS NZ.

---

[1] The term Island of Ireland is used in this book to refer to two separate national jurisdictions, the Republic of Ireland and Northern Ireland, the latter being administatively part of the United Kingdom. This convention is consistent with a decision by the Irish Men's Shed Movement and Assocation to 2015 to work collaboratively across national borders. Where the terms 'Irish' and 'Ireland' are used they refer to the Island of Ireland.
[2] Because of the way Ireland is defined as the Island of Ireland in this book, the term 'UK Men's Sheds' refers specifically to those Sheds on the island of Britain, comprising Scotland, England and Wales, not including those in Northern Ireland.

David Helmers and Ted Donnelly (Australia), Anne McDonnell and John Evoy (Ireland), Mike Jenn (UK) and Dr Neil Bruce (New Zealand) generously assisted researching and editing the Men's Shed histories in Chapter 5, as well as co-authoring Chapters 7 (Ireland), 8 (the UK) and 9 (New Zealand). I acknowledge the impossibility of selecting a small number of good and appropriate examples in the broad categories of 'early', 'innovative', 'remarkable' and 'new and cutting edge' Sheds for Part 3 without ruffling some feathers. While I have taken considerable effort to make this book accurate, I take full responsibility for the Sheds chosen for these case studies and for any errors that have crept into these accounts. What I have learned from this writing process is that while *all* Sheds are special, valuable and different, if all of the shedders that claim their Shed was the 'first' in some way were put in the one room, it would be a very crowded space. I acknowledge that there is no 'right' history: only the version that I have heard or read, based on my own experiences, filtered by what I have chosen to include and exclude as main author and editor.

I wish more broadly to acknowledge and sincerely thank everyone who contributed information, stories, ideas, advice, criticism and support during this intensive writing process in 2014-15. My sincere thanks to Ian Nelk, peer reviewers, editors and Common Ground Publishers. I acknowledge the invaluable support from my academic managers, Professor Lawrie Angus and Professor John McDonald as well as Federation University Australia (previously University of Ballarat) for giving me sufficient 'rope' to research and graze globally. My heartfelt thanks to Janet Bracks for her patience and support during the protracted writing and editing process, and also to Chris Bettle for generously reading and critically commenting on the draft manuscript.

I acknowledge that I come to this major writing project as both a researcher and 'insider', as Mark Thomson notes in the Foreword. It is impossible for me to be an objective and dispassionate observer of this Movement. I have been an active researcher of (and for) the Men's Shed Movement for nearly 15 years. I have often crossed the fictitious, objective, academic 'line' and become a passionate proponent, supporter and advocate of Men's Sheds. At times I have actively promoted and helped to shape the Movement in all four countries featured in the book, through conference presentations, academic papers and reports, conferences and Shed forums. In this sense, I am far from a benign and dispassionate university Professor and academic writer. While I have tried to get 'the facts' right, my apologies about whatever may be wrong or misleading.

I acknowledge that some of the many unknown men and women who actually got this Movement started will not have not been mentioned in this book.

Indeed some of them have already passed away or are very unwell up to two decades on. I also acknowledge that the Men's Shed Movement is far from running its full course, and that there needs to be more research into why and how it works: for men, families and communities.

Finally, I acknowledge that, in an ideal world, the debilitating dilemmas many men currently face, particularly when not in paid work for any reason, might be better addressed in the future in ways other than through Men's Sheds in community settings. Meantime, the Men's Shed Movement is meeting many men's otherwise unmet acute needs, overwhelmingly through committed volunteers. It is contributing positively to the lives of men, their families and communities, and also saving men's lives. Equally importantly, a wide range of service providers in very diverse fields are taking important lessons from the grassroots nature of Men's Sheds and the men's agency it encourages, and are now incorporating the growing evidence base into their everyday practice with men.

Professor Barry Golding
Federation University Australia
August 8, 2015

List of Tables, Figures, Photographs and Appendices

Tables

Figures

Photographs

Appendices

Foreword

Mark Thomson: Widely published author about Australian (backyard) sheds since 1995:

> The Men's Shed Movement book charts the rise of a remarkable social Movement from its unlikely origins in the backyards and streets of Australia to a global trend. As an insider in the creation of an immense network of community Sheds and meeting places, Barry Golding brings a unique perspective to a fascinating story. He reveals the immense untapped potential that lies within the grasp of ordinary citizens looking for connection and involvement in modern life and how they organized themselves into a powerful social force. The best part is that the Men's Shed story is still evolving. A timely and useful history.

Ted Donnelly: Founder of the best known early Men's Shed in Australia in Lane Cove, Sydney, Australia, first President of the Australian Men's Shed Association and widely respected 'Grandfather' of Men's Sheds:

> Although Men's Sheds have existed for a relatively short time there are many different versions of their history, because accurate factual information has not been available. This book, which for the first time definitively details and analyses the growth and development of Sheds in Australia, and now overseas, is very timely. Nobody is more qualified to write it than Barry Golding. Barry's research into Men's Sheds from their earliest days has given him a very wide range of contacts and information to access the data for this book. He has meticulously verified his data with the key people who were involved in the early development stages using original documents. The work that Barry has put into this book is impressive. This will become a very valuable resource for all involved in any way with Men's Sheds.

David Helmers: CEO of Australian Men's Shed Association (AMSA):

> This important book confirms that Men's Sheds in community settings did not happen overnight. It does three things. Firstly, it carefully honours and acknowledges the early Men's Shed 'pioneers' in Australia

and other countries that the Movement has since spread to. Secondly, it charts the incredible diversity of Men's Sheds. Thirdly, it considers the emerging evidence base about the wider value of the Movement and Men's Sheds to men and the wider community. It is very important after two decades to accurately tell this story: about how and where it happened, why it happened, who participates and with what benefits, as well as where this remarkable international Movement might now be headed. This knowledge is very important and timely for the future of Men's Sheds.

John Evoy: Founding CEO of Irish Men's Sheds Association (IMSA):

On behalf of the Shedders from across the Island of Ireland I would like to thank and congratulate our friend, Barry Golding, on the creation of this very valuable and insightful resource. It diligently outlines the growth and development of the Men's Sheds Movement across the globe. The arrival of Men's Sheds in Ireland was perfectly timed in terms of helping us manage some of the challenges we faced economically over the last number of years. This book outlines their evolution here including the tremendous support and guidance we received from our Australian friends who blazed a trail that we followed.

Mike Jenn: President of UK Men's Sheds Association (UKMSA) and founder of the Camden Town Men's Shed in London, the first 'grassroots' Men's Shed in the UK:

Men's Sheds have hit a nail on the head in a very timely and powerful way. The nail in this case is the need many men feel, particularly following retirement, to recreate critically important aspects of their former workplaces: particularly the social interaction, having a purpose, being able to learn and share experiences, as well as engage with tools, materials and ideas. This book documents how men and women have got together and created the resources and facilities needed. It chronicles how the idea has spread across the world, with remarkable success, and how the Men's Shed Movement has continued to evolve and develop. This book greatly informs and assists with this process.

Ray Hall: President of MENZSHED NZ, New Zealand:

MENZSHED NZ acknowledges the value of this timely book, which carefully places the Men's Shed Movement, including its development in New Zealand in the past decade, in its wider international context. It illustrates what has been achieved in New Zealand, when the simple but powerful concept of a Men's Shed in a community setting has been picked up, developed and implemented by a wide range of community groups. It charts the remarkable and rapid spread of Men's Sheds across New Zealand, achieved through the efforts of both men and women, mostly volunteers, working by establishing trusts or incorporated societies, gaining charitable status, getting building approvals and bringing together potential shedders. This has been achieved in the absence of central government funding, but supported by local councils and providers of community funding, acknowledging the huge value and potential benefits.

PART I

Introduction

Preface

WHY I HAVE WRITTEN THE BOOK

I have been privileged as a university-based researcher and Movement 'insider' to systematically document the first early decade of Men's Sheds from 1993, as well as to describe the rapid and remarkable spread of the Shed Movement across four countries during the past decade to 2015. My purpose is to summarise and share what I have researched, heard, learned and collected about Men's Sheds in the past two decades. My aim has been to create a comprehensive, informative, definitive but readable book about this recent and still rapidly expanding international Men's Shed Movement, as both an insider and researcher.

One of the remarkable and positive outcomes of the Men's Shed Movement I wish to emphasise and share in this book is the value of *agency*: people's choices and freedom to actively shape and create new places that meet their particular interests and needs, of particular value to their local communities. This book is my attempt to share the evidence of that agency, by and for men of any age and location. My intention is to debunk the myth that the only solution to 'the problem of men', including for men not in paid work or who are older, lies in the 'delivery' of more top-down services from deficit and ageist models of service provision, that assume all men '*are* the problem' and will only benefit if they are patronised as customers, students, patients or clients.

There are important reasons for documenting this story and its messages now. The main reason is because this new Movement is likely of wider value: to men, families and communities in other nations, facing many similar issues, particularly for men beyond paid work. Enough time has elapsed after two decades to be able to stand back and for the first time critically analyse what has occurred, where, how and with what impact. I anticipate that this analysis will be useful for shedders and Men's Shed stakeholders (Men's Shed organisations, communities, non-government organisations and governments) as well as students, historians and researchers, and encourage further research and debate.

Most of this history of Men's Sheds has not been written down before. What *has* been documented is often reliant on people's imperfect recollections and memories. The available printed information to verify dates and events is widely scattered, and located in ephemeral sources (in Men's Shed newsletters, local newspapers, posters, and reports as well as on websites and emails). Some of the earliest Sheds were set up for older men almost 20 years ago. Many potential key informants from these 'pioneer' Men's Shed organisations are unwell and others have passed away. As with all histories, even with a 'perfect record', there are many, sometimes contested versions of the same event. The events, Men's Sheds and people I have selected to write about in this book are basically those I already had information about, or had contacts to who were able to provide additional, accurate information.

Despite these problems and limitations, elaborated in Chapter 1, I have experienced a universal, strong interest from Australia, Ireland, the UK and New Zealand in getting this unknown (and sometimes contested) story down on paper. I hope you enjoy reading this book as much as I have enjoyed writing it.

WHY 'THE COMPANY OF MEN'?

The book's sub-title, '*The Company of Men*' has been taken from the name proposed by the late Dick McGowan and adopted by the group of men in Tongala, Victoria, Australia, who McGowan anticipated would take responsibility for self-managing what appears to be the first 'Men's Shed' ever opened *by that name* in a community setting. The Tongala Aged Care Centre, through the efforts and vision of the late Dick McGowan (that the Tongala Men's Shed was originally named in honour of), deliberately set out to allow Shed members to be as autonomous as possible through 'The Company of Men'. While this book identifies a wide range of Men's Sheds that have proliferated from this and other early Australian Shed and Men's Shed experiments, they share two common underpinning characteristics. The first is the empowerment of men to self-manage *their* Shed. The second is recognition of the positive value to men and the community of what can be achieved through their active participation in the Shed as well as its organization in the company of other men.

WHAT IS IN THE BOOK?

Part I, 'Introduction' comprises Chapter 1, 'Nailing Down the Men's Shed Basics'. This Chapter proceeds carefully along the definitional continuum from the personal backyard shed, through community 'Sheds' to 'Men's Sheds'. It highlights the importance of what a Shed organisation is actually called, as well as some of the difficulties creating a neat or simple Men's Shed history, chronology or typology with so many diverse variants in the 'shed space'. Finally, this introductory chapter analyses the distribution of all Men's Sheds registered with the four national associations to early 2015.

Part II, 'A Community Men's Shed History' explains how and where it all began in Australia in four broadly chronological Chapters 2 to 5. Chapter 2, 'Coming out of the Backyard Shed in Australia' teases out some of the thickest threads in the very early history of community Sheds and Men's Sheds, initially in South Australia. It focuses first on the context for early and tentative Australian experiments with Sheds in community settings in South Australia. It carefully considers the relevance of early workshop and Shed-based community organisations for men in Australia, some of which had been suspected as being the first, proverbial 'smoking gun' Men's Shed, but which had not been previously researched. In essence, the early history is about a number of very different threads and people coming together, both by serendipity and design in Australia during the 1990s.

In summary, this section of the book confirms that the first Shed organisation for men in a community setting was in existence in rural South Australia by 1993. The first Men's Sheds organisations by that name appeared five years later, as recently as 1998, in Victoria and New South Wales. It identifies some diverse elements and personalities associated with this 'perfect storm' that encouraged some community Sheds to publicly call themselves 'Men's Sheds' after mid-1998 in several Australian states. The latter part of Chapter 2, 'Early Australian Shed Experiments' explores some workshop and shed-based precursors to community Men's Sheds.

Chapter 3 examines 'Early Australian Men's Sheds and State Associations', chronicling the separate, overlapping and quite different early Australian Men's Shed developments in most Australian states after 1998, leading to the setting up of the first state associations. It closely examines the era between 1998 and 2005 during which Sheds were quietly spreading, mostly 'below the radar' in all Australian states except Queensland, and with very little sharing of information or linking up. Chapter 4 looks at how the 'Movement' began to gain significant traction in Australia after 2004, including with governments, service providers and the wider community, leading to the creation of the Australian Men's Shed Association (AMSA) by 2008. Chapter 5 documents the rapid and remarkable spread and adaptation of the Men's Shed model to Ireland, New Zealand and the UK since 2008, leading by 2015 to Men's Sheds opening in Canada and continental Europe.

Part III 'Men's Shed Innovation and Diversity' (Chapters 6 to 9) illustrates Men's Shed innovation and diversity, using case study examples from each of the four nations in which Men's Sheds are now firmly established. These examples are from Australia in Chapter 6, from Ireland in Chapter 7, the UK in Chapter 8 and New Zealand in Chapter 9. They each focus on 'early pioneer', 'innovative', 'remarkable' and 'new and cutting edge' Sheds, in effect as illustrative 'case studies'. The 'early pioneer' Men's Sheds in each country, Australian states, Irish or UK County and New Zealand region were all 'first' in several respects. Each one not only faced and overcame significant obstacles, but also tended to be used as models for later Sheds. 'Innovative' Sheds were selected from the many Men's Sheds that have 'broken new ground' and influenced subsequent Men's Shed practice in some way. The 'remarkable' Men's Shed examples have been selected because of some remarkable feature related to their location, venue, or the way they have interacted with the wider community. Finally, some examples of 'new and cutting edge' Men's Sheds are included for each country. They are seen as acting as possible trendsetters for future Men's Shed practice, both nationally and internationally.

Part IV, 'Conclusions after Two Decades of Men's Sheds' draws back from the specifics of individual Sheds to summarise and reflect on what is known (and not known) about Men's Sheds and the Movement globally. This summary is considered timely in 2015 after a decade of early Australian experimentation to 2005 and a decade of very rapid growth and international spread after 2007. Chapter 10, 'Research Evidence from Men's Sheds' provides a comprehensive and critical analysis of the still limited research evidence about Men's Sheds. Chapter 11, 'Men's Shed Theory and Practice' draws out some important theoretical and practical implications that Men's Sheds provoke. Finally, Chapter 12 discusses 'Men's Shed Issues, Trends and Possibilities' for Men's Sheds and the Movement. Appendix 2, 'Global Men's Shed List', includes a list of all Men's Sheds organisations registered with the four national associations and elsewhere in the world. Appendix 3, 'Articles about Men's Sheds, 1995-2014' lists articles specifically about Men's Sheds in community settings to early 2015.

WHAT'S NOT IN THE BOOK

By focusing on Men's Sheds in community settings that are registered with the four national associations, this book does not provide an account of personal men's sheds. Given that the Men's Shed Movement started in Australia and that its main author Barry Golding is based there, there is an inevitable bias in the account towards sources from Australia and towards his research interests, experiences and expertise. An account of the Movement from a men's health worker or a woman involved in the Movement, for example, might read very differently. No attempt is made to explore the hands-on, workshop-based traditions that are rich and varied in all countries and which are known by names other than 'Shed'. There are debates to be had about exposing future men to more diverse masculinities that are beyond the scope of this book. Given the availability of the AMSA (Australian) online manual *How to Set up and Run a Men's Shed*, this is not a 'how to' book.

POSITIONING MYSELF IN THE BOOK

It may be useful for readers to be aware of who the author is. I am a 65-year-old man and have lived for 35 years in the same very small town in a rural area an hour and a half drive outside of Melbourne. I was born in rural Victoria. I am married with three children in their 30s, including two boys. I am not a Men's Shedder, though I regularly visit local Sheds and have a passion for making and growing things, bushwalking and long distance road cycling. I did most of the renovations to our house, an abandoned municipal office, including the carpentry and plumbing (hot, cold, wastewater and gas). My formal education and work (in approximate order) have included geology, folk music, environmental science, wildlife research, education, secondary teaching and arts (philosophy and feminism). In the past 25 years I have worked mostly in universities exploring vocational and adult education research, men's learning and wellbeing, mainly using mixed method field research beyond the metropolis – which is how I found out about some of the early Men's Sheds in Australia from 2000. I am a proud honorary Patron of AMSA and was very recently President of Adult Learning Australia. My regular journeying in the past decade as an academic to all Australian states, New Zealand, Ireland and the UK has clearly informed my knowledge of Men's Sheds and led to my active contribution to the Shed Movement in these places as a researcher, enthuser and Patron. My late father and grandfather may have had different later lives in retirement if Men's Sheds had been around then.

CHAPTER 1

Nailing Down the Men's Shed Basics

Chapter 1 'nails down' the Men's Shed basics, proceeding along the continuum from the private or backyard shed through community 'Sheds' (from 1993) to 'Men's Sheds' in community settings (from 1998). It highlights the importance of what a Shed organisation is actually called, as well as some of the difficulties of creating a neat or simple Men's Shed history, chronology or typology with so many diverse variants.

SOME STARTING DEFINITIONS

A Shed

The word 'shed' has its origins in a 15th century, Old English word alluding to 'shade'. By the 1850s it referred to a light, temporary shelter. In Australia and many other English-speaking countries today, it refers generally to a building, room or garage where things are made, fixed or stored. In some countries, including in the USA and Canada, the term 'men's den' or 'man cave' might be used instead to describe more or less the same shed-like place or workshop space. It could be a sports shed, a fire shed, a tool shed, a wood shed, a shearing shed or a shed-based workshop. In each of these cases, while the shed may have been located in a community setting, the Shed was not an organisation *by that name* before the 1990s.

The personal or backyard shed is ubiquitous and culturally iconic in Australia and several other Anglophone nations. It was popularised in Australia in many formats, including through several popular books from the 1990s by Mark Thomson. John Williamson's *The Shed* song, exhorted that 'All Australian boys need a shed, A place where he can go, Somewhere to clear his head.'[1] Clare

---

[1] *The Shed*, John Williamson, lyrics http://www.songlyrics.com/john-williamson/the-shed-lyrics/#ebE9HmQevaHGYMJr.99, Accessed August 22, 2014.

Shann, then of beyondblue[2], the national Australian depression initiative, wrote on the Australian Psychological Society website in 2012 that:

> Australian country singer John Williamson's lyrics reflect the simple idea that is gaining support across Australia, particularly in helping to decrease social isolation and the health issues to which it can lead. The backyard shed is part of the Australian culture and regarded as a 'bloke's' space. But what about the men who don't have a shed? That's where the idea of a community shed emerged and it became the basis of the Australian Men's Shed movement.[3]

As this book will show in Part 2, Shann's backyard shed thread is only one of many strands of the history of how the community Shed and Men's Sheds actually emerged in Australia. The real story is actually much more interesting and complex.

Pre-1990s men's shed

A careful search of digitised Australian newspapers in the century to the 1980s[4] confirms that the uncapitalised term 'men's shed' was regularly and specifically used in the print media to refer to a men's room, typically a bathing, swimming or changing place for men on a beach or river bank, adjacent to a sportsground or in a workplace.

A Community Shed

As Part 2 will explain, during the 1990s a small number of organisations in Australia began to appear that were focused on shed-based activity mainly or solely for men in a community setting. However there is no evidence of Men's Sheds in community settings *by that name* in newspaper articles until the late 1990s. Even after the first Men's Sheds in 1998, several communities publicly and deliberately kept it simple by *not* naming their Shed or organisation as being just for men, even if that is what it effectively was. Occasionally they did this by simply calling it 'The Shed', such as in Hackham West (opened in South

---

[2] beyondblue is a not-for-profit organization working to increase awareness and understanding of anxiety and deparession in Australia.

[3] Clare Shann, 'Strengthening Men's Health and Wellbeing through a Community Shed', InPsych, August 2012, http://www.psychology.org.au/inpsych/2012/august/shann/, Accessed August 22, 2014.

[4] Trove http://trove.nla.gov.au/, Accessed April 22, 2014.

Australia in 1995) and Darkan (opened in Western Australia in 2005). Sometimes they got around the problem by adding either the venue or the name of a local identity on the front, for example 'The Boat Shed' (in Albany, Western Australia) and 'Clem's Shed' (in Minlaton, South Australia).

Some early Australian Shed organisations, particularly in small and relatively conservative communities in South Australia and Tasmania, called them 'Community Sheds' in order to include and not offend women in the community, as well as not to affect their chances of 'mainstream' funding. Some found a 'middle road' by calling it a 'Community Men's Shed'. A small number of other Sheds appear to have deliberately avoided becoming aligned with the Men's Shed Movement by finding another name that avoided using either the word 'Men' or 'Shed'. These national naming variations are returned to later in this chapter.

A Men's Shed

Men's Shed organisations (with the initial letters consistently capitalised in this book, to distinguish them from both personal sheds and buildings) in community settings first appeared from mid-1998 in Australia. They typically link a place name with 'Men's Shed' to create a community identity and organisation with all three words in the name. The early Men's Shed Movement in Australia first used the term 'community Men's Shed' generically from around 2005. This was for two main reasons. One was to distinguish the family of not-for-profit community Men's Shed-based organisations from private 'backyard' sheds. The second was to differentiate them from Men's Shed organisations set up by or with commercial arrangements associated with Mensheds Australia, as discussed in more detail in Chapter 4.

Some Men's Sheds in Australia, particularly those that received advice from Mensheds Australia, combined the two words in their shed name but dropped one 's' to become 'Mensheds'. A very small number of the earliest Shed organisations in Australia (in Donnybrook, Western Australia and Bendigo, Victoria) as well as in the UK, (particularly those associated with the Age UK initiative elaborated in Chapter 8), used the term 'Men in Sheds'. Indeed one quarter of all Sheds open in England to late 2014 (22 out of 81) were called 'Men in Sheds'.

Further complicating a simple definition, some organisations that function as Men's Sheds have deliberately left out the word 'Men', and some informal groups of men who have started a private men's shed have later thrown it open to other men in the community. For consistency, all specific Sheds, Men's Shed and

Community Shed organisations mentioned in this book have their initial Shed organisation titles capitalised.

The Men's Shed Movement

Men's Sheds in 2015 can certainly be defined as a 'social movement' in Australia, Ireland, the UK and New Zealand in that they comprise a large, informal grouping of individuals or organisations that focus on a specific social issue: the broad community involvement and wellbeing of men in community settings.

The term 'Men's Shed Movement' was first used publicly as Men's Sheds started to organise in Victoria, Australia from around 2007, and Australia-wide soon after. The Victorian Men's Shed Association (VMSA) 2007/8 Annual Report, for example, noted that the 'Victorian Men's Shed movement' had been incorporated. The veritable 'explosion' of Men's Sheds right across the Island of Ireland from the first Men's Shed in 2009, to 244 Sheds in January 2015 less than six years later, is certainly indicative of a powerful Irish Men's Shed *Movement*. So too is the rapid growth of Men's Sheds across Scotland from two Men's Sheds to 42 in less than two years between 2013 and February 2015[5].

While a very small number of social and religious causes and community organisations have created, sponsored, auspiced or attached themselves to particular Men's Sheds and Shed 'Clusters', it is important to note that the Men's Shed Movement has, with some exceptions, not come out of the 'Men's Movement', or from radicalised or party-politicised men. Rather the Men's Shed Movement has come from relatively conservative, mainly older men as well as diverse communities and professionals concerned about the wellbeing of men and their broader involvement in the community beyond the paid workforce. As Part 2 will demonstrate, some professionals and service providers were particularly desperate by the 1990s in Australia to find other, better ways to work with and provide appropriate support for some older and rural men. The traction achieved by the Men's Sheds in Ireland post the Global Financial Crisis is evidence of the particular appeal of the Movement to men not in paid work.

A Men's Shed Definition

Because of the many variants in 2015, it is difficult for one simple definition to fit all Men's Sheds. The national *Men's Sheds in Australia* study I conducted with

---

[5] Myra Duncan, *Learning about Community Capacity Building from the Spread of Men's Sheds in Scotland.* Dunvegan: md consulting, February, 2015.

colleagues, published by NCVER (the National Centre for Vocational Education Research) in 2007, defined Men's Sheds organisations as:

> ... typically located in a shed or workshop-type space in community settings that provide opportunities for regular, hands-on activity by groups deliberately and mainly comprising men.[6]

Because of these difficulties, researching a definitive history and chronology of Men's Sheds calls for an early elaboration of what a Men's Shed organisation is, in order to decide what to include and omit. The more elaborate Australian Men's Sheds Association (AMSA) definition:

> ... recognises as a Men's Shed any community-based, non-profit, non-commercial organisation that is accessible to all men and whose primary activity is the provision of a safe and friendly environment where men are able to work on projects at their own pace in their own time in the company of other men. A major objective is to advance the well being and health of their male members.

AMSA, in its Membership Definition, formally distinguishes between organisations that are 'in name a Men's Shed' (to which it grants full membership), and those that are not, which are defined as 'auxiliaries'. So far, so good. But what about Shed organisations in community settings that do not register with a national Men's Shed organisation but are accepted in their communities as Men's Sheds?

A Men's Shed generally (but not always) includes a workshop-type place or space in a community setting usually comprising all or mainly men. Importantly, as much as possible, men involved are equal and active co-participants in the activity. Ideally they are not treated from deficit or ageist positions as students, customers, clients or patients. To broaden this definition to include the whole and very diverse family of Men's Sheds internationally, the Shed organisation name usually (but not always, as identified later) includes one or more of: a place or locality, 'Men' or 'Shed' (or an equivalent term in another language) in the organisation title. These definitional issues are returned to at the end of this Chapter with my proposal for a broader definition of a Men's Shed that includes three other, quite different criteria.

---

[6] Barry Golding *et al.*, *Men's Sheds in Australia: Learning through Community Contexts*. Adelaide: NCVER, 2007, 7.

Meantime, it is as important to be as clear about what a Men's Shed *is not* as it is to define what it is. This idea comes from a leaflet prepared by the Armagh Men's Shed in Ireland in 2013, which on closer investigation turned out to have been derived from David Helmers's (AMSA CEO's) ideas, when he visited and officially opened the Armagh Men's Shed and talked about the Australian Shed experience. First, the leaflet provides a clear and concise account of what their Shed is:

Armagh Men's Shed is a dedicated, friendly and welcoming meeting place where men can come together and undertake a variety of mutually agreed activities. Men's Sheds are open to ... [7] men regardless of background or ability. It is a place you can share your knowledge with others, learn new skills and develop your old skills. New members are always welcome and can be assured that there is something of interest for everyone as the men have ownership of the projects and decide their own program of events.

The Armagh Men's Shed leaflet follows with a similarly clear explanation of what a men's shed is *not*.

- It is not a formal training program, but you may gain new knowledge and skills.
- It is not a sports club, but you could play sports.
- It is not a health programme but your health and well being may improve.
- It is not an information service but you can ask for info you need
- It is not a service for men, but activities organised by men.

This list of 'What a Men's Shed Is Not', combined with its novel suggestion that 'anything's possible' is consistent with the appealing idea of a Men's Shed as a free, 'third' community place (aside from the 'first' and 'second' places in paid work and at home respectively). All Men's Sheds arguably seek to create this 'third place' in the community for and with other men, particularly for men with much diminished first or second places. Sheds have generally resisted being 'pigeonholed' as being mainly about one thing, one activity, one program, for one

---

[7] In the original *Armagh Men's Shed* leaflet, the word 'older' was included here, as this is the demographic targeted by the organisations that supports the Shed.

purpose or for a one-dimensional outcome. They have deliberately fought to keep words about function or purpose out of the public name of the Shed organisation in order to keep many possibilities open.

WHAT'S THE BIG DEAL ABOUT MEN'S SHEDS?

While a history of Men's Sheds is not provided until Part 2 (Chapter 2) it is important at this early stage to briefly discuss why calling it a *Men's* Shed was (and sometimes still is) such a 'big deal'. For many communities, service providers, community workers and governments in Australia, calling a shed in a community setting a *Men's* Shed anywhere before 1998 was too hard and contentious. Research into fatherhood and family services from the UK in 2000 provides a neat and relatively simple way of explaining this difficulty. Summarising research by Ghate and others[8] in 2006, Sandy Ruxton, in a report for Age UK, identified three types of gender strategies adopted by centres that provided services for older men:

> ... the *'gender blind'* (where men and women are treated the same); the *gender-differentiated* (where men and women are treated differently) and the *agnostic* (which has no identifiable approach to working with men). ... [W]hile the first two [are] more effective, **having a strategy [is] more important than what the strategy [is].** Rather than be prescriptive, [it is better for] providers of services for older people [to] develop a strategic approach to working with older men that is appropriate to their individual circumstances and the needs of their communities.[9]

Men's Sheds challenge the acceptance by many service providers in health, aged care, welfare and adult education it is fair to treat all men and women in the same way (i.e. using 'gender-blind' strategies), while also providing other compensatory services mainly for and by women (i.e. providing 'gender differentiated' services but only for women). By doing so, *some* men's needs will not be properly accommodated. More importantly, such 'gender blind' strategies effectively mean that many older men are not even recognised as being gendered.

---

[8] Deborah Ghate, Catherine Shaw, Catherine and Neal Hazel, *Fathers and Family Centres: Family Centres, Fathers and Working with Men*. London: Policy Research Bureau, 2000.
[9] Sandy Ruxton, *Working with Older Men: A Review of Aged Concern Services*. London: Age Concern, 2006.

What the Men's Shed model does that is different, indeed revolutionary and transformational, is still too difficult for some service providers and countries to accept and adopt for three main reasons. Firstly, they would be using (and arguably reinforcing) the attraction of a stereotypically male-gendered activity (Men's Sheds) in order to help some men, particularly older men and other men not on paid work, to be empowered and to look after themselves, each other and their local community. Secondly, the service provider would be put 'at arms length' by fundamentally changing the power relationship, from older men being dependent clients, customers, patients or students of the professional or 'service provider', to their becoming active and equal participants in a community activity. Instead of the provider servicing the client from a deficit model, the Shed environment itself becomes *salutogenic* (health promoting and giving), and the men became agents of their own transformation.

Thirdly, the Men's Shed model is based around bottom up informality, approaches that can be anathema to increasingly top-down, outcome driven service organisations and governments. There is no place for mateship, happiness and friendship in such dry and clinical models of 'delivery'. Men's Sheds work precisely *because of* the informality and homeliness of the setting and the activity, not in spite of it, particularly because the informal aspect is not prescribed or named. The benefit to men occurs because of and *in spite of* there often being few professionals or programs. In some ways, it is this transfer of power, from females as professionals to men as shedders that many women, some men and some communities find most confronting, confusing and difficult to acknowledge and sanction.

While apparently simple, the Men's Shed model, as the history that follows in Part 2 suggests, developed progressively through widespread practice and local experimentation. The 'huge mind shift' for professionals and governments involved accepting a gendering of the space *and* standing back to provide an opportunity for shedders to develop agency. Both these hurdles and the risk management issues they provoke have posed a high barrier to Men's Sheds development for some men, women, governments, nations and communities.

MEN'S SHED NAMES: SOME NATIONAL VARIATIONS

It is important to acknowledge that the names that individual Shed organisations have chosen are important and have often been the subject of considerable debate. What follows summarises the naming trends to date in Australia, Ireland, the UK and New Zealand.

Shed Names in Australia

The title of most community Men's Sheds organisations, for example the 'Buninyong Men's Shed', has capitalised initial letters and typically includes:

- the name of the populated locality, town or city (and less commonly region) where the Shed is located
- the word 'Men'
- the word 'Shed'.

However around one quarter of Sheds registered with the Australian Men's Sheds Association (AMSA) depart from this general rule in some way. An analysis of 920 registered Australian Men's Sheds[10] showed that:

- Around one in five (19%) did *not* include the name of a town or city, though many of those that did not included instead:
  o an abbreviated place name (e.g. 'Island Shed' on Palm Island in Queensland
  o the name of a nearby river, mountain, street, local government area or region (e.g. 'Central Coast Community Shed' in Ulverstone, Tasmania)
  o the name of a community facility, such as the aged care facility in which it was located (e.g. the 'Good Shepherd Home's Men's Shed' in Queensland)
  o the name of a person (e.g. 'Willo's Shed' in Gawler, South Australia), particularly for Sheds in some parts of rural South Australia and Tasmania where there had been concern about naming the organisation as being only for or by men.
- Fifteen per cent included the word 'Community', though most (8 out of 10) of those that *did* use the word 'Community' also included the word 'Men' (for example 'Camden Community Men's Shed' in New South Wales).
- Thirteen per cent did *not* include the word 'Men', though a small number of these instead used the colloquial term referring to men, 'Blokes'.
- Four per cent did *not* include the word 'Shed' (though some included the word 'Workshop' or 'Museum', e.g. 'The Carpenter's Workshop', in Elanora, Queensland).

---

[10] Shed organisation names as registered with AMSA to early 2014 (N=920), including approximately 200 then in the process of opening.

- Three per cent of Shed organisations (29 in total) self-described as 'Community Sheds' without mentioning 'Men' (e.g. 'Malak Community Shed', in Darwin, Northern Territory).
- Around one in five Shed organisations (23%) included the word 'Inc.' in their formal registration, indicating that they had achieved formal status as an independent 'Incorporated Association'. Many other sheds were involved in auspice arrangements with a separate Incorporated Association.
- Some Shed names are very short (e.g. 'Woodies' in Whalan, NSW; 'The Workshop' in Youngtown, Tasmania; 'The Hub' in Brooklyn Park. South Australia).
- Some Sheds have taken on Aboriginal names (e.g. 'Mowun Marnu Men's Shed' in Hall's Creek, Western Australia).
- A small number of Sheds (around one per cent) include the word 'Veteran' or 'RSL', indicative of an association with or emphasis on war Veterans as participants.

Shed Names in Ireland

Irish Sheds have very consistently named their organisations as 'Men's Sheds' linked to the location of the Shed. Of 244 Men's Shed organisations registered in January 2015 by IMSA on the Island of Ireland (including the Republic of Ireland and Northern Ireland):

- only one Shed (Southill) did not include the word 'Men' or 'Shed'
- only three per cent (8 Sheds) included the word 'Community' in their organisation name, and all of those that did were Men's Sheds (e.g. the 'Drogheda Community Men's Shed', in County Lough).
- Other Irish variants include Sheds with Gaelic names, including *'Cumann bhFear'* ('Men's Shed'). Thus, the Irish heritage crafts-based Men's Shed in Galway is called *'An Seid Cumann bhFear'*. There is also the delightfully named *'Crann Go Beatha'* ('Tree of Life') Men's Shed in Belfast, Northern Ireland.

Shed Names in the UK

Men's Sheds in the UK show greater diversity and regional variations in naming. Of all 124 Sheds open and registered with UKMSA to January 2015, around two thirds (65%, 81 Sheds) were in England. One quarter of English Shed organisations (22) were 'Men in Sheds', related in some way to having been set by up or in an auspice arrangement with a local or regional Age UK branch. Many English Men's Sheds (29, 36%) avoided the term 'Men' in their Shed organisation name (e.g. 'Nailsea Social Shedders' in Bristol). Others (13, 16%) also avoided the term 'Shed', while several others made no reference to place. Several avoided both 'Men' and 'Shed' in their official name (e.g. 'Gerald's Room', in Diss, Norfolk, and 'Skills4Holme', in Holme, Yorkshire).

By contrast all 20 Sheds in Northern Ireland and the five Welsh Sheds registered with UKMSA were called 'Men's Sheds', though one in Belfast added the name 'Community'. Of 17 Sheds quite recently opened in Scotland, ten were 'Men's Sheds', while five others did not use the term 'Men'.

Shed Names in New Zealand

In New Zealand, the biggest difference in terms of the names of Sheds is the tendency to use 'Menz' instead of 'Men's', deliberately distinguishing them as NZ or New Zealand Sheds. Of the 61 Sheds registered with MENSHEDS NZ in April 2014:

- 44 per cent included the word 'Menz', including four Sheds that used Menzshed or 'Menz' at the start of the shed title.
- Only five (8% of) Sheds did not include the word 'Men', two of which used the word 'Bloke's' instead.
- Only two shed-based organisations did not include the word 'Shed', instead referring to it as a 'Workshop' or 'Store'.

MEN'S SHED DISTRIBUTION

This section includes maps showing the locations of all 1,330 Men's Sheds globally to January 2015. This section also includes an analysis and description of where these Sheds had spread. There is more detail in the analysis of Australian Men's Sheds by virtue of the fact that the Men's Shed Movement there is larger and around a decade older than in Ireland, the UK and New Zealand.

In the first four months of 2015 since this analysis was undertaken, an additional 86 Sheds had opened globally, mostly in the UK and Ireland. This extrapolates to annual global growth rate in Men's Shed numbers of around 20 per cent per year. Appendix 2 list all 1,416 Men's Sheds registered with Australian, Irish, UK and New Zealand peak bodies to May 2015.

Australia has a relatively 'mature' Shed sector, with 916 Men's Sheds registered and open to January 2015, with many others registered but still setting up. Figure 1 below confirms that Australian Men's Sheds are far from evenly distributed geographically, though relatively evenly distributed by State, once each State's population is taken into account. Sheds spread early and fastest in South Australia, but the growth there has slowed. By contrast, Sheds started around a decade later in southeastern Queensland from 2009, but have since spread very rapidly north and west.

Sheds in Ireland and the UK are still spreading rapidly, despite their respective national Movements being less than five years old. The most rapid, recent growth has been in England and Scotland. Despite relatively late commencement, Men's Shed densities across the Republic of Ireland (Sheds per head of total population) were similar to or above those in Australia in many Irish Counties by early 2014. The most likely next development of new Men's Sheds and the associated Movement is anticipated in both North America (Canada and the US) as well as in continental Europe.

Men's Shed Distribution in Australia

The distribution if all 916 Australian Men's Sheds registered with the national association (AMSA) and open to January 2015 is shown below in Figure 1. As well as being represented as individual dots, a 'heat map' has been generated which visually emphasizes where the dots (and Men's Sheds) are densest.

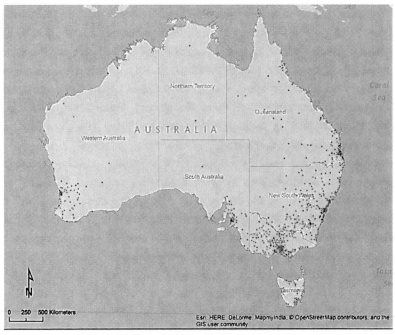

Figure 1 Map of Men's Sheds in Australia to 2015

A list of all Australian Sheds open to May 2015 is included in Appendix 2. Table 1 below summarises the Shed distribution and density of Australian by State and Territory across Australia. Shed density is expressed as the number of Sheds per 100,000 total population.

In summary, these maps and tables confirm that Men's Sheds in Australia:

- have rapidly and recently expanded in Queensland, the ACT and Northern Territory
- are found in most populated areas of the Australian southeast as well as the south west of Western Australia
- are differentially located in regional cities and smaller rural towns
- developed later in Queensland
- are differentially located in regions and Australian States (particularly Tasmania) with higher regional, rural or remote populations, such as in rural northern Victoria, western New South Wales and the Western Australian wheat belt
- have a relatively low density in Australia's capital cities.

While the average national Shed density across Australia to 2015 was approximately four Sheds per 100,000 total population, rural Shed density was often much greater. For example, the five Men's Sheds in the Buloke Shire in rural north western Victoria serviced a total of 8,000 people; equivalent to one Shed per 1,500 people, close to 20 times the national average.

Table 1 Men's Shed Distribution and Density across Australia to 2015

State or Territory	Number of Sheds 2015 (& 2007#)	Population (million, 2013)	Sheds per 100,000 pop., 2015 (& 2007#)	Year first Men's Shed established
New South Wales	292 (45)	7.44	**3.92** (0.35)	1998
Victoria	250 (64)	5.77	**5.91** (0.81)	1998
Queensland	159 (10)	4.68	**3.40** (0)	2009
Western Australia	95 (6)	2.54	**3.74** (0.26)	2002
South Australia	68 (51)	1.67	**4.07** (2.78)	1999
Tasmania	37 (13)	0.51	**7.25** (1.28)	2001
ACT	10 (1)	0.38	**2.89** (0.31)	2006
Northern Territory	5 (1)	0.24	**2.08** (0.5)	2006
Australia	**916 (191)**	**23.24**	**3.94 (0.65)**	**1998**

KEY: # from Barry Golding *et al., Men's Sheds in Australia*, 2007, NCVER, Table 1, 27; AMSA Data on AMSA registered Australian Men's Sheds to January 2015; ACT is the Australian Capital Territory which includes Canberra.

Sheds have established in some very small and remote Australian communities. For example there were Men's Sheds on Bruny Island in Tasmania and Snowtown in South Australia (both with a population of only 600) as well as in the very small and remote towns of Barellan, Tottenham and Trundle in inland New South Wales. The outer Western Australian wheat belt towns of Mukinbudin, Bencubbin and Wyalkatchem all had a Men's Shed, despite town populations of less than 400 people.

Men's Sheds in Distribution in Ireland

Figure 2 is a map of all 244 Irish Men's Sheds registered with IMSA and open to February 2015 across the Island of Ireland (including the Irish Republic and Northern Ireland. These Sheds are referred to in this book for simplicity as 'Irish').

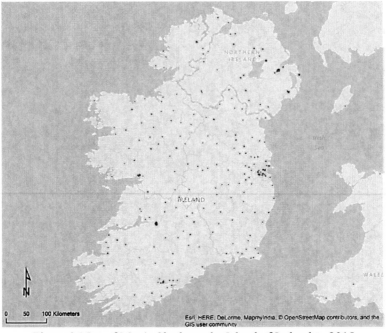

Figure 2 Map of Men's Sheds on the Island of Ireland to 2015

A list of all these Irish Sheds to May 2015 is included in Appendix 2. Table 2 below summarises the Shed distribution and density of Men's Sheds across the Island of Ireland, sorted by County. Shed density is again expressed as the number of Sheds per 100,000 total population.

When the Northern Ireland Sheds are separated from the Republic of Ireland Sheds, it is apparent that the Shed densities in the Irish Republic (227 Sheds, 4.93 Sheds per 100,000 population, total population 4.6 million) to 2015 was around five times greater than in Northern Ireland (17 Sheds, 0.94 Sheds per 100,000, total population 1.81 million). For comparison with elsewhere in the UK, the Northern Ireland Sheds, to January 2015, were seven times denser than in England (0.15 Sheds per 100,000) and three times denser than in Scotland.

Table 2 Men's Shed Distribution and Density across Ireland to 2015

Irish Counties	Population, 2011	Number of Sheds, January 2015	Sheds Per 100,000
Antrim	618,108	8	1.3
Armagh *	174,792	2	1.1
Carlow	54,612	4	7.3
Cavan	73,183	4	5.5
Clare	117,196	7	6.0
Cork	519,032	24	4.6
Derry *	247,132	3	1.2
Donegal	161,137	12	7.5
Down *	532,665	3	0.8
Dublin	1,273,069	23	1.8
Fermanagh *	61,160	1	1.6
Galway	250,653	16	6.4
Kerry	145,502	14	9.6
Kildare	210,312	8	3.8
Kilkenny	95,419	3	3.1
Laois	80,559	5	6.2
Leitrim	31,798	4	12.6
Limerick	191,809	9	4.7
Longford	39,000	2	5.1
Louth	122,897	3	2.4
Mayo	130,638	11	8.4
Meath	184,135	14	7.6
Monaghan	60,483	6	9.9
Offaly	76,687	3	3.9
Roscommon	64,065	6	9.4
Sligo	65,393	7	10.7
Tipperary	158,754	13	8.2
Tyrone *	177,986	4	2.3
Waterford	113,795	3	2.6
Westmeath	86,164	5	5.8
Wexford	145,320	11	7.6
Wicklow	69,098	7	10.1
TOTALS	**6.4 million**	**244**	**3.81**

Key: * Counties in Northern Ireland. All other Counties are in the Republic of Ireland.

In summary, the development of Men's Sheds has been earlier, more rapid and extensive in the Republic of Ireland. As in Australia, Men's Sheds in Northern Ireland and the Republic of Ireland are more prevalent in rural areas, away from the main cities. In broad terms, Men's Sheds in Ireland are in higher densities in Counties where a higher proportion of men are categorised as being in lower socioeconomic groups.

Men's Shed Distribution in the UK

Figure 3 is a map of all Men's Sheds open to February 2015 in Great Britain (England, Scotland and Wales, excluding Northern Ireland). A list of all UK Men's Sheds (including Northern Ireland) open to May 2015 is included in Appendix 2. UK Men's Sheds Association prepared a report on UK Men's Sheds open and planned by Region to January 2015[11], reproduced in Table 3a.

Table 3a UK Men's Sheds Open and Planned by Region to 2015

UK Regions	Open	Planned	Totals	% of Total
East of England	8	3	11	6.0
East Midlands	6	4	10	5.4
London	8	2	10	5.4
North East	4	2	6	3.3
North West	17	5	22	12.0
South East	21	10	31	16.8
South West	12	3	15	8.2
West Midlands	5	3	8	4.3
Yorkshire & The Humber	2	2	4	2.2
England	*83*	*34*	*117*	*63.6*
Northern Ireland	*20*	*2*	*22*	*12.0*
Scotland	*18*	*20*	*38*	*20.7*
Wales	*6*	*1*	*7*	*3.8*
ALL OF UK	**127**	**57**	**184**	100

Table 3b summarises the Shed distribution and density of Men's Sheds by County, specifically in England. Shed density is expressed as the number of Sheds per 100,000 total population. The table is sorted by Shed density, from highest Shed density (in Cumbria and Cheshire), to lowest Shed density (in London, Yorkshire and Manchester).

---

[11] 'UK Men's Shed Assocation Report', Patrick Abrahams, January 29, 2015.

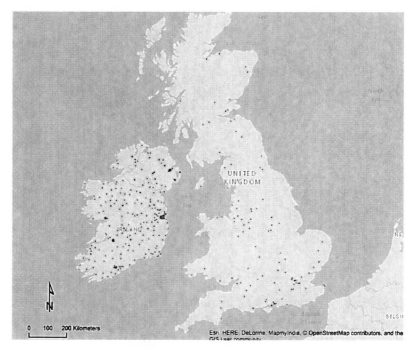

Figure 3 Map of Men's Sheds in Great Britain to 2015

Table 3b Men's Shed Distribution and Density in England to 2015

County	Number of Sheds	Shed density (population millions)	Population density (Rank#)
Cumbria	4	0.8 (0.50)	47
Cheshire	7	0.68 (1.03)	21
Hertfordshire	1	0.56 (0.18)	12
Bristol	2	0.47 (0.43)	2
Nottinghamshire	5	0.45 (1.10)	13
Hampshire	7	0.40 (1.76)	17
West Sussex	3	0.37 (0.81)	22
Devon	4	0.35 (1.14)	39
Wiltshire	2	0.29 (0.68)	37
Lancashire	4	0.27 (1.46)	15
Surrey	3	0.26 (1.14)	11
Kent	4	0.23 (1.73)	18
Norfolk	2	0.23 (0.86)	40
Buckinghamshire	2	0.23 (0.86)	24
Berkshire	2	0.23 (0.86)	10
Somerset	2	0.22 (0.91)	36
Durham	2	0.22 (0.90)	27
Shropshire	1	0.21 (0.47)	43
Staffordshire	2	0.18 (1.10)	23
Warwickshire	1	0.18 (0.55)	31

Essex	3	0.17 (1.73)	16
Bedfordshire	1	0.16 (0.62)	14
Suffolk	1	0.14 (0.73)	38
Northamptonshire	1	0.14 (0.69)	29
Dorset	1	0.13 (0.75)	30
Gloucestershire	1	0.12 (0.86)	32
Tyne	1	0.09 (1.10)	7
Greater London	6	0.07 (8.20)	1
Yorkshire	2	0.04 (5.0)	#
Greater Manchester	1	0.04 (2.69)	6
Birmingham	1	0.01 (1.07)	#
England	**81**	**0.15 (53.0)**	

KEY: Rank indicates the population rank for each English County between 1 (most densely populated = 1, least densely populated = 48); 31 counties had at least one Men's Shed, 17 English counties (not listed) had no Men's Sheds open. # Yorkshire and Birmingham were not ranked.

Of the 124 Men's Sheds open across the UK and registered with UKMSA to January 2015, with approximately 0.2 Sheds open per 100,000 population:

- approximately two thirds (65%, 80 Sheds) were in England, in 31 different Counties, with an average Shed density of 0.15 Sheds per 100,000 population.
- 20 Sheds were in Northern Ireland, in six different Counties, with a much higher average density of 1.1 Sheds per 100,000 people, well above the UK national average of 0.15 Sheds per 100,000.
- 17 Sheds were in Scotland, in 12 different Counties, with an average density of 0.32 Sheds per 100,000 people. This represents a Scottish Shed density three times that in UK, despite the more recent (2013) Scottish commencement. February 2015 data collected independently of UKMSA from Scotland suggest that 22 Scottish Men's Sheds were operating, with eight others acquiring premises and twelve others 'in active discussion' about starting a Shed.[12]
- 6 Men's Sheds were in Wales, all in different Counties, with an average density of 0.16 Sheds per 100,000 population
- one Shed was on the Isle of Man.

Given the large number of UK Counties and the relatively small number of Sheds open per County (as well as the large number of Counties without a Shed), it is

---

[12] Myra Duncan, *Learning about Community Capacity Building from the Spread of Men's Sheds in Scotland*. Dunvegan: md consulting, February 2015, 12-13.

too early to do a meaningful analysis by County across the whole of the UK. In general, based on the English data above and expressed with caution given the small, early numbers, Men's Sheds are more concentrated in smaller towns and rural Counties in the northwest and southeast of England, many in the vicinity of some of the earliest established English Sheds. To early 2015, only seven English Counties had four or more Sheds open, representing average Shed densities per 100,000 of:

- 0.69 in Cheshire (6 Sheds)
- 0.53 in Cumbria (4 Sheds)
- 0.45 in Nottinghamshire (5 Sheds)
- 0.40 in Hampshire (7 Sheds)
- 0.27 in Lancashire (7 Sheds)
- 0.23 in Kent (4 Sheds)
- 0.07 in London (7 Sheds).

While the growth of Men's Sheds across the UK has been quite recent and rapid (post-2009), the average Shed densities across the UK (including in Northern Ireland) to early 2015 remained very low compared to in Ireland. *If* average Shed densities were to eventually be achieved in the UK as exist on average in the Republic of Ireland in early 2015, one might anticipate as many as 3,000 Sheds in total across the whole of the UK.

Men's Sheds Distribution in New Zealand

Figure 4 shows the distribution of all 54 Men's Sheds registered with MENZSHED NZ and open in New Zealand to February 2015. A list of all open and registered New Zealand Men's Sheds to May 2015 is included in Appendix 2. Table 4 summarises the distribution and density of Men's Sheds in New Zealand by Shed Region (as defined by MENZSHED NZ). Shed density is expressed as the number of Men's Sheds per 100,000 people.

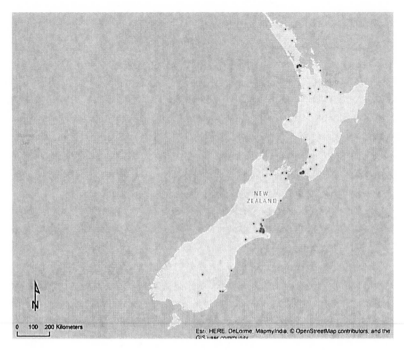

Figure 4 Map of Men's Sheds in New Zealand to 2015

Table 4 Men's Shed Distribution and Density in New Zealand by Shed Region

Shed Regional Zones*	Number of Sheds	Shed densities per 100,000 population (total population, million)
1 Upper North Island	7	
2 Central North Island	9	
3 Lower North Island	12	
4 Upper South Island	21	
5 Lower South Island	5	
North Island	*28*	*0.81 (3.45)*
South Island	*26*	*2.5 (1.04)*
New Zealand	**54**	**1.2 (4.49)**

Key: *New Zealand Shed Regional Zones are broadly defined on a map in Appendix 1 (p. 9) of MENZSHED NZ Constitution and Rules[13]. The Zones do not neatly fit any existing government zoning.

---

[13] http://menzshed.org.nz/wp-content/uploads/2014/06/MENZSHED-NZ-Constitution-June-2013.pdf, Accessed February 13, 2015.

The same data are presented in Table 5 by New Zealand Government Region.

Table 5 Men's Shed Distribution and Density across New Zealand by Region

Regions (population 2014)	Number of Sheds	Shed densities per 100,000 population
Northland (166,000)	2	1.2
Auckland (1,527,000)	5	0.3
Waikato (431,000)	5	1.2
Bay of Plenty (282,000)	2	0.7
Manawatu-Wanganui (233,000)	4	1.7
Taranaki (115,000)	1	0.9
Wellington (491,000)	8	1.6
Canterbury (474,000)	15	3.2
Marlborough (45,000)	3	6.7
Nelson (49,000)	2	4.1
Tasman (49,000)	1	2.0
Otago (212,000)	5	2.4
New Zealand (4.49 million)	**54**	**1.2**

NOTE: Three other New Zealand Regions had no Sheds registered and open to January 2015: Hawkes Bay, West Coast and Southland.

In summary, Men's Sheds are more than three times as dense on the New Zealand South Island compared with those on New Zealand's North Island. As in Australia and Ireland, Sheds are denser in rural areas. Shed densities in Marlborough, Nelson and Canterbury regions approach those already identified in some parts of Ireland and Australia. As for other national and regional analyses, this summary is based on a small number of Sheds per region and takes no account of the likely much larger number of men per Shed in many urban Sheds.

GLOBAL SHED DISTRIBUTION

Table 6 summarises Men's Shed distribution and density in all four countries with a large number of Men's Sheds open to February 2015. The very small number of other very recent Men's Sheds in North America and Europe are included in *italics* in the table but are excluded from the totals. Table 6 confirms that while Australia has the largest number of Men's Sheds open (916), 31 per cent of all Men's Sheds by early 2015 were located outside of Australia, mainly in Ireland (17% of all Sheds) and the UK (9%). When total national populations are accounted for, average Shed densities are highest in the Republic of Ireland: around 30 per cent higher than in Australia, four times higher than in New Zealand and 26 times higher than in the UK.

Table 6 Men's Shed Numbers and Density Globally to 2015

Countries	Men's Shed numbers	Shed densities per 100,000 population (Total population, millions)
Australia	916	3.81 (23.24)
Republic of Ireland	227	4.93 (4.6)
New Zealand	54	1.2 (4.49)
UK	124	0.19 (64.1)
Canada & USA	*4*	*0.0001 (319 & 35 = 354)*
Europe	*1*	*0 (745)*
TOTAL (4 countries)	**1,325**	1.38 (96.4)

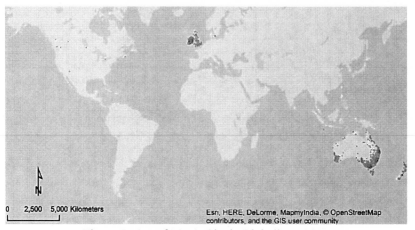

Figure 5 Map of Men's Sheds Globally to 2015

Figure 5 confirms that, globally to 2015, the distribution of most Men's Sheds was restricted to four Anglophone countries, two each on opposite (antipodean) sides of the globe. In general, in all four countries with established national Men's Shed Movements, Sheds have mostly developed in areas where the proportion of older men not in work is higher than average, in rural areas and also in areas which have experienced recent significant demographic and economic change, including population ageing, retirement and unemployment.

DIFFICULTIES WRITING A MEN'S SHED HISTORY

Definitional issues aside, the second main problem with writing a Men's Shed history is that much of what has happened is very recent, and is continuing to rapidly evolve and change. Very little of the history in Part 2 has previously been written down or critically analysed. In many cases when researching this book, I have had to rely on people's memories and recollections, as well as on some documents that included information that could not be readily checked. Writing a definitive, quite recent history like this is therefore surprisingly difficult. It was made much more difficult by the many different 'varieties' of Men's Sheds, including those that operate *as* Men's Sheds organisations without using either key word in their organisation name.

If this were instead a history and chronology of the spread of a particular fast food chain, such as 'McDonalds', for example, this would be relatively easy, because one could be confident that if someone said there was a hypothetical McDonalds restaurant open in Kyabram (in rural Australia) in 1996, it could be easily checked without confusion. However if a source or document mentioned (or someone recalled) a hypothetical 'Shed' organisation being open in 1996, it could have been any type of shed.

It may have been for men and/or women. It may (or may not) have been open to the public. Shed participants may have been restricted to members of other organisations (for example Vietnam War Veterans, or members of Rotary, Car or Angler's Clubs). It could have been a commercial workshop. At that time in 1996 it might have been: a 'sheltered workshop' for people with a disability; a personal or backyard shed or garage where local men used to 'hang out' informally; a local wood turners' club, a shed where men from a local agricultural museum, stationary engine or tramways preservation society met, formally or informally, to maintain their collections or carry on a traditional craft. It may have been a men's activity or occupational therapy room or annex of a hospital, residential aged care village, home or day care facility. Any of these 'sheds' could have had a sign outside in 1996 that said 'Shed', or much less likely, 'Men's Shed'. Those associated with any of these hypothetical Shed-based or workshop-based organisations might retrospectively make the claim to have been the first 'Men's Shed' in Australia (and therefore the world).

Any of these hypothetical sheds, if established over a decade ago, could, in 2015, subtly adapt what they do in order to change their organisation name to gain membership of a peak national Men's Shed body: by changing their organisational structure, activities, meeting place or rules for eligible participants. If they did nothing else but change the sign outside to 'Kyabram Men's Shed' (or 'Bob's Community Shed' or 'Bob's Blokes Den') and decided not to affiliate with a peak community Men's Shed body, would or should they be accepted in the shedder community (and included in this book) as a Men's Shed?

To continue the hypothetical 'Kyabram Shed' example, there could have been more than one shed in Kyabram, and in each case, if open in 1996, it could have been open for a decade or more, before Mark Thomson started publishing his widely read books about backyard men's sheds (from 1995), very subtly encouraging men to think about shed-based alternatives in community settings. The hypothetical Kyabram shedders in 1996 were much less likely to have read Leon Earle's early academic work (with others) in the obscure first issue *the Australasian Leisure for Pleasure Journal* about personal 'Sheds and Male Retirement' in 1995. However they may have heard of and been influenced by Earle or Thomson's ideas on the radio in South Australia, or by the half hour ABC TV documentary *Men and their Sheds* broadcast nationally in Australia in 1996.

However if any community Shed organization in Australia was open a few years later, say in 1999, it could have already begun to subtly or radically transform itself towards a community Men's Shed, motivated by anyone who had read the article circulated nationally about the Dick McGowan Men's Shed in Tongala, which opened in July 1998. Someone may have participated in or heard about the recently opened Bendigo 'Men in Sheds' and its 1999 'Shed Open Day,' attended by 4,000 people and publicised via the media. Alternatively, they may have seen something in the press or via the internet about either the Lane Cove Men's Shed (opened in late 1998 in New South Wales) or the Port Augusta Men's Shed in South Australia, opened in 1999.

The final, related difficulty with a definitive Men's Shed history is that a small number of early Sheds were reluctant to identify with the Men's Shed Movement. Most Men's Sheds to 2015 'Stand on the Shoulder of Giants'[14] and willingly incorporate the accumulated knowledge of the Men's Shed Movement, by identifying as 'Men's Sheds', registering and being accepted by the state or national peak bodies. In doing so they are accepted by shedders and the wider community as Men's Sheds, even if the word 'Men' or 'Shed' is not included in the name of the organisation. Other Sheds choose, for whatever reason, not to affiliate with Shed clusters or state or national peak Men's Shed bodies. This relatively small number of non-affiliated Men's Sheds is unable to be included in this history and analysis.

While it would be simpler to say that any community organisation without both the words 'Shed' and 'Men' in the name of the organization is not a Men's Shed, this would unfairly disqualify many other community organisations that have consistently been accepted by shedders and registered with peak body associations as Men's Sheds. Some very early Sheds in this category include

---

[14] The metaphor of dwarfs standing on the shoulders of giants (Latin: *nanos gigantum humeris insidentes*) expresses the meaning of discovering truth by building on previous discoveries.

Clem's Shed in Minlaton and Hocky's Shed in Snowtown, both in South Australia, and Pete's Community Workshed in Bridgewater, Tasmania.

It would also be unfair to exclude Shed-based community organisations that have, at a local level, often for good reasons, decided to admit and involve some or many women on equal terms with men. A good example is the St Helens Community Shed (Tasmania), which has consistently identified *with* and been accepted *by* the Shed Movement as a Men's Shed. In addition, to use the presence of a hands-on workshop as a definitional criterion for a Men's Shed would exclude several early, iconic and very influential Men's Sheds. It would also exclude Brimbank Men's Shed in Sunshine in suburban Melbourne, when in fact Brimbank has worked exceptionally effectively with no tools or workshop.

As a final example, the woodworking shed associated with 'House with No Steps' (a community organisation for people with a disability) near Alstonville (in rural Northern New South Wales) is one of many Australian examples of a wood workshop for men that existed before Men's Sheds *per se*. Similarly, the Ballarat Woodworkers, comprising almost all men, has been meeting in a shed at Ballarat Airport in regional Victoria for several decades. This problem of definition also applies in other countries beyond Australia. For example *Gal Gael* in Govan, in suburban Glasgow, has been operating since 1997 in Scotland as a workshop and has many Men's Shed-like attributes.

My Proposal For a Three-way Men's Shed Definition

In this final section in this introductory Chapter I propose a way of dealing with the definitional complexity and ambiguity identified above. I do this by suggesting three criteria that in combination define the essential essence of any community organisation being or becoming part of the Men's Shed Movement.

This proposal is consistent with what many communities and governments do in relation to other contentious issues of cultural identification. My proposal is to base the contemporary (and historic) definition of a Men's Shed in a community setting around a variation of the three-way (tripartite) definitional criteria (of *descent from, identification with* and *acceptance by the community*). A similar tripartite method is used, for example, to formally recognise Indigenous (Aboriginal and Torres Strait Islander) Australians.

The first criterion about '*descent from*' is easy to apply to all recent Sheds, since most new Men's Sheds organisations descend from, or are based on or around knowledge of Shed principles and practices developed by previous Sheds. Men's Sheds setting up in 2015 have the huge advantage of the knowledge base of over 1,300 Sheds, being descended in some way from all Sheds that have gone before them. Today's Men's Sheds also have an accumulating body of advice, manuals, research and program evaluation, much of it now available instantly and worldwide via the internet. As an example, around two thirds (66%) of Men's Sheds in Australia in 2013 acknowledged that they had used the Australian Men's Sheds Association (AMSA) *How to Set up and Run a Men's Shed* on-line manual, and 77 per cent of those who had accessed it agreed that the information it contained was 'useful'. AMSA confirmed in early 2015 that the download data for this resource also reveals a consistent, strong, recent interest in this Australian manual, particularly in the UK and Ireland.

Meeting the second and third criteria, of consistent *identification with* (effectively belonging to the 'family' or Movement of Men's Sheds), and furthermore *acceptance by* (that family or Movement *as* a Men's Shed) is perhaps more relevant here. The only problem is that it is impossible for the earliest Sheds (before there was a 'Movement') to demonstrate either. The criterion that the organisation identifies with the community of Men's Sheds can also be problematic. As flagged already, some Men's Shed organisations deliberately choose to remain fiercely independent and not join the national (or any) Shed-based peak body or association. While there are several financial incentives to join, such as access to discounted group insurance and funding via Men's Sheds associations, there should be no obligation in a truly 'grassroots' organisation to comply with any top-down directive.

My proposal is that being a Men's Shed in a community setting in 2015 should ideally be about 'ticking' all three boxes: consistently *identifying* with and supporting other Sheds in the Movement, being *accepted* by the Movement and *acknowledging the contribution* of those that have gone before in order to get the Movement up and running.

One could make a moral case that a Men's Shed that chooses to 'go it totally alone', and not acknowledge or identify with the Movement, is unfairly benefiting from the widespread community support generated by others who have toiled long and hard to get the Movement 'off the ground'. If a Shed (or peak body) is reluctant or unwilling to share its knowledge, to identify with or give back to the Movement by affiliating and 'paying its way', can it claim to be part of the Movement? There is an argument that individual Sheds (or organisations such as Mensheds Australia) that have relied on or benefited from shedder community or government goodwill, technical resources, Men's Shed data bases, research and accumulated wisdom, but do not identify with the Movement, or reciprocate and support other Sheds (other than for a fee), should not be accepted by the shedder community. In effect, if a Shed deliberately resists identifying, there is a case that it is morally problematic to accept it as being a part of the Men's Shed *Movement*.

INVENTION AND INNOVATION: A FRAMEWORK FOR THE BOOK

Having laboured above over the complex but important definitional issues, I turn in this final section of Part 1 to what the literature on innovation might say about whether we have an invention or an innovation here. This literature would draw a distinction between the *invention* of a Men's Shed and its subsequent *adoption* and *innovation*.

> *Invention* is the process by which a new idea [in this case, a Men's Shed] is discovered or created, and adoption is the decision to make full use of an innovation ... *Innovation* is not necessarily a fixed entity as it diffuses within a social system[15].

In essence, Part 2 that follows is mostly about the community Shed and Men's Shed *invention* and early *adoption* in advance of the Men's Shed Movement. Part 3 is mostly about subsequent, more widespread Men's Sheds *adoption and innovation*, including proliferation via the Men's Shed Movement. Parts 2 and 3 taken together confirm that, as for many inventions and innovations, Men's Sheds have been sensibly modified or 're-invented' by men and women, communities and stakeholder organisations in the process of their adoption and implementation in diverse contexts, cultures and countries, for diverse purposes, communities and groups of men.

The idea of one, 'smoking gun', 'original', spontaneous, prototypical, Men's Shed *invention* in a particular community setting in Australia is tantalising. However Part 2 will confirm that the first Shed and Men's Shed, in 1993 and 1998 respectively, were not invented by one person or organisation. They were created 'On the shoulders of Giants', informed by existing personal, social, professional, media, academic and community experience.

It is useful to finally but briefly distinguish between original invention, innovation and proliferation of Men's Sheds. The academic innovation literature acknowledges[16] that a number of prior conditions and stages typically precede the adoption of an invention. These prior conditions include previous practice, perceived need or an existing problem, as well as the innovativeness and norms of

---

[15] Everett Rogers, *Diffusion of Innovations*. New York: The Free Press, 1995, Chapter 5, 'The innovation-decision process', 1995, 174-175.
[16] Everett Rogers, 1995, as above, 163.

the social system. While it is still possible for one person or organisation in Australia to claim that they invented, 'hatched' (on more likely incubated) the first Shed or Men's Shed, many of the same preconditions (including: population ageing, perceived problems with men's health and wellbeing, disengagement of men from the community beyond their paid work lives, inability of conventional services to reach some men and reluctance to engage in later life learning) were already in place. In effect these same preconditions have encouraged the subsequent adoption of Men's Sheds (involving innovation and considerable re-invention) elsewhere in Australia and in other countries.

The evidence teased out in Part 2 will suggest that some of the earliest community Sheds did develop semi-independently with relatively slow adoption of the original invention. It was five years between the first Shed (in 1993) and the first Men's Shed (in 1998), and another six to seven years before the first Men's Shed gatherings were held to discuss Men's Sheds at a state or national forum (in Australia in 2004 and 2005 respectively). Indeed the principles of what a Men's Shed is (and is not) are still being hotly debated, defined and refined at these same national forums two decades after the first prototypical Men's Sheds, and a decade after the Movement began to gain momentum post-2005.

Thus the reason for writing the book and telling the story now is so that the set of circumstances that led to community Men's Sheds should be more widely understood and that the momentum the Movement has should not be lost. It is timely to learn, share and build on what early shedders and communities have invented and innovated. It is critically important and timely to document the process of subsequent innovation and proliferation after the remarkable first decade in Australia. It is both pleasurable and exciting to record the first five years of the Men's Shed Movement's rapid spread across Ireland, the UK and New Zealand and as I pen these words in early 2015, also to Europe and North America.

PART II

A Community Men's Shed History

Part 2 chronicles the slow, early development of shed-based organisations in community settings for men during the first decade from the mid-1990s, which preceded the rapid, subsequent proliferation of Men's Shed organisations across Australia in the decade after 2005, and to other countries, particularly to Ireland, the UK and New Zealand after 2008. In includes a comprehensive account of the creation of 'the Men's Shed Movement' as Men's Sheds in community settings came to wider public and government attention in southern Australia from 2007. Given this is effectively a 'grassroots' Movement, Part 2 emphasises the important part multiple origins, people, intentions and some serendipity have played, particularly in terms of the earliest service providers, places, people or organisations to 'pick and run with' the idea of a Shed, for and by men in the community. Part 2, in its totality, shows how the Men's Shed model has proved amenable to modification to suit a wide range of locations, groups of men and nations, for diverse purposes, It also shows how Men's Sheds and the Movement have progressed and continue to innovate and change.

The first part of Chapter 2 documents the early, tentative experiments by 'Shed pioneers' in a small number of places across Australia, particularly in South Australia in the first decade after 1993. It then teases out the several diverse strands of the 'Men's Shed story' as community organisations by that name started to appear from late 1998. A number of 'side stories' are critically examined about some early Sheds and workshops as well as people and organisations that sit somewhat ambiguously at the edges of the early Movement. Chapter 2 digs deepest into the fortuitous set of circumstances, people and agendas that led to the creation of a small number of prototypical community Sheds, particularly in South Australia before 1998.

Chapter 3 chronicles the creation, from 1998, of the first 'Men's Sheds', leading to the development of the first state Men's Shed Associations in Australia between 2007-9. It firstly explores early Men's Sheds in New South Wales and Victoria where the focus of the emerging Movement shifted to from South Australia after 2004. Secondly, it explores early Men's Shed history in all other Australian states. Chapter 4 explores how the national Men's Shed association and the national Movement began to achieve traction and funding by 2009. Finally, Chapter 5 documents the relatively rapid and remarkable spread of Men's Sheds and other national Men's Shed associations to Ireland, the UK and New Zealand after 2008. Some account of the early development of Men's Sheds in Canada, Sweden and Denmark completes the Chapter.

CHAPTER 2

Coming Out of the Backyard Shed in Australia

This chapter tells the story of how and why Men's Sheds in community settings were first created in Australia during the 1990s. The story has many diverse, fascinating and very early strands, most of them occurring in South Australia. The scene is set by going back to a little known conference held in South Australia in 1986, pondering how to improve services for men. It identifies the fertile bed for the first community Shed 'spark' to catch in rural South Australia after a major economic recession, in the context of population ageing and concerns about the wellbeing of men not in paid work. It tells about some early, prototypical community Shed experiments, including the first ever, well documented Shed for men in a community setting: the Goolwa Heritage Club Shed in rural South Australia in 1993.

Some thicker strands in the story appear in South Australia from the mid-1990s. Mark Thomson's *Blokes and Sheds* book was published in 1995. Dr Leon Earle discovered the value of the backyard shed and suggested that such sheds might play a role beyond the home. Health workers in rural South Australia were experimenting with shed-based services around the same time as grassroots, shed-based retreats and workshops were being set up by South Australian Vietnam War Veterans. A trickle of early, tentative Men's Shed experiments from mid-1998 became a rush in the new millennium as several other south eastern Australian states 'got the Men's Shed bug'. Chapter 2 turns to a number of earlier workshop and Shed-based organisations in Australia to explore which other threads of the Men's Shed story might have been incorporated into the Men's Shed invention and subsequent innovation. The story of how Men's Sheds began to share their knowledge and organise into national and state Movements in Australia is told in more detail in Chapter 3.

'A good historian can find a precedent for everything. But an even better historian knows when these precedents are but curiosities that cloud the big picture'.[1] Sapiens, Yuval Noah Hariri, 2014.

ACKNOWLEDGEMENTS

Part 2 is dedicated to Maxine Kitto (now Chaseling) and the late Dick McGowan, who are acknowledged for the first time via this book as important contributors to the many other strands of history and fate which led to The Shed in Goolwa, in South Australia in 1993, and the first Men's Shed in Tongala, Victoria in July 1998. Other important Australian Men's Shed pioneers, all recipients of the 2013 AMSA 'Hall of Fame' awards are acknowledged in Appendix 4.

KEY THREADS OF THE STORY IN SOUTH AUSTRALIA

The period prior to 2000, while critically important in telling the early community Men's Shed story, is the least known or understood, and ripe for this first serious historical study. Despite being relatively recent, this is the period that most current shedders[2], community members, students and scholars want to know much more about.

Prior to writing this book I had tended, in public forums, to flippantly suggest that the early development of the 'first Men's Shed' was akin to Aladdin rubbing his magic lamp and seeing a Men's Shed emerge, with the subsequent ones being copied or modified and spreading on the basis of their demonstrated utility and success. In truth it is much more complicated and interesting. While private, backyard sheds and some product-based workshops in community settings have been in existence for much longer in Australia than community Men's Sheds, as defined in Chapter 1, the fundamentals of the invention and innovation are embodied in the creation, from mid-1998, of a named *Men's* space in a *community* setting for diverse purposes. These purposes go well beyond workshop activity and products, including informally addressing men's *health and wellbeing*, very broadly defined.

The hard part of writing this book, and particularly this chapter, was deciding where and when to start the story. While the whole story about the attraction of

---

[1] Yuval Noah Harari, *Sapiens: A Brief History of Humankind*. London: Harvill Secker: London, 2014, 260.

[2] Ruth van Herk from Lane Cove Men's Shed in Sydney claims credit for the word 'shedders' as she used it 'very early in the history' in presentations and in the written word.

private sheds for men in Australia and elsewhere is much earlier, bigger and wider, this book deliberately focuses on *community* Men's Sheds organisations. Because the evidence of early Shed-based experimentation in community settings during the 1990s is particularly compelling in South Australia, this is where I start the story. To set the scene I go back to South Australia in the mid-1980s, where, for very good reasons, as in many other areas of the world, women's issues and feminism had come to the fore since the 1960s.

The Women's Movement made huge advances in many relatively developed nations, including Australia, Ireland, the UK and New Zealand related to gender equity during the latter part of the last millennium. These advances were well overdue after hundreds of years of men's total domination and hegemony over many areas of government, service provision as well as in private and public life. Until these advances, many women were effectively missing from the official public and historical record, from many areas of paid work, education, the media, politics and public life, including in Australia. The move towards gender equality, still incomplete even in relatively progressive and enlightened nations, took over a century of women's struggle. As an example in the Australian state of South Australia, women first got the right to vote and stand for State Parliament in 1894. It took 65 more years (until 1959) for the first South Australian woman to be elected to the Australian Parliament. By the 1970s services for women and by women had become widely accepted as being effective, necessary and important. What had not been factored in at this time was how *some* men and *some* men's services were faring.

EARLY DISCUSSIONS ABOUT MEN'S SERVICES IN SOUTH AUSTRALIA

By the mid-1980s the pendulum was beginning to swing back for some men and some services, and some of the early thinking and action in Australia was quietly happening, mostly 'below the radar', in South Australia. On March 7-8, 1986 a community services gathering, 'Linking Men's Services: A Conference on Men's Issues and Services in South Australia', was held at Noarlunga Health Village (in south suburban Adelaide). It discussed how to address the fact that while some men had acute needs, including during the process of later life ageing, most community and health services at that time were aimed at assisting women. This conference is of particular interest because of its links, explored later in this chapter, to the genesis of 'The Shed' seven years later in Goolwa, only 50 km southeast of where the conference was held. Maxine Kitto, the key player in the creation of the Goolwa Heritage Club Shed, then lived and worked in Noarlunga, participated in and was influenced by this early conference.

So what was the thinking about men's issues and services in the mid-1980s as captured in the 1986 conference proceedings? The rest of this section provides a snapshot of this thinking, by revisiting some of what was discussed by the one hundred South Australian participants (one quarter of whom were women). It included the views from the 22 invited presenters, 20 who were men, all of whom were from Adelaide. The conference participants were from diverse professional backgrounds, in health, hospital, welfare, counseling and aged care services as well as from prisons, War Veterans and men's services generally. The issues that were discussed neatly summarise the world of service provision that existed for men who were then in midlife (around 40 years) during the 1980s. These same men are now of median shedder age (around 70 years in Australia) in 2015. The issues discussed neatly set the scene for what was to later occur nearby in several places in rural South Australia during the next decade, including some early experimentation with Shed-based service provision.

The 1986 Conference proceedings record, in the 'Introduction', that the conference was held in the context of major social change for men in South Australia, including:

> ... changing patterns of employment, long-term unemployment, changing patterns of family life, the rise of the divorce and separation rate, and the women's movement with its questioning of traditional sex-role stereotyping and particularly male dominance in society, [which] has led many men to reassess their identities and roles. A special case of this is the men who came back from the Vietnam War with their perceptions of life permanently changed. This change process, while positive, is not without its share of stress, change and pathology. Reflective of these stresses is the growing interest in the development of programmes and services targeted directly at men. [3]

This 1986 conference was, 'to the best knowledge of the organisers ... the first conference of its type in Australia'[4]. The organisers were careful to stress that the conference:

> ... was not conceived as a forum for men to vent anger at particular women, or the women's movement in general but [as] a serious attempt

---

[3] *Linking Men's Services: A Conference on Men's Issues and Services in South Australia*, March 7-8, 1986, Noarlunga, Conference Proceedings, 1986, 3.

[4] *Linking Men's Services*, as above, 3.

> to address difficulties confronting men in today's society and to link services trying to meet these needs. ... Increasingly it is being recognised that many social phenomena classified as "women's issues" *cannot successfully be addressed without including men in the solutions.*[5]

In his opening address, the South Australian Minister of Health and Community Welfare, John Cornwall, observed that:

> To some extent, the Conference could be seen as a reaction to the increased emphasis placed on special health issues related to women. However looking at the topics covered by the many speakers ... [it] is surprising that it has taken until now for sufficient interest to be generated in men's community health.[6]

The Minister pointed to a number of good reasons to 'focus particularly on services for men'[7], including 'gender differences in rates of sickness and death', 'changing roles in domestic and work scenes [that] require considerable adjustment by men' and 'differences in use of community health services by men and women'. In that year, 1986, the average life expectancy in Australia of 71 years for men was significantly less (by seven years), than for women. It is of some note in retrospect that the life expectancy in 1986 for men was only one year older than the recently (2013) revised 70 year future pension age, at which age people born after 1965 will become eligible for the Australian age pension from 2035. This significant extension of life expectancy in many parts of the more developed world, particularly for men beyond paid work[8], is an important background to this Men's Shed Movement story.

Aside from acknowledging the many health issues related to 'men's relationships, excessive use of alcohol, or stress related problems'[9], the Minister noted that:

> Traditionally men have been seen as the providers for their families ... work was always central to men's identity ... they should be emotionally

---

[5] *Linking Men's Services*, as above, 3, *italics* added.
[6] *Linking Men's Services*, as above, 4.
[7] *Linking Men's Services*, as above, 3.
[8] Barry Golding, Rob Mark and Annette Foley, *Men Learning through Life*. Leicester: NIACE, 2014.
[9] *Linking Men's Services*, as above, 5.

> "in control" and invulnerable at all times … [A]ggression was seen as an
> important component of men's self-image. Many developments have
> challenged this traditional view of the male sex role[10].

None of the many presenters at this 1986 South Australian conference mentioned
private or community sheds for men as a health or other intervention. However it
is possible to retrospectively find pointers for what was to follow during the next
decade, including from presentations that focused on why men then used
community health services around half as much as women. There was a
perception, based on some local research reported to the conference, that some of
the differences observed in men accessing services was about accessibility,
opening hours and need. However much of it was about prevailing negative male
stereotypes, including perceptions about men not admitting to illness,
vulnerability to failure, and being afraid of becoming involved with health
professionals in clinical settings. Several of these broad stereotypes called
'hegemonic masculinities' were identified by gender theorists from field research
in Australian schools during the same era (from 1982) and were later reworked by
Bob Connell[11].

A health service reported to the Conference that it had experimented on a
small scale in suburban Adelaide with a range of services and programs targeted
specifically at men. This included programs for violent and isolated men,
including stress management and assertiveness training. It reported coming up
against some men who had expressed 'resentment of the women's movement'[12]
and who felt 'threatened by the new breed of women, particularly if they want to
maintain a traditional male-role'[13]. The workshop associated with this
presentation concluded that:

> … men's questioning of traditional role-definition and the need for them
> to adapt to a changing social and economic climate has created *a need
> for services designed specifically for men*[14].

In hindsight, it is evident that the deployment of these relatively informal
'courses' for specific groups of problematized men, including programs run by

---

[10] *Linking Men's Services*, as above, 5.
[11] Robert Connell and James Messerschmidt, 'Hegemonic Masculinity: Rethinking the
Concept', *Gender and Society*, 19: 829-859, 2005.
[12] *Linking Men's Services*, as above, 23.
[13] *Linking Men's Services*, as above, 24.
[14] *Linking Men's Services*, as above, 24, *italics* added.

women for male 'clients' based on a deficit model, was not the most appropriate or effective approach. However two fascinating findings lie in the detail of this early research and service experimentation. The first was the finding (and conclusion) that in '... all the courses, the most prominent aspect reported by most of the men was the contact with others in the course. ... Facilitating this type of contact may be a major function for Community Health workers'[15]. The second was '... the general consensus of the men attending the groups that they preferred men-only groups'[16].

Again in hindsight, the other particularly prescient conference presentation was about the way differential power relationships were affecting men in organisational structures in 1986. Workers from the Men's Contact and Resource Centre in Parkside (inner suburban Adelaide) suggested that ' ... men are so often out of touch with their feelings that they deny that these affect their perceptions and behaviour. *This in itself is a legacy of the lack of 'socialness' of many of our organisations and experiences as men*'[17]. Specifically they observed that:

> Men from low socio-economic backgrounds generally find themselves ... with limited opportunity and power. ... *Men from these backgrounds are generally de-powered by other people with greater 'authority'. They are the 'clients' rather than the service providers*; the subordinates rather than the bosses; affected rather than affecting.[18]

It is important to note in passing that these are very similar findings to those contained in many of my research papers about Men's Sheds in community settings to 2015.

The 1986 Conference Proceedings summary records that there was a 'preponderance of professional service providers', and that 'Some regret was expressed that more "ordinary" men were not present'[19]. The first of the three main issues identified in the 'Where to from here?' plenary session at the end of the conference included the perennial, 'hoary chestnut', 'The involvement of women'. While some participants suggested that 'it was very necessary for women to be involved because at present they are providing many of the services

---

[15] *Linking Men's Services*, as above, 22.
[16] *Linking Men's Services*, as above, 23.
[17] *Linking Men's Services*, as above, 80, *italics* added.
[18] *Linking Men's Services,* ss above, 78.
[19] *Linking Men's Services*, as above, 133, *italics* added.

for men', there was 'a general feeling that in the future it would be valuable to have men only groups and/or gatherings'[20].

My point in drawing out these prescient observations from this important, first meeting of mainly men's service providers, almost three decades ago in South Australia, is to stress that Men's Sheds organisations, like Aladdin's genies, did not magically 'come out of nowhere'. They were created and organised in the first instance by 'normal' men *and* women, including some professional service providers. They were mainly *for* men because of a deeply perceived need, including from professional service providers dissatisfied with the *status quo* for older men. Importantly, they did not, with some minor exceptions, spring from any of the Men's Movements of the day, a theme returned to in Part 4.[21]

It is no accident that the first, early, prototypical Sheds in South Australia would later be nested within health, aged care and hospital settings. They served a community health function, not only because they empowered men to work with and help other men, but particularly because they reached older and rural men from very diverse, isolated and often disempowered backgrounds. As will also be shown later, Men's Shed organisations had the capacity to challenge and reverse the *professional to client* service model of health provision, oriented mainly towards women by women, on the assumption that only women were gendered and that men did not need their own programs because they should and would access 'mainstream' programs.

It is not surprising, in retrospect, that some of the earliest informal Shed activity would be located in sheds in community settings increasingly at arms length from service providers and specifically for men. Backyard sheds and workshops were where many rural men during the 1980s simultaneously felt at home *and* productively worked. What the Men's Shed Movement started to do, nearly two decades after this 1986 conference, was create a familiar, workshop-type setting with other men, able to freely 'do stuff', often hands-on, practicing and learning new skills in familiar workshop situations, for the benefit of the community. What was not possible in their earliest iterations, until much later, during the late 1990s, was to take the next, quite radical step and publicly name the organisation and the space a *Men's Shed*.

---

[20] *Linking Men's Services*, as above, 134.
[21] Spase Karoski, in his 2007 PhD thesis, *Men on the Move: The Politics of the Australian Men's Movement* (University of Wollongong), identified four contemporary men's movements: the pro-feminist, fathers rights, mythopoetic and inclusive men's movements. Men's sheds were not mentioned in the thesis.

WHAT ELSE WAS CHANGING FOR MEN IN AUSTRALIA DURING THE 1990S?

While much of the very early action in the community 'Shed space' before 2000 will be shown later in this chapter to have occurred in South Australia, things were changing similarly elsewhere in Australia. There is evidence that some service providers during the late 1980s and early 1990s in Australia were beginning to question some aspects of the female-gendered nature of their provision for some men. Some were taking small but deliberate steps to try and address them for and by some groups of men. As an example, in October 1986 *The Canberra Times* reported that a group called 'Men in Transition' had been set up, run 'by men and for men' under the auspices of Belconnen Community Services in Canberra, Australia's capital city. Their stated interest was in 'talking with other men and looking at issues such as men's roles in society, relationships, communication and parenting.'

Another example from six years later (in 1992) comes again from Canberra, as reported in *The Canberra Times*[22]. The article was headed 'Men-only groups confront a social phenomenon', discussing Southside Community Centre's 'fortnightly men's group for over 60s', with activities that included 'discussions, picnics and visits to cultural and historic sites'. The rationale for setting up the small (five person) group was explained by Margaret Barraclough, who delivered games at the Centre for the Hungarian Australian Club.

> About 90 per cent of our clients, are women, and we have no trouble getting them to join in groups and activities. But somehow we just haven't been able to get this men's group off the ground, and I can't say I really know why.

'Dudley', one of the male 'clients' in this Canberra program, funded by Home and Community Care in 1992, was sceptical. "I said it from the start. ... You'll never get a men's group off the ground. It takes women to get this sort of thing organised." This is illustrative of prevailing attitudes and context in which the first community Men's Sheds were developed later the same decade. It is also important to acknowledge that women were then perceived as critically important to get some of the 'stuff organised' *for* male clients.

In the same place and around the same time, private men's sheds were being publicly recognised as a valid space for men to escape to. Paige Gordon put on a

---

[22] February 22, 1992, 40.

show called *Shed* in Canberra in 1994 with an all-male cast. It included 'Martin O'Callaghan, who trained in Adelaide but now farms (with several sheds in Braidwood)'[23]. The *Canberra Times* records that the show opened on a Canberra stage on February 22, 1994 at the Bogong Theatre. The article promoting *Shed* quoted Paige Gordon as saying:

> Sheds for men are sanctuary all their own. ... Whether in habitual use – or only intermittently – the shed remains a private place where [a man] can escape to. In a busy world filled with all sorts of pressures, the shed is a valid space for men.

The main social and economic influence in Australia during the early 1990s was the major economic recession, whose early seeds were sown in long tail of the world Stock Market Crash of October 1987. This recession affected much of the world in the late 1980s and early 1990s. The economy of Australia suffered its worst recession since the Great Depression in the 1930s. The Australian stock market lost 40 per cent of its value in the period. Many businesses around Australia collapsed and the unemployment rate continued to climb until 1992, putting people of all ages, including many older men, out of work, some forever.

South Australia was particularly hard hit by this recession by the early 1990s, and unemployment soared in many former industrial regions, towns and suburbs across the state. Rural and regional areas in South Australia and other Australian states were particularly adversely affected. Unsurprisingly, the available evidence points towards some of the earliest experimentation and regional development and use of sheds in community settings for men in rural and regional South Australia, centred on the most adversely affected areas *and* particularly impacted groups of rural, older men. This difficult and unusual set of circumstances and demographics, combined with a fortuitous set of persuasive people, will be shown to have created a particularly fertile opportunity for early shed experimentation in South Australia. Most of the earliest action and the key players were operating in personal and backyard shed settings and well beyond reach of academics and the media. It would be several years later, in 1998 in Tongala in Victoria and in Lane Cove in New South Wales, that the first community organisations would open under the name *Men's* Sheds, in July and December respectively.

Meantime a semi-independent set of fortuitous circumstances and people were coalescing in rural South Australia (around 1,400 kilometers, or 17 hours driving time west of Sydney). While the exact chronology is difficult to pin

---

[23] 'Dance Production Celebrates the Shed', *Canberra Times*, February 16, 1994.

down, there is evidence of an informal sharing of ideas about Men's Sheds and shed experimentation, some involving men as participants in quite diverse community settings. There were so many things happening after 1995 in the backyard and community Shed 'space' in South Australia in particular that it is difficult to completely disentangle them. In reality, several of the key 'players' and events in this eclectic mix, introduced below, likely influenced each other. Much of what follows in this chapter is about the shift in interest and locus of activity about sheds from the personal and private to the public, community and organisational sphere.

A BRIEF INTRODUCTION TO THE KEY 'SHED PLAYERS' IN SOUTH AUSTRALIA IN THE 1990S

One of the most visible and influential national players in the personal men's shed 'space' from the mid-1990s was Mark Thomson, a prolific grassroots researcher, writer and photographer of backyard men's sheds, who lived and worked in South Australia. Thomson was, in his own words, the first person to make '... a serious study of them ... clock[ing] up thousands of kilometres in search of backyard sheds'. The final selection for his *Blokes and Sheds* book published in 1995 was pared down from 170 to 45 mainly South Australian backyard and personal sheds, but it also included three sheds from Victoria and some from Queensland and New South Wales[24]. Thomson's widely circulated, popular books fired men up about their own backyard sheds, as did the half hour ABC TV *Men in their Sheds* documentary, produced in 1995 by producer Susan McKinnon and written by Ian Walker[25], broadcast nationally in Australia in 1996.

It is difficult to overemphasise the importance of popular culture and media in generating the interest that led to other very early sheds in community settings in Australia after 1995. This includes Mark Thomson's very readable and widely circulated books in Australia, the widely viewed national TV program broadcast in 1996, and as elaborated later, John Williamson's *The Shed* song, released in Australia in 1995. Around the same time an Adelaide-based academic gerontologist[26], Dr [later Professor] Leon Earle, whose research work on older people's recreation from the early 1990s had touched peripherally on backyard

---

[24] "Shedding Light on Our Blokes", *The Age*, October 24, 1995, by Alan Attwood, www.drillbits.com.au, Accessed June 5, 2014.
[25] *Men and their Sheds*, 1995 ABC TV, 26 minutes. http://trove.nla.gov.au/work/33004518?selectedversion=NBD21771281, Accessed June 5, 2014.
[26] Gerontology refers to the science of ageing.

men's sheds, had begun to enter academic discussions about the value of the backyard sheds by 1995. While publication of a relatively obscure academic paper of which Earle was lead author emphasised the role of backyard sheds in the lives of retired men, it was the widespread media promotion of his work rather than his academic publications that likely gave his work visibility and traction.

In the same era in the mid-1990s Vietnam War Veterans across several sites in South Australia, shattered from their war experiences, were struggling to find places and spaces (including workshops and sheds) where men could meet and regroup after being comprehensively shunned on return from serving their country overseas. Community health workers in the mid north of South Australia and the Yorke Peninsula were at the same time struggling to meet the acute health and wellbeing needs of some rural, older and unemployed men, some of whom were also war Veterans.

John Monten[27], a welfare worker, had stumbled across and become involved in early experiments with shed-based provision during the late 1980s as part of his previous work with former miners in the remote western New South Wales mining city of Broken Hill. Broken Hill is close to the South Australian border with many South Australian affinities. Some creative dementia workers in Adelaide including Keith Bettany, in his behaviour consultant's role with Alzheimer's South Australia in Adelaide, were becoming concerned about the inappropriateness of many of the care options for older men living with dementia in aged and day care settings.

Each of these people is separately and comprehensively introduced later, but not until one more piece of the shed story 'jigsaw' is added in the section that follows: the first well-documented early experiment with shed-based provision for men in South Australia. 'The Shed', set up in the rural Goolwa Heritage Club in South Australia, introduced next, is arguably the *first* Shed in the world deliberately created for men in a community setting. There is also evidence of a compelling link between the South Australian Men's Services Conference in 1986, The Shed in Goolwa in 1993 and planning for Manningham Men's Shed. Manningham, one of first Men's Sheds established in 2000 in suburban Melbourne (Doncaster) in Victoria is introduced later in Chapter 3.

---

[27] In 2015 John Monten was a Men's Health Worker for the Yorke and Lower North Rural Region: Clare Centre.

THE GOOLWA HERITAGE CLUB SHED: THE FIRST COMMUNITY SHED FOR MEN

The earliest Shed I can find that was deliberately set up and officially opened for men in a community setting through a community organization with unequivocal, clearly documented, direct links to later Men's Sheds is 'The Shed' in the Goolwa Heritage Club. Goolwa is a small rural town on the coastal barrages that mark the end of the Murray River in South Australia. Officially opened by the Hon Dean Brown, Member of Parliament on February 24, 1993[28], 'The Shed' was spawned from the Goolwa Heritage Club that commenced much earlier, in January 1984, later to be renamed the Alexandrina Centre for Positive Ageing.

The Shed's history was well documented locally as part of the Alexandrina Centre's published history in 2004. However no one involved in the more recent Men's Shed Movement had been aware of its role for two reasons, quite apart from its location in rural South Australia, well away from the later community Men's Shed 'action'. The first reason is because The Shed and its woodwork program, which with leatherwork comprised the core of the 'hands-on' activity, were in decline by mid-1996. The Centre's commitment to the Shed also waned after its founder, Maxine Kitto, left Goolwa in March 1998. The second reason is because documents suggestive of The Shed having been used by one of the earliest *Men's* Sheds (Manningham Men's Shed, opened in Victoria in early 2000) as a precedent in its planning phase had not previously been made public. For context, The Shed in Goolwa opened five years before the opening of the first two 'Men's Sheds' during 1998, in Tongala in Victoria and Lane Cove in Sydney. The Shed in 2015 is shown in Photograph 1.

---

[28] This is the date recorded in 1996 (and confirmed as correct) by Maxine Kitto in 'Goolwa Heritage Club: The Shed'. The previous year, February 1992, is indicated in M. Brown (Ed.), *A People's Place: The First Twenty Years 1984-2004*, 2004, 48.

Photograph 1 The Shed, Goolwa Heritage Club, South Australia, May 2015

Dawn Juers[29], the Historian at the Goolwa Library, reported that while the original Goolwa Heritage Club Shed was now used for storage in 2015, it still had a plaque above the door, "Ras' Retreat". It was placed in honour of the first helper and volunteer carpenter, Alf (Ras) Stokes who helped Maxine Kitto start The Shed, was integral to its success and died on July 27, 2006. The Shed was renamed 'Ras' Retreat' in 2008. After he died his family donated his tools to the Shed. Next to it is another, larger shed with workbenches that were still used for woodwork and leather work as part of the Alexandrina Centre's scheduled programs each Wednesday in early 2015, though The Shed stopped functioning briefly between 2010 and 2012 because of occupational health and safety concerns. While gender still does not come into the name of The Shed (it is theoretically open to women), Dawn Juers noted that no women were participating in early 2015. Ironically, to 2013, Goolwa was one of very few towns in Australia without a later version of the community *Men's* Shed[30].

---

[29] Dawn Juers, January 23, 2015.
[30] 'Armfield Slip and Boatshed - Armfield Wooden Boats Inc.' in Goolwa was registered with AMSA in November 2013. The Armfield Slipway developed the first South Australian Wooden Boat Festival at Goolwa Wharf from approximately 1990.

I was alerted as recently as March 2014 to the likely importance of a 'Shed' in Goolwa. It was specifically referred to as a 'precedent' buried in a very early Manningham Men's Shed proposal document in Victoria, provided to me by Ric Blackburn, its second Shed Coordinator. Drawing a complete blank with online searches for a 'Goolwa Men's Shed', a phone call in desperation to the Goolwa Tourist Information Centre was fortuitously answered by Helen Barclay, whose husband Peter Barclay, a volunteer in the History Room at Goolwa, found some of the information I was seeking.

In April 2014, a few weeks afterwards, a doctoral student, Alison Herron, fortuitously approached me at a research forum in Melbourne after I told an outline of this story, and said, "I think I may have the information you are seeking about the links between the Manningham and Goolwa Sheds". This conversation proved serendipitous indeed. Based on information Alison Herron subsequently sent me by email, there is evidence of a clear link between this very early South Australian shed, officially opened in 1993, and planning for the Manningham Men's Shed, one of the earliest Men's Sheds to open in Victoria in 2000.

While a more detailed history of early Men's Sheds, including the Manningham Men's Shed, is provided later in Chapter 3, one 'back story' is important to briefly tell here which links The Shed in Goolwa back to ideas that were being discussed at the 1986 Noarlunga Men's Services Conference discussed at the start of Chapter 2. Alison Herron was employed as a social worker/social support manager from January 1995 at Doncare (Doncaster Community Services) and provided some input into a funding submission being developed for the Manningham Men's Shed by Manningham Community Health Services by its CEO, Neil Wakeman, in the late 1990s.

Alison Herron attended the May 1996 Australian Association of Gerontology 'Successful Ageing' Conference in Hobart, at which she heard a paper presentation about The Shed in Goolwa written by Maxine Kitto, presented on her behalf by Councillor Bill Green, Chairperson of the Heritage Club Management Committee[31]. Green also presented his own paper about how the Heritage Club was shifting their programs 'from care-based to learning-based'. In Alison Herron's words, written in 1996, she 'came away enthused by the concept of a Men's Shed as an avenue to involve more men in meaningful community connections'.

Maxine Kitto's insightful words about The Shed in the Goolwa Heritage Club, below, were written in 1996, more than two years before the first Men's Shed (with those words in the Shed's name) opened at Tongala in Victoria in July

---

[31] Alison Herron, May 2, 2014.

1998. For context, the Heritage Club provided 'services to aged people to enable empowerment and quality of life while residing in their own community' [32]. Maxine Kitto confirmed in 1996 (with extra information added in square brackets in early 2015, by the now Maxine Chaseling) that:

> The concept of The Shed was developed from three sources of knowledge.
>
> 1. [As the Coordinator, Noarlunga Community Aged Care] I attended a National Conference in March 1986 entitled "Linking Men's Services", a conference on community services and issues relating to men.[33] I was in a minority group of [5 female amid 300 male] community workers. [At that stage] the vast majority of community and health workers [were] aimed at assisting women. The "macho" image of "I'm alright mate" was still evident, especially in the minds of funding bodies.
>
> 2. [Six months after attending the conference I became employed as Coordinator, Heritage Aged Care Services for the Goolwa and Port Elliot Council. At the Goolwa Heritage Club] I observed the custom of men driving their wives to the Club for services and then waiting in the car park. With up to a dozen men in the car park, unless they had previously met, there was no social interaction. They usually read the paper, with every man keeping to the territory of their own car. The same wives of those men soon became widows who we supported and provided transport. The women inside the Club were healthier than the men in the car park.
>
> 3. My third key source of knowledge was my Dad. I grew up in an average Australian family where Mum's territory was inside the house and Dad's territory was the shed. Dad still knows where every jar of nails and screws, or hammer and saw belongs in his shed. It is where he feels comfortable, it is where he continues his role as the handyman, the fixer, the craftsman, and it is where he goes to get away from it all.[34]

---

[32] 'Goolwa Heritage Club: The Shed', Maxine Kitto, Coordinator. The Heritage Club, undated fax to Alison Herron, July 5, 1996.

[33] The proceedings of this conference were published as *Linking Men's Services: A Conference on Men's Issues and Services in South Australia, 7th and 8th March 1986*, Noarlunga Health Village, copy in FAHSIA Library, Canberra. http://trove.nla.gov.au/work/16547795?q&versionId=19422633, Accessed February 16, 2014.

[34] Maxine Kitto (Coordinator, The Heritage Club), *Goolwa Heritage Club: The Shed*, 1996, 1.

Maxine Kitto's astute and powerful observations about her inspiration for The Shed confirm that they were based on a combination of three sources: professional knowledge, everyday observation and personal/family experiences. Kitto's other words below were penned in 1996, two years before the first community Men's Shed was created. They remain very relevant to the Men's Shed Movement several decades on.

> The Shed is a program aimed at promoting good health through empowerment for older men. The Shed provides an environment in which retired men are motivated to retain their skills and social interactions with other men. ... The Shed has far outgrown the original aims of the program and has become a key focus in educating the community as to the value of older men. The men have become confident and felt social respect, and the Shed program has branched out creating [other] programs and interest groups.[35] ... The Shed Project is a strategic health promoting resource, to ensure older men retain their role of productive and valued community member, preventing taking on the role of "sick person"'. This strategy has been very successful, regardless of the fact that we have no funding for the program. ... The Shed program ... started to soar to success when a group of men came to me and demanded that I tell them what's expected of them in the shed. "What do you want us to do?" I was astounded and told them so. "I'm a woman, how in the world do I know what goes on in sheds. The shed is there. You blokes sort it out", and they did.
>
> I had thrown them a challenge and suddenly it opened the door. They could do what they wanted, and what they wanted was to help others. They took on the role of breadwinner, Mr Fix-it, craftsman, inventor, and the roles grew, expanding in different directions[36].

Maxine Kitto identified a diverse range of men's groups that The Shed subsequently spawned beyond the 'core of woodworkers and leather workers'[37], including the F.R.O.G. (Fleurieu Railway Operators Group) and the Saturday 'men only' Crib Group that 'used the same crib board that they used in the trenches in World War II' as well as the Community Garden Project. Kitto wrote

---

[35] Maxine Kitto, as above, 1.
[36] Maxine Kitto, as above, 2.
[37] Maxine Kitto, as above, 2-3.

in 1996 that 'The Dementia Unit use the shed on a one-to-one basis with their men. Amazing results in the men's ability to name all the tools in the shed and their use. Very rewarding experiences'[38]. Importantly Maxine Kitto confirmed that:

> The Shed project worked because the men were empowered. I had no idea what the men did in a shed but I knew that they were healthier with a shed than without a shed. Very simple, but beware, the shed project is not without risks. Some men have got to be the boss. The shed contains machinery that can cut fingers off etc. All men regardless of disability are encouraged to use the shed, and I have to rely on mateship to ensure all men find a valued place in the shed. Consequently it has been a rather frightening journey that I have also traveled, in letting them go. My relationship with these men is mutually respectful but also light hearted. The Shed Project should be recognised as a health promotion resource and funding should be made available. Most importantly as health professionals, we should be constantly aware of the importance of a valued social role in the health of older men.[39]

This perceptive account, written before July 1996, is echoed in the official history of The Shed in Goolwa, penned around eight years later in 2004, which used phrases that have since become remarkably 'normal' to anyone involved in the Men's Shed Movement.

> Over the years, *the shed* has provided an outlet for retired men to use their acquired skills or to learn new ones and has become a place of their own for a chat and a 'cuppa'. The [Heritage] Club has also benefited by selling items that have been produced by these skilled members.[40]

Tantalisingly, the official history of The Shed in Goolwa, published in 2004 and reproduced below in Photograph 2[41], starts with:

> *Everyman needs a shed ... especially when they are retired.* Having attended a Seminar on this topic, Maxine [Kitto] was convinced that this

---

[38] Maxine Kitto, as above, 3.
[39] Maxine Kitto, as above, 3.
[40] M. Brown (Ed.), *A People's Place: The First Twenty Years 1984-2004*, Alexandrina Centre for Positive Ageing (Formerly The Heritage Club), Goolwa, 2004, 47-8.
[41] This 2004 article gives the opening date as 1992. Maxine Chaseling confirms the actual date was 1993.

was a much needed adjunct to the services already provided at the Heritage Club.

Over the years, *the shed* has provided an outlet for retired men to use their acquired skills or to learn new ones and has become a place of their own for a chat and a 'cuppa'. The Club has also benefited by selling items that have been produced by these skilled members.

For several years part of the shed housed the Model Train Club but as this group increased in size, a larger space had to be found.

Although the shed still has a Leatherwork program running, the Woodwork program ceased mid 1996. In 2001 GoolwaSkill commenced programs in the shed which, to date, have been very successful and well attended. GoolwaSkill volunteers and students were very involved in the 2003 State Regional Arts Conference *Navigating Community Through The Arts*. They spent months working on zany floats based upon bicycle components which were to be ridden, pushed, carried and even dragged in the Street Parade that heralded the start of the weekend.

48

THE SHED

Every man needs a shed ..... especially when they are retired!

Having attended a Seminar on this topic, Maxine was convinced this was a much needed adjunct to the services already provided at the Heritage Club. A new large shed would also solve the problem of garage space for the Club's new 12-seater bus. It was agreed by the Management Committee that this would be funded by $3,000 from the Special Projects fund with the balance coming from fundraising by the Support Group.

After settling a few problems over the style and type of roof required and accepting that the shed would conform to *Heritage* requirements, the building was erected and officially opened in February 1992 by the Hon. Dean Brown, MP. Once the shed was completed, the surrounding garden area needed to be planned and established. Thanks are due to the Council's Head Gardener, Kalan Dennis, for his advice and guidance. Thanks also go to Heritage Club Volunteers for help in planting bushes and trees.

The Management Committee and Club members agreed that Alf Stokes would be the Woodwork instructor and that Reg Vowles would be the Leatherwork instructor (Reg is still passing on his Leatherwork skills today). Alf compiled a list of necessary resources and put out a request to the community through the Goolwa Lions Newsletter for unwanted tools, wood, paint, benches, etc. Club members also donated some of their own tools and the Murray Bridge Day Centre Woodwork program donated samples of items which could be made by our frailer members.

Photograph 2 Brief History of The Shed (Goolwa, South Australia), published in 2004

Both accounts of the Goolwa Heritage Club Shed, penned in 1996 and 2004, preceded the start of 'the Movement'. And yet they sounded so familiar and accurate when David Helmers (in 2015 the CEO of AMSA) first heard them, in April 2014, he swore that they were from a more recent Men's Shed Movement source.

It is important to note that these 'every man needs a shed' sentiments come directly from John Williamson's *The Shed* song on his *True Blue* Album, released on the Gumleaf / EMI label in Australia in 1995. Part of the song's lyrics go:

Yeah, all Australian boys need a shed
A place where he can go, somewhere to clear his head
To think about the things his woman said
Yeah, all Australian boys need a shed.
To grow up as he likes, to grow anything under lights
A place to keep his tools, nuts and bolts and drills
To hang a hide, to hide the dry or hang to pay the bills.
Yeah, all Australian boys need a shed.

Unsurprisingly, some of the song's words and sentiments reappear in the rationale of several later Australian Men's Sheds, particularly in media reports associated with official Shed openings. This is strongly suggestive of the relevance of *The Shed* song popularised by John Williamson to part of the explanation about how and why backyard men's sheds gained such widespread and iconic public acknowledgement and appeal in Australia after 1995. While backyard sheds had been popular in Australia for decades with men, it was songs and books that publicly celebrated this fact during the 1990s that reinforced their popularity and were clearly influential and timely.

While The Shed in Goolwa, opened in 1993, is not *the* only, proverbial 'smoking gun', its presence amongst several early, nearby community Sheds in South Australia in the decade that followed its opening, combined with the people and events detailed below, seems far from coincidental. A very small number of community Sheds, some of them created as part of hospital and aged care centres, but none publicly called Men's Sheds before 1998, sprang up around the same time nearby in South Australia. As an example, Jack Ellis' 'The Shed' (discussed later) opened in Hackham West (south of Adelaide) only 50 kilometers north of Goolwa in 1995. It remains the longest continuously operating Shed in the world, though it did not identify until relatively recently as a *Men's Shed*.

Tracking down Maxine Chaseling (previously Kitto) to check the Goolwa Shed story took the author over a year until January 21, 2015, with contact generously assisted by Dawn Juers, acknowledged earlier. In Maxine Chaseling's 2015 words:

> I was a registered nurse, and then gained a Diploma in Community Health Nursing prior to working at Goolwa. It was a challenge to promote the concept of retired people being healthy people, and in control of their lives. I am thrilled to see the subsequent development of Men's Sheds throughout Australia and overseas, but think that it was time, and health services were looking in that direction. I was just in the right place at the right time to test it. Since leaving the Goolwa Heritage Club in March 1998, I have gained a Master of International Public Health, worked for ten years in Papua New Guinea, and then five years in remote Indigenous Health in the Northern Territory. I now live at the Gold Coast, Queensland and work in Continuous Quality Improvement with Blue Care Metropolitan South Aged Care Services. [42]

Maxine Chaseling was invited to check this mostly written story (based only on historical, documentary evidence) in 2015. She was also asked about other influences that might have spawned what appears to be the first community Shed specifically for men in the world. Chaseling was also asked what other Sheds she recalled might have visited The Shed in Goolwa aside from Manningham or that may have used it as a model. Her response was as follows:

> The Goolwa Heritage Club Shed was initiated in 1993, to enable retired men, often retired farmers, to socialise within their own comfort zone and to gain confidence to link into a range of health support. Once they were through the door of The Shed, men around them would chat about the Heritage Club, thus becoming informally connected to a range of health promotion services and health, aged and information resources. Suddenly, their support network in retirement flourished. The Heritage Club Shed was one section of a multi-disciplinary health service that relied on 60 volunteers to operate. The men liked being in the fix-it section that frail, aged people would wander into with a problem that needed fixing at home. Staff would often ask the men to have a look at some equipment issue in the centre; volunteer bus drivers would take the bus to the Shed and discuss adaptations needed to transport people with special needs and they were able to assist the Club with goods for sale.

---

[42] Maxine Chaseling, January 25, 2015.

The men felt needed, they made friends, they researched equipment, they had access to the council workshop staff for support, and they loved the morning and afternoon teas. They were valued and happily booked in for physiotherapy, attended the gymnasium and walking group, and lined up for their appointment with the podiatrist. If life became a bit difficult, they would sit near the fire with the "oldies", have a yarn and a laugh, and all was OK. If anything serious happened, they could ask to see [professional staff], behind closed doors. The Goolwa Heritage Club Shed provided the door to enable retired men to retain independence within a network of support. They decided what sections of support they needed. They retained control of their lives.

Between 1993 and 1998, I was contacted for information on the Shed by many community health services throughout South Australia including Victor Harbor (Encounter Centre), Tanunda (Barossa Valley) Community Health, Port Adelaide Community House, Port Augusta Health Services, Hackham Community Services and Milang Community Group on Lake Alexandrina.[43]

It is important to note that while the Tongala Men's Shed in Victoria, proposed in Chapter 3 as the first *Men's* Shed, appears to have developed independently of (and five years later that Goolwa Heritage Club Shed), the rationale and the setting for both in rural aged care centres are not dissimilar. It is quite feasible that one or more people involved in getting the Tongala Men's Shed established might have heard about The Shed in Goolwa, directly or indirectly.

THE ROLE OF BACKYARD MEN'S SHED WRITER, MARK THOMSON

As identified earlier in this Chapter, Mark Thomson, based in Adelaide, South Australia, was writing about backyard men's sheds in a popular and accessible format from 1995, the same year that John Williamson's *The Shed* song came to prominence in Australia. Also in Adelaide, at the same time, gerontologist Leon Earle, discussed in detail in the section that follows, was researching the benefits to men of backyard sheds. Indeed Earle was briefly acknowledged (amongst 14 others) in Mark Thomson's best-selling book, *Blokes and Sheds*[44], published in

---

[43] Maxine Chaseling, January 25, 2015.
[44] Mark Thomson, *Blokes and Sheds: Behind the Corrugated Iron Curtains of Australia's Sheds*. Sydney: Angus and Robertson, 1995.

1995, which included Thomson's evocative, personal, mostly backyard shed photos.

Along with his 1996 sequel, *Stories from the Shed,* Mark Thomson's books have arguably been very influential in 'preparing the ground' in the wider Australian community for the later blossoming of community Men's Sheds. While Thomson's work is written and presented in a very accessible format, *Stories from the Shed* in particular brings into play a deceptively powerful subtext suggestive of some of the problems caused through some men's social isolation in their sheds. Other acknowledgements in his 1995 book point to some of its wider influences that are otherwise not formally referenced. One example is the contribution from a marital and family therapist, Dr Michael Lee, who contributed some powerful words about the backyard shed's potential dark side. Lee, '… as a young doctor, fresh out of university', had come across a man who had committed suicide in his shed, later suggesting that:

> It is perhaps hard for some to appreciate the depth and significance of the relationship between the man and his shed. Should a man be separated from his shed prematurely, or unwillingly, a life-threatening withdrawal and grief reaction can occur. It can leave the man hopeless and helpless, with no sense of meaning or purpose, alienated from his family and, at times from life in general.[45]

Mark Thomson, in *Stories from the Shed,* as the Goolwa Shed story confirms, was not necessarily the first person to write about the value and future possibilities of sheds for men in community settings. However there is a power and accessibility about his two compact books. Thomson's brief but carefully chosen words and exquisite black and white photography about sheds and their community-oriented possibilities reached out to many men beyond the professions and academia. Thomson's work is unlike some later popular and illustrated shed books, magazines and websites, which can be prone to celebrate the backyard shed as an a quasi-religious, personal 'man cave' and 'man space', to retreat from life in the shed around the fridge, away from partner and family, sometimes verging on the misogynistic ('woman hating') and featuring 'girlie' posters.

By contrast, Mark Thomson's work and messages are sensitive, positive, carefully nuanced as well as family and community oriented. While Thomson celebrates the personal shed, he is also acutely aware of the risk of the personal shed becoming a dark space. While *Blokes and Sheds,* published in 1995,

---

[45] Mark Thomson, *Stories from the Shed,* 1996.

acknowledges 'The tragedy of the shedless'[46], it tails off with, 'There's probably a whole new range of therapy options opening up ... '. The book's 'social shed' page[47] notes that 'all these [social shed-based activities] help to reinforce family links and traditions, in addition to being good fun'. The 'Fathers and sons (and daughters too)' section presciently asks:

> Is there a secret knowledge that men hand on to their sons in sheds? What values are handed on by young men in the seclusion of the shed? Is there a case for saying that the shed is the equivalent of the Navajo smokehouse or the Papuan Longhaus, to which only men are admitted.'[48]

In *Stories from the Shed*, Thomson refers to the paradoxical theme of isolation[49] that he observes recur in men's backyard shed stories. While some men in their private sheds 'found the strength to get through life'[50], at the same time Dr Michael Lee noted that some men ' ... saw it as a means by which men legitimized their withdrawal from domestic, partnering and child rearing responsibilities'. Mark Thomson raises the notion of the backyard shed to another level when he suggests that 'A surprising number of men talk about sheds using words and images that show a strongly spiritual and religious aspect of shed ownership', before finally asking, 'Have we thought about a community shed?'

Mark Thomson recently (in 2014) reflected thoughtfully on the pre-community Men's Shed era, recalling that:

> In 1995 there were no Men's Sheds of the type we would recognise today. There was one attached to a retirement complex in Adelaide's northeastern suburbs (mentioned in the *Complete Blokes and Sheds*[51] book) but it seemed to be tolerated by the management as an initiative of the male residents rather than having any official status. I vaguely recall ringing up various aged care organisations and asking them if they had any facilities for men's hobbies. The one I found at Tea Tree Gardens Retirement Village (which is the only one I found at the time) was the nearest thing to what we might say now is a community Men's Shed. At

---

[46] *Blokes and Sheds*, 54.
[47] *Blokes and Sheds*, 56-7.
[48] *Blokes and Sheds*, 88-89.
[49] *Stories from the Shed*, 8.
[50] *Stories from the Shed*, 9.
[51] Mark Thomson, *The Complete Blokes and Sheds: Stories from the Shed*. Australia: HarperCollins, 2002, 110.

this stage I had not heard of Leon Earle's work to do with sheds, as it seemed to only exist in academic literature. ... My recollection was that quite a number of men's sheds sprung up from nowhere after the [*Blokes and Sheds,* 1995] book came out, principally out of service clubs such as Lions and Rotary and out of public health organisations that existed somewhere between state and local government level. I would have thought that before 2000 there would have been more than a couple in South Australia – more like ten or 15. But I was elsewhere working on my *Rare Trades* project so wasn't paying much attention.[52]

As a footnote to Thomson's recollection of the Tea Tree Gardens shed, I have since contacted the Tea Tree Gardens [Retirement] Village Manager, who confirmed that when the facility opened in 1987 in South Australia, it:

> ... attracted quite young retirees. The men enthusiastically embraced the idea of the shed and produced items we still use today i.e. the stage for entertaining. I came here 20 years ago and at that time the men spent a great deal of time working in the shed. The wives would take it in turns to bring them afternoon tea. Sadly the new era of wives are not enthusiastic about baking and serving afternoon tea![53]

THE ROLE OF SOUTH AUSTRALIAN GERONTOLOGIST, LEON EARLE

This section briefly explores the role of the South Australian gerontologist, Leon Earle, in making a conceptual early link between the value of backyard sheds to retired men, and the potential for community Sheds to become part of a wider strategy for ageing. Leon Earle's early research was in the field of gerontology (the study of ageing) in South Australia, specifically about productive ageing. By 1995 some of Earle's work had begun to focus on the role and value of personal sheds to older and retired men. Some of this published work was undoubtedly influential and academically interesting[54].

Leon Earle's published work from 1995-6, mainly about the value of backyard sheds, was used as evidence by some early Men's Shed pioneers in several states to support their claim for public legitimacy and government

---

[52] Mark Thomson, March 31, 2014.
[53] Jean Link, Village Manager, April 2, 2014.
[54] Leon Earle, *Successful Ageing in Australian Society: A Community Development Challenge.* Adelaide: Recreation for Older Adults Inc., 1996; Leon Earle, *Social Network Needs Among Older People.* Adelaide: Recreation for Older Adults Inc., 1992.

funding. Earle's research in the field of ageing goes back to his 1978 doctoral study about what happens to people who relocate in retirement. Earle retrospectively dated his 'light bulb moment' about the importance of backyard sheds in male retirement to 1985, during his South Australian study of what seniors were doing in their leisure[55].

Dr Earle with his son, Tony Earle, along with the US gerontologist Professor Otto von Mering (now deceased), published the suggestion in 1995 that the activities of many men in retirement were 'somewhat hidden'. They claimed to have partly solved 'the mystery', suggesting that 'They are ensconced in their sheds!' Their broader challenge, to ensure that this importance was recognized, was to community and recreation professionals. For context, their challenge was made two years after The Shed in Goolwa officially opened, and around the same time as Mark Thomson's first book came out (with some very similar ideas). Earle, Earle and von Mering specifically suggested devising 'programs to make sheds more socially inclusive and productive learning centres'. Given the timing, it is very hard to know to what extent Earle's academic work was influenced by Thomson's (and vice versa), and whether early Sheds nearby in South Australia had informed or affected the ideas of both. What is not in doubt is that Leon Earle and Mark Thomson had something of a significant disagreement about appropriate attribution of some of these ideas around the time Thomson's *Blokes and Sheds* was published in 1995.

In order to try and identify what data and experiences might have informed Leon Earle's and colleague's 1995 paper, Earle's earlier research was carefully examined. This examination included his substantial (107 page) *Social Network Needs among Older People* (1992) investigating 'the *social network support needs* among older people in facilitating a pleasurable and productive lifestyle'[56]. It reveals only one very brief mention of sheds for men, made by Earle as part of an elaboration of a general finding 'that social class and socialisation affected a person's social activities, social networks and leisure pursuits', specifically that 'working class men obtained continuing *satisfaction autonomy* and *creativity* through working in their sheds'. A similar very brief mention appears in Earle's 'Successful Ageing' article in the *Leisure Options* Journal in 1992, which noted

---

[55] Kate Legge, 'A Man and his Shed', *The Weekend Australian Magazine*, June 25-26, 2011, 11-14.
[56] Leon Earle
, 'Social Network Needs among Older People', *Leisure Options* 2 (4), 7-17, 1992, 1, original *italics*.

that 'Many working class men focused on the pursuit of autonomy, creativity and personal involvement in the seclusion of their sheds and gardens'[57].

While sheds were not amongst a long list of suggestions for future research[58] in Earle's 1992 book, sheds for men do begin to creep into Earle's thinking in his 1996 book, *Successful Ageing in Australian Society: A Community Development Challenge*. Sheds achieve particular prominence in Chapter 5, with 12 pages devoted to sheds as a 'compensatory strategy' in a section titled 'Sheds and Male Retirement: A place to go to ... and come back from'[59]. The new material about sheds incorporated in Earle's 1996 study was:

> ... prompted by the mystery of *what* older men and women were doing in their retirement. Because of the significant differences between men and women it was decided to investigate each sex separately ... Our follow up research in 1993-6 has revealed the activities of many men are somewhat hidden.[60]

Earle, Earle and von Mering published a later joint paper on 'Sheds and Male Retirement: The Place-to-go to and come back from'[61] in 1999. However it was essentially reproduced directly from their 1996 book. The 1999 article was read by and quoted by several early Australian community men's shedders looking for evidence of impact to bolster their case for community Men's Shed funding. And it was all the evidence there was, since the data for this 1999 paper came from earlier studies that preceded all known *Men's* Shed organisations.

---

[57] Leon Earle, as above 7, *original italics*
[58] Leon Earle, as above, 32.
[59] Leon Earle, *Successful Ageing in Australian Society: A Community Development Challenge*. Adelaide: Active Ageing South Australia Inc., 1996, 69.
[60] Leon Earle, 1996, as above, 69.
[61] Leon Earle, Tony Earle, and Otto von Mering, "Sheds and Male Retirement", *Australasian Leisure for Pleasure Journal*, 1999, 1 (1): 5-19.

Early Australian Shed Experiments

This latter part of Chapter 2 explores a number of tantalising, workshop and shed-based precursors to community Men's Sheds. During my research for this book, informants in many countries have pointed to a wide variety of shed or workshop-based community organisations involving hands-on, mainly men's craft or trade practice going back many decades, including woodworkers' clubs, volunteer fire and emergency services, sporting clubs and restoration-oriented museums. While all might be regarded as community Sheds in a broad sense, they are not named as *Men's* spaces or organisations. Nevertheless they share a tangible lineage with community Men's Sheds and the Shed Movement to 2015.

Given the diverse and sometimes inaccurate claims made in both the popular media and research articles about the first Men's Sheds and their origins, it is useful to carefully examine the history of several workshops and sheds for men in community settings that *definitely* preceded the first community Men's Shed in 1998. Each of the five candidates chosen for this close examination has been suggested at various times as *the* 'smoking gun' of Men's Sheds at different times by different claimants. Two are from New South Wales: The MAC in Albury (dating back to 1978, but languishing by the late 1980s) and the Broken Hill Workshops set up by the 1980s. Both workshops were briefly examined by Gary Misan in his 2008 *Men's Sheds: A Strategy to Improve Men's Health* report as perhaps the earliest Men's Sheds.

The three other candidates examined are again from South Australia. The first is the Encounter Centre in Victor Harbor, cited as *the* prototypical Men's Shed by gerontologist, Dr Leon Earle, discussed earlier, dating back to 1974 and still operating. The second is a toy workshop in suburban Adelaide, called T.O.Y.S., operating since 1990. The third is The Shed at Hackham West, which is indeed first in other, important ways. A small number of similar early workshops mainly for men are more briefly examined, dating from the 1980s in New South Wales and Tasmania, and from the 1990s in Western Australia.

These sheds and workshops, mainly for groups of men and set up by community organisations prior to mid-1998, when 'Men's Sheds' began to emerge and proliferate in Australia, are worthy of closer examination since they provide some possible Men's Shed precursors and parallels. The intention of this careful examination is to clarify previous claims about the 'earliest Men's Shed'. Most of these claims will later be shown to lead back to earlier community workshops that have been inaccurately claimed (or later renamed) as 'Men's Sheds'.

Gary Misan's *Men's Sheds: A Strategy to Improve Men's Health* in 2008[1] accurately acknowledged that, while the history of Men's Sheds in Australia had not been comprehensively documented at that stage, 'the 'bragging rights' about the 'first' shed is unclear. Misan concluded that either Albury or Broken Hill in New South Wales were sites of the first 'Men's Sheds', suggesting that in Albury the history had been better documented, with their shed opening earlier, in 1978.

While both the Albury and Broken Hill examples are therefore worthy of closer investigation in the sections below, the Albury example (actually the 'MAC', never called a Shed or a Men's Shed) is something of a 'mirage'. The closer one looks, the less one sees what might be thought of as a 'Men's Shed' in the 2015 sense. By contrast, the Broken Hill Workshops will be shown to stand up better to close scrutiny as an early and influential Shed, specifically for ex-miners. Importantly, the Broken Hill Workshops provide evidence of a tantalising professional connection to some later Sheds for men in nearby rural South Australia.

THE MAC IN ALBURY NORTH (NEW SOUTH WALES)

Gary Misan, writing in 2008, noted that:

> The then president of the Albury [North] Rotary Club, a Mr Jim De Kruiff patterned a retired men's space for Albury on a model he had seen in his hometown of Ede in Holland. The Rotary Club managed to secure land from the Council, a local draughtsman supplied the plans, local tradesmen donated material and labour, Rotary Club members and local businesses donated plant and equipment including heating oil; the Albury Men's Shed was born. The local Rotary Club met most of the costs until 1999 when the shed was handed over to the local Council.[2]

---

[1] Gary Misan, *Men's Sheds: A Strategy to Improve Men's Health*. Parramatta: Mensheds Australia, 2008, 32.
[2] Gary Misan, 2008, as above.

Misan's account is to this point accurate and consistent with the subsequently published history of the Rotary Club of Albury North[3], except that it was never called the 'Albury Men's Shed'. Its title was the MAC (Manual Activity Centre). What Jim De Kruiff saw and was enthused by in Holland in the early 1970s was spotted as an aside during a tour organised by the Rotarian manager of a factory that employed 2,500 workers making synthetic silk. The Dutch factory directors had observed that 'the workers who had worked at the plant for a long time [often] didn't have a good hobby and felt useless and lonely', and had 'opened a small part of a factory for retired workers where they could meet together and make something for themselves and their family'.

Jim De Kruiff had some spare land in Union Road, Albury (behind his own workshop) that he put aside as the site for a future 'workshop for retired workers' on the basis of his experiences in Holland. De Kruiff's plans for a workshop on the site shifted once the Health Commission and the Rotary Club got involved, though at one stage there were plans for it to become part of a day care centre 'encompassing a geriatric day care, social care and rehabilitation unit'. Mainly financed by Albury North Rotary Club fundraising between 1974 and 1977, it was finally sited 'off Nowland Avenue adjacent to the pool at Lavington'.

The MAC facility became a major North Albury Rotary Club project and was launched by the Albury Mayor in October 1978. In its first months, the MAC '... boasted programmes in carpet bowls, crochet, framework, soft toy making, paper mache, plant potting and woodwork'. While extended in the mid-1980s, the MAC languished from the late 1980s, in part due to health and safety issues, until Albury City Council took over the centre in 2002. In summary, while a brave and early experiment, there are many aspects that make the MAC an unlikely community *men's* shed. While it functioned as a men's workshop it was not publicly called a Shed or Men's Shed. Unlike the Broken Hill Workshops elaborated in the next section, there is no evidence that the MAC was used as a template for later Shed or Men's Shed experimentation.

THE BROKEN HILL WORKSHOPS

The second claim by Gary Misan about an early 'Broken Hill Men's Shed' is certainly worthy of closer analysis[4]. It goes back to a long time mateship and partnership in Broken Hill between Barry Fowler, a professional health worker

---

[3] *The Rotary Club of Albury North, 1963-2013: The First 50 Years.*
[4] Minutes of the Inaugural Meeting of Ex-Pasminco Employees, August 27, 2002, 200 Beryl Street, Broken Hill.

and Lifeline Board Liaison person in Broken Hill from 1980-1986, and Brian Fenton, a mine worker. Fowler and Fenton teamed up at the Centre for Community to create an early shed for men in Broken Hill[5]. Brian Fenton recently claimed that the 'Lifeline Workshop' in Mercury Street in Broken Hill 'was a men's shed started by Rev Brian Nicholls, Director of Lifeline for retired and retrenched men mainly drawn from the mining industry'[6], guessing that 'it would have commenced in the late 1970s and has continued at that location until [late 2013]'. The Lifeline Broken Hill history[7], published for its 50th anniversary in 2014, confirms that Lifeline began in Broken Hill in 1964. Nichols was appointed as its full-time Director in 1977 and retired in 1993. The 'Workshop site' at 186 Mercury Street referred to by Brian Fenton was purchased by Lifeline in 1977 but there is no evidence that it was referred to as a Shed or as a Men's Shed.

Brian Fenton was coordinator of a separate, later Broken Hill 'BH Men's Shed' group at the Centre for Community, 200 Beryl Street, that came out of a 1999 Broken Hill Community Roundtable and which was still in operation in 2014. It was set up as 'a shed without tools', regarded by Fenton as a:

> ... 'transfer station' ... that allowed men to meet socially and reconnect with other men. Often they became dislocated from work colleagues when the later [mine] retrenchments occurred from 1986 to 2004. Men moved on to join the fishing club, form a group to play golf or offer their services to community groups.

Around this time Lane Cove Men's Shed opened (in December 1998) was the only other Men's Shed Brian Fenton was then aware of.

Documentary evidence confirms that a meeting was held on August 27, 2002 in Broken Hill at which the '... concept of a Men's shed was discussed and how [the Beryl Street premises] could be used. Some suggestions were fishing trips, fixing things, table tennis, speakers etc.'. The meeting coordinator, Brian Fenton, explained '... that the intention was to retain connections to work mates and foster comradeship whilst working for [the mining company] Pasminco'. Ex-miners at the meeting noted that they '... no longer had access to mine halls and facilities' and were encouraged to 'dig out mine souvenirs and to bring them along to decorate the Shed or talk about them at the next meeting'.

---

[5] Brian Fenton, August 19, 2014.
[6] Brian Fenton, April 6, 2014.
[7] Lifeline Broken Hill, *Brief History 1964-2013*, 2014.

While Broken Hill is remotely located in western New South Wales, information about these Broken Hill sheds and the 'Big Boys Toys' Men's Expos, held in Broken Hill between 1999 and 2004, was communicated much more widely, with around ten radio broadcasts on ABC and commercial radio in Broken Hill and also west into South Australia. Brian Fenton recalled in 2014 that 'The Broken Hill Gallipoli Foundation provided funding for a study tour by four men down to South Australian Sheds. They recorded a video and interviewed men at each Shed they visited.'

These early Broken Hill (NSW) experiences with sheds helped inform Barry Fowler in his later (2004-5) role as Regional Manager for Health Promotion at Wakefield Health (on the Yorke Peninsula) in South Australia. Barry Fowler's professional role during this period included strengthening several existing early South Australian Sheds in: in Snowtown, Yorketown, Maitland and Minlaton, and establishing new Sheds at Riverton and Kadina. Barry Fowler also played a part in setting up the Regional Men's Sheds Forum, which included Men's Sheds in Port Pirie, Peterborough, Stirling and Port Augusta. Fowler went on in subsequent roles to establish other Shed networks in South Australia's Riverland for existing Sheds at Waikerie and Renmark, as well as to establish new Men's Sheds at Loxton[8] and Paringa.

In some important senses, these early rural South Australian Sheds with a Broken Hill connection through Brian Fenton and Barry Fowler, a mine worker and health worker respectively, comprise another strong strand in the early Men's Shed story. By the time Men's Sheds in Sydney and Victoria had collectively organised their state and national gatherings in 2004 and 2005 respectively, a first cluster of rural Sheds in the mid-north of South Australian was already very well networked. Several Sheds had at least five years of valuable, practical experience, actively shared through their Shed Cluster in South Australia. While South Australian Sheds shone brightest earliest, Chapter 3 confirms that by the mid-1990s much of the new locus of Men's Shed activity, growth and networking in Australia shifted mainly to Victoria and New South Wales.

THE ENCOUNTER CENTRE WORKSHOP IN VICTOR HARBOR

In a magazine article featuring Professor Leon Earle in 2011[9], Earle is quoted as saying that he played a consultant's role in the foundation of perhaps the earliest

---

[8] An undated newspaper cutting suggests that the Loxton Men's Shed opened in 2006 as a program within the Loxton Hospital Complex. Guest speakers included men from the already operating Renmark Paringa Men's Shed program.

[9] "Secret Men's Business", *The Weekend Australian Magazine*, June 25-26, 2011, 11-14.

'men's shed' in Victor Harbor in rural, coastal South Australia. This claim was checked with those responsible for the Encounter Centre in 2014. Any role or impact Earle may have had was not recalled by anyone involved in the Centre from that time. None of the older or remaining contacts recollect a visit from Earle though one person met him as a lecturer.

In fact the wood workshop facility at the Encounter Centre in Victor Harbor has a much older lineage, going back to the Hay, Johnston and Rymill families[10], and was not necessarily directly connected to the later development of Men's Sheds[11]. As Bruce Lindqvist, the Encounter Centre Manager in 2014 put it:

> By the time Leon Earle [claims to have] visited it in the early 1990s, the Encounter Centre had been in operation for approximately 15 years. I don't believe anything changed after his visit. My thought would be that he was looking at what had been established (and was working) and was looking at how the concept could be replicated elsewhere to help other men.[12]

Nevertheless Bruce Lindqvist suggested in 2014 that while:

> ... the "Men's Shed': name has only been invented or used in more recent years, the **concept** was what started [in Victor Harbor] in 1974 and on their own site in 1976. The making of wooden toys was originally to give the men a meaningful project for them to do. To work towards being partly sustainable, this developed into selling the products that they made.

The wood workshop's 2015 slogan was still 'The home of quality hand made wooden toys'. According to Lindqvist, the original idea for the wood workshop:

> ... was to help men with mental health issues. [It] has always been a place for men to share their stories and skills as they have made the items for sale, to provide funds to run our programs. This has helped them to improve their health by having the chance to be involved in meaningful activity and to mix with other men. (There have been some women involved in all areas, particularly painting toys, but the women

---

[10] http://encountercentre.com.au/history.html, Accessed January 8, 2015.
[11] Bruce Lindqvist, March 20, 2014.
[12] Bruce Lindqvist, August 18, 2014.

rarely sit with the men during their break times and their discussions seem to be quite different!)[13].

Documents confirm that the first meeting of interested parties in Victor Harbor to plan for what later became 'Encounter Industries' in July 1975 was held on June 17, 1974. From August 1976 it operated from a permanent base with art and craft and social activities for people 'with little to do with their time who were living in Rehabilitation Guest Houses in Victor Harbor'. Part of the veranda of the former ESTA[14] building was then enclosed and used as a carpentry area. Renamed the 'Encounter Craft and Social Centre' in 1981, it functioned as a wood workshop making wooden toys for sale to raise funds. Rob Jervois was the centre's first full time coordinator from 1983-1997. When Jervois started, 'the workshop was operating four mornings a week and was attracting quite a number of retired men'[15]. When Jervois left in 1997, 'the whole operation was still quite substantial and loyal to its roots.' In 2001 the workshop activities moved into a purpose-built Workshop and Centre that was built at the current site in Victor Harbor.

It is pertinent to note here that the Encounter Centre in Victor Harbor was only 20 kilometers from the former The Heritage Club in Goolwa (established in 1984), whose 'The Shed' for men opened in 1993. Maxine Kitto, the key figure in starting The Shed in Goolwa, was, from 1987, the Coordinator of the Heritage and Aged Care Services for the Goolwa and Port Elliot Council. Given these facts and the close proximity of these small coastal towns, it is possible that some aspects of the Goolwa facility may have been informed by earlier activities in Victor Harbor. It is relevant to mention here that the Victor Harbor facility has been used since 2012 by the 'new' Victor Harbor Men's Shed on Fridays, using the Encounter Centre Inc. workshop as its base.

So where does the Victor Harbor facility sit in terms of its lineage as *the* prototypical Men's Shed? In its earlier iterations the workshop was not exclusively a men's space, but neither were many later workshops or Community Sheds. The centre certainly involved much mentoring and mutual support between men in the workshop. Men who made toys for sale on workdays were entitled to come in on a different day to work on their own projects. It was called a Workshop rather than a Shed and, as the toy repair service examples from the same era below suggest, while it was certainly one of the earliest community wood workshops mostly attractive to men, it was not the first 'Men's Shed'.

---

[13] Bruce Lindqvist, May 27, 2014.
[14] ETSA: Electricity Trust of South Australia.
[15] Rob Jervois, July 24, 2014.

Contrary to Leon Earle's claim, he paid no significant role in creating or shaping it and, at best, is likely to have borrowed some of the ideas pioneered in Victor Harbor by the Encounter Centre 15 years prior to his visit some time in the 1990s.

T.O.Y.S. Workshop, Unley and Other Early Toy Workshops

T.O.Y.S. ('Together Offering Your Skills') in inner suburban Adelaide, South Australia is effectively a workshop-based, volunteer toy repair service for early childhood organisations. This section seeks to explore the possible relevance of T.O.Y.S. and other similar toy repair workshops from the same era in other Australian states to the history of community Men's Sheds.

T.O.Y.S. operated from many sites in an inner southwestern suburban area around Unley from the 1980s. Its main aim was to create and maintain a mutual assistance program involving aged and retired people who met in a voluntary capacity in the Unley district, creating, repairing and supplying toys for early childhood groups. Its secondary aim was to provide and enhance opportunities for inter-generational social interaction. The history of T.O.Y.S. goes back to 1980, when John Thurston, a social worker then working with local kindergartens, noticed the large number of wooden toys and puzzles that were being discarded, as there were no resources or funds to repair them. He recognized the untapped human resource amongst the elderly and retired members of the local community and began a small toy repair service catering for the children's centres in Unley.

T.O.Y.S. operated from diverse community sites for over 35 years. These sites include The Orphanage at Millswood, Princess Margaret Playground in Black Forest, The Abbey on King William Road and the Church of the Trinity Shed on Goodwood Road. In 2014 it was located at the Clarence Park Community Centre in Black Forest. From 1981 the program operated under a funding grant from the Department for Family and Community Services (FACS). After 1994 the program no longer fitted the FACS funding criteria and a half-year grant was given by the Department of Education to cover the coordinator's salary. Since that time the City of Unley and the Clarence Park Community Centre (CPCC) have operated a partnership agreement enabling funding of the program and a paid coordinator. T.O.Y.S. joined the Australian Men's Sheds Association in 2010, after which it was renamed 'The Shed (T.O.Y.S.)'. Since October 2014 the program, operating three mornings a week, has obtained most of its funding from the Board of Management of CPCC, with much reduced funding from the Unley Council.

Despite all these changes of site and funding, the focus of the program, including the involvement of men and women as volunteers, has not changed in close to 35 years. T.O.Y.S. continues to provide a vital service to the early childhood learning programs in South Australia, as well as its parallel and valuable social obligation to aged and retired volunteers who participate as volunteers in the program. While it is now a Shed in name, its main role was as a toy repair workshop.

Several similar wood workshops that fix toys date from the same era in New South Wales and other Australian states. For example the Sutherland Council in Sydney set up 'Sutherland Toy Restoration' in the 1980s, in an enterprise not unlike the Encounter Centre and T.O.Y.S.

> Retirees aged up to 93 worked at the toy restoration centre making, repairing and selling at affordable prices children's playthings, ranging from Barbie dolls and Wiggles cars to bikes and trikes. ... The building, which Sutherland Shire Council had provided for their use for 35 years, was once a ... furniture store.[16]

The Sutherland facility, run by older people, mainly men, provided the 'companionship and a very friendly atmosphere' characteristic of a wood workshop, at the same time running a shop to sell the restored toys and donating the money to charitable projects.

One early and now thriving Tasmanian facility that some Tasmanian shedders now point to as their contender for the 'oldest Tasmanian Men's Shed' is the Wooden Boat Centre Tasmania, initially established in 1990 as the 'Shipwright's Point School of Wooden Boatbuilding', to teach and preserve the skills of wooden boatbuilding[17]. In the same maritime vein, a Western Australian facility, called the Albany Boat Shed, with similar links to wooden boatbuilding as the one in Tasmania, was set up more recently through the Albany Maritime Foundation [18] in 1999. The Foundation is an incorporated, not-for-profit organization, which seeks to 'tell a proud story of achievement in the core activity of wooden boat construction and restoration within the Shed'. The Albany Boat Shed building was originally used in Fremantle to house the construction of a replica of the early Dutch exploring ship, the *Duyfken*. At the completion of the

---

[16] 'Cool comfort for the toy restorers at last', *St George and Sutherland Shire Lea*der, http://www.theleader.com.au/story/1966741/cool-comfort-for-the-toy-restorers-at-last/, Accessed April 2, 2014.

[17] The Wooden Boat Centre Tasmania, http://www.woodenboatcentre.com/, Accessed April 3, 2014.

[18] The Albany Maritime Foundation, http://www.boatshed.org.au/About.html, Accessed June 5, 2014.

project the facility was gifted to the City of Albany. While the purpose-built facility looks like and functions somewhat like a very large Men's Shed, importantly and deliberately it does not identify as one.

THE SHED AT HACKHAM WEST

'The Shed' in southern suburban Adelaide, established by the late Jack Ellis in 1995 in Hackham West, goes some way closer to the current Men's Shed model by being based in the community around a wood workshop, working semi-independently of health and wellbeing services and organisations and not located in an aged care setting. However, like The Shed in Goolwa that opened only two years earlier, only 50 kilometers away, it also stopped short of naming itself as a 'men's' space.

While it opened two years after The Shed in Goolwa, the identically named 'The Shed' in Hackham West appears to be one of the first work sheds in which former tradesmen specifically, deliberately and mainly worked with and mentored young people, including school resisters, mainly in woodwork. Its original slogan was "Working with and for the community". The Shed can certainly be regarded as a very early and important community Men's Shed precursor. It is perhaps the first Shed organisation to deliberately embed intergenerational mentoring involving young people. Early Sheds in other states that specialised in working with young people several years later included Donnybrook (in Western Australia) and Pete's Workshed in Bridgewater, Tasmania. Both are introduced later in Chapter 3. [19]

'The Shed' was set up in 1995 by the Noarlunga Community Action Group, later the same year changing its name to Southern Community Project Group Inc. It is relevant to note here that Hackham Community Services contacted Maxine Kitto, from The Shed in Goolwa, some time during the 1990s for information about their Shed.[20] Photograph 3 of the signage outside The Shed was taken in February 2006 during interviews for Barry Golding's national Men's Shed research.

---

[19] Michael Nelson presented to the 2005 Lakes Entrance Men's Shed Conference about 'Changing Lanes' (then known affectionately as 'Peg's Shed'), a community-based campus of Bairnsdale Secondary College for disaffected young people.

[20] This could only have occurred between the Goolwa Shed opening in February 1993 and Maxine Kitto leaving Goolwa in March 1998.

Photograph 3 The Shed, Jack Ellis Community Workshop, February 2006.

In 2011, in self-acknowledgement of its early origins, The Shed in Hackham West became "The-Original-Shed Community Volunteer Workshop' for marketing purposes'[21].

In a 2006 research interview I asked Jack Ellis whether he was aware of any other Men's Shed at the time his Shed set up in 1995. Ellis replied emphatically, "Nowhere. Not a Shed in sight, it came from nowhere, it just came from our own heads". The late Jack Ellis' full time unpaid involvement extended over 11 years, dating back to 1995. While 'The members of the Southern Community Project Group at Hackham West [now also called the 'Hackham West Men's Shed'] proudly boast they are 'the original Men's Shed', [22] it is a stretch for the organisation to claim that they are *the* 'original men's shed', or that 'The Shed' at Hackham West was used 'as a blueprint for Men's Sheds across Australia'.

Jack Ellis was awarded an OAM (Order of Australia Medal) before his death in January 2007. His work with young people in the City of Onkaparinga was acknowledged in 2007 by a $A4,000 per year 'Jack Ellis OAM Vocational

---

[21] http://www.the-original-shed.org.au/index.html, Accessed January 3, 2015.
[22] 'Hackham West Men's Shed Part of Zero Waste SA's Share N Save Program', *The Advertiser*, December 2, 2013.

Scholarship' to support two young local people in vocational training. The Council tribute in 2007 acknowledged Ellis as:

> ... the founder of the Southern Community Project Group, who made a significant contribution to The Shed at Hackham West. At The Shed, retired tradesmen assist disadvantaged young people to develop skills and knowledge in a range of areas including design, woodwork, metal work and teamwork. [The then Mayor noted that] "Jack was well known for his patience and non-judgmental approach, and even the most challenging students were encouraged to participate in practical projects that expanded their confidence and developed skills".[23]

CLAIMS ABOUT OTHER EARLY MEN'S SHEDS

There is a legitimate argument that volunteer fire brigades, which have until relatively recently comprised only or mainly men in rural areas in all four countries featured in this book, function very similarly to and predate community Men's Sheds. It is no accident that my research, with others, into fire and emergency services organisations in small and remote towns in Australia[24], published in 2004, led me to research the nature and value of Men's Sheds to men and the community. Many woodworking and wood turning workshops, as well as many community railway, car and motor cycle clubs, museums and technology preservation associations also function somewhat like Men's Sheds in very diverse community settings.

Around the same time Rick Hayes, a men's health academic from La Trobe University, himself a Vietnam Veteran, was involved in the early Darebin Men's Shed and was exploring pre-Men's Shed history and origins. Michelle Morgan with Rick Hayes and others in 2007 identified the 'growing awareness in Victoria, Australia and internationally of the need to provide socially supportive environments for men in the community'[25] as one factor that encouraged Men's Sheds and the development of men's health promotion strategies in this decade.

---

[23] 'Council Pays Tribute to an Outstanding Citizen', City of Onkaparinga, Press Release, March 21, 2007.
[24] Christine Hayes, Barry Golding and Jack Harvey, *Adult Learning through Fire and Emergency Service Organisations in Small and Remote Australian Towns*. Adelaide: NCVER, 2004.
[25] Michelle Morgan, Rick Hayes *et al.*, 'Men's Sheds: A Community Approach to Promoting Health and Wellbeing'. *International Journal of Health Promotion*, 9 (3): 50-54, 2007, cited from page 50.

Hayes had developed a strategic framework for men's health in 2001[26] in this decade. Morgan and Hayes with others also pointed specifically to the importance to early Men's Shed development of 'discussions at the 1995 and 1999 National Men's Health Conferences'[27].

In Rick Hayes' presentation to the Lakes Entrance Conference in 2005 about 'Victorian Men's Shed History and Evidence'[28], Hayes linked the idea of men and sheds to an eclectic range of people, historic places and spaces in which Victorian men had previously informally organised and gathered for their mutual benefit in community and work settings. These included 'Indigenous men's business', Joseph Furphy (as a bullock driver, 'on the track', as a foundry worker and father), shearing crews, Mechanics Institutes, men in the military, service clubs, fire brigades, unions and church fellowships.

Some sheds that men frequented in the pre-Men's Shed era (before 1998) in community settings were definitely not community oriented. From my own childhood in the 1950s-60s I recall a row of remote, corrugated iron, Sunday School picnic sheds near Little Lake Buloke in rural Victoria, otherwise used only one day a year, being used in the 1960s by a particularly 'wild' group of men that called themselves 'The Spasms'. They used the shelter of the isolated public sheds to 'escape' from their wives and families in nearby Donald and 'let off steam', mainly for antisocial bouts of drinking. Mark Thomson recalls another, similarly wild but slightly more community-oriented shed in South Australia from his childhood.

> ... called The Doghouse, in the Adelaide suburb of Seaton. It was a kind of Sunday morning club ... where men would gather in Sunday mornings, usually after a domestic argument about the previous night's activities. ... Apart from being a bunch of grumpy, misogynistic alcoholics, they also did all sorts of community building and fundraising activities. ... A bit like a locally-based neighbourhood service club.[29]

There are many other organisations in Australia and worldwide, set up in community shed-like places, 'man caves' and 'dens' (in the US and Canada) or workshops, mainly or wholly comprising men as participants, whose main, stated

---

[26] Rick Hayes, *Men's Health Promotion: Developing an Intersectoral Strategic Framework*. Melbourne: Victorian Health Promotion Foundation, 2001.

[27] Michelle Morgan, Rick Hayes *et al.*, 2007, 50.

[28] http://www.mensshed.org/SiteFiles/mensshed2011org/Rick%20Hayes1.pdf, Accessed January 15, 2015.

[29] Mark Thomson, March 24, 2014.

aim is to preserve skills, crafts and historical mechanical artifacts and associated processes, including for agriculture, mining and forestry. As one example, the Gal Gael project in Govan, organised around an interconnected series of workshops in a disadvantaged suburb of Glasgow, Scotland was established in 1997 to preserve Scottish traditional crafts and develop skills, capabilities and confidence amongst mostly male participants. Gal Gael was written up as a case study in *Men Learning through Life* in 2014.[30]

Many workshop-based organisations, most involving only men as participants, repair and restore stationary engines, trains, railways, trams, steam traction engines, timber milling, stone cutting or mining equipment, fire engines, trucks, cars, bicycles or motorbikes. Though superficially similar, the essential difference between community Men's Sheds and these workshop-based community organisations lies in their emphasis on naming the *activity* and the *artifacts*. In most cases there is little or no recognition of the specific value of the organisation or the activity to men. Nor are their stated aims about being truly inclusive of the needs and wellbeing of diverse men. What is different is that most Men's Sheds place men at the centre of the activity, and provide freedom for specifying (and changing) the activities conducted in the shed, by the men, and for the community.

That said, there are now considerable financial incentives in Australia, with national or state-based Men's Sheds-specific funding, for some of these previously established workshop-based organisations to strategically shift the emphasis from what they previously did, or previously espoused in their mission statements, and to simply change their organisation name to include 'Shed' or become a 'Men's Shed'. A good example of this strategic transitioning of a pre-Men's Shed organisation comes from the Men's Shed Group at the Brisbane Tramways Museum in Ferny Grove, Brisbane. The Brisbane Tramway Museum Society had operated since 1968, but it took another 12 years before an official opening on a new, permanent site in 1980. The TRAMS ('Tuesday Retired Active Men's Shed') Group within the Tramways Museum was formed 23 years later in July 2003. Their role is to 'do all of the vital and necessary tasks to build, maintain and operate the Brisbane Tramways Museum.'[31] The only prerequisite for participants is to be a financial member of the tramway museum. Other, similar examples include the Melbourne Tramways Museum at Bylands, near

---

[30] Rob Mark and Jim Soulsby, 'Men's Learning in the UK' in Barry Golding *et al.*, *Men Learning through Life*. Leicester: NIACE, 2014, 131-147 (citing 142-143).
[31] 'The Brisbane Tram Shed', www.brisbanetramwaysmuseum.org, Accessed March 25, 2014.

Kilmore in Victoria, which now has a Men's Shed adjacent to their site, as does the ANGRMS (Australian Narrow Gauge Railway Museum Society) at Woodford in Queensland.

The apparently simple demarcation between pre-Men's Sheds workshops and Men's Sheds post-1999 is made more difficult by the decision of some Sheds in 2015 that identify as part of the Men's Shed Movement *not* to put 'Men' in the Shed name, and of others to call their organisation a Men's Shed but deliberately not join a national association or collaborate with the wider Men's Shed Movement.

Some workshop-based organisations set up specifically for and by men after Men's Sheds began to spread in Australia, functioned almost identically to Men's Sheds in all but name and confound any simple definition. A good example is United Wood Cooperative (UWC), formed by a group of African-Australian men in North Melbourne and Flemington, inner suburbs of Melbourne, in January 2005, supported by Adult Multicultural Education Services (AMES) and the Ministry of Community Services and Housing[32]. UWC was set up around the specific needs and skills of African refugees who had '... experienced war, torture, and imprisonment [and were] working hard to rebuild their lives and provide for their families in Australia.' Setting out to make everyday wooden items in a cooperative workshop setting, the ' ... aim of the group [was] to create employment for the new migrants and refugees ... based on the need of the new settlers, [reflecting] African creativity and ingenuity.' Such organisations and programs could be called Men's Sheds a decade later.

OTHER SOUTH AUSTRALIAN SHEDS AND THEIR INTERCONNECTIONS

Very few early South Australian Sheds in this era appear, on the available evidence, to have had many connections with (or inspiration from) Men's Sheds and community Sheds commencing around the same time in south-eastern Australia and Western Australia. However these links cannot be ruled out, given the many interconnections available via professional and personal networks, the media and the increasing accessibility of information via the internet. What is clear and consistent is a common link and support network between community Sheds and Men's Sheds and health services, hospital and War Veterans' organisations. This section explores some of these common connections.

---

[32] African refugees: United Wood Cooperative,
http://africanrefugees.blogspot.com.au/2005_01_01_archive.html, Accessed January 15, 2015.

As with Tongala Men's Shed in Victoria, there are sometimes War Veterans (Department of Veterans' Affairs) funding connections to several early South Australian Sheds. As an example, Hocky's Shed opened in Snowtown, 160 kilometers south of Port Augusta, on September 7, 2000 with an official opening of the extension a month later on October 8, 2000[33]. Like the Port Augusta Men's Shed (opened in July 1999), it was set up by a grant through the Department of Veterans' Affairs after identifying 80 War Veterans in the region as well as three active Returned Serviceman's League (RSL) clubs that supported the application. Named after Dean Hoskin ('Hocky'), the hospital maintenance manager, it was based 'on the grounds of the Snowtown Hospital … and Lumeah Homes bus shed' that had previously been 'used by members of the community to restore and repair furniture'.

The Hocky's Shed project began in mid-2000 after enquiries from a Lumeah Homes resident asking to potter in the maintenance shed, with an inaugural meeting on May 16, 2000. Its rationale was that 'there are few activities for those in the community who do not, or can not play sport, cards and who are restricted by lack of transport' in the area. The name 'Hocky's Shed' was chosen 'to ensure that the Shed was open to both men and women in the community and consequently did not want to call it a Men's Shed'[34]. Participants included 'men and women from the community and residents from Lumeah Homes and Snowtown Hospital Aged-Care facility'.

Many of the Sheds opening soon after in the same area of South Australia used a similar naming strategy avoiding the term 'Men'. Clare Shed (also called Bazza's Shed) only 50 kilometers from Snowtown opened in 2001. Clem's Shed, in Minlaton, 175 kilometers south on the Yorke Peninsula, opened in March 2001[35] is shown in February 2006 in Photograph 4.

---

[33] 'Hocky's Shed Extension Opened at Snowtown', Helen Jamieson, Project Coordinator, October 8, 2000.
[34] AHA Baxter National Healthcare Innovation Awards Nomination, 2002-3.
[35] Transcript from Barry Golding's NCVER research interview in Clem's Shed in 2006, 9, records that The Yorketown Hospital donated the shed in 2000, and that March 2001 was when it 'virtually got started … after getting a grant through Ian McDonald, a physiotherapist at Community Health Minlaton' (p. 10).

Photograph 4 Clem's Shed, Minlaton, South Australia, 2006

The Rocky River Men's Shed (originally run by the Laura Hospital, attached to the Laura Campus of Southern Flinders Health and now called Laura Men's Shed) opened in Laura, 75 kilometers north of Snowtown in 2002. Port Pirie Men's Shed (run by Uniting Care Wesley, Port Pirie) opened only one hour south of Port Augusta '… as a very small enterprise in an old, run down mechanics workshop during 2005'[36].

Though not widely recognised elsewhere in Australia, the account in this chapter confirms that, by the time shedders from Victoria and New South Wales Men's Shed-based organisations had begun to gather and make plans for sharing their early experiences from 2004, South Australia had a relatively large number of diverse Sheds. Some had a particular emphasis and specialisation on community health outreach to men in small rural communities, others to older men in aged care settings including with dementia, and several to Vietnam War Veterans.

While some Men's Sheds had formed relatively early regional clusters in South Australia before 2005 as expanded on later in this Chapter, there was no active linking up in South Australia at a state level until much later in that decade.

---

[36] Heather Eglinton July 28, 2014 noted it was opened by Uniting Care Wesley Country South Australia (UCWCSA), rebadged in a new facility in 2014 as 'The Port Pirie Men's Shed and Training Centre'.

Keith Bettany, via his early role as a dementia worker with Alzheimer's South Australia in Adelaide, actively chronicled and encouraged Men's Sheds to spread from the early 2000s, and was briefly the 'lynch pin' between South Australia and the emerging national Men's Shed Movement from 2005-6.

Keith Bettany's early professional networking in South Australia was mainly about the value of sheds in aged care and hospital settings, particularly for people experiencing dementia. His invention of the portable 'fold away men's shed' (an early prototype was completed by August 30, 2004), combined with his extensive use of the print and electronic media between 2004 and 2006, were very influential in encouraging and shaping Men's Shed practice in South Australia. Keith Bettany unveiled his 'Foldaway Shed', shown in the 'open' position with Bettany in Photograph 5. It was officially launched in September 2004 at Alzheimer's South Australia in Glenside (Adelaide), with the opening conducted by *Blokes and Sheds* author, Mark Thomson.[37]

Photograph 5 Keith Bettany and his 'Foldaway Shed', Adelaide, 2006.

In Bettany's descriptive words:

> It's virtually a shed that folds into a little cupboard, and it has a shadow
> board attached to it with shelves on each side. It opens up to about 2

---

[37] 'Men and Sheds: Now You See it, Now You Don't – The Demo Fold-away Shed', *Alzheimer's SA Newsletter*, February, 2005, 6-7.

metres by 2 metres and when it's shut it's lockable and very safe and fits in with the décor so that they can be put in a day activity centre, in a community centre, anywhere. ... The staff can feel safe, it can be locked up when it's not being used.

In the early 2000s Keith Bettany[38] undertook a series of radio interviews (several of them national) espousing the virtues of Men's Sheds. As a follow up he personally distributed his brief and very accessible 'Blokes and Sheds' paper, contributed a full page article headed 'Alzheimer's Australia SA support backyard sanctuaries for men with dementia' in the *50s Lifestyle Paper*. [39] He also helped distribute Earle, Earle and von Mering's (1999) paper about the value of backyard sheds in retirement. Unbeknown to Bettany, some of the issues he was addressing had been discussed at nearby Noarlunga almost two decades before. In a research interview with the author in 2006, Keith Bettany suggested that he came to the idea of sheds for older men in aged care facilities:

> ... all out of my head. ... As a registered Nurse I have been taught not just to put a bandaid on a problem but also to look at a cause. I recognised that a lot of the men who were being referred to us by nursing homes due to 'behaviours of concern' were either bored or were forced to do tasks more suited to women. It became obvious that men were stuck in nice pretty lounges with nice décor for women and no familiar surroundings. They were surrounded by women ... and the staff were again women, so the poor blokes had nowhere to 'escape' to and no familiar surroundings. When they retired, they would have gone down to the shed. ... And then I started doing a literature research to back up my thoughts and Leon Earle cropped up and also Mark Thomson.[40]

As a specialist worker in Alzheimer's, Keith Bettany recognised that for:

> ... men with dementia, it's important to tap into their existing skills. ... Most men have had a shed, or they've helped their dad in his shed. You put a bloke in a shed and he starts talking. You put him in a nursing home without a shed and they clam up. ... Give a man a familiar tool

---

[38] Keith Bettany, March 11, 2014.
[39] *50's Lifestyle Paper*, Issue 6, Winter, 2004, 38.
[40] Barry Golding, research interview with Keith Bettany 2006, revised by Keith Bettany, December 23, 2014.

and give him a chance to do something useful and they open up. It's not rocket science!

Keith Bettany participated in the now historic, first Australian Men's Sheds Conference in Lakes Entrance in coastal East Gippsland in Victoria in November 2005, presenting a paper called *Easier Shed than Done: Meaningful Activities for Men with Dementia*. While Bettany presented and wrote passionately and persuasively, as illustrated below, with original capitalisation, he used four pages of academic references to support the contentions in his paper.

> **Thank goodness for sheds**. A man's domain. The last area where he has control. A virtual workshop of equipment, tools & hoarded goods gathered over the years. A place where strange smells, clutter, dust, disorder, and an accumulation of odds and ends is the norm. This is contrary to the well-ordered tidy house, where everything is in its place, except for the Tupperware[41] cupboard. ... By ensuring men are not disadvantaged and deprived of opportunities to engage in 'shed therapy' simply because they are old, frail, and live in an aged care facility, they can be assisted to enjoy a quality of life that **SHEDLESSNESS** would rob them.

Keith Bettany also spoke about 'Blokes and Sheds' at the June 2004 5th International Dementia Conference in Sydney and also participated in the Tasmanian 2006 (Pontville) Men's Shed Conference. Through his employment at Alzheimer's South Australia, Bettany was actively but informally networking with around 20 South Australian Men's Sheds to 2006. Many of the earlier (pre-2006) South Australian sheds and community workshops, listed in the approximate chronological order of official opening below, are mentioned in Keith's Bettany's professional diaries. Those Sheds clustered around either side of the Yorke Peninsula north of Adelaide in rural South Australia are marked with an asterisk (*)

- T.O.Y.S. in Black Forest, opened in 1980 discussed above, only very recently renamed 'The Shed T.O.Y.S'.
- 'The Shed' at Hackham West, opened in 1995 and was run by the late Jack Ellis, discussed above.

---

[41] Tupperware is a home products line that pioneered a direct marketing strategy, made famous by the 'Tupperware Party', usually conducted by women in their homes.

- The Sheds within the Peter Badcoe VC XMRC (Ex-Military Rehabilitation Complex) in a former air force base north of Adelaide near Salisbury, open before 1999, are discussed in the section that follows.
- Port Augusta Men's Shed opened on July 29, 1999. *
- Aldgate Men's Shed[42], Aldgate, auspiced by The Hut Community Information and Resource Centre Inc., in partnership with the Aldgate Church of Christ, whose premises had previously been Aldgate TAFE[43], officially opened on November 24, 1999[44].
- Hocky's Shed, run through the Snowtown Community Hospital, officially opened on October 8, 2000[45]. *
- Rocky River Men's Shed, in Laura run by Laura Hospital, opened in 2001. *
- Bazza's Shed, set up by Wakefield Health, opened at Clare in 2001[46], called Clare Community Shed in 2015. *
- Clem's Shed opened in March 2001 (or 2003[47]), set up by Southern Yorke Peninsula Community Health, initiated by the physiotherapist based in Minlaton. *
- Camden Community Shed opened in Camden Park in suburban Adelaide in 2004, taking two years from planning to completion.[48]
- Renmark Paringa Men's Shed, apparently open before 2005[49], was 'complemented by a shed run by the Renmark/Paringa Museum Community Group in 2005'[50].
- Ardrossan Men's Shed was purpose-built by the Ardrossan Aged Care Facility. *
- Great Eastern Men's Shed project launched in October 2005 involved ACH (Aged Care and Housing), Burnside Council, Eastern Region

---

[42] Started in May 1999, in Strathalbyn Road, Aldgate, as a joint project auspiced by the Aldgate Church of Christ and the Hut Community Centre, as confirmed by Jeff Whitbread, letter, May 10, 2000. From 2014 the Aldgate Men's Shed was independently incorporated.
[43] The Hut Community Information and Resource Centre Inc., letter from 'Peggy' to Chris Hoffman, Church Coordinator, May 10, 2000.
[44] An unsourced newspaper cutting confirms the Aldgate Men's Shed was opened by Hon David Wotton at Aldgate Church of Christ.
[45] Denise Fairbairn, May 31, 2011.
[46] John Monten, January 15, 2015.
[47] Tanya Short, March 7, 2014.
[48] Jo Smith, March 17, 2014.
[49] Men from the Renmark Paringa Shed attended the 2006 Loxton Men's Shed inaugural session.
[50] Barry Fowler, November 11, 2005.

Collaboration Project and St Matthews Anglican Church, providing a respite Shed for men with dementia.[51]

- The ACH Shed at Elizabeth House Over 50s Community Centre in Christie's Beach summarised later, specialised in respite for frail age men and men with disability and early dementia.
- Peterborough Veterans Shed. *
- Strathalbyn Wood Shed.
- Jingle's Shed at Riverton started because 'community nurses were seeing many homebound men'[52] A full page article about this 'new men's shed' appeared in August 24, 2005. (By 2015 the shed in Riverton was the Gilbert Valley Men's Shed).
- Des' Shed, Lameroo, a multi-purpose community shed used by community day care, hostel, nursing home and hospital, run by the Mallee Health Service.
- St Mary's Community Shed (The Project Centre), St Mary's.
- The Shed at the Fleurieu Peninsula Veterans Community Association, in McLaren Vale, opened in 2005.
- Maitland Men's Shed, run by the Maitland Progress Association, was established in 2005 with the assistance of Yorke Peninsula Community Health. *

There were sufficient Sheds by 2005[53] in the Yorke Peninsula area for Wakefield Health (based in Balaklava, a town of around 2,000 people approximately 90 kilometers north of Adelaide) to set up a Community Shed Support Network (CSSN). John Monten recalled in 2015 that:

> The CSSN acted as an informal conference of sheds in the area to share information, ideas, and support each other. It was started in 2004 by Peter Burford, a Men's Health Worker from Yorke Peninsula, in collaboration with Shed coordinators at the time. The first meeting was at Balaklava Golf Club and it progressed as a biannual event hosted by individual sheds.[54]

---

[51] Keith Bettany, December 23, 2014.
[52] Unsourced (approx. 2005) newspaper cutting 'Old Shed Gives New Lease of Life', citing John Monten.
[53] Undated leaflet, 'Community Shed Support Network Action Plan' indicated that the CSSN was 'Supported by Wakefield Health'.
[54] John Monten, January 15, 2015.

Some of CSSN's early roles included developing and implementing 'Policies, Procedures, a Manual of Operations and Code of Conduct for CSSN members', and 'seeking 'recurring and one off funding for projects'. On September 29, 2005 (a few months before the first national Shed Conference in Lakes Entrance in Victoria), John Monten confirmed that there were CSSN representatives in the northern rural and remote area in South Australia. In an email to Keith Bettany, John Monten presciently said, 'Wouldn't it be great if there was a state network of sheds that fed into an Australia wide network?' As an example of the CSSN's continuing early influence, the Shed Network in September 2007 lent support for the creation of the Balaklava Community Shed.[55]

What was striking about these pre-2006 Sheds in South Australia, in comparison with the early Men's Sheds in New South Wales and Victoria, is that, apart from being relatively early and numerous, many tended to have close associations or auspice arrangements with health services, aged care centres and hospitals rather than with churches as will be shown later to be the case with several of the earliest New South Wales Men's Sheds.

A newspaper article in *The Adelaide Advertiser* in May 2004[56] named six facilities. three of which were in rural South Australia, including two (Moonta and Maitland) on the Yorke Peninsula, which then had either trial sheds or 'were considering sheds and male-oriented activities'. The six facilities comprised:

> Narooma [NSW] Retirement and Aged Care Services, Hawkesbury Gardens [Salisbury North, SA] Aged Care, Moonta [SA] Health and Aged Care, Eldercare The Village [Maitland, SA], Ardrossan [SA] Nursing Home and Carinya [Frankston, Victoria] Residential Aged Care.

It is likely that some of these sheds embedded in residential aged care facilities were influenced by the downstream effects of Leon Earle's gerontological work on the relationship between backyard sheds and positive ageing from the late 1990s, and possibly also from former students in Earle's classes.

THE WAR VETERAN AND XMRC SHED CONNECTIONS

War Veterans (mainly from Australia's involvement with America in the Vietnam War, called the 'American War' in Vietnam) have been actively involved in many

---

[55] Wakefield Regional Council Newsletter, September, 2007, https://www.wakefieldrc.sa.gov.au/webdata/resources/files/200709Newsletter.pdf, Accessed March 29, 2014.
[56] May 14, 2004, 43.

of the earliest Men's Sheds in every Australian state. More than 60,000 Australian personnel served overseas during the course of this War between 1962 and 1973, of whom 521 were killed and more than 3,000 wounded. Of a total of 144,000 War Veterans in Australia in June 2014, South Australia had around 11,000 Vietnam Veterans, many of whom had retired to coastal suburbs or close to Adelaide military bases.

Several South Australian (mostly Vietnam) War Veterans organisations had Veteran-specific sheds open in South Australia prior to 2005. The XMRC (Ex-Military Rehabilitation Centre) Shed was part of the Peter Badcoe Complex in Salisbury, based since 1998[57] in part of the Royal Australian Air Force (RAAF) complex at Edinburgh. XMRC shared the site from 1998-2006 with the Vietnam Veterans' Association of Australia, Northern Suburbs Sub Branch (VVAA NSSB). While the XMRC was offered nearby defence buildings 'of a higher standard' by the federal government in April 2006, several Sheds were still open in 2006 on the site, and some Shed participants were interviewed by me as part of the first national Men's Shed research, *Men's sheds: Learning in Community Contexts*, published in 2007 by NCVER in South Australia.

'The Shed' at BIOC (Brain Injury Option Coordination) was set up on the XMRC site in approximately 2003[58]. BIOC specialised in supporting men with brain injuries acquired through accident, stroke or trauma including war injuries. In 2005 BIOC was described as:

> A humble shed in Salisbury ... where men who have suffered brain injury come to rebuild their lives. The shed is a State Government initiative in cooperation with Salisbury Council and Brain Injury Option Coordination. Craig Oswald is the boss, who is providing the guidance and knowhow, helping men regain their confidence to think and the ability to enjoy life. It's just like any other shed, full of great tools, talk and dreams. However the dreams in this shed are a reality, serving many families, providing rehabilitation to the men who through misfortune have had brain injury.[59]

---

[57] 'New Home for Vietnam Vets' Association at Edinburgh', Media Release April 5, 2006, Sandy Macdonald, Minister for Defence.
[58] Undated, pre-2006, unsourced magazine article, 'Life Goes on in The Shed', by Ian Rennie, says that the program 'started about 'two years ago'.
[59] Local Government Association of South Australia, January 8, 2005, https://www.lga.sa.gov.au/webdata/resources/.../Synopsis_series_1.doc, Accessed January 9, 2015.

BIOC provided:

> ... work on projects such as repairing motor bikes, building model train
> sets, building coffee tables, tending to a herb garden, building bird boxes
> and learning computer skills. Not bad for a place that started out life as a
> dilapidated tin shed, with limited funding support. ... In the two years of
> its operation, The [BIOC] Shed has seen people benefit from the simple
> social interaction.[60]

Signage to 'The Shed' at the XMRC at the time of Barry Golding's research
interviews at the XMRC in Salisbury in February 2006 is shown in Photograph 6.

Photograph 6 Signage to 'The Shed' at the XMRC, Salisbury, South Australia,
February 2006

As well as The Shed run by BIOC at the XMRC, a separate woodworking Men's
Shed was in operation in 2006 for War Veterans, many with PTSD (Post
Traumatic Stress Disorder). A third 'Shed' on the same site was at that time a
base for the Vietnam Veterans' Northern Suburbs Sub-Branch. Men interviewed

---

[60] 'Life Goes on in The Shed', undated, as above.

in the woodworking Men's Shed at the facility in 2006 linked the early development and use of their Sheds to the early Vietnam Veterans Movement in South Australia. The original concept of the XMRC Peter Badcoe Complex (Peter Badcoe was a Victoria Cross Winner decorated for gallantry in Vietnam) was conceived by Ian Campbell (nickname 'Patch') and other Veterans in 1995. They suggested that a broader spectrum of support services was needed for Vietnam Veterans than remote bush refuges in the rural Mallee. In 2006 the XMRC services included 'rehabilitation activities, pension and welfare advice, computer classes, fellowship for Veterans, hobbies, transport, youth employment and a meal service'.[61] In 2014 Patch 'was still running a place in the Adelaide Hills called the Grunt Club which help out Veterans that are in a bad place with PTSD-related stuff'.[62]

In the 2006 NCVER research interviews many of the men who were participating stressed that the Shed had been a lifesaver. As one Vietnam Veteran wisely predicted:

> I think places like the Shed definitely have their place in ex-military people's lives. I fear for the more recent ex-military people of this country because I don't think we have learned our lesson. I am still very angry over Vietnam. ... We are going to get people from East Timor .... and Afghanistan. ... This country has learned absolutely nothing: we need areas like this to help them when they get back.

There was a suggestion in a 2006 research interview at the XMRC in Salisbury that the origins of some of the earliest Sheds in South Australia, including the role and use of sheds and workshops by War Veterans, might be related in some way to the 'Grunt Clubs' (comprising ex infantry who had served in the Vietnam War[63]). Some Vietnam Veterans had set up 'bush camps in the Mallee' that formed part of a wider series of remote refuges, some still run by male War Veterans across south eastern Australia, as well as in the hills behind Adelaide. As one War Veteran interviewed at the XMRC in 2006 put it:

> I think we could say that the XMRC has been a template for a number of Sheds... because we have people come down from Burra, Kadina,

---

[61] 'New Home for Vietnam Vets' Association at Edinburgh', Media Release, April 5, 2006, Sandy Macdonald, Minster for Defence.
[62] Heather Hewitt, September 10, 2014.
[63] 'Grunt' is a colloquial name used within the military for someone who has served in the infantry.

MacLaren Vale. ... Men's Sheds are basically a new concept. ... These towns are now realising that they've got these older chaps floating around who have lost their wives or are separated, and the concentration has been on women's needs with the advent of feminism. ... I think a lot of men's stuff was forgotten.

Several early Sheds in Australia, for example in MacLaren Vale in South Australia, Kingsley, in northern suburban Perth in Western Australia, and Grenfell in rural New South Wales, were set up specifically for and mostly by War Veterans, usually affiliated with a Vietnam Veterans or RSL [Returned Services League] organisation. Other early Sheds overtly acknowledged the inclusion of a significant number of War Veterans in an otherwise 'mainstream' Shed, for example at Clem's Shed in Yorketown in South Australia. This recognition was in part about acknowledging the early and ongoing support from the Department of Veterans' Affairs for Men's Shed fittings (not infrastructure or staff). In late 2013 the Minister for Veterans' Affairs, Michael Ronaldson acknowledged at the 2013 AMSA Conference in Ballarat that:

> RSLs, Men's Sheds and many other Veteran and defence community organisations provide a central hub of support, recreation and comradeship for so many of our current and former servicemen and women. Since 1999, the *Veteran and Community Grants* programme has helped ex-service organisations continue to provide high quality services and support to the Veteran and defence community and their families, as well as assisting in attracting the next generation of members.[64]

EARLY MEN'S SHEDS AND CHURCH CONNECTIONS

It is important to acknowledge that in these quite early times for Men's Sheds some churches, particularly in New South Wales, but also in some places in South Australia and Victoria, were linking their informal ministry and community outreach with Men's Sheds. Indeed the second and third ever Men's Sheds, in Lane Cove and Bendigo, were auspiced through the Uniting Church and Salvation Army respectively. The Uniting Church and Catholic Churches (through UnitingCare in Sydney and Catholic Care in Newcastle) played pivotal early roles in the creation of many early Men's Sheds and provided invaluable

---

[64] Press Release, 'Grants Help Improve Veteran and Defence Community Life', December 24, 2013, http://minister.dva.gov.au/media_releases/2013/dec/va020.htm, Accessed March 21, 2014.

practical and financial assistance in setting up the Australian Men's Sheds Association. As a post script, late in 2014 UnitingCare Ageing (UCA) were backing away from auspice arrangements and support for Men's Sheds in Sydney, under 'their new and pragmatic 'funding package', business approach'[65], in part because of new federal government funding guidelines for various new Aged Care Packages.

A small number of churches opportunistically wound their informal practical support up a notch from an auspice arrangement to proselytizing. In March 2003, the Lutheran Church in South Australia was advertising a 'Men in Sheds ministry'[66] centred around congregations in rural areas, welcoming non-church goers, suggesting 'a shed (any size or degree of tidiness) as its meeting point' offering 'beer and barbecue catering', a wide range of activities 'from Bible study to motor maintenance ... hunting to recycling'.

AN EARLY COMMUNITY SHED HISTORY

In summary, a careful analysis of each of these early workshops and community-based Shed 'starts ups' before 1998 across all Australian states points to only a handful of precursor and proto-typical 'Sheds' in community settings. Whilst none put *Men* in the organisation name, several placed a primary emphasis on participation by and value to men. It is difficult to answer which of these might be the 'smoking gun' as the first or most influential early Australian Shed before the Dick McGowan Men's Shed opened in Tongala, Victoria in July 1998. What is obvious is that, by the end of 1990s, results of early and isolated experimentation with several of these Sheds began to be communicated within and between Australian states, and as the next Chapter suggests, several *Men's Sheds* organisations were created in community settings from mid-1998.

Importantly, while the early stirrings of a Men's Shed 'Movement' were still around five years off, and the start of the first state or national associations did not occur until almost a decade later, the anecdotal benefits of the Men's Shed as a grassroots, community intervention gradually came to be understood and recognised at the level of community, as well as by a small number of professionals and service providers.

As Chapter 3 will document, in terms of the date of its official opening, the Dick McGowan Men's Shed in Tongala, opened on July 26, 1998, was most

---

[65] Ruth van Herk, September 9, 2014.
[66] Lutheran Church of Australia: 'Church in Action, For Men', 'Men in Sheds', www.lca.org.au/Action/men, Accessed April 28, 2005.

likely the first ever *Men's Shed*. Another four Men's Sheds opened within 18 months in four other states, suggestive of at least some common inspiration and communication. Lane Cove Men's Shed opened in December of the same year. The Salvation Army in Bendigo in Victoria commenced the 'Men in Sheds' Positive Retirement Project in March 1999 that aimed at providing 'an opportunity to socialize with other men with similar interests in a relaxed setting'[67]. Port Augusta Men's Shed officially opened on July 28, 1999. Aldgate Men's Shed in Adelaide opened on November 24, 1999[68] also in South Australia. Donnybrook 'Men in Sheds' in Western Australia also has a long history, initially in a private shed, going back to the late 1990s.

Chapter 3 that follows documents early Australian Sheds for men in community settings, most (but not all) described publicly as Men's Sheds. It looks at each of the six Australian states in turn; illustrating how Men's Sheds commenced, spread and linked up somewhat differently and semi-independently at different times in different states. It confirms a slowing of growth in South Australia where most of the early Sheds had been concentrated. It also documents a very recent, veritable explosion of Men's Sheds across the rural areas of all other states, most recently in Australia's largest states, Western Australia and Queensland. Most of the impetus for the national Men's Shed Movement and coordination in the decade to 2015 originated from the most populous Australian states of New South Wales and Victoria during 2004-5 as outlined first in Chapter 3.

---

[67] Men in Sheds, City of Greater Bendigo website,
www.bendigo.vic.gov.au/Page/Page.sp?Page_Id=344&h=1, Accessed April 28, 2005.
[68] Confirmed by newspaper cutting.

Early Australian Men's Sheds and State Associations

Chapter 3 looks at how Men's Sheds and state associations began to develop in all Australian states after the first early, relatively independent community Shed experiments for men in South Australia. It examines how and why the earliest Men's Shed organisations in Australia opened, often in the face of considerable resistance. There was no template to follow, and minimal research evidence to justify why they might be helped to open. All prospective Sheds had to go on was what their members could glean informally from already established Sheds. For that reason, a number of quite different and innovative early Men's Shed models were trialed in each Australian state. Approximately 30 early Sheds and Men's Sheds are included as historical case studies. They are included for two reasons. Firstly, they illustrate the diversity apparent even at this very early stage of the Movement a decade ago. Secondly, they underline the innovation and continuing influence of many of these Sheds. Chapter 3 begins with the story of how some Men's Sheds organisations began to actively link up and network in both New South Wales and Victoria from 2004, culminating in the first national conference in Victoria in 2005, leading to the first use of the term 'Men's Shed Movement' and to serious discussions about the need for a future national Men's Shed Association in Australia. The latter part of Chapter 3 provides a history of Men's Sheds and state associations in the four other Australian states.

AN EARLY AUSTRALIAN MEN'S SHED CHRONOLOGY

An examination of Men's Shed official opening dates by state before 2005 summarised in Table 7 confirms that around 31 Sheds (18 'Men's Sheds', two 'Men in Sheds', as well as 11 other Sheds, without 'Men' in the organisation name) were open in community settings across Australia before 2005. These early Sheds opened in widely spread locations across five Australian states. Most were in South Australia (10), Victoria (8) and New South Wales (6), with four in Tasmania and three in Western Australia. Of all these Sheds open before 2005, two thirds (20) were located outside of Australian capital cities.

Table 7 does not include the unknown number of sheds that were set up informally in the same era without a community identity or community involvement within aged care facilities or as part of day care programs. The table includes Donnybrook and Kingsley Sheds in Western Australia each of which started in a private garage. The indicated year and month of an official opening (if there was one) does not account for the sometimes much earlier date that many shedders may have met informally. Brief case studies, *italicized* as they are introduced, are included for most of these early Australian Sheds. All were very influential in shaping the early Movement within their respective states. Several have also been influential nationally and internationally.

Pre-1999	*Lifeline Workshop, Broken Hill (1980s, NSW); Peter Badcoe XMRC Sheds (1998, SA);* The Shed, Goolwa (2/93, SA); *The Shed, Hackham West (1995, SA);* **Dick McGowan M,** Tongala (7/98, Vic); **Lane Cove M** (12/98, NSW) Donnybrook @ # (late 90s/WA).
1999	Bendigo # (3, Vic); **Port Augusta M** (7, SA); **Aldgate* M** (11, SA); Hocky's * [Snowtown] (6, SA)
2000	**Manningham M** (1, Vic); **Orbost M** (5, Vic); Pete's Bridgewater (5, Tas); **Nambucca Valley M** (8, NSW).
2001	**Kingsley@ M** (5, WA); **Creswick M** (9, Vic); **Ashfield* M** (6, NSW); **Dorset [Scottsdale] CM** (10, Tas); **Rocky River* M** [Laura] (SA); **Bazza's*** [Clare] (SA); Clem's Shed* (3/SA); The Shed, Christie's Beach ACH (7/SA).
2002	**Cobaw M** [Kyneton] (3, Vic); **Darebin M** (Vic); **Bowral* M** (NSW); **Albany* M** (6, WA).
2003	**Brimbank M** [Sunshine] (3. Vic).
2004	**Grenfell M** (7, NSW); Camden* C (SA); St Helens C (11, Tas); Deloraine C (Tas); The Shed, Mt Druitt (8, NSW).

Table 7 Opening Dates of Pre-2005 Australian Men's and Community Sheds
KEY: Vic: Victoria; Tas: Tasmania, NSW: New South Wales; WA: Western Australia; SA: South Australia. Those actually called 'Men's Sheds' are in **bold**; *italics* indicates doubtful inclusion; C=Community, M=Men's; @ indicates backyard start up; # Bendigo and Donnybrook were both opened as 'Men in Sheds'; Month of official opening / State are in brackets; * indicates Sheds not included as case studies in Parts 2 or 3.

Early Men's Sheds in each Australian State

This section examines the early history of Men's Sheds in each Australian state, commencing with some of the earliest Sheds in the two most populous states, New South Wales and Victoria, where the early Men's Shed momentum shifted from South Australia after 2004-5. It also looks carefully at some of the earliest Sheds in South Australia, Tasmania and Western Australia. Most of the early Sheds examined opened semi-independently before 2005 and many had a limited knowledge of what was happening in other States. The section on early Queensland Sheds is much briefer mainly because of the much later development and spread of Sheds to that state, with earliest Sheds opening in Queensland around 2009. The Australian Capital Territory (with 10 Sheds in early 2015) and the Northern Territory (with 5) are not separately examined, mainly because Sheds developed there somewhat later and in relatively small numbers.

New South Wales Men's Shed Early History

The *Lane Cove Men's Shed* is the first community Men's Shed to be opened by that name in New South Wales and second in the world after Tongala in Victoria. While it is quite a small shed it has always 'punched well above its weight'. It was certainly more influential than any other in terms of its active proliferation of 'how to' to other Men's Sheds in Australia in the first decade from its official opening in December 1998. Ted Donnelly has been actively involved in the Lane Cove Shed since it was planned in 1998.

When interviewed by Barry Golding in 2006 for the *Men's Sheds in Australia* [1] research, Ted Donnelly regarded Lane Cove as 'a complete experiment' [2]. Donnelly is fondly regarded by the Australian Men's Shed Movement (AMSA) as the 'father of men's sheds', with his active and continuous involvement in the Lane Cove Men's Shed stretching back nearly 20 years. AMSA's 'Ted Donnelly Award' was named in his honour (and awarded first to Ted Donnelly) for his 'Outstanding Contribution to the Men's Shed Movement'. It was Donnelly's tireless work, supported by the Shed's long time Project Coordinator, Ruth van Herk, in collaboration with David Helmers (formerly manager of the Windale Shed from 2004, later to first become first CEO of

---

[1] Barry Golding *et al.*, *Men's Sheds in Australia: Learning through Community Contexts.* Adelaide: NCVER, 2007.
[2] Ted Donnelly interview with Barry Golding, 2006, 12.

AMSA) that led, after much hard slog, to the creation of AMSA. It was Donnelly who first registered the national association, Australian Men's Shed Association, on January 22, 2007. Ted Donnelly was appropriately acknowledged nationally for his close to two decades of voluntary work for the Lane Cove Men's Shed and the now international Movement by being awarded the AM (Member of the Order of Australia) in January 2013.

The background and rationale at the time of the Lane Cove Men's Shed's opening in December 1998 are interesting to hear and reflect on, given that they presciently anticipated much of what has transpired in the Men's Shed Movement in Australia and internationally since. It is clear that some early Shed organisations and Shed project participants were setting themselves up well before any actual Shed openings, comparing notes over long distances and across state borders. As an example, Manningham Men's Shed (in suburban Melbourne, discussed later) was aware that Lane Cove and Tongala were setting up a Men's Shed long before its official opening. This is confirmed in the December 1997 submission from the Manningham Community Health Service, seeking funds for the Manningham Men's Shed, which did not officially open until 2000.

An article about the Lane Cove Men's Shed opening appeared in a local monthly publication, the *Village Observer*, in December 1998[3] headed 'Lane Cove Men's Shed: For Health and Well Being'. It outlined the project, its background as well as the health benefits. The article stressed, perhaps for the first time in print, that, unlike personal sheds, this was a *'Community Shed'*.

- **The project** – the Men's Shed is a community project, which seeks to improve the health and quality of life for older men in the Lane Cove Area.
- **Background** – The shed has an important part in Australian culture and mythology. Sheds are an integral part of Australian Life. For men sheds can sustain a meaning in life as it is a reservoir of memories and experiences, rich with satisfying layers of accumulated personal history. The shed is a place to escape to, to meet others and to teach others skills.
- **Health benefits** – Good health is based on a number of foundations including having self-esteem, a valued role in society and developing social networks. Social relationships

---

[3] 'Lane Cove Men's Shed: For Health and Wellbeing', *Village Observer* (Lane Cove and Hunters Hill areas, Sydney), December, 1998.

have long been believed to promote health and protect against diseases.

- **Why a Community Shed?** – When people retire they often down size their living arrangements and move into as flat or retirement centre, which often results in men losing their personal space such as a shed. There is often a realisation that domestic space is the domain of the female partner. Many men crave a space of their own, where they can maintain their identity and have an outlet for both creative expression and purposeful activity.

- The Men's Shed will be a meeting place where older men can: share common interests, make and repair handy craft items like furniture and toys, be provided with health care information, maintain social networks, teach younger people skills in handy crafts.

As the Lane Cove Men's Shed website put it, in what was by 2014 a huge understatement, 'In 1998 the Lane Cove Shed was an experiment. Now there are many more "Sheds"'[4]. Ted Donnelly and Ruth van Herk have been excellent at attracting friends and supporters nationally and enjoyed the strong support of UnitingCare from their Shed's inception. Its initial establishment was assisted with a Commonwealth grant from the Department of Health and Aged Services under the 'Healthy Seniors Grant Programme'. As its web site in 2014 explained, the Shed was originally:

> ... set up in 1997/98 to meet these needs and to provide a substitute space for "shedless blokes". Besides encouraging new social activities and friendships, the Shed also gives access to other networks for men, including local activities and men's health information.

The shed itself, being located in what used to be several car parking spaces under St Columba's Retirement Centre, is actually quite small and compact. Its early self-description was quite simple: 'THE MEN'S SHED is a fully equipped workshop where skilled and unskilled men can share time with each other, swap yarns and work together on community projects'[5]. In September 2005 Ruth van Herk wrote that:

---

[4] Lane Cove Men's Shed, http://www.mensshed.org.au/, Accessed April 15, 2014.
[5] http://www.mensshed.org.au/story1.htm, Accessed April 15, 2014.

Lane Cove prides itself on being the first leisure-type shed set up in a metropolitan area. Starting in 1998 it specifically responded to Aged Care needs for older men in the community. UnitingCare took on the project and to [2005] has auspiced / is currently auspicing six Sheds all modeled on the Lane Cove non-commercial model. The Lane Cove Shed has become an unofficial resource centre for many more Sheds situated all over Australia but particularly in NSW and Vic. Thus far we have shared information, been viewed, attended steering committee meetings, discussed issues by telephone and sent out e-mail information to twenty Sheds or intending Sheds. One of our earliest contacts was with the Nambucca [Valley] Men's Shed and the MacKillop Outreach Shed in Lewisham – both sheds of interest to researchers.

Like the Men's Shed that opened in Tongala in July the same year (1998), Lane Cove was established with a Commonwealth grant as a Men's Shed when it opened. As with most early Men's Sheds, there was a considerable lead-time between when the idea was formulated and the official opening. Discussions about a possible Men's Shed began at Lane Cove in 1997. There has been a reduction of the average lead-time for many Shed organisations, between the idea and official opening, in the almost two decades years since Lane Cove opened. This is in no small part due to the *'Setting up a Men's Shed'* manual that the Lane Cove Men's Shed, mainly Ted Donnelly, developed and circulated free, initially as a Lane Cove hard copy document[6], later via AMSA and more recently via AMSA's web site.

Lane Cove Men's Shed received many important community awards at local, state and national levels for its diverse contributions in and beyond the Shed, many going back over a decade. They included the Council of the Ageing (COTA) Award in 2001 for Good Practice as 'An outstanding initiative for the needs of older men in the local community', 2002 Aged and Community Services, Australia 'Award for Excellence'; National Award of Innovations in Local Government; Royal North Shore Hospital Certificate of Appreciation 'for generous support to the Children's Ward'; North Sydney Community Award in 2004 'for outstanding service to the community', as well as the Lane Cove Council 'Access and Disability Award' in 2005 'for work done in establishing 'The Wednesday Group.' The Wednesday Group was still active fifteen years

---

[6] In September 2005 the Lane Cove Men's Shed manual ran to 15 pages and was titled: *Manual: Information re Setting up and Continuing Men's Sheds*. It included five pages contributed by Mary MacKillop Shed, Lewisham.

later in 2015, providing a welcome, special help and supervision on projects that included leatherwork, simple woodcarving and bookbinding,

> ... to men with few or no skills, who like to be very leisurely about their projects or may need special help because of age or infirmity. ... The supervisor provides simple projects, helps with instruction [and] ensures safety standards in a friendly and patient atmosphere ...[7]

Lave Cove was directly or indirectly responsible for advising and mentoring many other early Men's Sheds as far away as Western Australia, mostly through phone calls and email, but also by visits and talks in the greater Sydney region. By September 2005 the Lane Cove Men's Shed had personally advised: Ashfield Council and Nambucca Valley Community Services (both in June 2000); Blue Mountains and Botany Bay City Council (both in November, 2001); Bowral Uniting Church (November, 2002); North Sydney Uniting Care and North Sydney Council, and Chatswood-Uniting Care / Willoughby Council as well as Central Coast and Shoalhaven (2005)[8].

From the early work in developing new Sheds, it was obvious to Ted Donnelly that there was a need to have a convenient way of exchanging information. Donnelly, in his words 'with the aid of several library books', produced a website with the aim of developing it as a communications hub where shedders could share ideas about projects, training, materials, and local events. It was basically a discussion forum but also included details of existing Men's Sheds. The costs involved in the development of this early website, managed by Donnelly through Lane Cove, were covered by UnitingCare Ageing (North Sydney Region). At the Lakes Entrance Men's Shed conference in Victoria in 2005 the website was introduced to and made available to any Shed that wished to use it.

While the discussion forum on the site was not widely used, the 'Shed Details' section became very important and formed the base for the AMSA database that Barry Golding from University of Ballarat (Federation University Australia from 2014) had begun to develop in 2005 as part of his research into Men's Sheds and learning, leading to the *Men's Sheds in Australia* report, published by NCVER in 2007. Once AMSA formed, Barry Golding's research database, developed as a consequence of the national Men's Shed research

---

[7] http://www.mensshed.org.au/wedgroup.htm, Accessed April 15, 2014.
[8] 'Help for New Sheds', www.mensshed.org.au/help.htm, Accessed September 23, 2005.

project, was transferred via Ted Donnelly to AMSA, and later put into the current searchable Shed Locator on AMSA's web site.

Through the efforts of Lane Cove Men's Shed and with the support of UnitingCare in North Sydney, by 2007 there was a cluster of very successful UnitingCare Men's Sheds across northern Sydney. UnitingCare also underwrote the first totally national Men's Shed conference, held in a magnificent former Catholic Seminary in nearby Manly in Sydney in September 2007.

Ashfield Men's Shed, was another influential and very generous New South Wales Shed, set up in this same early era in 2001 only 13 kilometers south west of Lane Cove, also in inner suburban Sydney. The Mary MacKillop Outreach of the St Vincent de Paul Society, through its manager and psychologist, Bob Nelson, spearheaded the workshop-based Ashfield Men's Shed, for 'Mateship and Meaningful Community Contribution.'[9] The original agreement between the Ashfield Council and Mary MacKillop Outreach, signed in November 2001, is shown in Photograph 7.

---

[9] Bob Nelson, 'The Men's Shed Concept: Mateship and Meaningful Community Contribution', Paper to NSW Elderly Suicide Prevention Network, 2005.

AGREEMENT BETWEEN
ASHFIELD COUNCIL *and*
MARY MACKILLOP OUTREACH (MMO)
(a special work of the St Vincent De Paul Society)
REGARDING THE ASHFIELD MEN'S SHED

This agreement is made on the _____ Fourteenth _____

Day of _____ November _____ 2001

between Ashfield Council and the Trustees of the Society of St Vincent de Paul (NSW). The purpose of this agreement is to provide a framework for the future of the Ashfield Men's Shed.

INTRODUCTION

What is the Men's Shed?
The Men's Shed is a social group for men. It will provide an opportunity for like-minded men to come together, mix and socialise while participating in woodwork activities. The group comprises a number of retired men from the Ashfield Municipality and Mary Mackillop Outreach clients who require some assistance with carpentry projects and who wish to join a mainstream men's activity program.

Once established, efforts will be made to broaden the activities of the project to include guest speakers on men's health and a mentoring program between the men and younger residents of local boarding houses. This mentoring program should also serve to improve the employment opportunities available to MMO clients.

Ashfield Men's Shed projects
The projects undertaken by the participants of the Shed will be non profit community projects, including specific projects for the St. Vincent De Paul Society. The goods produced by these specific projects (eg bed bases) remain the property of the Society, until delivered to people in need.

Hours of operation
The project will operate one day per week from 10.00am - 2.00pm for a trial of three months. If both parties wish to continue after the three month period, the project is to be expanded to two days per week from 10.00am – 2.00pm.
Date of commencement: Friday 9th November 2001.

TERMS OF THE AGREEMENT
The term of the agreement shall be for two (2) years commencing on _____ Friday 9th Nov. 2001

Ashfield Men's Shed Agreement
Ashfield Council and St Vincent De Paul Society

Photograph 7 Agreement to set up the Ashfield Men's Shed, New South Wales, 2001

The purpose of the Ashfield Shed was summarised in Bob Nelson's 2005 account, below.

In 2001, Mary MacKillop Outreach and Ashfield Council initiated a joint project aimed at meeting a number of the needs of retired men, through a social/woodwork program called the Ashfield Men's Shed. ... [S]ince the Men's Shed opened, many men have participated – retired men, those with mental health problems and substance abuse issues, men with disabilities and isolated men from boarding houses. Depression is common amongst this group and the risk of suicide is ever present, so the Shed operates as a lifeline. This venture utilises the skills of retired men, channels their energies and experience into creative activities producing items of benefit to the community, and fosters the development of supportive and social relationships. The important element is the sense of belonging and connectedness, and the self-esteem and fulfillment, which comes from building useful items for others in the local community. These elements appear to assist in making participants more resilient to stress and the effects of mental illness, which may also reduce the risk of suicide for those involved.

The original *Agreement Between Ashfield Council and Mary MacKillop Outreach ... Regarding the Ashfield Men's Shed*, dated November 14, 2001, clearly documents the Ashfield Council responsibilities, making this one of the first Men's Sheds to get significant local government funding. The agreement clearly defined a Men's Shed as:

A social group for men ... [providing] an opportunity for like-minded men to come together, mix and socialise while participating in woodwork activities. ... Once established, efforts will be made to broaden the activities ... to include guest speakers on men's health and a mentoring program between the men and younger residents of local boarding houses.

A critical analysis was undertaken by Bob Nelson,[10] penned in 2003 using mainly anecdotal evidence from the Ashfield Men's Shed program when the Shed was in its third year[11]. Because of Nelson's professional expertise, the report was bolstered by psychological insights and literature. Nelson recalled that Mary MacKillop Outreach had been operating '... since the early 1990s to provide

---

[10] Created October 20, 2003, updated as an evaluation for Ashfield Council, revised February 11, 2005.
[11] Bob Nelson, 2005, as above. 5.

recreational, educational and prevocational training programs for persons having a mental illness residing in licensed boarding houses and group homes of Sydney's Inner West'[12]. The aim of the Men's Shed program, as defined by Bob Nelson in 2005, was:

> ... to provide social opportunities and carpentry activities for retired men, war Veterans and male persons having a mental illness; to address the problem of isolation among elderly men in the community; to provide older men with a non-threatening means of accessing health professionals in a relaxed, informal and "male-friendly" environment, to offer an opportunity to men having a mental illness to integrate into a mainstream carpentry program; to facilitate the development of mentoring relationships; to provide social, recreational and meaningful employment training opportunities for male clients having a mental illness.[13]

Bob Nelson identified groups of men that the early Ashfield Men's Shed had effectively reached, including men with a disability and War Veterans with Post Traumatic Stress Disorder (PTSD). He also reflected that the 'Men's Shed model has had less success contacting and attracting retired and older men who prefer a more reclusive lifestyle' many of whom 'may be at greater risk of suicide.'[14] Nelson looked ahead in his report summary to future research about the potential of the Men's Shed project '... to rehabilitate Vietnam Veterans ... through the work of building wheelchairs for third world children injured in landmine accidents.'[15] Mary MacKillop Outreach / Ashfield Council Men's Shed was recognised for its contribution to the betterment of the mental health of its members with an award from the Australian Psychological Society in 2009.

Several other early (pre-2006) Men's Sheds in New South Wales, particularly in rural Nambucca and Grenfell but also in Windale (a suburb of Newcastle) and Mt Druitt (in outer Western Sydney) were similarly innovative, generous in helping other Sheds, influential in creating the practical knowledge base for the early Men's Shed Movement, and very influential in helping create, underwrite and support the first national Men's Sheds association, AMSA, physically located since its inception in the New South Wales city of Newcastle.

---

[12] Bob Nelson, 2005, as above, 1.
[13] Bob Nelson, 2005, as above, 1.
[14] Bob Nelson, as above, 7.
[15] Bob Nelson, as above, 9.

The Hon Ron Dyer MLC (second from right) officially opens the Nambucca Heads Men's Shed in a ceremony last Wednesday. In attendance were about 60 people who had been instrumental in the project coming to fruition.

Every man needs a shed and Nambucca blokes get theirs

Every man should have a should, or so the saying goes. And for Nambucca men it's official ... men of the Nambucca have their shed.

The Men's Shed at Nambucca Heads was officially opened last Wednesday, August 22 in front of some 60 people who gathered to celebrate the occasion.

From humble beginnings the shed has become a reality through a lot of hard work. Program coordinator Stuart Holmes is excited by the shed's future.

"There are plans to offer seminars on men's health issues as well as a regular

health check up servicde for men in the near future," he said on Wednesday.

"I can't thank enogh the wonderful group of blokes that have supported the project, volunteering their time and effort to make it the success it is.

"I'm sure that with their continued support this facility will continue to serve the Nambucca Valley for years."

General manager of the Nambucca Community Services Council, Glenys Munro, echoed Mr Holmes' thoughts when she said she was pleased with the way the shed had progressed and is confident the

project will continue to grow.

"The shed will offer many and veried services to the regular participants and to the general public alike," she added.

"The Men's Shed is a valuable asset to our community offering men a place to gather and share skills and experience, as well as providing a venue for ongoing training programs such as the fathering course due to start early next month."

For anyone interested in The Men's Shed or the training and health seminars offered at the shed, contact Stuart Holmes on 65685090 for more information.

Photograph 8 Newspaper Article about the opening of Nambucca Heads Men's Shed, 2001

Photograph 8, above, is an article about the opening (on 22 August, 2001) of the *Nambucca Heads Men's Shed*. Located in the coastal Nambucca Shire with a current population around 18,000, it was briefly called a 'Bloke's Shed' and later 'The Men's Shed Nambucca'. It is often confused with the more recent, nearby Nambucca Heads Men's Shed. Planning for the first Shed in Nambucca was well underway by John Scott, its project manager, in August 2000. Either Scott or the newspaper reporter had read the Dick McGowan Men's Shed story (opened in Tongala, Victoria in mid-1998), as some of the same words from the November

1998 *Community Link*[16] article about Tongala were used in the *Mid-Coast Observer*[17] news story in 2000 about the Nambucca Valley 'Bloke's Shed'. The newspaper reported the Shed was being set up for blokes to 'build, fix, socialise, snooze and proudly leave tools and unfinished projects on the bench'. The same article also noted that the Nambucca Shed was modeled on a similar project in Lane Cove, and its header again drew on words from John Williamson's *The Shed* song.

A small, rented shed was opened in coastal Nambucca (midway between Sydney and Brisbane) on November 8, 2000[18]. It moved to larger premises, another rented industrial bay in Nambucca Heads, on August 22, 2001,[19] this time clearly badged as a Men's Shed. The thinking for the Shed came in part from Jill Stowe, first employed in 1995 as part of the 'Assistance with Care and Housing for the Aged' (ACHA) program. ACHA, then federally fully-funded program, had set up a pilot program across the three local government areas of Coffs Harbour, Bellingen and Nambucca. The Nambucca Men's Shed was:

> ... targeted at financially disadvantaged aged people who were homeless or at risk of homelessness to meet both their accommodation and support needs. The majority of clients in the program were men with issues of drug abuse, mental illness, post-war traumas, community and social isolation and dislocation from families and friends due to lifestyles and relationship breakdown. This subgroup of men ... did not feel comfortable in the usual socialisation outlets such as Senior Citizens and Adult Day Clubs ... [and] often had trade or skills backgrounds. Through [Stowe's] consultation with the older male clients [through Nambucca Valley Community Service Council (NVCSC) in 1999], she was told that a Shed, a place to go and socialise with other men and a place to use tools and make things, would be great for them.[20]

With Narelle Haycroft (then a Neighbour Aid Coordinator from Bellingen), Jill Stowe convened a public meeting in Bellingen in 1999 to generate interest for the

---

[16] *Community Link* was a magazine published by the National Australia Bank from 1997-2000, devoted to community service and volunteer groups.

[17] 'All Australian Blokes Need a Shed', *Mid-Coast Observer*, August 9, 2000, 3.

[18] 'Blokes Shed Opens', *Mid-Coast Observer*, November, 2000, reporting opening in new premises 'last Wednesday' (November 8).

[19] 'Every Man needs a Shed and Nambucca Gets Theirs', *Mid-Coast Observer*, August 29, 2001, no page number.

[20] 'Concept to Reality: Nambucca Valley Community Men's Shed' (4 pages, no date or author).

Shed concept and also wrote a 1999 article for the Mid North Coast Regional Council for Social Development's Regional newsletter seeking a group of men to assist her in developing the ideas. At that stage no one was willing to take up the challenge. In March 1999 Stowe 'researched whether there were any other Men's Sheds in the country and found a recent opening of one in Lane Cove NSW and liked the concept'.

Nambucca Valley Community Services Council Inc. (known as Lifetime Connect Inc. in 2015) supported the concept, and in 2000 submitted a successful application for start-up funds. The first male worker, John Scott, previously a TAFE Welfare Studies student, and before that working on a local Blokes Media project, was sent to Lane Cove Men's Shed to speak to their coordinator. The Nambucca project was based around the Lane Cove model, but with a more local focus addressing disadvantaged males of all ages in the community.

In February 2001, a few months after the first Shed had opened, Stuart Holmes was employed to involve broader community services including schools, to try and transfer older men's skills, though mentoring, to younger men. By August 2001 the Shed needed larger premises, and in September 2001 it had started a boat-building program. In 2001 the Shed was also visited by Hugh Wright, then from the University of Western Sydney, who gathered information from the Nambucca Shed to use in a successful funding submission for a shed in Western Sydney. By 2002 the Nambucca Shed had trialed a cooking program 'for blokes'. It had also started working with Professor Bill O'Hehir, a psychologist at the local Southern Cross University, drawing upon a report by O'Hehir about the Nambucca Valley Men's Shed model, focusing on ageing men.

Bill O'Hehir's *The Men's Shed: A Practical Analysis of a Therapeutic Intervention Process into Men's Health*, written in 2004[21], included broad conclusions and implications from considerable '... empirical and non-standardised information ... collected from participants over the past two years (2002-2004)' at the Nambucca Valley Men's Shed. O'Hehir '... spent approximately 800 hours over two years attending the Men's Shed'. Hugh Wright contended in 2014 that O'Hehir's:

> ... formal research and evaluation of the Nambucca Shed ... was groundbreaking and miles ahead of anything done previously as this was

---

[21] Bill O'Hehir, 'The Men's Shed: A Practical Analysis of a Therapeutic Community Intervention Process into Men's Health', Unpublished paper, 2004.

the first time a Shed [had] been researched and evaluated by an academic.[22]

Stuart Holmes joined the first, interim AMSA Board in 2007. Holmes recalled in 2014 that his previous work 'as an activist and organiser in the Metal Workers Union' helped him recognise the potential of Sheds as 'the best place to engage men and get them to open up about what was going on, standing next to them while they worked and talked, not dragging them off to some room for an interview'[23].

The Nambucca Shed was relocated from the coastal town of Nambucca Heads (population approximately 11,000, approximately 500 kilometers north of Sydney) to smaller Macksville (population about 3,000) in 2012 and was still open and active in early 2015 as the Nambucca Valley Community Men's Shed[24].

Grenfell Men's Shed is an early rural New South Wales Men's Shed, located in the small rural town of Grenfell (population around 2,000, 370 kilometers west of Sydney). Though not officially opened until July 17, 2004, the Shed has a longer informal history and was something of an 'early pioneer' in New South Wales, particularly because of the way it worked with War Veterans. Its success was due in no small part to the late Len Wallace, and more recently to Ray Cawthorne, the Shed's 2015 Vice President. Wallace, a Vietnam War Veteran and prolific metal sculptor, generously made the Grenfell Shed the focus of his community work in later life. While it had its community baptism in a public meeting held to gauge interest for a Men's Shed a year earlier (on June 23, 2003), Len Wallace had been working informally supporting other Vietnam War Veterans in Grenfell for much longer, since 1985. Indeed the 2015 Grenfell Shed website suggests that 'The concept of the Grenfell Shed [originated] in 1987'[25].

Events came to a head in 2002 when, as Wallace put it, "My wife's cooking was disappearing at a fast rate and I was losing my own shed. Something had to be done". Wallace learnt at a meeting at the local community health facility in 2002 that grants might be available through Department of Veterans' Affairs (DVA) to assist with a Men's Shed. With DVA funding and significant community support, the pigeons were evicted from the former Railway Goods Shed and the Grenfell Men's Shed was born. Its Mission Statement, written by

---

[22] Hugh Wright, July 30, 2014.
[23] Stuart Holmes, July 24, 2014.
[24] http://nvcsc.org.au/nambucca-valley-mens-shed, Accessed January 8, 2015.
[25] http://www.grenfell.org.au/mensshed/, Accessed January 8, 2015.

Len Wallace, read: 'To enjoy each others company, promote self-worth and work ethics, while developing and sharing skills for the benefit of both the individual and the community'. [26] The concept of the Grenfell Shed, penned and deliberately underlined by Wallace in 2007, went quite a bit deeper than the 'hands-on'. Wallace saw it as being about:

> ... enabling men, from many social and ethnic backgrounds to mix and
> learn. It's a place for men of all ages getting together, sharing fellowship
> and discovering the satisfaction of *creation through the hands, and in
> turn changing the perception of the Mind.*[27]

Sadly, in 2013, despite his own heroic work with others, Len Wallace became the victim of the 'Black Dog', depression that had stalked many former war Veterans. His work with Men's Sheds was a passionate attempt to help other men. The bottom of the 2007 document referred to above had the words 'Please be advised, the Grenfell Shed is not a member or associated with (Mensheds Australia)'. Documenting the bitter experiences of the Grenfell Men's Shed and its committee in dealing with what amounted to a management takeover by Mensheds Australia from 2004, expanded on more broadly in Chapter 4, could fill many pages.

Unsurprisingly, Grenfell still uses the words 'Independent Men's Shed' to form the roof as part of its logo. By 2014 Grenfell enjoyed support from the many rural Shed organisations in South West Men's Sheds Alliance (also comprising Boorowa Men's Den, Canowindra Men's Shed, Cootamundra Shed for Men, Temora Men's Shed, Young Men's Shed, Murrumbateman Men's Shed, Ariah Park Men's Shed, Harden Men's Shed, Cowra Men's Shed and Blayney Men's Shed)[28].

The Shed at Windale (operating in 2015 as Windale Men's Shed and Community Group Inc.[29]) opened several years after Lane Cove, Nambucca, Ashfield and Grenfell (in 2006) but is included here because it played a pivotal role in the formation of the Australian Men's Shed Association. It is also an illustrative example of how Sheds often take several years to get everything in place. The Shed at Windale was also something of a pioneer in discovering and sharing the benefits of a Men's Shed organisation becoming an Incorporated Association[30].

---

[26] 'Explaining the Grenfell Shed for Men', 1, 26 March, 2007.
[27] As above, 2.
[28] Grenfell Men's Shed, http://www.grenfell.org.au/mensshed/, Accessed March 20, 2014.
[29] Windale Men's Shed, http://www.windalemensshed.org.au/, Accessed January 7, 2015.
[30] 'The Windale Men's Shed Story', Roger Greenan, President, March 20, 2014.

The Shed at Windale opened in 2006 in one of the most disadvantaged socioeconomic communities in urban Australia. The idea for a Shed originated around 2003 at the completion of a 'community renewal scheme', implemented after a national report was published in 1999[31], identifying Windale as being ranked:

> 1st on unemployment, 2nd on long-term unemployment, and 3rd on 'left school before aged 15 years'. The least disadvantaged rankings attained by Windale were 12th on court convictions, and 15th on low birth weight.

The community renewal scheme, introduced to improve the health and wellbeing of Windale residents, appeared in 2003 not to have provided many opportunities for men, hence the focus on the creation of a Shed for men.

> Progress was very slow until the Two Bishops Trust [32] in Newcastle was given the mandate to focus on establishing the project through CentaCare, a local Catholic Service provider.

According to a Media Release from the Catholic Diocese of Maitland-Newcastle, the funding for the project was originally intended for two Sheds as part of the Windale and Booragul/Bolton Point Shed Project. The Lake Macquarie Men's Shed Project Coordinator, Kerry Thompson noted on May 5, 2004 that one Shed was proposed east of Lake Macquarie adjacent to the Windale Police Citizens Youth Club, and the other one in Westlake's Neighbourhood Centre west of Lake Macquarie at Woodrising.[33] There was a big cast of early stakeholders aside from the Two Bishops Trust by 2004, including Family and Community Services, Premier's Department, Hunter Community Renewal Scheme, Department of Transport and Regional Services, Lake Macquarie City Council and Lake Macquarie Police Citizens Youth Club.

Importantly, many of AMSA's later operational and practical insights were drawn from a combination of the Lane Cove Men's Shed experience, outlined

---

[31] Tony Vinson, *Unequal in Life: The Distribution of Social Disadvantage in Victoria and New South Wales*. Richmond: Jesuit Social Services, 1999.

[32] The Two Bishops Trust was a collaborative venture between the Hunter's Catholic and Anglican Churches. Its broader aim was to 'inspire and unite the whole community in finding workable, just and creative solutions to unemployment', TBT – Men's Sheds Media Release, Diocese of Maitland-Newcastle, June 16, 2003.

[33] 'Lake Macquarie Men's Shed Project: Background Information', Kerry Thompson, Project Coordinator, May 5, 2004.

earlier in Section 2, and David Helmers's experiences helping to manage the early, difficult and protracted set-up phase of the Shed at Windale. It is to the credit of this project that AMSA's difficult, early and formative years were generously nested, both administratively and logistically, in this arm of the Catholic Church through the Diocese of Maitland-Newcastle. David Helmers tells a great (true) yarn that his first AMSA mobile phone was 'gifted' to him by the then Bishop. As Helmers acknowledged in 2014, the Windale Shed 'set some revolutionary processes in place in regards to self sustainability both in financial and management systems that were subsequently utilised by AMSA'. At the same time, it made a major contribution to AMSA by 'allowing for the diversion of allocated resources such as the funded position and funding for the Shed project to be diverted to the establishment of AMSA'[34].

With the strong support of the Department of Family and Community Services (which regarded the Windale Men's Shed project as 'one of the most viable and successful community initiatives it had funded'), a number of very broad 'deliverables' were strategically embedded in the Lake Macquarie Windale Shed Project work plan. This created the essential groundwork for the progressive development of a national Men's Shed Association in Australia. It included promotion of the Men's Shed Project to all levels of government, actively pursuing funding sources to continue to work on the national peak Men's Shed body, the development of the Hunter Valley Shed Cluster Group, development of the AMSA website and planning for the Hobart AMSA Conference in 2009.

To support these broader initiatives, the Shed at Windale undertook essential national networking from 2006 via *TheShed@Windale* Newsletter. It also undertook the first Australian Men's Shed Survey in June 2007, auspiced by CentaCare Newcastle[35]. Volume 1, Issue 1 of the *Australian Men's Shed Newsletter* produced after the Manly Conference in 2007 was also produced by The Shed at Windale, effectively coordinated by David Helmers and the Shed at Windale executive.

The end result was also positive for Windale Shed, which 'evolved from within a low socio-economic community from the outset, thereby providing constructive, cost effective planning opportunities to develop within the group that contained a local focus'[36]. After an inaugural meeting of The Hunter Valley Shed Cluster Group in November 2007, the Association was formally launched

---

[34] David Helmers, March 14, 2014.
[35] Australian Men's Shed Survey, June 2007, The Shed@Windale and CentaCare Newcastle.
[36] Roger Greenan, *The Windale Men's Shed Story*, 2014.

on May 26, 2008 by then Minister for the Aged Christine Keneally (later to become NSW Premier). The Press release for the launch[37] records that:

> After the 2007 Men's Sheds Conference in Manly, the idea of a National Men's Shed Association (AMSA) was tabled. The idea [was for] a unified body to represent the shed community to raise funds and provide assistance to existing sheds, but more importantly, to help communities to develop new shed projects.

As a postscript, in early 2015, the Windale Shed was still going strong.

This brief account of early and influential Sheds in New South Wales would not be complete without inclusion of *The Shed* in Mt Druitt in outer suburban western Sydney. The idea for 'The Shed' began in approximately 2002 with a conversation about 'getting a couple of old [Aboriginal] and homeless blokes together ... off the streets to have a good yarn and see how we could help each other'[38]. The Shed was the first in Australia to deliberately and actively work with Aboriginal men at risk. While many people imagine Indigenous Australia as a rural and remote phenomenon (which it is, by percentage of local residents), in fact Sydney has the largest Aboriginal community in Australia by number of people (around 40,000), disproportionately located in lower socio-economic, outer western and southwestern Sydney suburbs like Mt Druitt. The Shed was officially opened by the New South Wales State Governor, Mari Bashir, in August 2004.[39]

The Shed was backed by the University of Western Sydney (UWS) through Professor John Macdonald, later to become an AMSA Patron[40], and Anthony Brown, active in the UWS Men's Health and Information Resource Centre, with the support of the Holy Family Parish, Mt Druitt. It grew out of the particular and often acute needs of Aboriginal men, many at risk of suicide. In 2006 it was committed to 'bringing services to the community, and not making men go to the services'[41]. In 2014 John Macdonald described The Shed, ably coordinated and innovatively managed by Rick Welsh, as:

---

[37] Media release, May 20, 2007, The Hunter Valley Shed Cluster Group, Inaugural Meeting.
[38] 'The Shed' (Hackham West), Barry Golding interview transcript, 2006, 1.
[39] http://www.uws.edu.au/mhirc/mens_health_information_and_resource_centre/research_p rojects/the_shed, Accessed January 8, 2015.
[40] The third Patron was Tim Mathieson, partner of Australia's then Prime Minister, Julia Gillard.
[41] 'The Shed' (Hackham West), Barry Golding interview transcript, 2006, 3.

... a place for men, though women often attend, especially on the day of the week when service providers attend. The philosophy of this Shed is that the pathway to despair and suicide is often an accumulation of difficulties related to housing, relationships, the law etc. Service providers come to meet the men there including the mental health workers. It seems a popular place for men and belongs to them.[42]

THE DEVELOPMENT OF THE NEW SOUTH WALES MEN'S SHED ASSOCIATION[43]

The New South Wales Men's Shed Association (NSWMSA) name was formally registered on November 17, 2008 by the Australian Men's Shed Association (AMSA) together with all other state Assocation names. However, at that time, the New South Wales members who were interested in setting up the Association were heavily involved in establishing AMSA and little progress was made.

Calls for members for a working committee in New South Wales were advertised in the *AMSA Newsletter* in April 2009. From the few volunteers who responded, together with the original organisers, a Steering Committee was established. This group formally established the Association in February 2010 at a meeting held at Lake Macquarie. Their objective was to organise elections throughout NSW so that the Steering Committee could be replaced by elected representatives. In November 2010 a two-day "Gathering" was held at Myuna Bay, which about 100 members of Men's Sheds throughout NSW attended. A major purpose of this meeting was to elect a committee for the NSWMSA. This had been planned over many weeks, but only five candidates were nominated, less than the nine Committee positions required, so no election was held. Instead, there was a very 'robust discussion' on the legality of the Constitution and the proposed election.

It was agreed that the five people who had been nominated would form a "transient" committee and that they were to investigate the queries raised at the Myuna Bay meeting and organise an Annual General Meeting by mid-2011. It was also clear from the discussions that members would prefer future elections to be carried out on a regional basis, and the committee set out to develop a procedure for this to occur. Following the "Gathering", the Committee and AMSA had a number of discussions with the Department of Fair Trading to ensure that the Association had been properly set up, to confirm that this

---

[42] John Macdonald, December 31, 2014.
[43] The historic details of NSWMSA were supplied by Ted Donnelly, August 18, 2014.

arrangement was not in conflict with the Department rules and to seek advice on how to proceed. The advice from the Department was that the Transient Committee was acceptable to them as a management committee of the Association, and that an AGM could be held to confirm acceptance of the new Constitution. All Sheds that had registered with AMSA, and were geographically in NSW, would then automatically become members of the NSWMSA.

The Department's acceptance notice for the new Constitution was received on January 19, 2011. As requested, the Committee prepared a plan for regional elections. The NSWMSA defined nine geographical Zones. The nine Zone representatives comprised the NSWMSA Committee. This ensured full coverage and representation of the whole State, removing the need for representatives of all Sheds in NSW to travel extensively to attend meetings, and also eliminated the need for statewide elections. Completion date was July 8, 2011 and the first elected Committee for NSWMSA met briefly at the Brisbane AMSA conference on August 22, 2011 to elect Officers. The first full committee meeting of NSWMSA was held on October 6, 2011 at The Shed at Windale. This proved to be extremely successful with all committee members attending. The new committee was enthusiastic and keen to develop both their specific regions and the overall State network. They agreed that there were advantages to be gained by using the name "NSW State Branch of AMSA".

By January 2015 there were 292 Sheds open and registered with AMSA in New South Wales as shown in Figure 6. The map also includes the 10 Sheds open in the Australian Capital Territory (ACT), including Canberra.

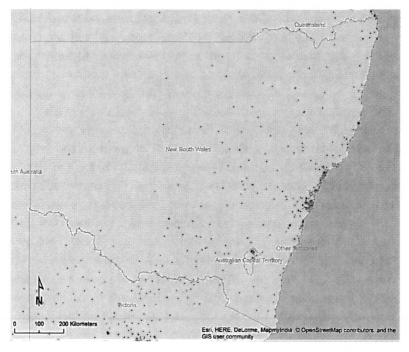

Figure 6 Map of Men's Sheds in New South Wales and ACT to 2015

VICTORIAN MEN'S SHED EARLY HISTORY

This section about early Men's Sheds history in Victoria focuses on three of the earliest Victorian Men's Sheds: the Dick McGowan Men's Shed in rural Tongala, 'Men in Sheds' in the regional central Victorian city of Bendigo, and Manningham Men's Shed in the Melbourne suburb of Doncaster. It also includes a discussion of the contribution of several other diverse, early and influential Men's Sheds in Victoria.

The *Dick McGowan Men's Shed* in the small rural fruit growing town of Tongala (population 1,000) is likely to be the earliest Men's Shed (by that name) to open in a community setting the world. It was officially opened by the local Federal Member of Parliament, Sharman Stone, on July 26 1998. The importance and downstream impact of this first Men's Shed was first established while this book was being finalized in mid-January 2015. The critical leads came from David Read and Ric Blackburn, from 'Men in Sheds' in Bendigo and Manningham Men's Shed in Melbourne respectively. Both recalled that they had separately visited a Men's Shed 'somewhere out the back of an Aged Care Centre' in either

Tongala or Kyabram before their own Sheds opened, in 1999 and 2000 respectively.

Jean Courtney, then the Director of Nursing at Tongala and District Bush Nursing and Memorial Aged Care Complex (and in early 2015, still Director of Nursing and Manager of the Tongala and District Memorial Aged Care Service) emailed in response to a letter by Barry Golding. Her email contained copies of all the local newspaper cuttings to confirm the detail and opening dates plus an article from the National Australia Bank magazine, *Community Link*, reproduced in Photograph 9.

There's a place for us

One man's personal philosophy that **people with good ideas and those with resources can achieve anything** has given a small Victorian town an unusual asset for its ageing men. *By Richard Snashall*

Dick McGowan is well known in the northern Victorian town of Tongala for putting his ideas on the table. And when it came to building a unique aged-care facility for men – in the form of a backyard shed – the former Tongala Primary School vice-principal's idea not only attracted the resources, but was appreciated to the extent that today it bears his name.

"All Australian boys need a shed," John Williamson sings in "The Shed". While that lyric may seem quaint and nostalgic to city people, McGowan knew that in the bush this was a serious sentiment.

When Jim Sargeant moved into the Tongala and District Bush Nursing Memorial Aged Care Complex in 1996, he brought his tool box. He was soon disappointed to find that his spanners and screwdrivers weren't seeing the light of day. This triggered McGowan, a member of the complex's committee, to consider the lack of resources for older men in care. "Men go from their roles of being the breadwinners

Simple yet sacred: *the shed "out the back" of the Tongala Aged Care Complex.*

and a central part of the community into aged-care, which is very female-oriented," he says. "That's not a criticism, it's just the way it is."

McGowan was also acutely aware of the high rates of male suicide in regional Australia, which he feels relate to the pressures of life on the land.

"Many people don't realise the

extraordinary losses farmers can suffer."

In most aged-care residences, things work – so there's very little offering for men who like to tinker. "Jim ended up giving his tool box to his son," McGowan recalls. "As much as he loved it, he had no need for it."

At the next committee meeting McGowan suggested the idea of a "shed" for older men – a place set up for blokes to build, fix, socialise, snooze, and proudly leave tools and unfinished projects on the bench. Also aware that older men's needs were not being served by traditional aged-care was director of nursing at the complex, Jean Courtney, who loved McGowan's proposal. "On the surface it's a shed," Courtney explains, "but it represents a move to a more sophisticated philosophy in care."

Jack Prowse Kerang Nursing Home

Jim Slevytt – Rochester (centre)

Alan Robinson RN McHale Hostel

*The shed is a place
set up for blokes to build,
fix, socialise, snooze,
and proudly leave tools
and unfinished projects
on the bench*

After researching every funding possibility through state and federal agencies, a submission was accepted by the Commonwealth Department of Veteran's Affairs.

"There were additional donations from the local Masonic community and individuals," McGowan says. "All in all, it cost around $25,000".

So where was the shed to be located? Where else but "out the back" of the complex, where there was enough space to erect the earmarked 40 by 25-foot kit shed. McGowan is quick to point out that elderly gentlemen don't work in metric!

While funding paid for the raw materials to build the shed, wherever possible the construction and fitting out was performed by volunteers. With a town population of 1000, the concept excited and involved just about everyone. "We had 76-year-old members of the local Uniting Church painting beams, while residents in

wheelchairs from the complex assisted with the lining and decorating," McGowan says.

Numerous tradespeople volunteered their services, including a plumber whom McGowan had taught. "Everything about it was voluntary and local," he says.

Also remarkable was the commercial generosity – the shed now houses about $7000 worth of donated equipment. Chatting with regulars at nearby Moama Bowling Club, where he plays the keyboards, McGowan was soon offered air tools, lathes and compressors by Norm and Carole Healey, owners of Bendigo-based Peerless Products, one of Australia's biggest industry equipment manufacturers. They wanted nothing in return, except for the men to occasionally pop on a Peerless cap while "at work".

While there are purposefully few luxuries, the men have allowed themselves a small pleasure in their transportation to and from the shed – a Rolls Royce! The six-

Boys' own: *Dick McGowan (left) saw that in a female-oriented environment, the men needed a resource just for them.*

BUILDING A SHED

- Know exactly what you want to achieve – have a vision.
- Research all possibilities of funding, and contact all state and federal departments.
- Prepare a submission, considering every angle relevant to your community.
- Establish good links with your funding source.
- Draw on the local community for volunteers to assist in the building and running of the shed.

CONTACT

Jean Courtney (03) 5859 0800

seater golf buggy was built in the style of the famous car for a Queensland resort and wound up in southern NSW before being bought by the complex. Being true gentlemen, the Roller is also used to take "the girls" from the complex around the gardens.

The shed is managed by a sub-committee, the Company of Men, made up of residents and the wider community. But

it is by no means a closed shop – the shed is open to any of the male species wanting to get among the sawdust.

All of the men who run programs at the shed do so on a voluntary basis. Even complex maintenance officer, Craig McGill, is a volunteer of sorts. Though a part-time employee, Courtney says "he always goes way beyond the call of duty". Due to the equipment, volunteer education and training is highly important, and much of it is handled by McGill.

A number of the shed's regulars were accomplished tradesmen in their working lives and are now reviving skills in everything from clock restoration to woodwork. Some are even taking orders. "There was a rocking-horse in the complex foyer," Courtney says. "It disappeared to the shed where the

men are using it as a prototype to build more!"

The Dick McGowan Men's Shed was officially opened on July 26 this year, and every volunteer who worked on the project was presented with a certificate of appreciation, while donors received brass plaques.

Despite this extraordinary achievement, Tongala's volunteers aren't resting on their laurels. Work has already begun on an activities centre at the complex.

"And eventually we'll put in a hydrotherapy pool," McGowan adds, sticking firmly to his philosophy that good ideas can always come to fruition. ♦

Community Link **23**

Photograph 9 Article about the Dick McGowan Men's Shed, Tongala, Victoria, 1998 in *Community Link.*

This turned out to be the same cutting that Bob Nelson, from the Ashfield Men's Shed in New South Wales (opened in 2000), recalled seeing and being influenced by, but could not source or locate. It's a great story, confirmed in a visit to the now Tongala Men's Shed on May 11, 2015. The visit included extended interviews Ruth McGowan and Jean Courtney for the Community Sheds Oral History Project for the National Library of Australia, conducted by Rob and Olya Willis[44].

The Men's Shed all goes back to the great insight and energy of the late Dick McGowan, a former Vice Principal of the Tongala Primary School, and in 1996 on the Committee of the Tongala and District Bush Nursing Memorial Aged Care Complex. Dick was a shaker and mover, whose 'personal philosophy was that people with good ideas and those with resources can achieve anything'[45]. He believed that all men needed three things, particularly beyond paid work: somewhere to go, something to do, and someone to talk to. McGowan was moved to act when Jim Sargeant moved into the aged care centre with his toolbox and was disappointed he would not be allowed to use his tools there (but stored them under his bed anyway). McGowan was acutely aware of the high rates of male suicide in regional areas and the extraordinary losses farmers can suffer in retirement. He wrote clearly and passionately, with ideas that have now become very familiar to all shedders:

> The Men's Shed is a way of thinking, a particular set of precepts about what constitutes fulfillment and a sense of worth in males. ... The physical setting ... is a well equipped and comfortable mature men's cubby house, dog house, club, cave – whatever you wish to term it. The most important factor is not what goes on there. The 'what goes on' is the cheese, the bait if you like to encourage our male population, both resident and community-based, to come together in a familiar setting, to have somewhere to go which is theirs, to do something of male interest, or choose not to, and to have contact with their fellow residents and the wider community. It may be a place to come into contact with a younger age group. In short, the most important factor is engendering the DESIRE to go there, to have reason for getting out of bed in the morning, to have a sense of achievement of production, of security in knowing they are still people of worth. ... We are not looking for a class-room with aged pupils. The leader does not have to be a highly

---

[44] This national project has involved audiotaped interviews in the past five years Australia with many of the early Men's Shed pioneers.
[45] 'There's a Place for Us', *Community Link*, National Australia Bank, 21-23, 1998.

skilled tradesman or craftsman, or woman. Rather, the leader needs to be able to talk with other people and help organize something[46].

The article in *Community Link*, penned by Richard Snashall for the National Australia Bank and published in November 1998, disseminated this rationale and way of working nationally in great detail at what was opened (as a surprise to and in recognition of McGowan) as the Dick McGowan Men's Shed. McGowan envisaged all management and involvement being voluntary in 'a totally community owned and operated organization', mainly 'for men of mature years – anything from 50's to mid 80's', involving mentoring (what McGowan described as a 'buddy system'), involving 'male-oriented activity in the shed on a monthly timetable' including 'light woodwork ... gardening, ... having a yarn, a cup of tea and so on'. The Men's Shed was also featured on the Australian television program *A Current Affair* (in 2000) and *The Weekly Times* newspaper. Despite being the first Men's Shed by that name in the world, it embedded and clearly communicated all of the characteristics that are now widely understood to be fundamental to Men's Sheds to 2015, as teased out throughout this book. McGowan's vision, powerfully embedded in his written 'Project Summary', was to restore a man's:

> ... feeling of worth, a feeling of familiarity in their every-day life, and a feeling of mate-ship. It sets out to give a reason why he should get up in the morning, and a feeling of going to work in his shed.

To continue the story of Jim Sargeant's dilemma:

> At the next committee meeting McGowan suggested the idea of a "shed' for older men – a place for blokes to build, fix, socialise, snooze and proudly leave tools and unfinished products on the bench. ... Jean Courtney, who loved McGowan's proposal [said]: "On the surface it's a shed ... but it represents a move to a more sophisticated philosophy in care" ... The shed is managed by a sub committee, the Company of Men, made up of residents of the wider community. But it is by no means a closed shop – the shed is open to any of the male species to get amongst the sawdust. All the men who run programs at the shed do so on a voluntary basis ... Due to the equipment, volunteer education and

---

[46] 'The Men's Shed at Tongala Aged Care Complex', Dick McGowan, undated (early 1999).

training is highly important. ... A number of the shed's regulars were accomplished tradesmen in their working lives and are now reviving skills.[47]

News about funding for constructing a Men's Shed[48] appeared in a newspaper cutting dated December 19, 1997[49]. Photograph 10 is a newspaper cutting two months later, from February 18, 1998, about Dick McGowan's rationale and progress towards what he then referred to as a 'bloke's shed'.

Photograph 10 'Life is for Living' Article about Dick McGowan and his Plans for a Shed in Tongala, February 1998.

Sharman Stone explained the federal government's rationale for supporting a Men's Shed project Tongala in *Hansard*, the Australian Federal Parliamentary record, on June 24, 1998, a month before the official Shed opening.

---

[47] 'There's a Place for Us', *Community Link*, November 1998, Issue 6, 21-23.

[48] A$22,595 came from the 'Federal Government's Community Care Seeding Grant Program run by the Department of Veteran's Affairs'. Other donations came from the Freemasons of Victoria Benevolent Fund and a local family.

[49] The cutting does not identify the newspaper, but appears in 'NEWS', Friday, December 19, 1997, 20.

I refer ... to what is called the men's shed at the Tongala aged care hostel. As you know, often in elderly people's hostels there is a predominance of women, and men sometimes do not have a range of activities to keep themselves busy. There is recognition at Tongala that many of the men, who have perhaps come off farms, or been active in workshops in their backyards, in the small towns, enjoy working with woodturning equipment and other bits of machinery. Instead of the older men, particularly the older Veterans, at Tongala sitting and watching the women do their craft work, they can now go out to the men's shed. It is a terrific facility built just beyond the garden at the edge of the very homely facility at Tongala.

[The Department of] Veterans' Affairs helped to fund that men's shed. The equipment inside has been donated very generously by machinery manufacturers. The door is big enough for wheelchair access. Those Veterans and other elderly men of the Tongala district can go into the big shed, smell the sawdust and talk to each other about things that matter to them. Volunteers from the community help them if they are not able to handle some of the machinery. They hope to be able to make little bits and pieces, such as Christmas presents, or do some basic maintenance at the Tongala aged persons hostel that might be within their ability. It is an innovative initiative and one that is very important for the older men in that community. Veterans' Affairs, through this government, saw it as an important thing to do. They have funded that initiative, and it is perhaps a model for other places.[50]

The final sentence is certainly an understatement, given the international spread of the Movement within two decades. This strong Veterans' Affairs support, in part about the War Veterans living in the Complex and in the community, was enhanced since the Tongala Aged Care Complex it was to be sited at was the local War Memorial. As Ron Macleod stressed in July 1997 in his letter of support for the proposed Men's Shed on behalf of the Returned and Services League Sub Branch:

---

[50] *Hansard*, June 24, 1998, 5271,
http://parlinfo.aph.gov.au/parlInfo/search/display/display.w3p;db=CHAMBER;id=chambe
r%2Fhansardr%2F1998-06-
24%2F0027;query=Id%3A%22chamber%2Fhansardr%2F1998-06-24%2F0051%22,
Accessed January 15, 2015.

It is fitting that this type of facility be made available at what is, after all the town War Memorial. I know that Rocky McHale [a former Prisoner of War from Tongala who worked alongside 'Weary' Dunlop on the Burma railway] would have been right behind you in your move to improve the life-style of his mates.[51]

In the space for 'Description of the Project' as part of the acquittal and evaluation for this pilot project, Jean Courtney wrote in longhand:

To provide a shed equipped with hand woodwork, lined and heated [as] a gathering place for male residents [in the Aged Care Complex], men from the town and male residents from Deakin Village. Men potter in sheds, and the loss of lifestyle upon entering aged care strikes at the feeling of self-worth and usefulness. Senior men from the wider community do their thing in the shed on a daily basis.[52]

One day someone will write more about the many other facets of Dick McGowan, who as his widow Ruth McGowan, explained in our May 2015 interview, was educated in Castlemaine, became a versatile pianist, dance band musician and entertainer, set up a School for Conductive Education (based on an Hungarian model for children with neurological disorders) and was instrumental in the Country Education Project (CEP[53]) in Northern Victoria with Don Edgar, Foundation Director of the Australian Institute of Family Studies[54]. This link to Don Edgar is particularly interesting, given that Edgar published *Men, Mateship, Marriage*[55] in 1997, the same year as McGowan approached DVA for funding his Men's Shed, and also wrote a sociogy text coauthored by Leon Earle in the 1990s.

McGowan took early retirement from schools at age 55 and launched himself passionately into his Men's Shed project during 1997, with no obvious template to follow. The quotes for the work constructing the new Men's Shed were completed in mid-1997. He brought together an astonishing range of community

---

[51] Ron Macleod, Tongala RSL Sub-Branch, July 4, 1997.
[52] Fax from Tongala and District Bush Nursing to Department of Veterans' Affairs, Victorian State Office, August 5, 1998.
[53] CEP originated in rural Victoria in 1977, focusing on the needs of schools in rurally isolated areas. It became a not-for-profit community organization in 1994 dedicated to a grassroots innovation, advocacy and support of rural schools and communities.
[54] Professor Don Edgar's work through the AIFS from 1980 had a profound influence on the Australian government regarding family policy, family and work, welfare policy and family law.
[55] Don Edgar, *Men, Mateship, Marriage: Exploring Macho Myths and the Way Forward*, Sydney: Harper Collins, 1997.

and government organisations and benefactors including the Aged Care Complex, Department of Veterans' Affairs, Masonic Lodge and many local companies and trades people. His networks extended to local, state and national politicians.

The sad postscript is that Dick McGowan was unable to attend the official opening due to ill health (following a massive heart attack) and passed away only eighteen months later on December 18, 1999. Much of his work was unfinished. In 1999 McGowan, restricted to a wheelchair, wrote about his plans for a proposed national conference in 2000 'the major thrust of which is to address the area of Care of Ageing Males, with a Focus on Rural Communities[56]'. He noted in a one page, typed postscript after the opening titled 'Men's Shed: A Great Beginning'[57], shown in Photograph 11, that he regretted not being able to attend due to ill health, but was honoured to have the shed named after him.

THE MEN'S SHED - A GREAT BEGINNING

The men's shed was officially opened by Sharman Stone on Sunday, 26th. of July. I was not able to attend due to ill health, but I am honoured to have the shed named after me. It is a facility of great interest and potential in the challenge of providing a 'seamless' transition for men, from an active, familiar life in the wider community, to life in a protected environment, with the unavoidable changes to daily habits this brings about.

The building is magnificent. It is a testimonial to the workers who have turned it from an idea into a reality. The on-site work done by many people, under the 'foremanship' of Craig McGill, has produced a 40' X 25' building, fully lined, cooled and heated, with a light and airy feel. Throw in the equipment provided by Norm and Carole Healey of Pioneer Products of Bendigo and we have a second-to-none home for the development of activities, interests and friendships between men of all walks of life.

The challenge really starts now!

Providing the building was easy. I know this may sound a bit trite but, things that can be seen and felt are easy to describe, to visualise and to gain support. We thank the people who provided the finance for this - the Department of Veteran's Affairs, the Grand Masonic Lodge and the Renner family. We thank all the volunteers who contributed their time and skills to the building. We thank the donors of equipment. NOW THE REAL CHALLENGE BEGINS, and that is to USE the facility in order to BUILD the daily achievements of COMPANIONSHIP, A FEELING OF WORTH, PHYSICAL ACTIVITY AND PRIDE OF ACCOMPLISHMENT. This will be the result if we can successfully combine the time, skills and interests of men, and dare I suggest also women in some aspects, from both the Complex Residential community and the wider town / district community. An age-mixture will add to this, as will different interests from woodwork to gardening to mechanics to pottering and so on.

The Company of Men is the umbrella organisation, and a sub-Committee of the Complex Management Committee, for the daily running needs of the shed. I'm sorry I am not able to take the role I had envisaged in this, at this time, but Tongala has the capacity and people to achieve a successful, on-going program. So, there's the challenge! Let's make life more interesting for ALL men who choose to be part of the activities.

Almost twenty years ago, the facility on the North-West corner of Tongala - The Cottage - came into being for the purpose of providing "somewhere to go, something to do, someone to talk to". It has achieved these aims admirably and is an integral part of life for many people in this area. The Men's Shed can do the same.

Dick McGowan
Convenor
Company of men

---

[56] 'The Men's Shed at Tongala Aged Care Complex', Dick McGowan, undated (early 1999).
[57] Jean Courtney, Tongala Aged Care Complex, 23 April, 2015.

Photograph 11 'The Men's Shed: A Great Beginning', Dick McGowan, August 1998

Presciently, McGowan wrote that:

> It is a facility of great interest and potential in the challenge of providing a 'seamless' transition for men from an active, familiar life in the wider community, to a protected environment, with the unavoidable changes to daily habits this brings about …

McGowan identified, in his original capitalization:

> NOW THE REAL CHALLENGE BEGINS, and that is to USE the facility in order to BUILD the daily achievements of COMPANIONSHIP, A FEELING OF WORTH, PHYSICAL ACTIVITY AND THE PRIDE OF ACCOMPLISHMENT. This will be the result if we can successfully combine the time, skills and interests of men, and dare I say women in some aspects, from both the Complex Residential Community and the wider town / district community.

Before he signed off as 'Dick McGowan, Convener, The Company of Men', McGowan was explicit about the way the shed would run.

> The Company of Men is the umbrella organisation, and a sub-Committee of the Complex Management Committee, for the daily running needs of the shed. I'm sorry I am not able to take the role I had envisaged in this, at this time, but Tongala has the capacity and people to achieve a successful, ongoing program. So there's the challenge! Let's make life interesting for ALL men who choose to be part of the activities for not being able to take the role I had envisaged in this.

McGowan tantalizingly pointed to an earlier inspiration dating back to around 1980 for his Men's Shed vision:

> Almost twenty years ago, the facility on the North West corner of Tongala – The Cottage – came into being for the purpose of providing "somewhere to go, something to do, someone to talk to". It has achieved these aims admirably and is an integral part of life for many people in this area. The Men's Shed can do the same.

Dick McGowan's widow, Ruth McGowan, emailed me in January 2015 and recalled, with understandable pride, that her late husband '... was very passionate about this project and worked very hard to make it a reality'.[58] For the past 14 years, two days a week, Ruth McGowan has participated as an 'honorary bloke', the only woman in the Shed, hand turning wooden pens on a lathe. Jean Courtney, still managing the Tongala Aged Care Centre in 2015 reported that many of the residents in the Tongala complex were '... now much frailer than when the shed commenced ... with many of those who originally attended the Shed having passed away or getting frailer'. Nevertheless the Tongala Aged Care Men's Shed was still functioning in 2015. Photograph 12 shows Ruth McGowan working in the corner of the Tongala Men's Shed in May 2015.

Photograph 12 Ruth McGowan working on her hand-turned pens in the corner of the Tongala Men's Shed, Victoria, 2015

---

[58] Ruth McGowan, January 20, 2015.

The Men's Shed in Tongala is, on this evidence, the oldest and longest continually operating community Men's Shed (so called) in the world, though less than 17 years old in early 2015. Jean Courtney noted that management at the Tongala Aged Care Centre had deliberately and 'historically endeavored to allow Shed members to be as autonomous as possible' through the Shed's Sub-Committee. This simple but powerful idea of Men's Sheds being run by the men themselves is consistent with now fundamental ethos of all successful community Men's Sheds, constrained only by a recent need for 'increased regulatory compliance for more risk management'.[59] This book is subtitled 'The Company of Men' for all of the above reasons, with a huge debt to Dick McGowan.

Men in Sheds Inc. Bendigo officially opened in November 1999 (coincidentally the Year of the Older Person). It is the second oldest Men's Shed to open in Victoria after Tongala, and only 100 kilometers southwest of Tongala. Bendigo, 150 kilometers north of Melbourne in central Victoria, is a former gold mining city, with a population of over 80,000, making it the fourth largest inland city in Australia. Like the most other early Men's Sheds, once carefully examined, they did not simply 'come out of nowhere'. Young people were 'doing woodwork and computers' as part of a Salvation Army training program on another site in Bendigo from as early as 1993[60]. It was in late 1998 that the Salvation Army approached the City of Greater Bendigo to use part of the former Gravel Hill Primary School site as part of a Positive Retirement strategy for men, called the 'Men in Sheds Project'. The opening of the facility was in November 1999. Photograph 13, 'Shed Meets Men's Need', is a cutting from late 1999 that provides a summary of its rationale and set up. David Reid was appointed as Supervisor/Coordinator from 2000 and has continued a close association with the Shed ever since.

---

[59] Jean Courtney, January 15, 2015.
[60] '20 Year Celebration Bendigo Salvation Army Workshop', September 23, 2013. Gravel Hill: Bendigo Salvation Army.

Photograph 13 'Shed Meets Men's Needs' Article about Men in Sheds, Bendigo, December 1999

The author of an evaluation for the nearby Cobaw Men's Shed (in Kyneton, introduced later) in 2003[61] suggested that the original rationale behind the Bendigo Men in Sheds program came from Earle, Earle and von Mering's (1996) *Sheds and Male Retirement* paper.[62] Specifically it cited Earle's suggestion that 'community and recreational professionals should devise programs to make [backyard] sheds more socially inclusive and productive learning centres.'

The 2001 evaluation of the Bendigo Men in Sheds program, published as *Bendigo Shedding the Light on "Men in Sheds" Report 2001*[63], written by Kaye Graves[64], is one of the earliest formal evaluations of a Men's Sheds program. It was based on survey data from 61 men (age 47-84 years) and one six-person focus group interview. The evaluation was the first to provide evidence of the now almost 'taken for granted' main benefits: meeting new people, developing confidence, having a place for 'blokes' (men) to go and sharing knowledge and learning new things.[65] In the same year, April 2001, the Bendigo Men in Sheds

---

[61] Robyn Jones and Lyn-Marie Richards, *Men's Shed Survey Report*. Kyneton: Cobaw Community Health Service, 2003, 7.
[62] Leon Earle, Tony Earle and Otto von Mering, 'Sheds and Male Retirement'. *Australasian Leisure and Pleasure Journal*, 1: 1, 1996, 5-19.
[63] 'Shedding the light on 'Men in Sheds''. Bendigo: Community Health Bendigo with La Trobe Department of Public Health.
[64] Kaye Graves was then employed by Community Health Bendigo.
[65] 'Shedding Light on Men in Sheds', 4.

program held one of the earliest ever shed 'Expos' with 4,000 people attending.[66] David Reid, still Men in Sheds (Bendigo) Coordinator in 2015, presented a comprehensive account of the Shed's history to the Family and Community Development Committee in Victoria on November 18, 2012.[67]

Manningham Men's Shed in suburban Melbourne, referred to earlier in the section about very early South Australian sheds is examined here in some detail because of its many early important connections, including to some of the earliest Sheds in other Australian states. Manningham Men's Shed was a program that originated from Manningham Community Health Service (MCHS) in Victoria. The Shed is located in suburban Doncaster within the Manningham local government area only 12 kilometers from the centre of Melbourne.

Manningham is arguably one of the most influential early Men's Sheds in Victoria. It began operation without an official opening in January 2000[68]. Manningham is of particular interest because its early start up was informed in active communication with several other influential, very early Sheds that were setting up at the same time. Those planning the Manningham Men's Shed were certainly in conversation with those planning the Lane Cove Men's Shed. Manningham also looked to 'The Shed' in Goolwa in South Australia as a 'useful precedent'. Maxine Kitto from Goolwa faxed Alison Herron from Doncare (Doncaster Community Services) on July 5, 1996, providing a copy of a presentation Kitto attended at the Australian Association of Gerontology Conference in Hobart in May 1996 about the Goolwa Shed program[69]. This insight about 'The Shed' in Goolwa and the information shared by Maxine Kitto in July 1996 were included in a submission that Neil Wakeman later put together for Home and Community Care (HACC) funding to establish the Manningham Men's Shed.[70]

Alison Herron spoke with Neil Wakeman (CEO at Manningham Community Health Service from 1995, later to join the interim AMSA Board in 2007) about the idea of a shed for men. In Herron's words, 'I received an enthusiastic response as it resonated with his own 'blokey' handyman interests. He was a

---

[66] Cited in *Men's Shed Survey Report*, Cobaw Men's Shed, 2003, 7.

[67]

http://www.parliament.vic.gov.au/images/stories/committees/fcdc/inquiries/57th/iopvs/Tra nscripts/18_NOVEMBER_2011/T051_Men_in_Sheds_18-Nov-11_.pdf, Accessed February 2, 2015.

[68] Neil Wakeman suggested it may have been January 17, 2000, but there is no verification of a definite date.

[69] AAG was unable to locate a copy of this presentation or paper in May 2015.

[70] This program was still HACC funded to 2014: Ric Blackburn, August 8, 2014.

Shed man in his own right.' Neil Wakeman recalled in 2014 that he actually visited the Goolwa Shed:

> ... during my holidays in the late 1990s. I was also 'informed' by the Tweed Heads [likely Nambucca Heads] Shed, which I also visited on another holiday trip in the same period as well as the Bendigo Shed and another attached to a nursing home in Tongala.

The first Coordinator of the Manningham Men's Shed from late 1999, before the Manningham Shed building was completed, was John Heritage. Neil Wakeman gives John Heritage much of the credit for developing the Shed. According to Wakeman, Heritage's role:

> ... was a unique one and there was no precedent to draw upon. We put him in a tin shed, and he and the first group of clients and volunteer leaders did the rest. They built the workbenches, laid out the equipment, sought out additional sources of funding, and matched clients to tasks. John [Heritage] set up the first systems, developed the first set of safety rules and shed conduct, and created the culture, none of which has changed a lot over the years.[71]

Neil Wakeman and John Heritage therefore broke much 'new ground' in getting the Manningham Men's Shed up and running, ably carried on from 2003 by Ric Blackburn, who in 2013 became Victorian Men's Shed Association's (VMSA's) first paid Executive Officer. While Manningham effectively began its Shed in early 2000, the underlying rationale behind the Shed program was established earlier, influenced also by:

> ... the 1997 State Government: *Planning for Positive Ageing* Report, which outlined the difficulties men face as they retire and their preference for engaging in useful and meaningful activities such as what the shed offers, as opposed to learning programs such as those run by the Senior Citizens or University of the Third Age.[72]

At that stage the 1997 report was regarded by Neil Wakeman, in Alison Herron's words, as '... something of a bible, and the section on men's lack of participation

---

[71] Neil Wakeman, July 25, 2014.
[72] Robyn Jones and Lyn-Marie Richards, *Men's Shed Survey Report*. Kyneton: Cobaw Community Health Service, 2003, 6.

in community learning and recreation activities provided a solid rationale for a men's shed.' Wakeman admitted in 2014 that 'this is about the only Government report I have ever read voluntarily'[73]. In particular, Wakeman recalled that:

> Chapter 13 of the report contained a wealth of expert evidence about men and ageing – dealing with men's issues such as transition from the workforce into retirement, recreation and leisure, opportunities for social interaction, male specific health conditions and the specific needs of men as carers, and of widowed men and ageing single men.[74]

The 1997 *Inquiry Into Planning for Positive Ageing* report itself did not mention Sheds for men, but did cite research in Chapter 13 about 'Men and Ageing' that in some senses anticipated what was about to happen in the creation of the Manningham Men's Shed.

> Submissions to the Committee suggested that men were only interested in recreational activities that were traditionally viewed as male. ... Gerontological research suggests that older men are reluctant to participate in 'female dominated activities'. ... [T]he activities pursued by men are those typically associated with traditional male interests. ... Many men dislike being 'organized' and 'regimented' in their recreational pursuits, preferring instead to 'do their own thing', in their 'own time' and at their 'own pace'.[75]

The same report noted that 'Men actively seek out the company of other men in other ways', avoiding joining organized groups but instead forming 'around specific activities or 'tasks'', including:

> ... practical 'projects' which utilize men's handy-man skills such as toy repair, carpentry home maintenance and gardening. It has been argued that men are more willing to participate if the activity results in a benefit to another person ... [with] an alignment between pre-retirement

---

[73] It is very likely (without evidence) that this report would have been read by and incorporated into Dick McGowan's plans for the Men's Shed in Tongala.

[74] Neil Wakeman, July 25, 2014.

[75] *Inquiry into Planning for Positive Ageing*, Report by the Family and Community Development Committee. Melbourne: Victorian Parliament, December 1997, 256.

employment and interests and more generally a desire that all activities even social interaction have some practical utility.[76]

Referencing the 1996 National Men's Health Conference, Chapter 13 of the same 1997 report also observed that:

> Given that men die earlier than women and the relatively high incidence of male suicide, it is surprising men's patterns of visiting general practitioners and of social relations outside of the workplace have only recently received attention.[77]

The early planning for the Manningham Men's Shed was therefore based around Neil Wakeman's excellent knowledge of:

> ... health outcome statistics, especially those relating to the health experiences of males over 60 compared to females – I seem to remember the suicide rate for males at that time was 3 or 4 times that for females, and that men's health outcomes, including life expectancy, were generally inferior to women's across a whole range of criteria.

This evidence was used as part of Men's Health Information nights conducted by Manningham Community Health Service between 1997 and 2000. As early as 1995/6 Manningham Community Health Service (MCHS) was beginning to seek out areas of opportunity:

> ... to explore Men's health as an area which MCHS might be able to provide leadership. ... [H]aving read an article about a Shed in Goolwa, South Australia and inspired by his own interest in woodworking, car restoring and other handyman activities Neil [Wakeman, CEO, MCHS successfully] applied for funding.

It was a long battle, as Neil Wakeman explained in 2014.

> I applied (unsuccessfully) for funding for two or three years from government departments, philanthropic trusts and others. Because men's sheds were a new idea and therefore had no track record, funding bodies

---

[76] Report as above, 1997, 257.
[77] Report as above, 247-8.

weren't prepared to take the risk. Eventually HACC [78] [Home and Community Care] recurrent funding of [A]$35,000 was granted in about 1998/9... Half of that money was used to buy the Shed building, a 6 metre x 6 metre kit with steel sheet cladding on a steel frame. The balance of the initial grant was sufficient to employ John Heritage for two days of each week ... commencing in January 2000.

In subsequent years I applied successfully for further bits of HACC funding – MCHS was allocated some money to run a weekly session for men from a non-English speaking background and I engaged an Italian speaking leader for a group of Italian men. Subsequently, we received a further grant to provide a day for men at risk of homelessness, so we formed a group of men from a special accommodation home in Manningham, who met on Saturdays. Under a contract with Manningham Council, we provided a Planned Activity Group (PAG) for frail aged and men with disabilities. [79]

The December 1997 submission from the Manningham Community Health Service seeking funds for a Manningham Men's Shed used a quote from Mark Thomson's 1995 *Blokes and Sheds* book. It specifically envisaged a Men's Shed 'based on a similar project in Goolwa South Australia and another being established in Lane Cove (NSW)'. Importantly, it cited the Goolwa Shed as a 'Precedent', noting that:

The Goolwa Shed has provided an environment in which older men have been motivated to retain their trade skills and social interaction with other men. Several new activities (such as crib club, walking group and a model railway enthusiasts groups) have evolved out of the Shed workers, and the program has also helped bridge the generation gap, with older men passing on their handicraft and trade skills to local school children. The observed outcome of the Goolwa project has been a marked improvement in the general health and self-esteem of the participants in the program, and recognition by the wider community that older people

---

[78] The HACC Program was first set up in Australia in 1985. To 2015 it was still operated by the Australian Government in all states and territories except Victoria and Western Australia (where it was funded jointly by both states).

[79] Rick Hayes and Michelle Williamson, *Men's Sheds: Exploring the Evidence for Best Practice*. Bundoora: School of Public Health, La Trobe University, 2007.

still have an important role as productive and valued community members.[80]

As in many later Shed startups including at Lane Cove, some women played critically important facilitation and support roles. Alison Herron was manager of a Doncare social support program funded by HACC (Home and Community Care) and worked closely with other local HACC service providers including at MCHS. Neil Wakeman recalled in 2014 that:

> .... 'the Manningham model' was different to any sheds that existed at that time, in that it catered for frail aged and older men with disabilities, the criteria for HACC funding. Other sheds, like Bendigo's and Goolwa's, were more like wood working clubs or male social clubs, catering for able bodied and self-sufficient participants.[81]

Manningham Men's Shed was the only shed that Neil Wakeman knew of[82] that was successful in securing recurrent State Government funding specifically for its shed through the combined Commonwealth/State HACC program. Wakeman reflected in April 2006, a year after his retirement as CEO, that:

> Manningham was very fortunate in that the HACC Program in 1998-1999 encouraged and funded program proposals that were different and innovative [which Men's Sheds were at that time] and the enlightened folk in the [Department of Human Services] regional office could see the value of a shed program and supported the funding bid.

Like Bendigo Men in Sheds, Manningham undertook a very early formal review.[83] It is certainly the first Shed in the world to have a short film made totally about and within the shed, also actively involving the shedders as actors in the film. *Men's Sheds: The Movie* in 2005[84] is simultaneously funny and moving, focusing in a light hearted but powerful way on the lives and disabilities of several of the men then participating in the Shed. The commercial film catalogue entry about the DVD from 2008 noted that:

---

[80] 'Manningham Men's Shed: A Submission to the Healthy Seniors Initiative 1997/98'. Doncaster: Manningham Community Health Service, December, 1997.
[81] Neil Wakeman, July 25, 2014.
[82] Email from Neil Wakeman, to 'Bob', April 9, 2007.
[83] 'Men's Shed Report', Manningham Community Health Service, 2003.
[84] Leah Dobrejcer and Novak Ristov, *Men's Shed: The Movie* (DVD). Directed by Peter Muizulius. Melbourne: Dobrejcer and Ristov Films, 2005.

Community Men's Sheds bolster mateship as well as community spirit. They are places where men can simply be men whilst exploring their creativity through woodwork, metalwork and anything that needs fixing. The program profiles one shed and its frequent visitors. It provides an insight into how community, mateship and engagement can contribute towards healing and an individual's sense of prosperity.[85]

Manningham Men's Shed is perhaps the earliest Men's Shed to open six days a week (though by 2014 it was back to five days) and has been the subject and site of considerable research[86]. It was the site, in 2007, for the celebratory launch of the most cited piece of research on Men's Sheds, *Men's Sheds in Australia: Learning through Community Contexts*[87], that Manningham participated in. Photograph 14 taken at the launch in May 2007 includes Ted Donnelly (centre) and Ruth van Herk (second from left).

Photograph 14 Launch of the *Men's Sheds in Australia* Research, Manningham Men's Shed, May 23, 2007 (centre Ted Donnelly; Ruth van Herk, second from left)

---

[85] VEA Public Health Catalogue, 2008.

[86] For example, Matt Moylan *et al.*, 'The Men's Shed: Providing Biopsychosocial and Spiritual Support', *Journal of Religion and Health*, 2013, 221-234.

[87] Barry Golding *et al.*, *Men's Sheds in Australia: Learning through Community Contexts.* Adelaide: NCVER, 2007.

Manningham Men's Shed was also one of two HACC-funded study sites that Alison Herron used for collecting data in 2003 for her Masters Thesis [88] (completed in 2007) that explored the role of the creative arts as leisure. As part of her thesis, four of the older men attending the Manningham Men's Shed were interviewed, as well as John Heritage and Ric Blackburn.

Herron's pen picture from 2003, included in her 2007 thesis might be useful to those who have never seen or been in a typical, workshop-based, Australian Men's Shed.

> The Men's Shed is a purpose-built over-sized version of a typical suburban backyard shed constructed of Colorbond [painted, corrugated steel]. There are workbenches, shelving full of timber, jars of nails and screws, hand tools, power tools and saws that make a lot of noise. At one end are a kitchen table and chairs and a kitchen sink. In the corner is the co-ordinator's office space – a desk and filing cabinet. Outside is a small vegetable patch. The main activity is woodwork. The men may be engaged in their own individual project (such as making bird boxes) or else as part of a group project (such as making wooden toys for a local kindergarten or wooden wheelbarrows to be sold at a market as pot plant holders). Others might get involved in jobs such as repairing a broken toy or fixing a broken gate at the next door community centre.[89]

The key findings in Alison Herron's thesis, based on data collected from both the Manningham Men's Shed and a visual arts project are powerful and particularly instructive about repositioning leisure more positively in discourses about ageing. In acknowledging the leisure value of the Men's Shed in her conclusion, Herron was critical of problem-oriented and deficit-based approaches to aged care. She concluded that the Men's Shed incorporated:

> ... many well-recognised principles about serious leisure ... [demonstrating] that leisure can be a powerful means of enhancing ageing well. Serious leisure can focus on older people's strengths and

[88] Alison Herron, *It Opens a Whole New World: Older People's Perceptions of the Role of the Creative Arts as Leisure in their Lives*. Masters of Arts Thesis. Footscray: Victoria University, 2007.
[89] Alison Herron's Masters Thesis, downloaded July 29, 2014 from http://vuir.vu.edu.au/1487/1/Herron.pdf, 52.

capacities, provide flow[90] experiences, and contribute to life purpose and meaning. It can also reopen doors to a world that can close in as people's health, mobility and meaningful social roles are under threat. Such a leisure model has far more potential for promoting ageing well than the traditional aged care model on which most services to older people are based. The aged care model is problem-oriented and deficit-based. It focuses on dependency needs, assuming that the level of independence of older people is the most relevant measure of health and well-being.

[These] findings indicate that there is potential scope for the arts, leisure, and aged care fields to provide a more stimulating and developmental range of creative programs, so that older people can have more opportunities to lead enjoyable lives that provide them with meaning and purpose. Instead of delivering mediocre programs to meet minimum standards, service providers should be supported to be innovative and inspirational in finding ways for older people to age well, no matter what their situation.[91]

The briefer history of several other early Men's Sheds in Victoria: Orbost, Creswick, Brimbank (Sunshine), Keysborough, Cobaw (Kyneton) and Mansfield are discussed below to illustrate how different and diverse their relatively independent, early approaches were. It also illustrates how other very early Sheds in Victoria began to organise and innovate between 2000 and 2005. All these Sheds and their Shed coordinators were influential in the development of the Victorian Men's Shed Association. Most contributed to or participated in the first 2005 Lakes Entrance Men's Shed Conference. All but Brimbank and Keysborough are located in rural Victoria. Collectively, combined with the insights above from Men's Sheds in Tongala, Bendigo and Manningham, these early Sheds illustrate several similarities but also significant differences in the way Sheds were conceived and developed for quite diverse participants across widely separated parts of Victoria.

Unlike in New South Wales, church-based organisations played a relatively minor auspice role in most early Victorian Men's Sheds. Most early Victorian Sheds were in auspice arrangements with community health or adult education organisations. Victoria is more compact and more densely settled than all other

---

[90] 'Flow' is the psychological idea of single-minded immersion, as defined and theorised by Mihály Csíkszentmihályi.
[91] Alison Herron, Thesis as above, 2007, 156.

Australian states. There were therefore more opportunities for Victorian men's shedders to collaborate, visit each other's Sheds and regularly meet to create the first peak body Men's Shed association, Victorian Men's Shed Association (VMSA), as discussed in the section that follows. In doing so, and producing evidence of impact from research and evaluation, many of these early Victorian Sheds were able to leverage significant funds from the state government in Victoria by 2006. The funds were for start up and Men's Shed development, including establishing new Sheds, a program that was ongoing and strongly supported by VMSA to 2015.

Orbost is a small rural town of around 2,000 people located in East Gippsland, 375 kilometers east of Melbourne. The *Orbost Men's Shed* originated from the Far East Gippsland Health and Support Service (later to become Orbost Regional Health) with support from the Orbost Rotary Club. A Men's Health Steering Committee meeting chaired by Gary Green, then the Community Health Nurse, had been considering the question of how to more effectively attract and engage with older men post-retirement.

Green recalled one of its Committee members, John Mundy, saying that, "My shed is my sanctuary". Further discussion revealed that most other men had used their own sheds as places of sanctuary, where as Green put it,

> ... they could dwell for a little 'time out' from life's demands. The idea of a Men's Shed (or similar space where they might gather and undertake shed-type activities) was arrived at independently as none of the committee was aware of any other Men's Sheds. However some searching on-line revealed around four other Men's Sheds 'out there'.

Gary Green recalled phoning the Men in Sheds coordinator in Bendigo (opened in 1999), as well as Stuart Holmes at the soon to open Nambucca Men's Shed, prior to the official Orbost Shed opening on May 3, 2000.[92] A vacant shed was located within the Orbost town boundary on the site of another service provider at minimal rent. 'The Shed', as it was called when it officially opened[93], operated one day a week, from 10am to 3pm.

---

[93] The *Snowy River Mail* called it 'Orbost Men's Shed' in the leader about the opening, May 10, 2000, 3.

Photograph 15 'Community "Shed" to Open', Article about the Opening of
Orbost Men's Shed, April 2000

The Orbost Men's Shed, as it soon came to be known, aimed to create a man-
friendly space for mainly older men to socialise. It is interesting that the *Snowy
River Mail* led its article "Community 'shed' to open" (shown in Photograph 15
above) with:

> "All Australian boys need a shed", John Williamson sings. While that
> lyric may seem quaint and nostalgic to city dwellers, here in the bush it
> is a serious statement.[94]

Orbost Men's Shed's philosophy was to make the shed as 'men friendly' as
possible and to keep the rules and regulations to a minimum. Democracy
prevailed, with 'the blokes' being consulted before decisions were made
effectively 'in control' of their own Shed. Before the Orbost Shed opened, it was
envisaged that the men would undertake tasks for themselves. This soon changed
to most of the work being carried out in aid of community groups.

This early Shed's ethos of evolving with the interests and wishes of the men,
as distinct from being prescriptive and 'top-down', became very important for
later Sheds. This 'bottom-up' ethos and encouragement for men to 'just bring
your sense of humour', and stay in the Shed 'for five minutes or five hours' came

---

[94] April 19, 2000, 3.

very much from Gary Green, its first and long-time coordinator. Many other communities in Gippsland in eastern Victoria started a Men's Shed of their own, based in part on the Orbost template.

The Orbost Men's Shed's initial double garage-size shed proved inadequate over the next few years due to steadily increasing numbers attending. At first the men brought tools and equipment from home, but small grants allowed the purchase of some shed equipment. Orbost Regional Health allocated funding to build a larger shed on the same site in 2007, which again proved inadequate. While a large, disused factory was purchased in 2010 and redeveloped into a Men's Shed, it was gutted by a major fire on January 8, 2012 and required total replacement and refurbishment.

The Orbost Men's Shed became an important springboard for the national Movement in Australia by hosting the first national Men's Sheds conference in 2005. The Shed's founder, Gary Green, with the East Gippsland Men's Health Group and Primary Care Partnership, hosted the conference in Lakes Entrance on November 10-11, 2005. Many of the people, ideas and contacts who assembled for the conference were brought together by Gary Green who later became the first Community Engagement person for AMSA from 2010.

Creswick Men's Friendship Shed is located in Creswick, a rural former gold mining town around the same size as Orbost (approximately 3,000 people) in central Victoria 130 kilometers northwest of Melbourne (and only 10 kilometers from the author's home in Kingston). Aside from being amongst the earliest five Men's Sheds in Victoria, it remains one of the only Sheds to aptly have 'Friendship' as part of its organisation title, despite the ubiquity and importance of the company and friendship of other men in the life of all Men's Sheds. The Creswick Shed was commenced informally in September 2001 through Hepburn Community Health by its Welfare Officer, Jackie Slade[95] with other staff and a few 'male clients'. The Creswick Shed was coordinated by John Quinlan for a decade from 2004-14. Jackie Slade summarized the Shed's informal beginnings.

> A few guys were having a cuppa together in the unused quarters at the local [Creswick] hospital's disused Nurses' Home. This gave them somewhere to meet and a chat while they explored the idea of a backyard type of shed to make items including community projects. In

---

[95] Jackie Slade, July 29, 2014.

January 2002 [they] were offered the use of a dilapidated garage behind
the Hepburn Health Service's Emergency Accommodation House.[96]

Extensively renovated and expanded by 2015, the Creswick Men's Shed was set
up specifically to address men's social isolation. With one of the best views
possible from the open shed door above the historic Botanical Park Lake,
accessed along a gravel track through a grove of huge pine trees, it was perhaps
the first[97] Shed to put together its own book, called *Tales from the Shed:*
Collected Wit, Wisdom and Tales from the Creswick Men's Friendship Shed,
launched at the Creswick Shed in July 2007.[98] It documents the often very
personal life and experiences of men who then participated in the Shed.

Mansfield Community Shed, like Orbost and Creswick is located in the small rural
town of Mansfield (population around 4,000 people) 200 kilometers north east of
Melbourne. Mansfield is one of the closest 'gateways' from Melbourne to
Victoria's 'high country'. Though not officially opened until August 25, 2005,
like many other early Sheds, its planning phase goes back several years, to mid-
2002. *The Shed@Windale Newsletter* (the precursor to the *AMSA Newsletter*)
reported in 2007 that:

> Mansfield resident Don Hodges visited his local doctor to act upon his
> depression as a result of boredom after retirement. Don had been on the
> land for many years prior to retiring into town and quickly became
> frustrated at the limited opportunities for retirees in the town. "I had
> heard of Men's Sheds in other towns and thought that as there are many
> retired blokes with a lot of knowledge in Mansfield, we should have one
> of our own", said Don, who is the voluntary coordinator of the shed.[99]

Hodges wrote to the local Mansfield newspaper on August 13, 2002 seeking
community support for a Shed[100]. Two weeks later the Board of Mansfield Adult
Continuing Education (MACE) Board agreed to auspice a Mansfield Shed. By
late 2002 the Delatite Shire had agreed to a 30-year 'peppercorn' lease to MACE
for council-owned land on which to site the shed, and plans were drawn up. The

---

[96] John Quinlan, April 15, 2014.
[97] Dubbo Community Men's Shed, *A Shed Load of Stories*, 2012.
[98] *Tales from the Shed: Collected Wit, Wisdom and Tales from the Creswick Men's*
Friendship Shed, Creswick. Creswick: Hepburn Health Services, 2007, coordinated by
Jackie Slade.
[99] 'Feature Shed: Mansfield Community Shed', *The Shed@ Windale Newsletter*, Issue 4, 1.
[100] Paul Sladdin, August 19, 2014.

initial July 2003 submission for funding to the state Department of Infrastructure for a *Men's* Shed was not successful, but the feedback suggested to apply the following year as a *Community* Shed. The re-application to the federal Department of Transport and Regional Services via the Regional Partnerships program was successful, with additional State government funding.

Mansfield was one of very few early Sheds to get sufficient funding from both federal and state governments to build a new purpose-built shed. In fact two separate, adjacent sheds were built, one for woodwork and one for metalwork. Another Australian Shed organisation around the same time that received federal funding to build a new purpose-built shed was 'The Shed' in rural Darkan in Western Australia. Like several other early Sheds in relatively conservative rural areas, while the local committee in Mansfield was mainly comprised of men, the pragmatic decision to call it a 'Community' Shed also worked at a community level. As Hodges said, "We don't want to exclude anybody and we have plenty of ladies who come in to do both woodwork and welding projects"[101].

The Mansfield Community Shed was also one of the earliest to enter into an auspice arrangement through an Adult and Community Education (ACE) provider. MACE (Mansfield ACE) was at that time also a Registered Training Organisation, Neighbourhood House and Childcare Centre operator. This trend to auspice with an adult education centre set by Mansfield was repeated in mainly Victorian Sheds. In part, this is because it has had the most comprehensive networks of ACE and Neighbourhood House providers of any state in Australia. It is also because the original source of Victorian State government Men's Shed funding came from the Department of Planning and Community Development that then managed and funded Adult and Community Education in Victoria. The Mansfield Community Shed was used as a case study by the Department of Victorian Communities for the development of the Victorian Government's Men's Sheds Funding Program announced at the 2nd Australian National Community Men's Sheds Conference in Manly, in suburban Sydney in September 2007.

The Mansfield Men's Shed became an Incorporated Association in January 2013. Paul Sladdin, the long time MACE CEO, who played an important role helping to set up and manage the Mansfield Shed, was an important leader of the Victorian Men's Shed Association and very active AMSA Board member and VMSA's President to 2015.

---

[101] *The Shed@Windale Newsletter*, Issue 4, 1.

By contrast, *Brimbank Men's Shed* began operation in Sunshine, a suburb of inner western Melbourne in March 2003, as part of the outreach of UnitingCare Sunshine Mission. Brimbank was one of the first Sheds in Australia to work successfully with newly arrived refugees and asylum seekers [102]. The demographics of Sunshine made it an important site for involving men from a range of disadvantaged and lower socio-economic backgrounds. Around four out of ten men in the area are from non-English speaking backgrounds, and many have significant health and welfare issues. Rick Hayes and Michelle Williamson summarised the early history of the Brimbank Men's Shed to 2006:[103] 'Men with relationship breakdown, mental health, loneliness/ socialisation, homelessness, financial, recreational and other issues were seeking the Mission's assistance'[104]. Brimbank Men's Shed is distinctive in that it is not based around a workshop, focusing instead on providing a welcoming social space for men.

Brimbank Men's Shed hosted an evaluation by a final year university student in 2005/6[105] as part of his studies, a trend that has since become common in several other Sheds. Other higher degree students, including Masters by research and PhD students in several countries, have since studied aspects of Men's Sheds in fields as diverse as social work, community development, adult education, gender studies, psychology, men's health and management.

Brimbank Men's Shed became a leader supporting the Victorian Men's Shed Association (VMSA). The Shed hosted VMSA's inaugural annual general meeting in 2008. Lyn Kinder, coordinator of the Brimbank Men's Shed from mid-2005 to 2010, played pivotal roles in VMSA from 2005 until late 2013, ensuring that both the men who participated and Men's Shed organisations were empowered to self-manage and connect by means of networks and partnerships locally, regionally, state wide and nationally. As an example of how the Shed encouraged participation, a minibus of Brimbank shedders drove to and fully participated in both the Lakes Entrance (2005) and Manly (2007) national conferences, and many of the men regularly attend VMSA meetings. Lyn Kinder, working from the Brimbank Men's Shed until 2010, was a wise and important influence in the development and management of the Victorian Men's Shed Association, taking the role of first VMSA Secretary from 2007-8. Lyn Kinder acknowledged in 2014 that:

---

[102] Anthony Lai, January 23, 2015.
[103] Rick Hayes and Michelle Williamson, 2007, 53-6.
[104] Rick Hayes and Michelle Williamson, 2007, 53.
[105] John Dostine, *Brimbank Men's Shed: Evaluation 2006*. Sunshine: UnitingCare Sunshine Mission, 2006.

The Brimbank men have been integral to the formation and development of VMSA. It is a part of who and how they are and was a catalyst for their own shed development. It was their way of giving back.[106]

Cobaw Men's Shed, located at Kyneton, Central Victoria, a town of around 6,500 people 85 kilometers north of Melbourne, commenced operation in March 2002,[107] starting as an unfunded program supported by the Cobaw Community Health Service. Alan Taylor, the CEO of Cobaw Community Health, was the main instigator and was actively involved for the next decade to 2012. Des Rees was the first coordinator for the Shed's first five years to August 2007, and presented about the Shed to the 2005 Lakes Entrance conference. The original aim of the Cobaw Men's Shed was to:

> ... promote the health and wellbeing of men by providing a supportive and stimulating environment: that engages men in woodwork and other practical activities; that encourages a sense of belonging; and in which men feel valued.[108]

Cobaw Men's Shed was one of the first Men's Sheds to undertake a survey-based formal evaluation[109]. The main value of the Shed was identified as 'the ability to interact in an environment that is conducive to what many men enjoy and [that] addresses confidentiality and ease with other "blokes."' The survey used the PRECEDE Model[110] to identity the enabling factors created by the Shed. These factors included: a sense of purpose; availability of tools and machinery; meeting new people; sharing of knowledge and skills; opportunity to discuss social and emotional problems, and availability of a supervisor who listens and respects confidentiality.[111] These factors have become familiar in practice to many later Men's Sheds.

---

[106] Lyn Kinder, August 6, 2014.

[107] A Cobaw Community Health Service media release dated June 19, 2002 invited men over 50 'from far and wide ... to come along and inspect the workshop'.

[108] Cobaw Community Health Service. 'Community Workshop: Application to Victorian Department of Human Services for Rural Health Innovation Practice', 2002.

[109] The evaluation involved an interview and survey from 16 participants. The *Men's Shed Survey Report,* December 22, 2003, was produced after the Shed had been operating for 18 months.

[110] PRECEDE is a theoretical framework for identifying positive and negative behaviours.: see Penelope Hawe *et al., Evaluating Health Promotion: A Health Workers Guide.* Sydney: MacLennan and Petty, 1990.

[111] *Men's Sheds Survey Report*, 2003, as above, 4.

Cobaw Men's Shed was also the site for a definitive and regularly cited early Masters thesis completed in 2007 by Megan Ballinger[112]. The Shed program was coordinated from August 2007 to 2013 by John Quinlan[113]. In 2008 a new 18m X 10m 'barn style' shed was built on the original site in Kyneton to improve access and safety. Photograph 16 is a view through the Shed taken in August 2009.

Photograph 16 Cobaw Men's Shed, August 9, 2009

By 2015 the Shed became independently incorporated and was renamed Kyneton Men's Shed Inc.

THE DEVELOPMENT OF THE VICTORIAN MEN'S SHED ASSOCIATION

One of the recommendations of the 2005 Lakes Entrance Conference in Victoria was to set up a wider Men's Shed network with a view to building on the relationships and links forged at that conference between many of the Victorian

---

[112] Megan Ballinger, Lyn Talbot and Glenda Verrinder, *More than a Place to do Woodwork: A Case Study of a Community-based Men's Shed.* Bundoora, La Trobe University, 2009. Based on interviews with eight shed participants. the thesis findings were published in the *Journal of Men's Health*, 20-27 in 2009 under the same title with Ballinger's La Trobe University supervisors, Lyn Talbot and Glenda Verrinder.
[113] Quinlan worked until late 2014 in a similar role for the Creswick Men's Friendship Shed. discussed above, 70 km west of Kyneton.

Sheds mentioned above. Lyn Kinder, then at Brimbank Men's Shed, recalled in 2014 that:

> With one of my partner agencies, and encouragement from Gary Green [who had facilitated the 2005 Conference] and others we organised the first meeting in Brimbank to discuss 'Where are we now? Where do we want to be? How can we get there?' on March 30, 2007. Another follow up meeting was organised in Ballarat [June 15, 2007] and the decision to incorporate was endorsed. Paperwork was completed and the first Annual General Meeting of VMSA was held in Bendigo in November 2007.

The strength of interest in a Victorian State Association by the time of the March 2007 meeting at Brimbank Men's Shed in Sunshine was large. Sixteen Sheds sent representatives to the meeting and a further fourteen sent apologies [114]. The Victorian Men's Shed Association was registered as an Incorporated Association on September 24, 2007 to represent community Men's Sheds throughout Victoria. By this time Victoria had, with Sydney and Newcastle in New South Wales, become epicentres of Australian Men's Shed activity and the emerging Movement, with approximately 70 Sheds open in Victoria of the more than 180 then open across Australia.

The March 30, 2007 VMSA meeting minutes record the presentation of a 'national overview' by Gary Green. Green reported that, as an outcome of the Lakes Entrance Conference in 2005, a decision was made to form a National Association, and that:

> At present there are 8 people involved who email and telephone each other exchanging ideas. [A] Committee [has been] formed to organise details for approval to attendees at the conference 13th and 14th September 2007, in Sydney, as yet nothing definite.

VMSA's aim in 2007 was included in its invitation to the then Victorian Governor, Professor David de Kretser, to become its Patron and to be guest speaker at VMSA's inaugural Annual General meeting. The stated aim was to '... promote and publicise the Men's Shed Concept throughout Victoria, ... working with the Australian Men's Shed Association to provide the local touch' [115]. As

---

[114] From 'Minutes of Men's Shed Co-ordinator Network Meeting', Brimbank Men's Shed, Sunshine, March 30, 2007.

[115] VMSA email to Professor David de Kretser, November 20, 2007.

with the emerging national body, VMSA explicitly stated that it would 'not have any direct control or responsibility for any individual shed'. Lyn Kinder recalled in 2014 that the Governor's acceptance as Patron 'was a welcome surprise when he accepted, given the VMSA was in the very early stage of development. I feel this gave all involved a boost of enthusiasm and commitment to make it work.'[116]

One of VMSA's significant, early achievements was working closely with the Victorian Government to secure the first round of state funding in 2007-8 through the Department of Planning and Community Development via a 'Men's Sheds Program'. Its first round of funding was consistent with the Australian Labour Party policy [117] for the 2006 Victorian election, which included a commitment of A$2 million for 25 new Men's Sheds. A second round of the program in 2009 provided an additional A$2 million, whose rationale was that:

> Men's Sheds provide a broad program of community strengthening activities for men that support health and wellbeing, provide social interaction for men in transitional or life-changing circumstances and improve skills through life-long learning or vocational education and training. [118]

By the time of the VMSA Inc. 2008 Annual Report, with Iain Beggs from Ballarat as its President, VMSA had 86 Sheds as members. Beggs reported that VMSA was 'continuing to strengthen [its] links with the emerging AMSA', and that 'our relationship with AMSA will only grow and strengthen from here'. A Media Release from June 2013 about the funding for Men's Sheds through the Victorian government, supported by VMSA is shown in Photograph 17.

---

[116] Lyn Kinder, August 6, 2014.
[117] ALP (Australian Labour Party) Policy for 2006 Victorian Election.
[118] DPCD (Department of Planning and Community Development) Men's Shed Program 2009, 5.

Media release

The Hon Mary Wooldridge MP
Minister for Mental Health
Minister for Community Services
Minister for Disability Services and Reform

Monday 17 June 2013

Coalition Government's $1.5 million boost to build new Men's Sheds across Victoria

Grants of up to $60,000 are now available to help local communities build new Men's Sheds across Victoria, Minister for Community Services Mary Wooldridge announced today.

Ms Wooldridge said that $1.5 million is available to build up to 25 new sheds through the latest round of grants from the Victorian Coalition Government's *Strengthening Men's Sheds* initiative.

"Men's Sheds are valuable community facilities that give men a place to meet, establish social networks and work on meaningful projects that benefit the community," Ms Wooldridge said.

"They also provide a place where men can discuss important wellbeing and health issues and develop new skills."

The new funding round is part of the $4 million *Strengthening Men's Sheds* initiative introduced by the Coalition Government.

"Through the first two rounds of funding we have provided $290,000 to strengthen the sustainability of Men's Sheds and $700,000 for the refurbishment of existing Men's Sheds," Ms Wooldridge said.

"Now we are supporting the establishment of new sheds in areas where they are most needed."

Victorian Men's Shed Association President Paul Sladdin said the funding was an outstanding opportunity to expand the Men's Sheds program into new communities across the state.

"Demand for Men's Sheds continues to grow in both regional and metropolitan areas," Mr Sladdin said.

Applications for grants open on 17 June 2013 and close on Friday 6 September 2013.

More information, including details of information sessions, is available at:

www.dhs.vic.gov.au/for-business-and-community/community-involvement/men-in-the-community/strengthening-mens-sheds

Media contact: Michael Moore 0400 719 355   michael.moore@minstaff.vic.gov.au

Visit www.premier.vic.gov.au for more news

Photograph 17 Media Release about Funding for Men's Sheds through the
Victorian Government, June 17, 2013.

VMSA has been one of the most consistently active State Men's Shed associations in Australia. It was meticulously and deliberately built as an organisation that fully and regularly involved affiliated Men's Sheds in Victoria.

It strongly valued a grassroots ethos, volunteerism and collaborative, inclusive, community-based approach to shedding. In the decade to 2015 it adopted a deliberately decentralised meeting strategy, with meetings held alternately in rural and city locations. VMSA also adopted a purpose statement that was deliberately broad and inclusive of women who participated in and worked for some sheds. By January 2015 there were 250 Men's Sheds open and registered with AMSA in Victoria as shown in Figure 7.

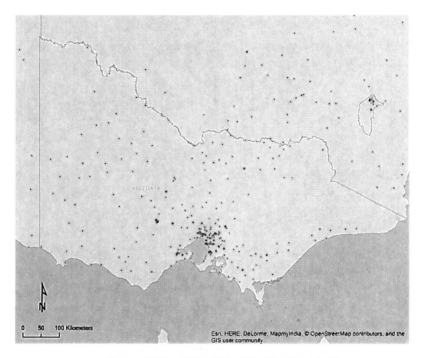

Figure 7 Map of Men's Sheds in Victoria to 2015

SOUTH AUSTRALIAN MEN'S SHED EARLY HISTORY

It is apparent, from the many early (pre-2005) Shed startups documented in Chapter 2 that South Australia developed a very early interest in sheds for men, (though the word 'Men' was not always included in the name of the Shed). The South Australian Sheds were very active in practice at a community and cluster level, particularly in rural areas. However South Australian Men's Sheds were relatively late to organise as a state. Indeed the 'first South Australian Men's Shed get-together', as it was advertised, took place in Tusmore in suburban Adelaide on May 23, 2011. This reluctance or inertia to organise as a state is curious, given that South Australia was the epicentre of early Australian Shed experimentation and thinking for much of the decade from 1993.

Several very early South Australian Sheds, including those in Goolwa (opened in 1993) and Hackham West (opened in 1995) have already been mentioned in the early history in Chapter 2. For this reason the history of only two other early and influential Sheds in South Australia are included here. One is the Port Augusta Men's Shed. The other is the Aged Care and Housing (ACH) Community Shed, located adjacent to the Elizabeth House Over 50s Centre at Christie's Beach. Elizabeth House happens to be 'just down the road' from Jack Ellis's Shed and very close to the Noarlunga site of the 1986 'Linking Men's Services' conference.

Port Augusta Men's Shed, officially opened on July 29, 1999, appears to be the earliest South Australian Men's Shed, and perhaps the third ever to open as a Men's Shed in the world. Its early history, like many Men's Sheds, is subject to slightly different recollections. Neil Edwards, the original and current Older Men's Project Coordinator Volunteer, recalled (in 2014) that 'the concept of having the shed came from two sources. One from a Shed in Horsham and the other from a Veteran's Shed in Adelaide.'[119] While no early Shed has been identified in Horsham (in 1999 it is more likely to have been in Bendigo), the Veteran connections are definitely to one of the Peter Badcoe XMRC sheds, already discussed, north of Adelaide.

Maxine Kitto (until March 1998 associated with Shed in Goolwa) also recalled being contacted about their Shed by Port Augusta Health Services. Leanne Tripodi confirmed in 2014 that:

> The concept/program was designed by Ian Reid (then manager of Domiciliary Care) and myself after visiting the Peter Badcoe [XMRC] Centre in Adelaide [that] was predominately based on social inclusion. [We] really wanted to create a new concept around a men's health service.

Michelle Baluch, who later became the first Port Augusta Men's Shed Coordinator, initiated the search by Read and Tripodi '... after proposing that we build a small shed on the premises so that the older men could brew beer'[120]. Tripodi was then employed by the Health Focus Day Therapy Centre for Older

---

[119] Bronwyn Filsell, March 26, 2014.
[120] Leanne Tripodi, September 9, 2014.

Adults through the Port Augusta City Council. Leanne Tripodi, the Shed Coordinator since 2002, recalled in 2014 that:

> We were always conscious of health services being highly feminised so [we] sat down one evening after dinner and began exploring the idea of combining health services with social programs. We met with [some other people including Vietnam Veterans, and] following some research came across the Peter Badcoe Centre for Veterans ... run more or less as a drop in centre. ... Our idea was to have a two-pronged approach: to have health professionals come to the site (this didn't happen) and to create meaningful work to give back to the community. [We] created the overall project, created the partnerships and wrote the funding proposal. Port Augusta Mayor, Joy Baluch secured the site, the Veterans developed the Veterans' Information Centre and [the rest of us] developed the older men's program. We gave the proposal and program information to the Department of Veterans' Affairs to distribute to anyone who would like to set up the program: that was part of the funding deal.[121]

Bronwyn Filsell, the current (2015) Shed Coordinator (since 2002), suggested that the professional thinking behind the early Port Augusta Men's Shed:

> ... started after a discussion between Health Focus Day Therapy Centre staff [Michelle Baluch and Leanne Tripodi] and Flinders and Far North Community Health Domiciliary Care Team identified the need for a program aimed at improving men's health status by addressing need such as social isolation, specific gender needs and improved access to community services. The Department of Veterans' Affairs provided a seeding grant of A$19,685 to implement the project. EDI Rail was approached regarding the old "crib room" at the entrance of the main railway workshops. This is an area that men could strongly identify with.[122]

Leanne Tripodi critically reflected[123] in 2014 on which elements of her original, personal vision were realised (or not) by the Port Augusta Men's Shed. The elements that *were* realised were the Older Men's Program (for both the Veteran

---

[121] Leanne Tripodi email to Bronwyn Filsell, May 16, 2014.
[122] 'Port Augusta Men's Shed', undated sheet provided by Bronwyn Filsell.
[123] Leanne Tripodi, Daw House Hospice Foundation, July 28, 2014.

and non-Veteran communities), the Veterans' Information Centre, as well as the manufacturing section to assist community services and raise income. It is of interest, given the contested nature of the role of health in Men's Sheds elaborated in Part 4, that the elements Tripodi concluded were *not* realised were health promotion sessions and basic health testing for men conducted on site.

The Port Augusta Men's Shed, generously supported and run through the Port Augusta City Council as well as by volunteers and the community for over 15 years to 2015, still operated out of a Crib Room [124] adjacent to the EDI Railway Workshops, offering …

> Retired men over 65 years of age and Veterans a place to go where they can enjoy physical and social activities. The Men's Shed is a self-sufficient community project, which relies upon production and sale of items by participants and kind donations and support from the local community. [125]

The Aged Care and Housing (ACH) Shed at Elizabeth House in Christie's Beach was not only early in South Australia, opening around 2002 [126], but also broke much new ground nationally by specialising in frail aged men and men with a disability and early dementia in a stand alone, purpose-built woodwork Shed with appropriately modified equipment and tools. The ACH Shed, simple signed as 'The Shed' was built next to the Over 50s Learning Centre. [127] Located on Elizabeth Road in the Noarlunga area south of Adelaide, it is coincidentally close to the site of the 1986 'Linking Men's Services' Conference discussed in Chapter 2. 'Trish' who helped set up the Shed in 2002 remarked in 2006 [128] that "We went down to [look at] the Encounter Centre [in Victor Harbor], it is a lot more productive than this Shed, and it's very strictly run so they are very different".

In 2006 three different groups used the Shed on different days, comprising a group with acquired brain injury, a 'Kookaburra Club' group for frail, older people from Elizabeth House and a group of men with dementia. The equipment

---

[124] A 'crib room' is a traditional term for a place to eat lunch in a workplace.

[125] Port Augusta City Council, Services, Men's Shed Web site, http://www.portaugusta.sa.gov.au/page.aspx?u=958, Accessed March 28, 2014.

[126] The Shed at Elizabeth House had been 'running for four years' at the time of Barry Golding's research interviews there in 2006.

[127] This is sometimes referred to as the Noarlunga Shed. In December 2005, Keith Bettany reported that 'On Monday and Wednesday the Shed was used as a disability program for people with Brain Injury. On Tuesday the Shed was called the Kookaburra Club for a frail age support program and for people in the early stages of dementia.'

[128] Barry Golding research interview with 'Trish', mid-2006.

and tools were all carefully selected and adapted with the safety of these groups in mind. By late 2014 The Elizabeth House Positive Ageing Centre still had a Shed Project Disabilities Group meeting in the Shed on Monday, Wednesday and Friday mornings, with a Women's Shed Group on Friday afternoons.

THE DEVELOPMENT OF THE SOUTH AUSTRALIAN MEN'S SHED ASSOCIATION

Sheds proliferated relatively early in South Australia and Men's Shed-based organisations in that state were more numerous per head of population than in any Australian state until around 2005. However it was one of the last states to formally set up a State Association. AMSA experienced considerable difficulty during its founding years getting representation from South Australia until Evan Reay joined the AMSA Board on November 1, 2010, to be replaced on July 17, 2012 by Bryce Routley.

The South Australian Men's Shed Association (SAMSA) was finally formally registered on August 16, 2013, two decades after The Shed opened in Goolwa. South Australia's first state Men's Shed 'get-together' was badged as 'Shed Talk'. This event, held prior to SAMSA's formal incorporation, was held in the Burnside Council ballroom in Tusmore, Adelaide on May 23, 2011. It included, as guest speakers, Men's Shed researchers, Barry Golding (from Ballarat) and Gary Misan (from University of South Australia, Whyalla campus). The South Australian Men's Shed Association (SAMSA) adopted a novel 'Where men work at play' motto. By January 2015 there were 68 Men's Sheds open across South Australia as shown in Figure 8.

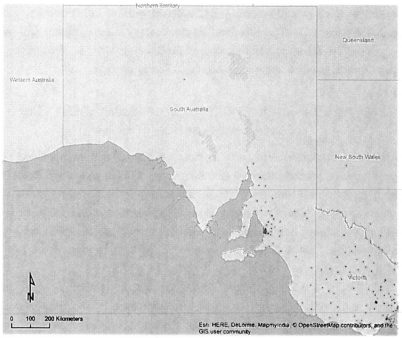

Figure 8 Map of Men's Sheds in South Australia to 2015

Tasmanian Men's Shed Early History

The island State of Tasmania has a relatively small proportion (2.4%) of the Australian population. While its total state population was only around 420,000 in 2014, it had a much higher proportion of its population than other Australian states living in rural areas outside of the state capital, Hobart or its 'second city', Launceston. Given the tendency for Men's Sheds to get more traction in rural communities, Tasmania had twice the Shed density per head of total population by 2015 (9 Sheds per 100,000) of any other Australian state, matched only by the elevated densities in the Irish rural counties of Donegal, Kerrie and Monaghan. Tasmanian Sheds developed relatively early, though, as in South Australia, few included 'Men' in their organisation name until after 2005.

Pete's Community Workshed, located in Bridgewater, in outer suburban Hobart, was the earliest Shed established in Tasmania. It commenced in the socially and economically disadvantaged Bridgewater-Gagebrook area in May 2000 [129]. It followed a chance conversation in the waiting room of a doctor's surgery between

---

[129] Helen Manser, Jordan River Service, July 31, 2014.

a handyman and a model maker. Bill Griffiths, the original founder of the Shed, tells the story.

> I got talking to a fellow at the medical centre. He seemed really depressed so I asked him what he did and he said, "Nothing". I told him I make furniture and model boats. He said he wasn't capable of doing anything. He said he was too bloody stupid. I didn't believe him so I told him I would show him how... [Three weeks later] he was amazed by what he had achieved. I later saw his wife and she said it had changed him completely. She said he was making toys and had also received a job offer. ... So I thought, "If it works for one ...".

Bill Griffiths approached the Brighton Council who supplied, free of charge, the use of a building that had housed the local fire station, and Pete's Community Workshed was born. Initial funds for tools and equipment came from a Housing Tasmania grant with support from Brighton Rotary Club. Soon after, the Department of Education's Derwent Support Service requested assistance to involve a group of "at risk" young people in Pete's Workshed activities as part of their Work Place Mentor Program. For much of the next decade, five mornings a week, Pete's Workshed specialised in collaboration with local schools including in-Shed mentoring by older men of young people and young single mothers, school resisters and people with a disability in an area where unemployment, single parenthood and poverty are relatively high.

The Workshed's early highlight was winning News Corporation's 'Pride of Australia Medal' in the 'Mateship Category' in August 2006. Pete's Community Workshed helped facilitate the Tasmanian Men's Sheds Conference on September 16-17, 2006 at nearby Pontville as well as the 2009 AMSA National conference in Hobart. John Waters played an important role in the Workshed as well as bringing the Tasmanian Men's Shed Association together. Waters served until 2013 on the AMSA Board, withdrawing through ill health and being formally recognised for his significant contribution to the Shed Movement with admission to the 'Men's Shed Hall of Fame' at the 2013 Ballarat AMSA Conference[130].

Pete's Workshed in Bridgewater was spearheaded in practice by three wise and enthusiastic older men. All were battling their 'own demons' including health issues: John Waters, Jeff White (in 2015 working at the West Moonah Shed) and

---

[130] All other recipients of this 2013 award, most mentioned in this book, are included in Appendix 4.

the late George Startup. From its inception, Pete's Community Workshed provided a valuable service to community nursing homes, schools, people with a disability and young people. Like many Sheds, Pete's Shed:

> ... decided not to 'go it alone' with incorporation and operated under the management of the Jordan River Service Inc. – this was mainly due to the fact the guys just wanted to concentrate and work on what they enjoyed and not be concerned too much with the formalities of incorporation.[131]

The Workshed's recent purpose was comprehensively self-described in 2014 as follows.

> Pete's Community Workshed provides a free of charge resource for the wider community to build, repair or be creative. It is open to the entire community, regardless of gender, age and ability. The Workshed also provides assistance to other community organisations and offers hands-on, skill-based education, practical opportunities for learning to children who are at risk of leaving the education system prematurely, and diversional therapy for the aged and disabled. It offers a supportive and accepting environment run by long-serving community volunteers, which enables community members to met, improve skills and socialise. The Workshed is a widely used resource for building community capacity and social capital in the area. It proves that a simple, practical and low cost idea based in the local community, and meeting needs by finding local solutions to local problems, can have a remarkable, positive impact on the wider community.

> Pete's Community Workshed is unique in that it serves a far broader cross-section of the community than does the 'average' Men's Shed in Australia. While research indicated that the majority of Men's Sheds are mainly used by partnered, retired men and younger single men not participating in the paid workforce, the Work Shed at Bridgewater runs several tailored programs involving at-risk, school-aged children, the elderly, women, people with spinal/brain injuries, those with disabilities,

---

[131] Helen Manser, January 30, 2015.

> as well as offering a valued resource to all members of the community.[132]

The history of four other relatively early and influential Tasmanian Sheds: in Scottsdale, St Helens, Deloraine and Devonport are included more briefly below. Collectively, they illustrate diverse, early and relatively independent approaches on a common theme to Men's Sheds, including a trend towards *Community Men's Sheds* in Tasmania.

Dorset Community Men's Shed is located in rural Scottsdale (population 2,000, in the Dorset Shire, 60 kilometers east of Launceston). Located in inland northeast Tasmania, Dorset was the second shed to open in Tasmania. A Community Men's Shed was:

> ... established in October 2001 after a carload of men from the Hilltop Christian Church visited Pete's Shed at Bridgewater in Southern Tasmania. Pete's Shed was [then] basically based on boat repairing and it was decided [by the five men] to establish a shed and utilise the pine timber that was available from the local sawmills. Hilltop Christian Church assisted with paying rent and the insurance for the first four years. The men first met in a double garage at the Community House and everyone brought along their own tools. The current premises were hired to the Shed by the local council from 2005. Don Rockliff was the coordinator and he was the inspiration for getting the Dorset Shed established.[133]

The Dorset Shed had a paid part time coordinator, Mervyn Chilcott, for nearly six years from 2006. In 2015 it was operating as Dorset Men's Shed – Scottsdale three days a week with volunteers, with 25 Shed members and around eight men in regular attendance. Mervyn Chilcott was continuing as coordinator in a voluntary capacity. There were card and board games on Wednesdays and mentoring was undertaken with students from the local high and primary schools. The Shed had woodworking displays in June each year. Its 2014 vision was 'To create a workshop environment where men of all ages can share a common interest, learn new skills and enjoy social interaction and networking'[134]. The

---

[132] Helen Manser, July 31, 2014.
[133] Mervyn Chilcott, April 21, 2014.
[134] Dorset Community Men's Shed, leaflet, 2014.

Dorset Shed set out to provide 'A workshop environment where men (& women) of all ages, backgrounds and abilities can share common interests, learn new skills and enjoy social interaction and networking.'[135]

St Helens Community Shed on the rural Tasmanian northeast coast, is distinctive in that it opened as a *Community* Shed without Men in the organization name, and made women equally welcome in the Shed. St Helens is a town of around 2,000 people, and like many rural areas, its population is significantly older (by 14 years) than the Australian average. The Shed was set up in an auspice arrangement with the St Helens Neighbourhood House. It was officially opened on November 1, 2004 by Gerard Loughran, Chair of the Tasmanian Community Fund[136]. The Shed sent a delegate to the 2005 Men's Shed Conference and in 2006 obtained funds from Department of Veterans' Affairs for a project officer position[137]. Photograph 18 is an article about the Shed one year after it opened in 2006.

Photograph 18 'Shed Going Great Guns', Article about The Community Shed at St Helens, Tasmania, 2006

---

[135] Dorset Community Men's Shed, http://www.dorsetonline.org.au/menshed.htm, Accessed April 3, 2014.
[136] St Helen's Shed, Barry Golding interview, June, 1996, 7.
[137] 'Shed Going Great Guns', *East Coast News*, 2006 (undated).

Almost a decade after its opening in 2014, the Shed was called the St Helen's Men's Shed and was:

> ... completely self-sustaining through the sale of items made at the shed and construction of items for community groups and people in the local area. [In 2014] it has a core group of around 25 members as well as regular visitors, and caters for all members of the community.[138]

The *Deloraine Community Shed* was purchased and set up as part of the Meander Valley Centre for Health and Wellbeing (MVCHWB) project in 2004.[139] The Shed's biggest breakthrough was getting ongoing funding from the Home and Community Care (HACC) program for a Coordinator. As a result, many of its participants were members of the 'HACC target group', frail aged and older men with disabilities. Lester Jones, Director of Nursing at the Deloraine District Hospital and Manager of Community Health Service that managed the Shed in 2015, explained that:

> One of the main motivations for the instigation of the shed concept in our community was that the recently set up Day Centre was not accommodating the needs of the men in our community over 65. They felt the Day Centre was female-focused in activities, and the men felt disengaged. This information was useful in gaining funding from HACC in the co-ordination of a place mainly men could meet.
>
> MVCHWB knew of a couple of other men's sheds, including one at Bridgewater [Pete's Shed], and we knew of another one for Vietnam Veterans that was at Salamanca somewhere on the wharf [in Hobart]. Ours was one of the initial sheds [in Tasmania] that proved to be positive and took off after that time. Once the ongoing [HACC] funding was

---

[138] Department of Premier and Cabinet, 'Case Study: Community Shed-St Helens Neighbourhood House', http://www.dpac.tas.gov.au/divisions/siu/reports,_research_and_data/state_of_our_community_2007/4._what_were_doing_now/6, Accessed April 3, 2014.

[139] http://sydneynearlydailyphot.blogspot.com.au/2007/11/community-shed-deloraine.html, Accessed April 3, 2014.

secured the MVCHWB handed management of the Deloraine
Community Shed over to the Deloraine District Hospital.[140]

Its 2014 public leaflet had 'The Community Shed, Deloraine: The Backyard Shed
Comes Back to Life in the Meander Valley' on the front, with no specific
emphasis on men. The fully equipped workshop-based Shed welcomes all
members of the wider community to participate and was open Monday to
Thursday, 9am-2pm in 2015.

Though officially launched relatively late in May 2007, planning for the
Devonport Men's Shed started several years earlier via the Mersey Community
Men's Group that met first in November 2003, organised by Steve Brodzinski
and David Cameron. The Men's Group met monthly in the Devonport
Community House before moving into the shed/garage at the back of the
Community House around 2005[141]. They started to meet weekly in October 2006
when power was put onto the shed. The Men's Group Secretary, David Thomas
("Foxx") 'was struggling with depression when he joined' and said, "It got me
out of the house and gave me something to do." Thomas was enthused to set up
programs at the Men's Shed after attending the 2005 Lakes Entrance Conference.
The Devonport Men's Shed was reopened on May 7, 2012, with Fairbrothers
donating a building extension, tripling its size[142]. Its 2014 programs included
'Cooking with Blokes', monthly bus trips, a mental health 'Project Bloke'
initiative with Anglicare and Men's Shed mentoring with secondary school boys
at risk.[143]

THE DEVELOPMENT OF THE TASMANIAN MEN'S SHED ASSOCIATION

Pete's Community Workshed (in Bridgewater) set up an informal Tasmanian
Men's Shed Association (TMSA) in 2006, after the Tasmanian Community and
Men's Shed Conference, held at Pontville Hall on the outer edge of Hobart in
September 16-17, 2006. However the Tasmanian Men's Shed Association
(TMSA)[144] was not formally constituted until July 6, 2009. Its formation was
hastened by a dispute between the informal TMSA committee and the auspice

---

[140] Lester Jones, May 21, 2014.

[141] Kate Beer (Manager Devonport Community House), March 29, 2014.

[142] Kate Beer, July 24, 2014.

[143] http://www.devonportcommunityhouse.com.au/the-mens-shed, Accessed January 8,
2015.

[144] http://www.tasmensshed.org/page13885/What-is-TMSA.aspx, Tasmanian Men's Shed
Association, Accessed March 13, 2014.

body of Pete's Workshed over the hosting of the AMSA 2009 Conference. John Waters' important foundational work for TMSA from 2009-13 was an inspiration to other Sheds being developed around Tasmania. A well-known Tasmanian men's health professional, Jonathan Bedloe, assisted John Waters before he retired as President of TMSA in 2013.

The TMSA aim was to provide assistance locally through support, information and auspicing, through the efforts of volunteers from various Sheds around Tasmania, organised into three broad regions: North West, North East and Southern. The TMSA Committee lobbied local governments and the Tasmanian state government in 2014 for funding on behalf of registered Men's Sheds and offered a local link to the national body, the Australian Men's Shed Association. The Tasmanian government allocated A$130,000 via Communities, Sport and Recreation Tasmania for two rounds of the TMSA Grants program in 2014-15, with up to A$5,000 available to TMSA members for Men's Shed development.

By early 2015 the Tasmanian Association had a strong and active committee with 48 registered member Shed organisations across the State. The TMSA was instrumental in obtaining State Government funding for Tasmanian Sheds for a three-year period from 2015. It had a very strong focus on the development of statewide activities and projects that support the diverse membership of Tasmanian Sheds. The TMSA obtained State Government funding for a part-time Executive Officer in 2015 to play a supporting role in individual and collective Shed programs. As of January 2015, 37 of the 48 Men's Sheds registered with TMSA were also registered with AMSA, as shown in Figure 9, despite relations having soured between the two bodies in early 2014, causing the Tasmanian Association to resign from AMSA.

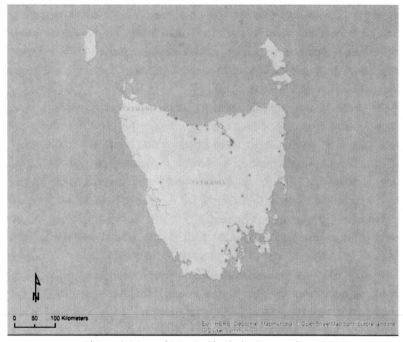

Figure 9 Map of Men's Sheds in Tasmania to 2015

WESTERN AUSTRALIAN MEN'S SHED EARLY HISTORY

Two of the earliest Western Australian Men's Sheds were initially set up privately. One was in rural Donnybrook and the other was in suburban Kingsley. Both were partly or mainly for and run by Vietnam Veterans, with the support for Shed infrastructure through the Department of Veterans' Affairs (DVA). Most other Men's Sheds in Western Australia opened slightly later than those in southeastern Australian states. As in Queensland, the subsequent growth was very rapid, particularly in rural and regional areas in the Western Australia's southwest.

Western Australia began to recognise the relatively low use of adult and community education centres by men several years before this began to be recognised elsewhere in Australia, including in Victoria[145]. Western Australia's Adult and Community Education (ACE) sector, then organized through Learning Centre Link (LCL), noted the highly female-gendered nature of the sector in Western Australia. LCL supported a small research project, begun in July 2001, resulting in a booklet called *Bringing in the Blokes: A Guide to Attracting and*

---

[145] Barry Golding, Jack Harvey and Adele Echter, *Men Learning through ACE and Community Involvement in Small Rural Towns.* University of Ballarat: Ballarat, 2004.

Involving Men in Community Neighbourhood and Learning Centres[146], first published in 2002. This guide is something of a 'world first'. While the Western Australian guide was too early to include Men's Sheds in the suggested solutions, the principles of service provision for men identified in the guide were consistent with the Men's Shed model and the later rapid growth in community Men's Sheds across the state.

The *Donnybrook Men in Sheds* program was started informally by Damien Dixon in his backyard shed in the late 1990s. It received its first DVA (Department of Veterans' Affairs) funding through the Donnybrook RSL in July 2002. It moved from private premises to a community location in Egan Park by creatively compressing and relocating the floats previously stored in the shed for the annual Apple Festival. Photograph 19 was taken in February 2006.

Photograph 19 Donnybrook Men in Sheds, Western Australia, February 1, 2006

Donnybrook Men in Sheds cultivated a strong collaborative link between the RSL Veteran community, the local school, local government and the community for around 15 years. Donnybrook was particularly innovative in terms of the way it mentored young local school resisters and also home-schooled children in woodwork. In 2015 it was registered as 'Donnybrook Men's Shed Inc.'.

---

[146] Perth: Learning Centre Link, 2003.

The men involved in the *RAAF*[147] *Vietnam Veterans Men's Shed* in the northern Perth suburb of Kingsley were also meeting regularly in a private garage as early as 2001. The Kingsley shedders received their first Department of Veterans' Affairs (DVA) funding in July 2002. Lions Community Care also received DVA funding towards a Men's Shed in Albany a few months earlier in March 2002, which was operating by mid-2002.

ThVeterans Men's Shed Kingsley, shown in Photograph 20, aside from being one of the first in Western Australia, is unusual in that it has operated out of Peter Robinson's backyard shed/garage in suburban Perth since May 2001. The purpose of the Shed project, initially under the banner of the RAAF Vietnam Veterans Association of Western Australia, but later called 'Veterans Men's Shed Kingsley', was described by Robinson in 2014 in the Shed Online as:

> ... a Men's Shed for ex military/war Veterans only. This is due to space and rules of Constitution/Insurance of our parent military association. Our Shed is purely mechanical, refurbishing mowers and the like. Bikes are donated to the Children's Home Parkerville. Our Shed prides itself by members not having to commit to a 'work' situation: they can do something or sit and chat over endless coffees. The atmosphere is very friendly and compassionate towards those who are suffering[148].

Photograph 20 The Veterans Men's Shed Kingsley, Western Australia, February 2, 2006

---

[147] RAAF: Royal Australian Air Force.
[148] https://www.theshedonline.org.au/mens-sheds/profile/veterans-mens-shed-kingsley, Accessed May 29 , 2015.

The Kingsley Shed's purpose, summarised by Robinson, was quite simple:

> To create a place for T&PI Vets (Totally and Permanently Incapacitated [War] Veterans) to socialise, join in friendship and camaraderie, to help increase their skills and to overcome some of their own problems. ... After each 'semester' of our Tuesday and Friday morning 'get-togethers' a barbecue has been held to bring together the guys and gals.[149]

The *Fremantle Community Men's Shed*[150] (originally called the Fremanshed), while not the earliest in Western Australia has been one of the most consistently innovative and influential, both in Western Australia and nationally. It is located in a former pigeon racing facility in White Gum Valley, a suburb of the historic port city of Fremantle, south of Perth. Plans for the Shed were being discussed as early as January 24, 2004,[151] as recorded in the meeting Agenda in Photograph 21.

---

[149] 'The Inception of the RAAF Vietnam Veterans Association of WA Project: Now Called Veterans Men's Shed Kingsley'. Peter Robinson, Kingsley, September 6, 2006.
[150] Freo Men's Shed, http://www.fremanshed.org/, Accessed April 3, 2014.
[151] Fremanshed Inc., 'Agenda. Shed Meeting, Monday 24th January, 2004'.

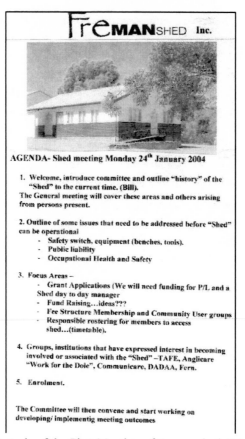

AGENDA- Shed meeting Monday 24th January 2004

1. Welcome, introduce committee and outline "history" of the "Shed" to the current time. (Bill).
The General meeting will cover these areas and others arising from persons present.

2. Outline of some issues that need to be addressed before "Shed" can be operational
   - Safety switch, equipment (benches, tools).
   - Public liability
   - Occupational Health and Safety

3. Focus Areas –
   - Grant Applications (We will need funding for P/L and a Shed day to day manager
   - Fund Raising...ideas???
   - Fee Structure Membership and Community User groups
   - Responsible rostering for members to access shed...(timetable).

4. Groups, institutions that have expressed interest in becoming involved or associated with the "Shed" –TAFE, Anglicare "Work for the Dole", Communicare, DADAA, Fern.

5. Enrolment.

The Committee will then convene and start working on developing/ implementig meeting outcomes

Photograph 21 Agenda of the First Meeting of Fremanshed, Western Australia, January 24, 2004

Fremanshed began operation one year later in February 2005, spearheaded by ex-teachers Bill Johnstone and Allan Gowland. Johnstone, the Shed's original Project coordinator, explained in 2006, during Barry Golding's *Men's Sheds in Australia* research interviews, that he came across the Men's Shed idea 'in the Eastern states of Australia while traveling on long service leave as a teacher'. He had heard about Men's Sheds and:

> ... was interested from an educational perspective. I just happened to pop in and have a look ... at Nambucca Heads [Men's Shed]. Our two-hour stay turned into two days because I was really fascinated by what was happening. Nambucca Heads was very like Fremantle. It's a place where lots of people retire [or move to]... I realised what it could

potentially do for the guys when I came back... and [we] started looking for a shed.

After discussion with his close friend Alan Gowland, a TAFE [Technical and Further Education] Building and Construction lecturer, both agreed that men in the Fremantle area could benefit from having a "tooled up" shed facility to work on projects, their own or community ones. Both men, together with a committee of 12 local men helped to establish the first metropolitan Shed in Western Australia. The Shed refurbished the building owned by the previous Pigeon Racing Federation[152], retaining the 'pigeon holes'. The Fremanshed Inc. opening effectively marked the slow start of the later explosion of the Men's Shed Movement in Western Australia after 2005.

In the Fremantle Shed members own words in the history of their Shed:

> A priority focus of the Shed has become men's health and wellbeing. The Shed has assisted men from all walks of life, including retired, unemployed, single-parent fathers, and isolated men. The Fremanshed Inc. has become a catalyst for involving men ranging in age from 9 to 90 with their community. It has helped to foster men's self esteem, create "active" social networks and worked on creating valued roles in society, particularly for men who have become disengaged with their community. These active social relationships have enhanced the health and well-being of countless men in ways that formal learning environments did not. These engagements have assisted in protecting against physical and emotional sickness including stress, depression and mental illness.[153]

The combined knowledge and skill of Bill Johnstone and Alan Gowland in mentoring boys and young men and their creativity with programs and community events made this one of the most consistently innovative Men's Sheds in Australia. Enjoyment, including through music, has often been an important focus in the Shed as illustrated in Photograph 22 from 2012.

---

[152] 'Men's Shed Marks Decades Work', *Fremantle Gazette*, February 10, 2015, 4.
[153] History of Fremanshed Inc.: Fremantle Men's Community Shed.

Photograph 22 'Striking a Chord', Newspaper Article about Freo Men's Shed
Guitar Making Workshop, July 2012 (Bill Johnstone second from right)

Johnstone played early and important leadership roles in the national and state associations (AMSA and WAMSA) as well as within the Fremantle Shed. Johnstone also assisted in many Shed start-ups across Western Australia, including in Rockingham, Mundaring, Albany, Melville, Karratha, Mandurah, Canning, Swan and Kalamunda (to name but a few). As a recent (2014) example of the diverse projects the Fremantle Shed has supported, Bill Johnstone as President of the Shed reported that one if its 73 year old members, Mike Pauly, had set out to walk unaided around Australia to raise funds for men's mental health and arthritis research, returning to base from remote Fitzroy Crossing to recuperate from a hernia after 2,500 kilometers![154]

The role of two other relatively early Western Australian Men's Sheds is also briefly examined. Both were established in the very small rural towns of Darkan and Mukinbudin in Western Australia's inland southwest.

The Shed at Darkan, a very small rural town (population 500) in the Shire of West Arthur (population 900) is located in a huge, shed, purpose-built for both metalwork and woodwork. It stores the Darkan Heritage Preservation Group's

---

[154] Bill Johnstone, July 28, 2014, http://ozsoulwalk.com/, Accessed August 1, 2014.

large agricultural machinery collection. Like most Sheds, it needed a lot of discussion, community and government lobbying, hard work and multiple funding sources (DVA, Positive Ageing, Lottery West, Regional Partnerships, West Arthur Shire), covering a reasonably long lead-time (3.5 years from first meeting to official opening). The detailed history of this formative period, painstakingly recorded by John Putland prior to its opening day, covered 22 typed pages[155], from which the rest of this history quotes from and summarises.

The first meeting to set up the Darkan Shed goes back to June 12, 2002, instigated and convened by Phil Harrington, 'after he had perused a pamphlet or article from NSW in which the Lane Cove Community Men's Shed is featured'. In Barry Golding's research interview in The Shed in 2006 for the *Men's Sheds in Australia* research, Harrington explained how Lane Cove ' … sent over some information on how they run their Shed and how they got started, and that was a big help as we didn't have a clue'. Within a month the five-person steering committee had drawn up plans, and in March 2003 the men took a small bus to visit the Albany Lions Club Community Day Care Workshop that had been open since mid-2002. By August 2003 they had also visited the Donnybrook Shed, mentioned earlier. Like several other early Australian Sheds, they were concerned that to call it a 'Men's Shed' would be discriminatory, eventually staying very safe and simply calling it 'The Shed'. The Shed in Darkan, shown in Photograph 23 soon after its opening, was officially opened by a well-known Western Australian federal politician, Wilson ('Ironbar') Tuckey on November 5, 2005.

Photograph 23 The Shed, Darkan, Western Australia, January 31, 2006

---

[155] John Putland, 'The Shed Diary', Darkan, 2005.

The *Mukinbudin 1950s Working Farm Shed* in the tiny town of Mukinbudin (2014 population 480) proved to be very important in the establishment of the WA Men's Shed Association. The whole town, with the support of Mukinbudin Shire and the 'Mukinbudin 1950s Working Farm Shed' hosted 'Western Australia's First Men's Shed Conference, 'Blokes building better communities' on September 3-4, 2009 [156]. Photograph 24 is of a sign at the Mukinbudin conference, an event fondly recalled by all 140 delegates including several guest interstate presenters.

Photograph 24 'Western Australia's First Men's Shed Conference' Sign, Mukinbudin, September 2009

Those contributing included AMSA Patrons, Professors John Macdonald (Sydney) and Barry Golding (Ballarat), AMSA CEO David Helmers and Gary

---

[156] Western Australia Men's Sheds 2009, Conference Program.

Green (Orbost Men's Shed). All visitors were generously welcomed and billeted in the tiny town, which actually ran the 'blue carpet' across the train line between the Shed and the main street, as shown in Photograph 25.

Photograph 25 'Blue Carpet' over the Railway Tracks, First Western Australian Men's Shed Conference, Mukinbudin, September 2009 (The Mukinbudin Shed on left, Conference marquee on right)

This large and important first State-wide Western Australian conference gathering, enthusiastically supported by the entire small wheat belt community as well as by AMSA was ably organised by Anne Brandis. Some enthusiastic shedders drove the 1,500 km down from Paraburdoo in the Pilbara. It started with a local fashion parade and included many memorable presentations including by Julian Krieg of Wheatbelt Men's Health. Anne Brandis says she took up the challenge to host the gathering '… in response to a visitor from Beverley who had visited the Men's Shed to try and start one in his home town and said we need to have a meeting of all men's sheds in WA'[157]. The Mukinbudin Conference led directly to the creation of the Western Australian Men's Shed Association. The 'Mukka Shed' was revisited in late 2014 by AMSA staff Gary Green and Mel White, who reported that they were 'met by a full house and were fed cakes, pies and a huge array of treats … This is a total community shed, and you could really feel the community within.'[158]

---

[157] Anne Brandis, October 16, 2014.
[158] 'AMSA staff visit WA Sheds', *AMSA Newsletter*, November 11, 2014.

THE DEVELOPMENT OF THE WESTERN AUSTRALIAN MEN'S SHED ASSOCIATION

The decision to form the Western Australian Men's Shed Association (WAMSA) was made at the September 2009 Mukinbudin conference, discussed above. An initial twelve-person steering committee was formed, led by Bill Johnstone from the Freo (Fremantle) Men's Shed. WAMSA became incorporated on July 7, 2010 and held its inaugural Annual General Meeting in Perth in July 2010[159]. The Association, formed to represent all of the Men's Sheds in Western Australia, coordinates and disseminates information to all Sheds and assists in setting up new Sheds. Meetings are held with politicians and funding bodies to get the maximum benefit for Western Australian Men's Sheds. WAMSA commissioned a *Strategic Business Plan* in 2014[160]. In 2015 WAMSA received financial support from the Western Australian Department of Health and was affiliated with the Australian Men's Shed Association, the national peak body.[161]

As of early 2015, the Patron of WAMSA was His Excellency Malcolm McCusker, Governor of Western Australia. Of all the national associations, WAMSA along with VMSA in Victoria has been most active in lobbying State governments and maintaining contact with Men's Sheds at a State level, in part because of Western Australia's relative isolation and its tendency in many areas of government policy to 'go it alone'. Its regular newsletter, *The Warbler* 'provides the catalyst for networking between sheds'.[162] By January 2015 there were 95 Men's Sheds open and registered with AMSA in Western Australia as shown in Figure 10.

---

[159] http://www.wamsa.org.au/ Western Australian Men's Sheds Association, Accessed March 13, 2014.

[160] Guildbridge Pty Ltd, *Western Australian Men's Shed Assocation Strategic Business Plan 2014*. Wembly, Western Australia, 2014.

[161] http://www.wamsa.org.au/ Western Australian Men's Sheds Association, Accessed March 13, 2014.

[162] http://www.wamsa.org.au/, Accessed January 8, 2015.

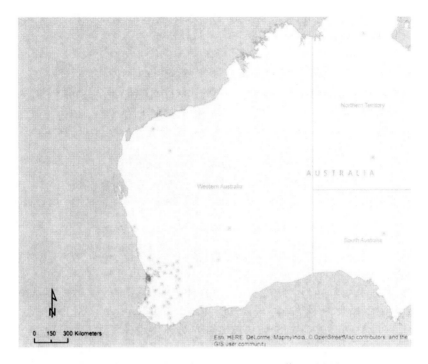

Figure 10 Map of Men's Sheds in Western Australia to 2015

QUEENSLAND MEN'S SHED EARLY HISTORY

Community Men's Sheds came relatively late to Queensland. Few, if any, officially opened before 2009. However there is evidence of an early and 'successful shed project ... set up for residents at Nambour's Sundale Garden in Queensland[163] that was still part of the complex in 2014.[164] The spread of Men's Sheds has since been very rapid. Thirteen Men's Sheds were registered (most still setting up) in Queensland by the time the Queensland Men's Shed Association (formally registered on June 18, 2009) hosted the 2011 AMSA Conference in Brisbane on August 22-23, giving Shed numbers in Queensland a significant further boost.

The three brief early Shed histories below, all from southeast Queensland, confirm that their relatively late start-ups (between 2009-10) were typically quite rapid. By 2009 AMSA was becoming very active, AMSA's early 'Starting a

---

[163] Leon Earle, *Men in Sheds: Life Long Therapy*, 2005, www.accreditation.org.au, printed November 31, 2005. Also see *The Weekend Australian,* September 17, 2005, 4.
[164] 'A fully equipped hobby shed' was mentioned on Sundale Garden Village website, http://www.sundale.org.au/locations-sundale.htm, Accessed April 2, 2014.

Men's Shed' manual had become widely accessible, and Men's Shed web sites were by then very common in other Australian states.

Coral Coast Men's Shed is an example of one relatively early Queensland Shed start up. The Shed opened in 2009 in Bargara, a satellite town (population 7,000) on the coast east of the large regional city of Bundaberg (population 71,000). The Shed Secretary, John Murdoch tells the short and simple version of the story.

> Bernie Daniels, its first President was traveling around Australia when he noticed a Men's Shed. Upon arriving back to Bargara he, with several others, made enquiries and soon the Shed was established on a Church property.

By 2014 the Coral Coast Men's Shed had four different day care support groups regularly attending it. The local secondary school regularly involves a small number of boys in the Shed's activities with the assistance of a carer. As at many Sheds, John Murdoch reported that 'the morning cuppa when everything stops is rather important', including for some participants who can only do very minor tasks.

The *Arana Hills Men's Shed* also commenced operation in July 2009. Arana is an outer northwestern suburb of Brisbane. It again illustrates how simple and effective the Men's Shed model was proving to be a decade after the earliest Men's Sheds had begun to be to set up elsewhere 'down south' in Australia. Don Scott, its Shed Coordinator recounted the Arana Shed's story.

> I was coming up to retirement ... and what was I to do after working? I realised that my Church had activities for women and not for men. ... I called a meeting of men in the Church to try and address this missing group. During this period I had purchased the Manual for starting up a Men's Shed, and when the Men's Shed Manual arrived we were listed [on the AMSA website] as Arana Hills Men's Shed. ... Our Shed is not a tool or manufacturing shed. We meet in the Church premises and socialise and mentor each other. We are auspiced by the Arana Hills Uniting Church, which has many advantages for members: we have rent-free space and our insurance comes under the Church's policy.

> We often go out for trips to various museums and places of interest, Sausage sizzles are our biggest event in the Shed calendar. Since our

inception with only eight members we now have 76 on our books that could be called 'regulars'. We do not charge a membership fee, just a gold coin donation for morning tea and all other activities are on a [Pay-As-You-Go] basis. When I am asked, "What do we do in our community since we are not tool oriented?" I say, "We are open to all men in our community and offer a safe and relaxed place for local men to come together and re-establish individual reconnections with like-minded men after leaving the workforce or after recovering from serious health conditions."[165]

While the *Shed West Workshop* in Brisbane did not officially open until February 20, 2010, their Shed members had been meeting regularly under the name of 'Shed West Community Men's Shed Inc.' at a local, disused Scout Hall since December 2007 and occasionally worked at each other's home workshops from early 2008[166]. In 2008, as a test to see if Men's Sheds would be viable in Brisbane, the Brisbane City Council provided an initial grant of $12,000 in seeding funds to the Shed West Community Men's Shed Inc. and also to the Sunnybank RSL so that each organization could set up a Men's Shed in their respective Council Wards. In 2015 the shed organisation in Kenmore Hills on Brisbane's western outskirts was known as Shedwest Community Shed Inc.

THE DEVELOPMENT OF THE QUEENSLAND MEN'S SHED ASSOCIATION

Community Men's Sheds first came to Queensland almost a decade later than in other Australian states. A Men's Shed Forum was held in Brisbane in December 2008. Hosted by Brisbane City Council, the forum coincided with the launch of the Brisbane City Council (BCC) Men's Shed-specific grant program mentioned above, that allocated A$50,000 to develop Men's Sheds within Brisbane, the state capital city. David Helmers was invited to the forum to represent AMSA. While this meeting heard some resistance to developing a State Branch, the Queensland Men's Shed Association (QMSA) was formally registered on June 18, 2009.

Meantime a small number of early Sheds forming in the Brisbane area received a boost from the BCC seeding funds. Two interested groups trialed the viability of Men's Sheds in two different Brisbane suburbs: Sunnybank (SE of the city) and Kenmore (SW of the city). As part of a Community Development Program, the BCC continued to encourage and support the establishment of Men's

---

[165] Don Scott, April 7, 2014.
[166] Graeme Curnow, March 8 and August 9, 2014.

Sheds, providing a A$100,000 pool for Shed Establishment Grants each year. It also assisted, from June 2010, with the formation of the Queensland Men's Shed Association (QMSA) in the lead up to the 2011 AMSA Conference in Brisbane.

QMSA to 2014 received no direct financial support from any branch of government, being entirely run by volunteers on the Committee. In 2012 the Queensland Supply Chain and Logistics Conference decided that QMSA was an organisation deserving of support, and raised A$10,000 for the organisation at their Conference. QMSA had been operating only with these funds until the 2014 introduction of an AMSA levy. Despite the lack of direct support provided to its State Association, many individual Sheds in Queensland received establishment grants through the Queensland Gaming Fund and from other community support funds.

During 2014, QMSA was involved in several community projects with Arthritis Queensland and The Premier's Department in the lead up to the G20 Summit held in Brisbane in late 2014. The high profile G20 project involved eight Queensland Men's Sheds each building a huge decorated letter, three metres high, spelling out 'BRISBANE' installed in the Southbank parklands on the riverbank opposite the CBD. The structural design was by an 84 year old shedder and structural engineer[167]. By January 2015 there were 159 Men's Sheds open and registered with AMSA in Queensland, as shown in Figure 11.

---

[167] Graeme Curnow, November 10, 2014.

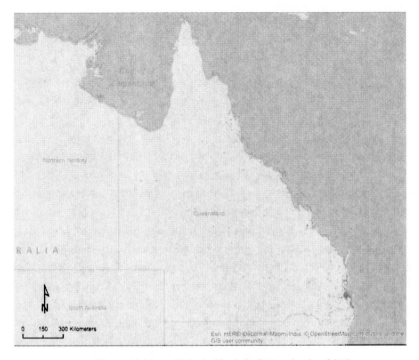

Figure 11 Map of Men's Sheds in Queensland to 2015

Chapter 3 focused on the setting up and progressive spread of Men's Sheds, primarily in the decade to 2009, to all Australian states and the later development of state associations. Chapter 4 looks at how Men's Shed organisations, shedders and some early state bodies began, in this same period from 2004, to link up and plan for a national Men's Shed organisation in Australia.

CHAPTER 4

The Men's Shed Movement in Australia

Chapter 4 documents how Men's Sheds, originally developed semi-independently across southern Australian states, began to gather together for mutual benefit and, by 2007, to form a national association and hold biennial national conferences. While the first of several state gatherings was held in 2004 in New South Wales, the first conference involving several states was held in Victoria in 2005. Much of the early momentum and work 'on the ground' towards a national association in Australia, as 'the Men's Shed Movement' began to take hold from 2005, centred on Sydney and Newcastle in New South Wales. This chapter documents the early pioneering work of the Lane Cove Men's Shed, the critically important role of The Shed at Windale, and the linking together of the main early players involved in Men's Sheds in each Australian state. This chapter identifies a number of impediments that had to be overcome, particularly getting sufficient funds and a secure organisational base to set up and run the fledgling national association during a time of exponential growth of Men's Sheds. The key breakthrough, documented late in this chapter, was getting the support of the national government in Australia and securing national funding to run the Australian Men's Shed Association from 2009.

SOME EARLY 'LINKING UP' FROM 2004

In the first decade of early Men's Sheds experimentation and development before 2005, several Australian Sheds actively shared their experiences. While Lane Cove Men's Shed in particular had generously and informally but actively mentored and supported Sheds as far away as Darkan in Western Australia, few attempts had been made, before a New South Wales Shed Conference Planning Meeting in 2004, for Sheds to link up in any Australian state. While one early 'Shed cluster' was in place in rural South Australia before 2004, most other early Sheds were too busy battling with their own, often common, local issues related to early Shed establishment. There was a gradual realisation by 2004-5 that sufficient Men's Sheds had already been established in some Australian states to enable the valuable sharing of information and that there was no need to completely 'reinvent the wheel' to create new Sheds.

In 2004 the first state and national associations, as the latter part of this Chapter reveals, were still some years off. The first meeting of Shed-based organisations in 2004 was originally intended as a precursor for a Men's Sheds conference in New South Wales, though it did not eventuate. Inviting shedders from other states to the first ever, highly successful Men's Shed Conference in Lakes Entrance in Victoria in 2005 was a move that enthused and informed many previously disconnected Men's Sheds. It also led to many new Sheds and provided evidence to all who attended that this could indeed become a national Movement. Both events are revisited in the sections that follow.

The 2004 New South Wales Conference Planning Meeting

While the Lakes Entrance Men's Shed Conference in Victoria in 2005 is widely regarded as the first 'national' conference, a handful of early Men's Sheds in New South Wales (NSW) was quietly planning for a state conference (that did not eventuate) over a year before. By 2004 there were sufficient Men's Sheds in New South Wales to convene a Men's Shed 'Conference Planning Meeting'. The South West Area Health Service Centre for Population Health and the UTS (University of Technology Sydney) Centre for Continuing Education (CPE) wrote up the August 16, 2004 event as follows in 2006.

> Hugh Wright, the second Katoomba Program Coordinator organised and convened the first NSW statewide Men's Shed Planning Morning held in St Mary's in 2004. This was jointly funded by the Mid-North Coast Area Health Service, St Clair Youth and Neighbourhood Team and the Nambucca [Valley] Men's Shed. Over 21 men from across NSW attended, including the existing Katoomba Men's Shed Office bearers.

Hugh Wright (working in Scotland in late 2014) confirmed that this 'Men's Shed Statewide Conference Planning Meeting'[1] was actually co-convened by John Kurko (Wentworth Area Health). In Wright's then role as part of the St Clair Youth and Neighbourhood Team, he noted that:

> This followed a visit by me (one of many fantastic visits to Stu[art Holmes] and the Nambucca Shed starting in early 2001 when I came to

---

[1] N. Hall, *Report on Men's Shed Statewide Conference Planning Meeting*. Blaxland: All In Community Consultants, 2004.

OZ as a [student]) to talk to Stu about the possibility of organising such an event.[2]

This early New South Wales meeting, including a session led by Stuart Holmes from the Nambucca Shed, identified several of the issues that would become very important as Sheds began to compare notes and organise state and national associations during the next decade. These issues included: 'Whether there is a need for a new association / peak / umbrella body'; the need to '… create an audit list of Men's Sheds projects … to somehow measure outcomes as well'; that 'there is no specific pool of funding … for men's stuff at any level of government'; 'Because no arm of the sector covers it all … under which auspice [they might] apply for funds; Are the Sheds 'run by professionals or are they more 'hands on'?' and 'Are the two mutually exclusive?'. Finally but importantly, there was recognition that 'To increase the likelihood of more funding, is it important to raise the public profile of Men's Sheds, look to collaborative partnerships, and consider a uniform method of monitoring and evaluation?'.[3]

   The session run by Stuart Holmes, based on his extensive experiences at Nambucca Men's Shed since it opened in 2000, shone a light on other important 'should' issues and themes that have been recurring in the decade since in most Men's Sheds, that are critically returned to in Part 4. For example: Should a Men's Shed be structured or unstructured? Should it be self-contained or should it seek community collaboration? Should it work with specific target groups? How might the Shed 'move blokes on' beyond the crisis and intervention stage? Should it be for men only, and how can the limited funding be most effectively used? The 2004 session notes ended with the highlighted quote, 'The men's shed is not about building stuff, it's about building better blokes'[4]. This theme was later critically analysed in the final session of the meeting, with some concerns that, if the discourse of 'Building better blokes' was used as part of the title of a future conference, 'it could possibly imply a value judgment that blokes are not good enough as they are.'

   It is of some interest to note here that despite these early and very positive state plans in New South Wales, quite a few Sheds already operating (including Lane Cove) were not invited or present. New South Wales did not formally register its state association until November 17, 2010, and was less successful *as a state* organization in reconciling early internal and regional differences or

---

[2] Hugh Wright, July 30, 2014.
[3] Report on Men's Shed Statewide Conference Planning Meeting, Session 2, 5.
[4] Report on Men's Shed Statewide Conference Planning Meeting, Session 1, 4.

organising and supporting its own state sector. The author attended a most acrimonious meeting on November 27, 2010 as part of a 'State Gathering' of the NSW Men's Sheds Association organised by AMSA at Myuna Bay[5]. The January 2011 *AMSA Newsletter* simply records that the election of the NSWMSA at this meeting 'was planned to be completed and announced, ... [but led] instead [to] a robust discussion on the constitution and election which raised a number of legal queries.'[6]

The specifics of this 'robust discussion' have since been resolved, as the NSW peak body (NSWMSA) history earlier attests. However it is a reminder and evidence that there are several strands to the Shed Movement in New South Wales and elsewhere, as in other grassroots social movements, where resolution of conflicting agendas, roles and strong individual personalities by consensus is sometimes very difficult to achieve. In essence, some is about particular regions and Sheds seeing themselves as separate and different. Some of this is about the ongoing dilemma about which entity should lead and for which purposes: the shedders, the Shed, the Shed cluster, the state peak body or the national peak organisation.

Several dilemmas identified at this early state peak body gathering in New South Wales have surfaced again in other Australian states and other countries. The issues typically at play come back to what the Shed is or should actually be about, a theme picked up in Part 4. At one extreme, for some shedders, it is just about 'doing stuff', often hands-on, in an exclusive and tight workshop clique with existing friends. At the other extreme, it is about being highly inclusive and reaching out to the community beyond the Shed and the current shedders to *all* men, many who may have no interest or skills in 'hands-on', but desperately seek a place simply to feel at home somewhere and to make friends.

As Part 4 will show, some professionals (and many governments) see Men's Sheds as a place to 'reach out to' and service the needs of some men who are otherwise difficult to reach by conventional models of men's 'service delivery' (of health, education, aged care and welfare, for example). By contrast, some shedders want to keep as far away as possible from the long arms of government funding, programs and the inevitable requirement of downstream accountability.

As evidenced in this first early Men's Shed gathering in New South Wales, some men will come to Sheds with agendas that preclude the idea of interacting

---

[5] New South Wales Men's Shed Association State Gathering 2010, Program.
[6] New South Wales Men's Shed Association, Newsletter, January, 2011, http://www.nswmensshed.org/SiteFiles/nswmensshed2012org/Newsletter_-2011_Jan.pdf, Accessed March 20, 2014.

with or being inclusive of women. Most men 'towards the centre' will recognise that 'bringing women' with them by participating with women's (typically their partner's) active support and encouragement is also in men's best interests. A smaller number of men and Men's Shed organisations will actively support women to join and participate in most aspects of the Shed. All of these issues and polarities will be shown in the rest of the book to be perennial and pervasive.

The 2005 Lakes Entrance Conference in Victoria

Most shedders in Australia identify the first significant national gathering as the one that occurred in Lakes Entrance, Victoria in 2005. Then simply badged as 'The Men's Shed Conference' and held on November 10-11, 2005, it was the point at which previously poorly connected shedders, early Shed innovations and findings during the first decade of isolated Shed development began to coalesce statewide in Victoria as well as nationally. This conference, organised by Gary Green of the Orbost Men's Shed through the East Gippsland Men's Health Network was something of a watershed in terms of a growing public recognition of Men's Sheds. By connecting and sharing their experiences, shedders began to acknowledge the capacity to develop considerable 'bottom-up' momentum and Movement status across Australia.

The aim of the Lakes Entrance Conference was 'to provide a forum to share information and ideas, problems and solutions, within the rapidly growing men's shed community.'[7] It involved 'an extensive range of speakers and Men's Shed enthusiasts'. Keynote presenters included Rob Moodie the CEO of VicHealth; Rick Hayes from La Trobe University; Bruce Hurley the CEO of Gippsland Lakes Community Health and Barry Golding from University of Ballarat. Shed organisations (including many shedders) that presented were from Orbost, Creswick, Kyneton (Cobaw), Bendigo ('Men in Sheds'), Sunshine (Brimbank), Doncaster (Manningham) and Lane Cove (Sydney), all already discussed.

The conference connected many experienced Men's Shed practitioners, coordinators and researchers from all states except Queensland and Western Australia. They included Ted Donnelly and Ruth van Herk from Lane Cove Men's Shed (Sydney, NSW), Anthony Brown, from University of Western Sydney and Keith Bettany from Alzheimer's South Australia, making it the first truly interstate Men's Shed forum. The Panel Discussion, 'Men's Shed blokes and their partners: What it's like for them?' was particularly moving, as was the

---

[7] The Men's Shed Conference Program, 2005, 3.

Conference Dinner entertainment at the Lakes Entrance Surf Club from the local Nowa Nowa Men's Choir.

DEVELOPMENT OF THE AUSTRALIAN MEN'S SHED ASSOCIATION[8]

The Importance of the Early Men's Shed Conferences

This section briefly teases out the importance of the 2005 Lakes Entrance Conference (in Victoria) and the subsequent biennial national conferences in Manly (2007), Hobart (2009), Brisbane (2011), Ballarat (2013) and Newcastle (2015). In essence, these conferences led to a national linking up process, including the creation of the first national database of Men's Sheds, recognition of the need for better data and research evidence and the formation of a national Australian association.

Aside from the huge networking value of these Conferences, the Brisbane and Ballarat conferences were both followed by 'Shed Crawls' a concept developed and organized by Barry Golding in Victoria in collaboration with AMSA and VMSA. Repeated at the 2015 Newcastle Conference as well as in Ireland, the idea is to expose delegates beyond the confines of the conference venue to a number of 'real' Sheds on a day tour, sharing transport, food and ideas and being hosted and informed by the shedders themselves.

Sheds had been developing semi-independently in several southern Australian States well before the 2005, though informal Men's Shed groups representing several geographically or organizationally connected sheds in Sydney, the Hunter Valley, Victoria and rural South Australia. Gary Green from the Orbost Shed organised the Lakes Entrance Conference to bring Sheds together and encourage sharing of some of the emerging research about the advantages that were already becoming apparent anecdotally in Men's Sheds. Though not 'badged' at the time as a 'national' conference[9], it was the first time that "shedders" began to realise that there were already many Sheds in other states. In a sense, this was the early beginning of a national 'shed consciousness' which preceded and anticipated the later Movement. In the networking conversations outside the formal presentations at Lakes Entrance, suggestions were made that Sheds should join together to form a national Association.

---

[8] Ted Donnelly generously supplied much information for this section from an 8 page document he wrote in 2011 called 'Australian Men's Shed Association (AMSA): A Chronological History'.

[9] There were 120 participants at the 2005 Lakes Entrance Conference from all Australian states except Queensland and Western Australia.

However it was not clear in 2005 how a national association might work or what it would do. Though the seeds had been sown, germination was delayed.

In a 2006 research interview for the *Men's Sheds in Australia* research at the Lane Cove Men's Shed, Ted Donnelly presciently remarked that:

> The main thing about Men's Sheds is getting men together for a reason ... [not just for talk]. ... [W]hat that reason is ... is going to be rather difficult to get [organised into] an Association, because it wouldn't be an association of woodwork, it's just a group of men.

The second national conference at the time of this 2006 interview had already been allocated to the Lane Cove Men's Shed, and was held at nearby Manly in September 2007, attended by representatives from all Australian states as well as from New Zealand. It was the first conference badged as being national. The Shed concept had been growing rapidly in Australia since the 2005 Lakes Entrance conference, and by the time of the 2007 Manly conference the national website database listed 214 Australian Men's Sheds. Around 40 per cent of the Sheds on this early database were still in the researching, planning or starting up stages and many were seeking information and advice. Because there was no central reference source, a great deal of duplication and "wheel re-invention" was occurring. A lot of interest was shown before and during the Manly conference for the first time by 'outside' bodies such as State and Federal Government Departments, non-government community organisations, men's health groups and the media.

Distinguishing AMSA from Mensheds Australia

It was the dilemma of how to deal with the not-for-profit company Mensheds Australia Limited, informally and effectively masquerading as the peak national body, and at the same time touting for business with unwitting new Men's Sheds on its website, that triggered and hastened the need for a truly representative, community-based national association. The Victorian Men's Shed Association (VMSA), formally incorporated in September 2007, carefully drew a firm 'line in the sand' when it developed its *Position Statement on Mensheds Australia Limited*[10] in 2007, reproduced in part below. VMSA recognised that:

> Men's Sheds should be community driven.

---

[10] 'Victorian Men's Sheds Association: Position Statement on Mensheds Australia Limited', VMSA, 2007.

Some of the major components of the appeal and success of Men's Sheds revolves around:

- a sense of ownership that individual Men's shedders have about their Men's Shed;
- the satisfaction of being able to freely give and contribute to their local communities, while at the same time being involved in social activities, that are, in themselves, health promoting;
- [not] running Men's Sheds as small businesses [that] reduces the health impacts of Men's Sheds, as by necessity, they need to become production focused.

We understand that the limited liability company Mensheds Aust Ltd:

- implies 'peak body status' for Men's Sheds, yet research evidence disputes this
- charges a fee for service to member Sheds, yet most of the services offered can be had free of charge from the community based AMSA and/or VMSA
- is not recognised by most Men's Sheds as the peak, not for profit men's shed body in Australia.

Mensheds Australia, discussed in more detail later in this Chapter, was also having a detrimental effect on planning for the national conference in Manly in 2007. Some people in the wider community and some Shed organisations were under the mistaken impression that the Manly conference organisers were a part of the Mensheds Australia Company that was actually organising a parallel conference. Mensheds Australia was also creating confusion among the media and other organisations with their skillful online marketing. It was also gaining a public relations and commercial advantage via the several companies that sat behind its not-for-profit shell and very professional website.

From a Shed Movement perspective, Mensheds Australia was arguably using the intellectual property and contacts created and shared generously and freely by community-based Sheds. The potential positive side of the Mensheds Australia agenda was that the business or self-supporting model it advocated, if it worked, might potentially avoid the problems associated with financial dependence on government and other bodies, with their external policy-based expectations about outcomes and associated key performance indicators.

It nevertheless became important and urgent that a separately defined, national Men's Shed peak body be created that could speak for and be representative of community-based Men's Sheds. The Australian Men's Shed Association (AMSA) was, for simplicity and to save money, formally registered as a NSW Incorporated Association in January 2007, enabling the Manly conference committee to put out a disclaimer notice similar to the VMSA one above, stating that there was no relationship between the two organisations. Similar actions were taken by several state associations as well as by some Men's Sheds.

The Initial AMSA Workgroup and the Lane Cove Connection

The Manly Conference Organising Committee members in 2007 were already heavily involved with Men's Sheds. Many points incorporated into AMSA's aims came from the Committee's suggestions as well as from discussions between Ted Donnelly and Ruth van Herk. Both had been actively involved in the Lane Cove Men's Shed for nearly a decade at that stage, and had been actively advising other Sheds nationally since 2000. Ruth van Herk, as the conference sponsors' representative, was mainly involved with the conference, whilst Ted Donnelly took on the development of AMSA. The 'Aims of the Association', subsequently approved by the national workgroup, were still the basic aims for AMSA to 2015.

- To maintain communications between "Sheds".
- To publicise and promote the Men's Shed concept.
- To represent Men's Sheds to Government Funding sources etc.
- To provide start-up information, documentation and assistance.
- To assist in training, OH&S [Occupational Health and Safety], funding and insurance advice.
- To act as a neutral body where overall collective decisions are required regarding the Association.
- The Association will not have any direct control or responsibility for any individual "Shed".

In July 2007 it was suggested that the existing interim national workgroup be approved as the interim committee for a year. All Sheds that expressed an opinion were in favour of this action, and this was the proposal voted on at the Manly conference. The interim committee representing the six states with Sheds open at that time (not including Queensland) comprised Gary Green and Neil Wakeman (Victoria), John Waters (Tasmania), Bill Johnstone (Western Australia), Keith

Bettany (South Australia) and Stuart Holmes and Ted Donnelly (New South Wales). Between them, they shared around 40 years of Shed experience. This interim committee had, as a major aim, the setting up of elections in 12 months, including helping to develop regional groups of Sheds to improve personal knowledge of whom they might nominate as their representatives for future committees. As AMSA had not received any funding to August 2007, all of AMSA's early communications with the several hundred Australian Men's Sheds were through Ted Donnelly's home computer and the 'free' use of the telephone at Lane Cove Shed.

In August 2007, however, AMSA received its first, small donation from a small engineering company based in Lane Cove (Chamberlain Australia Pty Ltd.) and a Government grant for A$1,500. This enabled the fledgling Association to cover the "one off" set up costs of a computer, printer, telephone and stationery and to establish a direct AMSA email link.

In September 2007 the startup information Lane Cove Men's Shed had created and widely disseminated informally was refined and rebadged as an AMSA manual, *Setting up a Men's Shed*. It had been developed by both Donnelly and van Herk over a long period of time. After some degree of involvement with the start-up of about 60 new Sheds, it was clear to these early Shed pioneers that many of the same questions and problems were occurring with most Men's Sheds. The manual was developed using their accumulated experience of helping and advising other Sheds covering all the aspects that typically occurred from startup. The manual also included standard administrative and occupational health and safety forms together with appropriate safety signs for machines and workshops. The manual was released at the 2007 Manly Conference. The Shed sponsors (North Sydney Region of UnitingCare Ageing) covered the costs of the first printing and offered proceeds of all sales to AMSA.

The Manly Conference was organised by the Lane Cove Community Men's Shed together with their sponsor, UnitingCare Ageing (North Sydney Region). However by the time of the conference AMSA had been established and became a co-organiser, effectively making it the first *AMSA* national conference. The event proved to be very successful. The Lakes Entrance conference in 2005 confirmed that Shed members were not alone and that other Sheds existed. The Manly conference, because of a heavy publicity campaign, showed the community and the 'world outside' that Men's Sheds existed.

On September 13, 2007, during the conference, a meeting was held to explain the basic aims and objectives of AMSA and to formally establish the Association by a vote of national representatives. This inaugural meeting consisted of 60 people representing 28 Sheds from around Australia. The following motion was carried unanimously: "That this meeting of representatives of active Men's Sheds from around Australia move to form the Australian Men's Shed Association Inc.". The meeting formally agreed that the interim committee should remain in place for another year and that an election for a national executive should occur by October 2008. The AMSA committee also confirmed that the 2009 National Men's Shed Conference would be held in Tasmania.

Whilst Ted Donnelly had concentrated on developing AMSA, other members of the national AMSA committee had been attempting to establish associations in their own States (Gary Green in Victoria, John Waters in Tasmania and Bill Johnstone in Western Australia). VMSA in Victoria had already held three meetings and was well on the way to formal Incorporation (achieved by September 2007) but wanted to link in with AMSA. It was agreed that there was merit in having state branches as well as the national organisation. AMSA aimed to be a communications hub where Sheds could share ideas on projects, training, materials, local events, committee business and other relevant information. Whilst this would partly be via the website, it was obvious that a regular newsletter was required. David Helmers from the Windale Shed offered to organise this, producing the first *AMSA Newsletter* in October 2007.

In the first half of 2008 the administration of records, database, website, printing and sending out manuals and answering general queries was, incredibly, still being carried out by Ted Donnelly working voluntarily from home. A number of organisations were approached for funding AMSA, but the interest that had been shown before the Manly Conference evaporated. As a result of a lack of funds, no Committee meetings were held during 2008. An AMSA Constitution was drafted during 2008 to replace the Model Rules that were accepted for the original incorporation. Because the election details had not been resolved it could not be finalised. Discussions were held with insurance companies and quotes obtained for an AMSA scheme but it proved difficult to get the numbers of interested Sheds and this did not progress. To this point all the huge amount of administration and background work for AMSA had been voluntary.

The Manly Conference had decided that the Interim Committee would set up a suitable structure, organise elections and hand over a functioning Association to the newly elected committee. This proved to be very difficult because the Committee members were all heavily involved in other activities including developing and managing their own Men's Sheds and state associations. In addition AMSA had no funds to enable people to get together to discuss and carry out this plan. It was obvious that AMSA could not develop using only voluntary help. For an Association of this complexity, which was growing so rapidly (239 Men's Sheds were listed on the AMSA website by this stage, in mid-2008), to progress quickly and efficiently, funds were required and staff would have to be employed.

'Embedding' into the Shed at Windale

In July 2008 an opportunity arose to set up and staff a national association. Over the previous four years, CentaCare[11] in Newcastle had received funds from Federal Government grants to set up Men's Sheds in their area, and they employed David Helmers to set up the "Shed @ Windale". Since this was successful, Helmers' brief was extended. In July 2008 CentaCare decided to use the remaining funding to cover the employment expenses for David Helmers for a year to properly establish AMSA. This offer was unanimously accepted by the Interim Committee and Helmers joined AMSA as Executive Officer on August 1, 2008.

An AMSA Committee Planning Meeting was held in Canberra on November 10-11, 2008 to discuss the progress of the Association, involving members of the AMSA Working Committee from all States[12]. Because of cost restraints, this was the first meeting that had been held since the Manly conference in 2007. The aim was to plan a future strategy and prepare a presentation for the Federal Government. A draft constitution was discussed, but a major point that required clarification was the legal structure of AMSA.

When AMSA was established it had to be "Incorporated". The obvious and cheapest way to do this was to set up an "Association". This structure specified the number of office bearers and committee members and implied a large bureaucratic structure. Organizing this on a national basis had proved difficult. Advice was sought from a number of legal sources. They recommended that AMSA, being a national body, should be set up as a "Not for Profit Company Limited by Guarantee", and not as an Association. Initially this did not seem to coincide with the will of shedders, but further investigation clarified that this was a way to use the less bureaucratic structure of a company. It was different from a conventional Trading Company that owned capital and earned and distributed profits/dividends.

---

[11] Every Catholic Diocese in Australia in 2015 had a 'CentaCare', the social service arm of the Catholic Church. Also called 'Centacare' and rebranded as CatholicCare in 2011.

[12] The Australian Men's Shed Association, Canberra Meeting Working Document, November 10-11, 2008.

Guarantee Companies are very widespread in Australia. This is the structure used by clubs, peak body sports associations (Cricket Australia), worker's cooperatives, Non-Government organizations (NGOs) and charities (Oxfam). Guarantee Companies do not have share capital and, in the case of AMSA, the shareholders would be the State Associations who would hold one share per State. They would appoint their representatives to the AMSA Board of Directors. The November 2008 meeting gave approval to convert AMSA to the simpler company structure and the Constitution was modified to permit this change.

The Funding Breakthrough with the Australian Government

Following the November 2008 planning meeting, three AMSA delegates met with senior staff at the Canberra offices of the federal Department of Housing, Families Community Services and Indigenous Affairs (FaHCSIA). This was to introduce AMSA and explain its future plans with the aim of seeking future funding from various national government agencies. There had been several previous unsuccessful submissions for funding (including to FaHCSIA and the Department of Health and Ageing: DoHA). Behind the scenes, AMSA was desperately trying to fit 'a square Shed' into a series of 'round government silos'. In David Helmers's words, the challenge was:

> ... to find a government funding stream to fit into an environment (being Government) where there was simply no box for us to fit. Getting government to agree to do so as a collective body was one of AMSA's (and Sheds') greatest achievements, our finest hour.[13]

Meantime, by January 2009 the AMSA office at Windale (near Newcastle in New South Wales) became functional. This facility, together with a dedicated 'freecall' telephone number, greatly increased the quantity of enquiries and calls from Shed members. By 2009 there were over 300 Men's Sheds across Australia registered with AMSA and, with 100 inquiries per week, there was an urgent need to secure ongoing support and funding for AMSA beyond its temporary bases in Lane Cove and Windale.

On March 10, 2009 David Helmers was invited as AMSA representative to a Male Health Policy Roundtable in Canberra. The 28-page AMSA submission was prepared by David Helmers and Ted Donnelly. Together with support for Men's Sheds contained in public submissions to the Senate Hearing on Male Health

---

[13] David Helmers, July 23, 2014.

during early 2009, the submission had a big impact on securing funding for AMSA in 2010. The success of the second AMSA Conference in Hobart on August 24-25, 2009 and the November 2009 launch of AMSA's Group Policy Insurance Scheme, as well as the huge interest in Men's Sheds from the popular press, confirmed that the continuing growth of Sheds far exceeded AMSA's resources. A full-page article in Melbourne's *Sun Herald* in March 2010 [14] headed 'Men's Sheds facing closure' placed further pressure on the federal government to provide financial support. On March 19, 2010 David Helmers was contacted by the Department of Health and Ageing and was involved in a series of subsequent meetings that culminated in AMSA being requested to provide a funding submission.

AMSA's successful *Funding Submission to the Department of Health and Ageing* in April 2010[15] was a 'game changer' for the Men's Shed Movement in Australia. The successful submission anticipated a three-year plan of work commencing in three stages from May 2010. The objective was for AMSA to provide practical support to Men's Sheds as well as deliver health services to Sheds in a project that was later called 'Spanner in the Works'. Stage 1 was about recruitment of staff and revising AMSA's constitution and corporate entity. Stage 2 related to setting up the corporate structure, a risk management program, networks and communications and revision of the Shed Manual. The necessary compromise included an obligation to allocate funds to Sheds in areas of perceived men's health risk. Other health service 'deliverables' were identified including involvement in the Men's Health Week project in 2012.

The Department of Health and Ageing responded belatedly but very positively to this funding submission. The announcement that AMSA would receive this funding was made at the launch of the Australian Male Health Policy on May 7, 2010 by Prime Minister Kevin Rudd at Whittlesea Men's Shed in outer suburban Melbourne. On June 9, 2010 the Department of Health and Ageing offered AMSA a funding agreement to the value of A$3.3 million 'to provide practical on the ground support and assistance to local Men's Sheds and assist AMSA in securing its financial sustainability.'[16]

On June 28, 2010, once AMSA had been registered as a Company Limited by Guarantee, David Helmers and Mel White from AMSA left Catholic Care to begin work for AMSA. Liz McDonald, who had also been doing AMSA work,

---

[14] March 25, 2010, 2.
[15] AMSA, Funding submission to the Department of Health and Ageing, April, 2010.
[16] Department of Health and Ageing, Canberra, letter from Melinda Bromley to David Helmers, June 9, 2010.

continued to work for CatholicCare but transferred to AMSA during 2012. All were still employed by AMSA to 2015, providing much needed continuity at a time of huge growth and change.

The Confusion Created by Mensheds Australia

Mensheds Australia (MSA)[17] was briefly mentioned in an earlier section as being a major irritant to the Men's Shed Movement as it was setting up in 2005-7. The Company has a history that goes back to 2003. One of its Company Directors explained 'how it all started' in a 2006 interview conducted for the NCVER *Men's Sheds in Australia* research:

> We were in the town of Grenfell in New South Wales, doing another job, and we came across this Shed with a whole bunch of cars around, an old railway shed, and someone said, "There's a bit of activity there. We'd better go and look". We were immediately surrounded by eight or nine elderly men with all this enthusiasm and they couldn't wait to ... tell us what they were doing. ... They asked us to do a few things and we agreed that perhaps we will act as a sponsor for them and give them a hand and we can move them along. ... Then as a few months rolled by we said, "Well I think we can put this together", and we started to put [together] all the various aspects that we thought were the [five] pillars of making it work across Australia. So we started a company.[18]

These 'five pillars' that Mensheds Australia subsequently adopted were teased out in the same 2006 research interview as being about men's health, occupational health and safety, community connection, sustainability and an application of business principles to Men's Sheds, specifically through 'economic gardening'. While these five pillars were broadly desirable principles for most Men's Sheds, the first problem was that the Mensheds Australia Company did not invent or own them. Indeed, they were developed by Len Wallace and others and generously shared by the Grenfell Men's Shed.

Amongst these five pillars, the Mensheds Australia Company saw economic gardening as 'their trump card'. These pillars were defined by the Company directors as being about 'growing organisations and businesses 'from the inside out to help that community grow and thrive'. They saw a problem with Men's

---

[17] Mensheds Australia http://www.mensheds.org.au/mens-shed-story, Accessed March 27, 2014.
[18] Barry Golding research interview in Sydney with three MSA Directors, 2006.

Sheds being run by what they described (patronisingly) as 'unreliable older men'. They saw an opportunity for their company strategically 'cornering the Men's Shed market', negotiating directly with the federal government, and bringing in corporate sponsors. As one of the Directors said in a 2006 interview in Sydney for the *Men's Sheds in Australia* research:

> Of course the government says, "You have to have the grassroots support", and we're saying, "If you are waiting for the grassroots support, this will never get off the ground".

Some of this story about the way Mensheds Australia Company and Directors moved in on Grenfell Men's Shed largely for its own purposes, raising issues of intellectual property was discussed from the Grenfell Men's Shed perspective in Chapter 3. A Mensheds Director admitted in 2006 that: "We let Grenfell make a lot of mistakes and in hindsight we are sorry we did. ... We got it wrong." Having had their 'fingers burnt' and with their reputation badly tarnished in the Men's Shed community, the Company turned its back on Grenfell. Mensheds Australia next turned their attention north and invested heavily in a new business venture in Armidale, New South Wales. It was envisaged as a commercial joinery with a Men's Shed attached, which they anticipated would give their Company '... a much bigger critical mass to be able to test our ideas and programs'.

Mensheds Australia since 2006 has undergone a number of changes of ownership and directorship. The Company described itself on its website in 2014 as:

> ... a not-for-profit Australian Public Company, Limited by Guarantee, dedicated to supporting and resourcing men's sheds across Australia. ... MSA formed in 2006 as an organisation to support the early initiatives to establish sheds. The purpose was to help sheds use the experience of other men's sheds and provide access to expertise about the formation, structure and operation of men's sheds. MSA facilitated the formation of new sheds through collating information and providing information to men's sheds.

Aside from not being representative of Men's Shed organizations or cognizant of the grassroots movement, what distinguished MSA from AMSA was the way it placed an emphasis on the commercial function of Men's Sheds and the way it charged for its advice and services. MSA was still tapping into the financial vulnerability of grassroots Sheds by claiming on its website in 2014 that its focus:

... is on building the sustainability of men's sheds. We believe that the sustainable shed will have assured financial resources and that their own commercial activities will be an important element. Men's sheds are a social enterprise that create value and that value should form the basis of assured revenue from those that benefit from shed activities.[19]

Mensheds Australia created its professional website, including the first 'Shed Locator', in October 2007, listing 210 Australian Men's Sheds. While the company used many of the same Shed organisation contact details created via the grassroots community Men's Shed Movement, it has never acknowledged either AMSA or the state Shed associations. Nor has it sought permission from Men's Sheds to be listed. Given that Mensheds Australia had a comprehensive online presence before AMSA, many early and prospective Sheds found the MSA website first, and established links with MSA, not realising that only Company Directors, not member Sheds, controlled and ran the Company. The same thing happened frequently to people and organisations overseas. Sheds with active links to the Company have typically put 'Mensheds' in the organisation title and also made use of the MSA logo (which features a green hammer). It is important to note that while MSA never mentions or acknowledges AMSA, it has purported (by complete omission) to be the only Australian peak Men's Shed body.

In 2012 AMSA were still experiencing what they perceived as unhelpful actions by Mensheds Australia. In letter to the federal Minister for Health and Ageing, Warren Snowden, on 6 February 2012, AMSA complained that Mensheds Australia was continuing 'to create further confusion between the two organisations, capitalising on our efforts to collaborate'. AMSA was until that time required by the Federal Government under its funding contract to work collaboratively and provide support for Sheds registered with MSA. Some of the words of The Waifs (Australian band's) song *Fourth Floor* seem particularly apt here:

> For every good seed she plants in the soil, there's a dozen bad waiting to grow. To strangle the goodness she's trying to nurture, and kill all the seed that she's sown. Every time you water the garden you also water the weeds ...

Mensheds Australia was creating most confusion with AMSA on-line. When users searched for their 'nearest Menshed' on the MSA website, they were

---

[19] Mensheds Australia http://www.mensheds.org.au/, Accessed March 27, 2014.

looking at Shed organisations that had no associations with MSA and which were generally listed without each Shed's knowledge or consent. The tensions caused within the emerging community-based Men's Sheds Movement in the period between 2006 and 2009, by the way Mensheds Australia played its hand, cannot be overemphasised. It actively bid against AMSA on several occasions with contracts for services to the Australian government and caused public and Shed Movement confusion. It also caused significant angst for Men's Sheds organisations that were buying advice and services that were effectively available elsewhere free. Those most adversely and unfairly affected included the men of the Grenfell Men's Shed, not the least the late Len Wallace.

This contentious role played by 'Mensheds Australia' (MSA) during the development of the Movement in Australia was so divisive it is something some shedders won't even talk about. It goes back to the way MSA effectively colonised the Grenfell Men's Shed for its own purposes, after becoming involved with the Shed via an associated company called *Ironbark Country* in 2004. After paying a third associated company *Front Row Media* for a new website in January 2005, the Grenfell Men's Shed website content and logo was effectively appropriated by MSA, despite the Shed expressing serious concerns about loss of control and intellectual property. Though MSA made a strategic withdrawal from Grenfell in 2006, it was not before it had created great personal and community harm. The Directors moved straight on to set up its new Men's Shed in Armidale on the so-called 'economic gardening' principles around a run down joinery business. This shed in Armidale also struggled despite a significant injection of MSA funds pumped in by the Company, ironically in an attempt to demonstrate its sustainability. Again, many of the men involved as participants in the Armidale Shed were aggrieved and confused.

It was something of a 'David and Goliath' battle at its peak in 2007. Mensheds Australia had much deeper pockets than the recently created VMSA (established in 2005, finally incorporated in 2007) or the fledgling AMSA. As a consequence, for several years AMSA and most state associations in Australia used the only free and legal weapon at their disposal: careful but strong disclaimers on their websites that they had no association with MSA. Barry Golding penned a document[20] presented to FaHCSIA in 2009, around the time that AMSA was negotiating its service contract that summarised the problematic role and status of the Mensheds Australia Company. AMSA's contract from 2009 required it to act in the interests of all Sheds, including the very small number of

---

[20] Summary of Evidence about the Problematic Role and Status of Mensheds Australia Ltd., 2009.

Sheds still in the MSA fold, leading to the removal of the disclaimer. While much of this is now history, MSA continued to represent itself in a similar way. It was only after AMSA said 'enough' to Minister Snowdon in early 2012 that the federal government rewrote the funding agreement to eliminate sections referring to AMSA having to collaborate with MSA. The story, while not pretty, is worth telling, if only as a lesson to subsequent Men's Sheds Movements in other nations.

In 2015 Mensheds Australia continued to position itself as 'Helping sheds find the resources they need'. It still provided a national Shed Locator, though it listed only four Sheds as 'Our Sheds' in its website: Airds Bradbury Menshed (included later as a case study in Chapter 6), as well as two Sheds in Aradale (Western Australia) and its joinery business in Armidale, mentioned above, in northern New South Wales.

The Difficulties, Achievements and Tensions in Australia to 2015

There have been many important achievements, difficulties, tensions and outcomes in Australia in the past five years. These include the increasing coordination of Men's Sheds, formalisation of national, state and cluster bodies, funding of Sheds from multiple sources and increasingly diverse research outputs. There has also been increased internationalism of the Movement in the wake of the 2009 (Hobart, Tasmania), 2011 (Brisbane, Queensland) and 2013 (Ballarat, Victoria) AMSA conferences and also as a consequence of several national conferences in the UK, New Zealand and Ireland.

David Helmers, CEO of AMSA, was asked to reflect on the difficulties, achievements and tensions as perceived by AMSA to February 2015. His extended response is as follows.

> The Australian Male Health policy was launched in May 2010 at Whittlesea Men's Shed noting the importance of the role Men's Sheds play in preventative health. At this launch the then Prime Minister, Kevin Rudd, announced, as part of the policy, that funding would be provided to the Australian Men's Shed Association to provide practical support for Men's Sheds. At this time there were approximately 350 Men's Sheds in Australia and a small handful starting to develop in other countries. By January 2015 there were 916 men's sheds open and registered nationally with the AMSA and an estimated 400 plus open and operating in many other countries all of which have replicated the Australian Men's Shed model. The history of the Men's Shed Movement

is now in the realm of the academics and researchers to publish but what had started organically in a few isolated pockets of our nation has now grown into a world recognised and highly effective initiative.

From the outset, amongst the dust and the tools, Men's Sheds have been providing men with a safe, male friendly environment for men to come together and have a meaningful purpose, to share experiences and sometimes share their problems. Most importantly Sheds are providing men with a place of belonging, a place they have ownership of well after they have left the workplace. Sheds have encouraged a strong element of friendship with new mates and a strong focus on supporting their respective communities. It is somewhat harder to describe what a Men's Shed achieves than what one is. Men's Sheds are recognised as a male health initiative by preventing social isolation but they are also an important part of community services. Some are special interest and social groups; some could be described as hobby clubs. Some, such as the 'Shed Online', exist in a virtual world. The common denominator is that they all involve men and are filling a void for many who find themselves no longer engaged in the social culture of the workplace.

The AMSA acknowledges and is extremely proud of the remarkable work being undertaken in Men's Sheds across the country. Sheds are making such valuable contributions to their communities and are changing lives. We encourage all Sheds to continue to highlight these contributions that Men's Sheds are making within their community to their elected Federal Parliamentary representatives. There is an important need for continued government support, as the overall return far exceeds current government contributions.

The AMSA was formed in 2007 with the aim of providing information and support to Men's Sheds. Since the implementation of our first funding Service Agreement with the Commonwealth in 2010 we have seen a dramatic rise in the number of Sheds developing. This, however, has come with its own challenges from an organisational perspective. The amount of resources available to deliver such services continues to diminish, despite the increasing numbers of inquiries and requests that go along with such growth. As Shed numbers have grown our funding has remained constant.

From a Shed organization perspective there emerges the issues of sustainability. Financial viability and administration/operational matters are among the many challenges that are constantly facing Sheds. There are also issues as to what exactly constitutes a 'Men's Shed'. This is constantly an issue for Sheds seeking funding in a very competitive and limited marketplace. After lengthy debate, in 2014 AMSA introduced membership fees for all AMSA registered Sheds and enhanced the basic criteria for registration in an effort to validate the numbers of Sheds registered. As the AMSA has grown so has our credibility including our membership in being recognised as a true Men's Shed. It is now our responsibility to maintain this credibility.

To early 2015 the AMSA escaped the federal government's budgetary cutbacks and received a new service agreement for a further two years (with marginally less funding than in previous agreements). The AMSA continues to make application for further funds to provide adequate service to member Sheds. All to date have proven unsuccessful. It is also worth bearing in mind that such applications are an expensive process on their own. Besides the issue of financial resources, AMSA faces many more challenges. As AMSA grows it will require continual review of our structure and operations while remaining true to our core objectives and our grassroots heritage. The word "Association" is a challenge in itself. It gives funding bodies the impression that like all Associations, AMSA is a member-funded organisation. Currently AMSA relies on the government for 90 per cent of our operational budget. A move to a member-funded system would flow directly through to Sheds and in turn to individual members resulting in a counterproductive scenario of men not being able to afford to go to the Shed. As Men's Sheds grow in prominence and numbers a focus is required on protecting the brands of "AMSA" and "Men's Sheds" to maintain our good name and reputation. Whatever challenges lie ahead for AMSA and Men's Sheds, both will continue to grow for the foreseeable future, providing meaningful purposes for all men involved.

Chapters 2 to 4 have summarised the first 15 years of Men's Sheds, from some of the earliest Shed experiments in South Australia in 1993, and the first Men's Sheds by mid-1998. They have charted the progressive development of Men's Sheds and associations across all Australian states as well as nationally. Up to 2007, all of the Men's Shed development had been in Australia. By 2008 'the secret was out' internationally, encouraged by the dissemination of information and people through attendance at conferences, inter-country visits, the internet and research. Chapter 5 that follows provides a history of quite recent but very rapid Men's Shed development in Ireland, the UK and New Zealand, where 'the ground' proved particularly fertile for Men's Sheds to spread, by making culturally appropriate but subtle changes to the model established by the early Australian Men's Shed Movement.

CHAPTER 5

The Men's Shed Movements in Ireland, the UK, New Zealand and Elsewhere

Chapter 5 examines way that Men's Sheds started and proliferated in Ireland, the UK, New Zealand and elsewhere after 2008. While the Australian Men's Shed model had been fairly well documented by this time, this chapter emphasises how the Men's Shed Movement took hold somewhat differently in each country. In summary, it shows that how Sheds develop and translate to a new national setting depends on a range of factors. It includes who 'picks up' the idea, when and where. It also depends on the extent to which the Men's Shed model is perceived as 'bottom-up' or 'top-down', and particularly on the national, regional, cultural, economic and demographic context for its translation.

The speed and extent of the Men's Shed 'explosion' across the Island of Ireland, documented first in this chapter, is remarkable. It was driven by the skills in translation of a dedicated community entrepreneur as well as by the exceptionally fertile cultural ground in Ireland post the Global Financial Crisis. Men's Shed development in the UK was considerable slower, in part caused by an early 'top-down' attempt at translation by Age UK and by a lack of government support for the sector to 2015. This UK account includes the story of parallel grassroots Shed innovation and rapid spread, firstly in England, but very recently also in Wales and Scotland. The growth of the New Zealand Men's Shed Movement has, by contrast been relatively slow but steady, taking account of the critically important and quite different cultural and national accommodation, including with Maori people in Aotearoa. The final part of the Chapter looks at the very early development of Men's Sheds in Canada, Demark and Sweden.

MEN'S SHEDS IN IRELAND

This section provides a history of Men's Sheds in the Island of Ireland (Northern Ireland and the Republic of Ireland), referred to for simplicity as Ireland (and Irish). The history starts from the first discussions at Dublin airport in 2008 and the first Men's Shed opening in Tipperary Town in August 2009. There were at least two hundred Men's Sheds open across Ireland only five years later. The section highlights includes the important role since played by John Evoy, to

February 2015 as the CEO of the IMSA (Irish Men's Sheds Association), in the innovative but accurate interpretation of the Australian concept to a quite different demographic on the opposite side of the globe.

The Beginnings in Ireland

The speed of development of Men's Sheds across the whole Island of Ireland has been phenomenal; from one Shed in August 2009, to 244 less than six years later to February 2015. While the Men's Shed model in Australia provided a clear and inspirational model to translate in an Irish context, the cultural and social acceptance in Ireland is particularly noteworthy. As with many social movements, the Irish Men's Shed Movement Ireland began not with one specific event, but with a number of circumstances in tandem. The story of Men's Sheds in Ireland has many parts, and has involved many organisations and people, some of which are described below.

In June 2008, Barry Golding and Mike Brown, both from the University of Ballarat (Victoria, Australia), presented a seminar at Queens University Belfast, in Northern Ireland about men's learning and Men's Sheds in Australia. Golding and Brown's presentation[1] was the first public event discussing Men's Sheds to take place in Ireland.

Soon after, Barry Golding was invited to meet at Dublin Airport with a group of community development workers and adult and community education practitioners from New Ross, County Wexford in the Republic of Ireland. The group of service providers and community representatives included John Evoy (then from County Wexford VEC: Vocational Education Committee) and Conor Dervan, of New Ross Community Development Project, who was the original 'driver' for the Men's Shed idea locally. This group were actively exploring the Men's Shed concept for translation to their local context, as a means of involving men in community learning. Golding's expertise was sought by this group, which included several members who would eventually go on to set up the Irish Men's Sheds Forum.

This conversation at Dublin Airport in June 1998 occurred at a time when the community development and adult and community education sectors were beginning to acknowledge the relative dearth of men within community learning environments. For example, in 2009, AONTAS (the National Adult Learning Organisation in the Republic of Ireland) observed that;

---

[1] http://www.qub.ac.uk/schools/SchoolofEducation/Events/EventsArchive/Events2008/, Accessed, February 16, 2014.

> ... in Ireland men are under-represented in the Adult and Community
> Education sector generally. ... A 2008 report emphasises the fact that the
> overall participation of men in adult and continuing education remains
> low in Ireland.[2]

The impact of the severe and sudden post-2008 economic downturn in Ireland as
part of the broader international financial crisis of 2007-8 resulted in an increased
focus on unemployment and men within the adult learning sector, but also among
community organisations. New ways were being sought to involve men whose
lives had been drastically and recently changed by unemployment and consequent
social isolation. In 2008 Dr Ted Fleming (then Head of Department, Adult
Education, National University of Ireland, Maynooth) contributed an article to the
Autumn 2008 edition of *Explore*, published by AONTAS, the Irish national adult
learning organisation, noting that 'from Australia comes the exciting possibility
known as 'Men's Shed' which is a unique way of engaging men in community
education ...'[3].

   The National Irish Men's Health Policy 2008-2013 provides insights into the
dialogue that was taking place concerning Men's Sheds. This 2008 policy
acknowledged that Men's Sheds as developed in Australia were one solution for
improving men's health and wellbeing. The Irish policy was the first statutory
men's health policy in the world, and also the first to actually describe Men's
Sheds. It identified

> ... 'Men's Sheds' organisations in southern Australia [as] another good
> example of community-based health promotion targeting men. ...
> Through the provision of 'mateship' and a sense of belonging through
> positive and therapeutic informal activities, 'Men's Sheds' achieve
> outcomes of positive health, happiness and well-being for those men
> who participate, as well as for their partners, families and communities.[4]

At this policy level, Men's Sheds from Australia were being noticed for what the
model could potentially do for men's health, wellbeing and learning across
Ireland. At a community level, similar things were happening. By August 2009,

---

[2] AONTAS, June 2009, 'BTEI - Best Practice Guidelines for Increasing Men's
Participation in BTEI'.
[3] Ted Fleming, 'From No Man's Land to Men's Sheds', *Explore*. 9. Dublin: AONTAS,
2008.
[4] Department of Health and Children, *National Men's Health Policy*. Dublin: Department
of Health and Children, 2008.

the first Men's Shed in Ireland was being set up in Tipperary Town at the Knockanrawley Resource Centre, inspired directly by the experience of Men's Sheds in Australia[5].

The Irish Men's Shed Movement from 2010

The Men's Shed Movement across the Island of Ireland effectively emerged with the founding of the Irish Men's Sheds Forum in 2010. John Evoy had participated and presented at the 3rd National Men's Shed Conference[6] in Hobart, Tasmania, Australia in August 2009 as Co-ordinator of the ENGAGE Programme. During this visit to Australia, Evoy visited several Men's Sheds in Victoria and New South Wales and found them to be truly inspiring. On his return to Ireland Evoy and several community activists founded the Irish Men's Sheds Forum, formally launched at the Moynalty Threshing Museum Men's Shed, Kells, County Meath in Ireland in October 2010. The Forum aimed to become a mechanism for the flow of information to support the development of Men's Sheds across Ireland.

Barry Golding was back in Ireland to speak at the launch, by which time there were already seven Men's Sheds in existence across Ireland[7]. The Forum became active in promoting Men's Sheds at a national level, and supporting communities at a local level to set up new Men's Sheds. A 2010 excerpt from the website of the Men's Health Forum in Ireland gives an account of the ethos and vision of the Forum group. It included an explicit focus on maintaining the core values of Men's Sheds as modelled in Australia.

> A "Men's Shed" is any community-based, non-commercial organisation which is open to all men, and provides a safe, friendly and inclusive environment where men are able to gather and/or work on meaningful projects at their own pace, in their own time, and in the company of other men. The primary objective is to advance the health and well-being of participants. The Irish Men's Shed Forum is a small, voluntary group, who share enthusiasm for the development of Community Men's Sheds in Ireland. The Forum is supported by the Australian Men's Shed Association whose vision and work the Irish Forum wishes to adapt to

---

[5] 'Men's Shed in Tipperary Town,' *The Nationalist*, August 6, 2009.
[6] http://www.mensshed.org/SiteFiles/mensshed2011org/Shed_Development_-_Ireland.pdf, Accessed March 20, 2014.
[7]
http://www.mensshed.org/sitefiles/mensshed2011org/Australian_Mens_Shed_Association_Newsletter_October_2010.pdf, Accessed March 20, 2014.

our local situation. It is hoped that, eventually, the Forum will facilitate the growth of a Men's Sheds Organisation, which will serve the whole Island of Ireland. [8]

Very quickly, enthusiasm for the development of Men's Sheds in Irish communities was apparent. Eighty-five men attended the Shed Forum meeting that followed in Tipperary Men's Shed on December 7, 2010. In January 2011, The Irish Men's Sheds Association (IMSA) was founded as a company limited by guarantee, to replace the Irish Men's Sheds Forum and ensure a sustainable structure for the development of Men's Sheds in Ireland. IMSA was founded as a member-based national organisation with the purpose of supporting the development and sustainability of Men's Sheds across the Island of Ireland, including the Republic of Ireland and Northern Ireland,

> ... sharing information freely between sheds, and supporting communities and organisations wishing to establish a shed. IMSA works towards a future where all men have the opportunity to improve and maintain their health and well-being by participating in a men's shed. [9]

2011 was a significant inaugural year for IMSA. With early funding from the Arthur Guinness Awards, John Evoy was at the helm as CEO of IMSA, and in a position to begin to bring the Men's Sheds Movement together, assisted by communities and Men's Sheds across Ireland. In this first year, IMSA supported the development of 40 Men's Sheds. As CEO, Evoy worked hard to promote the core ethos and values of Irish Men's Sheds, as well as their wellbeing benefits, particularly in the context of growing unemployment and a climate of recession increasingly impacting on men across Ireland.

The 'Men's Sheds' model promoted by IMSA became a key feature of dialogue and action at every level where men's health and wellbeing was a concern; individual, community, social and political. In 2011, a significant report of the Institute of Public Health, set up to promote cooperation for public health between the Republic of Ireland and Northern Ireland, suggested that 'strong causal links exist between unemployment, recession and deteriorating economic

---

[8] http://menssheds.ie/2010/11/30/irish-mens-sheds-forum-meeting-tuesday-7th-december-at-tipperary-mens-shed/, Accessed March 20, 2014.
[9] Irish Men's Sheds Association, Memorandum and Articles of Association, 2011.

circumstances; and the health and wellbeing of men in Northern Ireland and the Republic of Ireland.[10]

Positive Public Reaction from across Ireland

As Men's Sheds began to develop across the Island of Ireland, the wider public in turn responded positively, as illustrated by the five quotes from 2011-2 below, all from Irish sources.

June 2011: Institute of Public Health

Successful Australian initiatives where the old model of men's working clubs was adopted to what were called 'men's sheds'. Key here was the facility developed whereby older men could communicate with younger men about health issues. An organisation has been recently established in Ireland to promote the men's shed concept.[11]

February 2012: Fianna Fáil Policy Paper

There is a particular issue for older men in responding to social isolation as in general they have less inclination to develop social networks and share their feelings as compared with women. The Irish Men's Sheds Movement which encourages men to use their skills in a community social setting is one such commendable programme. Fianna Fáil will give specific recognition and support to these age friendly initiatives as their benefits include reducing social isolation.[12]

February 2012: Aware

Did you know that communities across Ireland are setting up Men's Sheds – places where men can socialise, network, make friends and share skills? Men's Sheds aim to recreate the atmosphere of "real life" sheds – safe spaces where men can feel confident to discuss and exchange information. We all know that men are less likely to talk about

---

[10] Institute of Public Health, *Facing the Challenge. The Impact of Recession and Unemployment on Men's Health in Ireland*, June 2011.
[11] Institute of Public Health, 2011, as above.
[12] Mary White, *Active Ageing and Quality Caring: A Policy Paper to Promote the Human Potential and Human Rights of our Older Irish Citizens*, A Fianna Fáil Policy Paper, February, 2012.

their problems or feelings than women, which can aggravate problems with mental health. The Men's Shed Movement, which originated in Australia, wants to help men to reach out to other men and become valued and valuable members of their community.[13]

March 2012: Manager, Kerry Mental Health

Men's Sheds provide an ideal environment for the promoting and fostering of positive mental health leading to an improvement in one's overall health and wellbeing. This can be done through the provision of mental health information leaflets and literature within the shed itself or through talks on the topic delivered by guest speakers. More importantly, the shed provides an opportunity for men to socially interact and integrate with other men, encourage conversation and share problems, learn and develop new skills, enhance self esteem and be occupied. These are key factors, which contribute to positive mental health leading to a greater level of overall health and wellbeing.[14]

July 2012: Family Resource Centres

At the outset of the recession in 2008, Family Resource Centres were heavily involved in supporting jobseekers with CV preparation and information about welfare entitlements. ... However, the nature of people's engagement with us has shifted. While there is still a demand for jobseeker support, many people are now looking to us for ways to connect with their community. In particular, people are seeking to be involved in initiatives such as men's sheds and support groups for people in long-term unemployment or with mental health issues.[15]

THE ROLE OF THE IRISH MEN'S SHEDS ASSOCIATION (IMSA)

There has been significant and steady growth each year in the number of Men's Sheds forming across both Northern Ireland and the Republic of Ireland. A majority of Sheds in both Irish jurisdictions have been set-up by community

---

[13] https://depressionaware.wordpress.com/tag/mens-sheds/, Accessed July 12, 2014.
[14] http://menssheds.ie/2012/03/31/men%E2%80%99s-sheds-and-positive-mental-health/, Accessed July 12, 2014.
[15] 'Family Resource Centres Report Increased Demand for Services', Press Release, July 11, 2012, http://www.familyresource.ie/documents/1342026905.pdf, Accessed July 12, 2014.

members since the first Irish Shed opened in August 2009. In the earliest days of the Shed Movement in Ireland, the setting-up of Men's Sheds was largely the domain of service providers in partnership with local communities. It was only after Sheds became established and national dialogue became more prominent that groups of men began to see and believe that they could do it for themselves.

The Irish Men's Sheds Association (IMSA) has played a vital role in the development of Men's Sheds in Ireland, together with communities and service providers[16]. In 2013 IMSA and John Evoy received a major boost by winning a Social Entrepreneurs Ireland (SEI) Impact award, which led to the Irish Shed sector's biggest financial investment to date. SEI's involvement also brought high levels of positive media attention that helped to initiate many new Men's Sheds. In September 2014, IMSA was allocated funding from POBAL (a not-for-profit company with charitable status that manages programmes on behalf of the Irish Government and the EU) under the Support for National Organisations fund. In addition, both the National Office for Suicide Prevention and the Health Service Executive (HSE) were providing small-scale funding to IMSA.

What distinguishes many Irish Sheds and communities along the Irish Republic – Northern Ireland border as well as in Northern Ireland is the way Sheds have been involved, albeit in a low key way, in post-Troubles, cross-community relationship building. The Irish Men's Sheds Association website summarised their role and rationale, below, to March 2014.

> The Irish Men's Sheds Association was set up in January 2011 with the purpose of supporting the development and sustainability of Men's Sheds on the Island of Ireland. ... IMSA is a member-based organisation formed to share information freely between Sheds and support communities and organisations wishing to establish a Shed. The IMSA as a national organisation represents the collective issues of Men's Sheds in Ireland. The Irish Men's Shed Association will work towards a future where all men have the opportunity to improve and maintain their health and well being by participating in a community Men's Shed. We are a grassroots organisation and we base our actions directly as a response to the needs, as expressed by the Men of the Sheds, so that we can make it is as easy as possible for any group of men to set up and run a Men's Shed.

---

[16] Lucia Carragher, *Men's Sheds in Ireland: Learning Through Community Contexts*, 2013.

ORIGIN AND DEVELOPMENT OF MEN'S SHEDS IN THE UK

This section provides a brief history of Men's Sheds in the rest of the UK (England, Scotland and Wales), from the first discussions with NIACE in England in 2007. The first Shed opened in England in early 2009. Six years later, by late 2014, there were close to 100 Men's Sheds open across many parts of England, Scotland, Wales and Northern Ireland[17]. Northern Ireland, though part of the UK, is only referred to briefly in this section as the Men's Sheds there to early 2015 had actively networked across the border with the independent Republic of Ireland. The early history of early Northern Ireland Sheds is included in the first section of this Chapter, entitled 'Men's Sheds in Ireland'. This section includes an outline of the early role played in England by both the parent and local organisations of Age Concern and Age UK in developing and promoting 'Men in Sheds'. It also documents the parallel, rapid growth of grassroots Men's Sheds, firstly across parts of England. It also highlights the very recent and rapid uptake of Men's Sheds in Scotland and Wales, the formation of the UK and Welsh Men's Sheds Associations in 2013 and the emergence of the Scottish Men's Sheds Association in 2015.

The Role of Age Concern (Age UK)

Age Concern in the United Kingdom (which later renamed itself 'Age UK') described itself on its website in 2014 as the 'country's largest charity dedicated to helping everyone make the most out of life'. It commissioned a report, published in January 2007 called *Working with Older Men: Improving Age Concern's Services*[18], based on the findings from a research seminar held on September 26, 2006. The report concluded that '… addressing the specific needs of older men has been a somewhat neglected area of Age Concern's practice, particularly in terms of outreach and service development'[19]. It acknowledged that the majority of Age Concern's service users … tend to be older women', and suggested that there was a need 'to develop more clearly gendered approaches to outreach, particularly with older men who are socially isolated'[20].

---

[17] While the UK Men's Sheds Association lists the Northern Ireland Sheds, these same sheds are included in the Irish Men's Sheds Association list, as a deliberate move towards an 'Island or Ireland' approach to managing and developing sheds for men in Ireland as part of the peace and reconciliation process after centuries of conflict.
[18] Age Concern, *Working with Older Men: Improving Age Concern's Services*, Report of a Research into Practice Seminar, September 26, 2006. London: Age Concern, England.
[19] As above, 25.
[20] As above, 25.

The 2007 report referred back to Sandy Ruxton's 2006 report for Age Concern on *Working with Older Men: A Review of Age Concern Services.*[21] Men's Sheds were not mentioned in either report. Ruxton's message to service providers began very cautiously. It noted that developing 'activities that are attractive to older men ... posed the danger in reinforcing stereotypically 'gendered' activities'. However it also acknowledged that:

> Although men-only groups are not attractive to all men, they have a place in a menu of options. For some men they provide vital encouragement, support and friendship in a safe environment. Having the space and autonomy to initiate their own activities is crucially important for some older men.[22]

Ruxton concluded that, for Age UK, 'having a strategy mattered more than what the strategy was.'"

Given the thinking above, it is unsurprising that England, through Age Concern, discovered Men's Sheds and, by late 2008 had found some funds to create a fully funded national pilot 'Men in Sheds' project by 2009, with the first 'pilot' Sheds open by 2010. This essentially 'top-down', initiative discussed in more detail later, while well intentioned, was not the only or ideal way to start a new Men's Shed Movement in the UK. It is important to note that at this time Age Concern nationally had sought minimal advice or assistance from the already rapidly growing Australian Men's Shed Movement, or from the recently formed national association in Australia, AMSA. Indeed there is evidence, from some Men in Sheds established as part of the Age Concern initiative, that some the ideas and logos used by Age UK and some of its affiliated Sheds were derived from Mensheds Australia.

Age UK was approached numerous times in 2014 during the writing of this book to contribute documents and commentary about their 2009-10 Men in Sheds project, but supplied no documents, information or advice. In early 2015, almost a year later, a Senior Media Officer for Age UK emailed to apologise for the delay, noting that:

---

[21] Sandy Ruxton, *Working with Older Men: A Review of Age Concern Services*. London: Age Concern, 2006.
[22] As above, 3.

Age UK no longer runs the Men In Sheds scheme on a national level however, that this is run by some of our partners at a local level.[23] Therefore it would be best for you to contact one of the below local Age UKs. Just to be clear these fall under the Age UK umbrella but operate as individual charities with their own budgets and activity, hence why they will be best placed to help you on this occasion to help get the story right.[24]

Nevertheless, in 2015 Age UK still featured its 'innovative Men in Sheds project' on its website, listing Sheds in Kendal, Blidworth and South London as three Sheds that 'were managed by Age UK', with the added note that 'Age UK no longer runs the Men in Sheds project at a national level. However a number of our partners run it at a local level.'[25]

Men in Sheds Hartford

Cheshire, the English County south of both Liverpool and Manchester, was the site of the earliest 'on the ground' Men's Shed activity in England, independently of and just preceding the Age Concern initiative. An awareness of the Australian Men's Shed Movement had been growing in the UK including through annual academic adult education presentations about Men's Sheds in several parts of the UK including visits to NIACE[26] in Leicester by Barry Golding from 2005. The first proposal to actually create a Shed came from Malcolm Bird in Cheshire. Bird had been a technical assistant in schools and felt that Men's Sheds would be assets for the elderly in his area. A proposal was made to a charity, Age Concern Cheshire, one of many affiliated organisations that formed the then main charity for older people in England. While 'Age Concern' is now known as 'Age UK' nationally, not all affiliated organizations followed suit.

Dr Neil Bruce, a Shed expert then visiting from New Zealand, interviewed Malcolm Bird at Men in Sheds Hartford in rented industrial premises in the suburb of Hartford, on the outskirts of the Chester very close to the Welsh border, in late 2009. Bruce recorded that Bird:

---

[23] http://www.ageuk.org.uk/professional-resources-home/services-and-practice/health-and-wellbeing/men-in-sheds, Accessed January 15, 2015.

[24] Hannah Barker-Green (Age UK Senior Media Officer), January 9, 2015.

[25] http://www.ageuk.org.uk/professional-resources-home/services-and-practice/health-and-wellbeing/men-in-sheds/, Accessed January 8, 2015.

[26] NIACE: National Institute of Adult and Continuing Education.

... had the time and skills to develop the project further and after a period of discussion, Age Concern were prepared to give the idea a go. Grants were approved of £10,000 a year to employ a Coordinator, £5,000 to cover consumables such as heating, lighting and rent and a further £10,000 as a setup grant to purchase plant tools; most of the tools were of a portable nature to minimise the danger.

Malcolm Bird was appointed as Coodinator. 'Men in Sheds' opened in Hartford (just west of Chester) two days a week in mid-2009. Neil Bruce recorded after his visit that:

> While no charge was made to use [the Men in Sheds] workshop, a donation was expected for tea/coffee. Typically there was a merry mix of personal, community and fundraising projects such as bird box construction. For community projects there was a charge for materials and bit also for time that went back to the shed. Projects were aimed to generate funds for the shed. A donated pile of wood was used to build chicken coops. They had also encouraged two members to get their training certificate for testing electrical goods ... which could then be sold back to the public for further shed funds. The building they leased in an industrial complex with other Age Concern programmes had two offices on a mezzanine floor, one the electrical testing room and the other the office of the supervisor. ... One shed member, a former wood turner ... could no longer turn wood, so he was now teaching other men. Malcolm's office had a fine collection of his handiwork ... It was therapeutic for him to pass on his skills and knowledge to others in the shed, members in turn were reciprocally gaining new skills from him.

While the Age Concern Cheshire 'Men in Sheds' project in Hartford preceded the Age Concern national pilot, by first opening in January 2009, it had, by later the same year, received Age Concern funding for its existing Shed from the national pilot. A separate organization, Age Concern East Cheshire also put a Shed 'on the ground' in Macclesfield (40 minutes drive east of Hartford) in September 2010. As a postscript, to early 2015 Age UK Cheshire had four 'Men in Sheds' open: in Northwich, Ellesmere Port and Crewe, as well as its original Shed in Hartford[27].

---

[27] http://www.ageuk.org.uk/cheshire/our-services/every-man-needs-a-shed, Accessed January 8, 2015.

The Age Concern Men in Sheds Pilot

The project launch of the Age Concern/UK Men in Sheds pilot took place on January 30, 2009. It was conducted by Sir Trevor Baylis, the inventor (in 1992) of the 'wind-up radio'. Aside from funding the already established Hartford Shed, the £493,000 from the UK Lottery pilot, via the 'Jules Thorn' Age Concern grant, enabled the start up of Men in Sheds pilot programs in Kendal (South Lakes District, Cumbria), Blidworth (in Nottinghamshire) and Eltham (in London).

By August 2010 an Age UK publication called *Age UK Promoting Mental Health and Well-being in Later Life: A Guide for Commissioners of Older Peoples,* outlined their Men in Sheds pilot program. By then the pilot included three new sheds as well as the Age Concern Cheshire shed in Hartford. The program was based on:

> ... an Australian model – Australian Men's Shed Association' (AMSA) – 'Men in Sheds' is the model for three similar Age UK/Age Concern projects across the country. It is a very simple concept and offers something different – all men over the age of 55 are welcome. It was launched in January 2009 as a 'social men's project' and is not promoted as a mental health project (although people with mental health problems do attend). ... Attendees are called 'learners' and are part of Age Concern Cheshire's large education department. There are many add-on service opportunities and evidence is being collected on the outcomes of the project and the potential health savings. *What benefits and outcomes does the service provide?* [It] offers access to information and advice; promotes healthy living; tackles loneliness; provides opportunities to make friends.[28]

The publication emphasised that The Age UK Men in Sheds pilot project was designed as:

> ... a two year initiative, funded by the Sir Jules Thorn Trust ... [which] Age UK is developing, piloting and evaluating ... in three locations. We are funding three contrasting projects to explore how the model can

---

[28] *Promoting Mental Health and Well-being in Later Life: A Guide for Commissioners of Older People's Services.* London: Age UK, http://www.ageuk.org.uk/Documents/EN-GB/For-professionals/Care/Mental%20Health%20and%20Wellbeing%20in%20later%20life_pro.pdf?dtrk=true, Accessed March 27, 2014.

work (such as rural and urban), with specific groups such as BME [Black and Minority Ethnic], elders, older men with mental health problems) and involving different activities (such as repair restoration, manufacture, hobbies). The three organisations we are partners with to deliver the project are Age Concern Nottingham and Nottinghamshire, Age Concern Greenwich and Age UK South Lakeland.[29]

The Kendal (South Lakes) Shed opened in June 2010, followed by Eltham in the south-east London in October 2010, and in Blidworth, a rural location near Nottingham, during November 2010. Each of these 'pilot' Sheds was fully funded, including a full-time paid coordinator on a service-provider basis. In two cases industrial sheds were leased at commercial rates. The shedders were regarded as their clients, as are all other Age UK service users, and generously had their travel to the Shed subsidised. The initial model did not set out to empower the men to self-manage: it simply planned to run as long as the pilot funding was available.

Two years later, at the end of the grant period, the South Lakes Shed faced a problem (and solution) familiar to other Sheds well-funded only in their start-up phase. The South Lakes Shed Coordinator, Claire Park, recalled in August 2014 that, since:

> ... the funding was coming to an end and no continuation funding was available, we consulted with the 70 shed members on what the future could look like. The shed members suggested becoming volunteer-led, and eight shed members volunteered to form a shed liaison committee to work with the management team at Age UK South Lakeland. Two years later, we have a hugely successful, volunteer-led shed that has also started to bring in their own income, and have extended their work into a number of community projects including some intergenerational projects with local primary schools.

The funding for these pilot Sheds was unusually generous. It guaranteed only their short-term success and was never going to be a sustainable model for a wider national rollout of the pilot. While these pilot Sheds had no Age UK/Concern central directives, being relatively 'top-down' and client oriented, the model did not factor in men's interests and agency over the Shed, which was an essential success criterion in Australian Men's Sheds. Given that the pilot

---

[29] Age UK 'Men in Sheds' information leaflet (undated).

scheme was planned around 2008, any wider roll out became even less likely in the wake of the subsequent Global Financial Crisis.

While Age UK as a central organisation effectively withdrew from the national Men in Sheds 'space', many local Age UKs continued to operate locally run Men in Sheds, with over 20 such Sheds open across England to early 2015. Age UK Lakeland, for example, had:

> ... successfully managed a transition from a grant-dependent model to a volunteer-led Shed which ... continues and thrives thanks to the support of Age UK South Lakes. By early 2015 the South Lakes Shed Liaison Committee had hosted groups from two new Sheds in Scotland, with a researcher seeking to develop a Shed in the Scottish Borders area and another in North Yorkshire. In a further initiative, support was being given to a community organization in Ambleside, Cumbria where a volunteer-led shed was proposed.[30]

Early 'Bottom-Up' Men's Sheds in England

Despite obvious initial shortcomings as a fully funded, top-down model, the four Age UK pilot Men in Sheds in England, developed between 2009 and 2010 as part of the Age UK/Age Concern regional Men's Sheds program and national pilot, greatly increased awareness of wider 'grassroots' Men's Shed possibilities. Those people and organisations already involved in Men's in Sheds in England to 2011 sensed that there must be less expensive other ways to run Sheds that were more bottom-up and sustainable. The story of how the first English Men's Sheds developed and began to network closer to the Australian community Shed model goes back to January 2011.

Mike Jenn, based in London, was planning his retirement. As this account will expand on, the same story leads, relatively seamlessly, to the creation of the UK Men's Sheds Association (UKMSA). On becoming aware of the Shed idea via his son in Sydney, Australia, Mike Jenn visited two Age UK Sheds and three others in Ireland as the guest of John Evoy. Jenn had a strong background in the voluntary sector and decided to try to develop a community Men's Shed where he lived. Additionally, as his field research had only found the staffed Age UK model in Great Britain, he also aimed to show that men could get together and create their own, lower cost and more sustainable Shed. With this in mind, all

---

[30] John Harris, Men in Sheds Kendal, January 20, 2015.

stages of the development of the Shed he subsequently created in Camden Town were recorded as a basis for later advice to others.

The Camden Town Shed Association was formed by Mike Jenn and his friends Robert MacGibbon and Ruth Hawthorn on February 4, 2011. Jenn recalled in 2014 that:

> This small initiating group opted to look for premises so that there was a firm basis for implementing the idea and it opened twelve weeks later (April 26, 2011) in a hired room in a community centre. This quick start was made possible by negotiating an initial rent-free period, on the basis that it enhanced the community centre's profile with its local authority funder, by attracting a 'hard-to-reach' target group. A 20-word 'News in brief' appeal in the local paper brought in almost all the small tools needed, and donated wood allowed us to build the benches. The room was small, at 70 square metres, was self-contained, and had a south-facing wall of glass that opened onto first-floor balconies. We opened two days a week: one day was 'men only' and the other day was mixed to see what that taught us. After a couple of months a £3,000 public grant paid for the next nine months of room hire plus some new equipment. Gifts from philanthropic individuals and two small trust grants enabled the Shed to complete fitting out and to be secure for the following year.

The initial publicity described The Camden Town Shed as 'a development of a typical shed in the garden, where a man pursues practical interests in independence and ease, by adding in better tools and resources and more interaction.' It advertised itself very simply as:

> ... a club offering a workspace where older people can work on practical projects with others. People are welcome from anywhere in London. The space was equipped with tools and materials donated by the public or local businesses. The club is run by the members who decide when they come and what they do. We learn from each other and contribute voluntarily to the club's future. It's free to attend. [31]

The Camden Town Shed was featured in an October 8, 2014 article in *The Guardian*, which described the Shed as being:

---

[31] The Camden Town Shed, http://www.camdentownshed.org, Accessed April 15, 2014.

... Tucked away inside a community centre ... Under low ceilings, planks of wood reels of tape and tiny plastic boxes full of screws sit surrounded by red wood shavings and half sanded fruit bowls, evidence of the week's work. ... [T]he 20 or so people who use the shed, which is open two days a week, roughly fit into two groups – those that come on occasion to get a job done, and those who come regularly for the interaction.[32]

Mike Jenn recalled in 2014 that:

We had anticipated that publicity in the local press would attract many people, but in the event people just trickled in. Fortunately this included a very skilled woodworker from Queensland [in Australia] who became the main voluntary supervisor. The Shed's initiators believe this was the sixth Men's Shed and the first community Shed in Great Britain on the Australian model. The Shed's basic running costs (rent, insurance, consumables) would be £5,000 p.a. compared with the average of £43,000 per year of Age Concern Cheshire's four Sheds.

It is pertinent to acknowledge that not everyone supported the idea of Men's Sheds. A positive response to an earlier article critical of Men's Sheds, posted on *The Guardian* website on October 7, 2012, observed that:

My father regularly goes to one in Australia and they are a wonderful idea. After the awful, flippant –and frankly misandristic[33] [earlier] article [in *The Guardian* by Lucy Mangan] about the Men's Shed movement a couple of years ago, I'm really pleased to see this fine movement being given the positive coverage it deserves.

The Development of UK Men's Sheds Association

Later in the same year that Camden Town Shed started, Age UK and NIACE (the National Institute of Adult and Continuing Education) hosted a conference in Leicester on Men's Sheds. Held on September 29, 2011 and attended by about 150 voluntary and public sector staff from across many parts of the UK, it had the effect of very effectively disseminating the idea. The conference was initiated by

---

[32] 'If I Didn't Come to the Shed, I'd be Alone, Watching TV', *The Guardian*, October 8, 2014 (web version).
[33] Misandry is dislike for men.

Barry Golding, who had been in regular contact with and presented seminars at NIACE in Leicester, about the growth and potential of the Australian Shed Movement since 2005. The following day a small group of mainly Age UK staff and academics plus Mike Jenn met with Australian and Irish Association representatives   (Photograph 26) to make plans for an independent national association of Men's Sheds in the UK.

Photograph 26 Participants in the First Meeting to Discuss a UK Men's Sheds Association, September 30, 2011

It was agreed that a major vehicle for Shed growth would be the creation of a website. Age UK offered some staff time to implement these plans, but were later unable to carry this forward.

In early 2012 Mike Jenn, encouraged by Age UK, set up a website which aimed to promote Men's Sheds and support their development in the UK. It described what a Men's Shed was with some examples. It also gave start up advice, showed a map with contact details and locations of all open or planned Sheds in the UK and provided a means for readers to register their interest in joining or starting one. Individual registration allowed the introduction of people interested in planning or forming new Shed groups. Publishing the contact details of Sheds and groups online enabled enquiries to go directly to Sheds and not via a central point. At that time, twelve Men's Sheds were known to be open in the UK, with others being planned.

In early 2013 after sounding out all known Shed groups, Mike Jenn called a meeting to see whether forming a national association was desirable. Twenty-six people from 17 Sheds and planning groups met in London on March 15, 2013 from all parts of the UK (other than Northern Ireland) and agreed on objectives, a constitution and a Steering Committee. By then 26 Sheds were open across the UK, including in England (17), Scotland (2), Wales (1) and Northern Ireland (6).

The public launch of the UK Men's Sheds Association was held in London on November 6, 2013, attended by 130 shedders and people wanting to find out more about the Men's Shed Movement. Publicity included a 700-word article in *The Guardian* newspaper. Shortly after (December 30, 2013) the Men's Shed Movement was featured on BBC TV's high profile *Breakfast Show*. Throughout 2014 information and advice on starting-up issues were given to anyone seeking them and many new Shed groups were helped to form. Many people registered on the website following the BBC broadcast.

The UK Men's Sheds Association's (UKMSA's) first annual general meeting was held in London on June 23, 2014 with 26 participants from 19 Sheds attending. A management committee of nine was elected. Plans were approved to seek funding to hire freelance staff, to update its website and hold eight regional events to promote and support Men's Shed development. The meeting also welcomed the creation of other national Associations. By that time 87 Sheds were known to be open across the whole of the UK, including seven in Scotland, four in Wales and 20 in Northern Ireland (Northern Ireland Sheds were able to also be members of the Irish Men's Sheds Association). Of the 56 English Sheds, around one third (18) were Age UK-affiliated. In October 2014, following on from the first International Men's Shed Conference in Ireland, the Movement received international coverage when the BBC World Service interviewed David Helmers (AMSA CEO), John Evoy (IMSA CEO) and Mike Jenn (UKMSA's Chair) and several shedders at a conference in Hampshire. In November 2014 the UKMSA started to hire administrative help for 7.5 hours per week. Up to this point it was totally voluntary.

In February 2015 the UKMSA committee could see that UKMSA's role was likely to change due to the emergence in 2014 of other national associations. These included the creation of a Scottish Men's Sheds Association. It also included a Welsh Association teaming up with Hafan Cymru, a domestic violence charity that had raised enough funds to hire four staff to promote and develop Men's Sheds in Wales. In Northern Ireland, a government tender to develop

Men's Sheds there had been won by Groundwork. These developments led the UKMSA committee to decide its focus would shift towards work in England so as to stand on equal footing with the others. While in early 2015, its role was still to be agreed upon with the membership, UKMSA is likely to become a federation of national associations.

Men's Sheds Crymru (Welsh Men's Sheds Association)

The start of thinking about Men's Sheds in Cymru /Wales came through an invitation from Trinity University, Carmarthen, to John Evoy of the Irish Men's Shed Association, to give a talk on the Shed Movement to interested parties in Wales in May 2012. Having run a successful Men's Group for four years, Robert Narayan-Taylor was invited to attend. John Evoy proved to be highly inspirational and after a one-week reciprocal visit to Ireland (paid for by the Irish Men's Sheds Association), Narayan-Taylor put the idea of starting the first Welsh Shed to his Men's Group. The first Welsh Men's Shed was formed six months later in January 2013.

Many of the members of the original Men's Group were drawn from the mental health sector, either as service users or health sector workers, and at least four of the nine Sheds in Wales to February 2015 developed with strong inclusive links to these sectors. This desire to make Welsh Sheds 'all inclusive' posed difficulties in deciding how an all men in an all male environment might cope with any unexpected behavior in the Shed. This difficulty led to the development and adoption in many Welsh Sheds of specific inclusion guidelines addressing the challenges that can arise from unhelpful or difficult behaviour. How the Welsh Sheds deal with these critical areas of inclusion and open door policies will be of interest and value to the Men's Shed Movement more widely.

As an example, the incorporation of "buddy" or mentoring systems for all voluntary officers, necessary if forced through changing mental states to take long periods off to recuperate, is proving very important in some Welsh Sheds. Similarly, guidelines have been developed covering the temporary exclusion of Shed members, albeit with compassion and understanding, if their behaviour requires it. The existing resources from both the Australian and Irish Men's Shed Associations in these areas were a useful starting point but, from the Welsh experience, might need to be clarified and extended.

So what is particularly 'Welsh' about this relatively small cluster of Welsh Sheds and the approaches they have so far adopted? One of the first requests to all new Sheds in Wales was that they consider an early group project, specifically the building of a 'coracle', a traditional Welsh river craft made from green ash and tar. The intention was to have as many Sheds as possible build such a craft for racing in the annual Carmarthen River festival in late July. This 2014 event included two Shed coracles participating. By 2015, the aim was for at least seven.

By August 2014 there were nine quite diverse Men's Sheds across Wales (which has a total population of approximately three million) with three other Sheds in the process of forming, These Sheds were loosely and informally coordinated by Men's Sheds Cymru, which formed on St. David's Day 2013 (March 1). The most important development in 2014 was the awarding of a large Lottery grant to Hafan Cymru on behalf of Men's Sheds Cymru, creating four part-time positions in Hafan Cymru[34], Hafan Cymru is a charitable organisation operating across Wales, providing housing and support services to women, men and their children, particularly those escaping domestic abuse, increasingly helping male partners involved either as perpetrators or victims of abuse. Hafan Cymru acknowledged the potential value of the Men's Shed concept to help men, women and families, and lent its expertise in obtaining the grant. The four part-time positions, including a project manager, two regional coordinators and an administrative position, were funded for three years, the sole object being to establish as many Men's Sheds as possible across the whole of Wales.

Scottish Men's Sheds

There have been many exchanges and visits between Scottish and Australian men's health workers and academics during the past decade, including through Australian Men's Shed Association Patron, John Macdonald, himself a Glaswegian, as well as through its other Patron, Barry Golding. In the last decade Golding presented about Men's Sheds several times in university forums about Men's Sheds in Glasgow, Aberdeen and Stirling. Golding discussed the value of Men's Sheds with a group of men's health workers from Glasgow at the nearby Bridge of Allan in 2007, set up by Jim Leishman, a Glasgow-based Men's Health training and development worker, as a follow up to Leishman's presentation to the Australian Men's Health Conference in Melbourne.

While there was interest, no one in Scotland actually 'ran with the idea' locally until 2009, after Dr Neil Bruce gave a talk in the Wyness Hall in Inverurie, Aberdeenshire. Bruce talked about the Men's Sheds Movement and his involvement in New Zealand as part of his Churchill Fellowship world tour visiting Men's Sheds. It was from this 'spark' that the Westhill Men's Shed (near

---

[34] Hafan Cymru http://www.hafancymru.co.uk/content/public/aboutus/Whoweare.aspx, Accessed August 21, 2014.

Aberdeen) became established as the first Men's Shed in Scotland. A fuller account of its establishment is included later in Chapter 8 as one of four 'early pioneer' UK Sheds. The Westhill Men's Shed played an important role in encouraging the development of an independent Scottish Men's Sheds Association by 2015.

On May 28, 2013 the recently opened Westhill Men's Shed hosted the first Scottish Men's Shed Conference. Called 'Shedding Light on Services for Older Men'[35], the event was organized by Age Scotland in partnership with Aberdeenshire Council (Garioch Community Planning Group). Of the 74 conference attendees, 30 were from Aberdeenshire and 44 were from other parts of Scotland. Participants from Inverurie, Ellon, Perth, Kinross, Moray and Glasgow indicated that they were planning setting up Sheds in their areas.

A meeting to explain and explore Men's Sheds was arranged in Glasgow on February 21, 2014 by Mike Jenn and UKMSA. It was based around a visit to Glasgow by AMSA Patron Barry Golding. Sixty people including some existing and potential shedders attended a Men's Shed forum at the University of Strathclyde in Glasgow, immediately after the launch of the *Men Learning through Life*[36] book. The book's editors included Dr Rob Mark from the University of Strathclyde, who offered a venue for several subsequent Glasgow Men's Shed working group meetings during 2014. The book included a case study of the GalGael project operating since 1997 based in Govan, a former shipbuilding area of Glasgow. GalGael, while not a Men's Shed, was identified in the book as an important Scottish pre-Men's Shed model for the Scottish Shed Movement to also learn from.

Interest grew from other communities around Scotland who attended subsequent meetings of both the Glasgow Area Men's Shed working group at the University of Strathclyde and the Lanarkshire Men's Shed Network. A workshop by the Ecology Centre Men's Shed, Fife was included in the 'Generations Working Together Conference' held in nearby Stirling in March 2014. Many individuals and groups visited the Westhill Shed as well as other new and emerging Sheds around Glasgow and the Scottish Borders. Due to the growing demand and pressure put on Westhill Men's Shed volunteers to help and advise other communities, a position of a dedicated Men's Shed Development Worker for Aberdeenshire was created, through the Council for Voluntary Services,

---

[35] 'Shedding the Light on Services for Older Men',
http://www.otbds.org/assets/uploaded_files/project/Mens_Shed_Conference_report_2013.
pdf, Accessed August 19, 2014.
[36] Barry Golding *et al.* (Eds.), *Men Learning through Life*. Leicester: NIACE, 2014.

Aberdeenshire and funded by the Change Fund for a two year period from September 2013. This position was taken up by Jason Schroeder.

Due to the demand for Shed information from across Scotland in his first nine months, the Aberdeenshire Men's Shed Development Worker set out to create a Scottish grassroots Men's Shed support network. The aim was to create an Association model similar to that used very successfully in Australia and Ireland and to support the emerging needs of Men's Sheds across Scotland. After consultation with John Evoy of the Irish Men's Sheds Association and in consultation with men across Scotland who were setting up their own Sheds, they were invited to join the proposed Scottish Men's Sheds Association Charity. By October 2014 their application had been approved by the Scottish Registrar of Charities (OSCR). In the same month the Scottish Joint Improvement Services (JIT[37]) commissioned research to see why and how the Scottish Men's Sheds Movement had grown so quickly. In January 2015 the Third Sector Interface (TSI) Aberdeenshire Voluntary Action (AVA) agreed to support a three-year national development plan proposed by the Scottish Men's Sheds Association.

As the report of the March 2014 Scottish Conference concluded, 'there appears to be a real hunger to continue and coordinate work on Men's Sheds [in Scotland] so that people can continue to learn from each other'[38]. Two reports in February 2015 summarized the rapid and remarkable developments in Scotland to that date: the *Men's Sheds in the Scottish Borders*[39] report and *Learning about Community Capacity Building from the Spread of Men's Sheds in Scotland*[40]. The latter report confirmed 42 Men's Sheds either in existence or being developed in Scotland to February 2015, 22 of which were in existence, with eight others acquiring premises and twelve others involved in active discussion.

The UK Situation to 2015

The Men's Shed Movement in the UK started gradually but Shed numbers increased rapidly, doubling in a year from 31 Sheds in December 2012 to 63 Sheds in December 2013, and doubling again to 127 Sheds by January 2015. In the three months to February 2015, two new community Men's Sheds opened

---

[37] JIT is a strategic improvement partnership between the Scottish Government, NHS Scotland, COSLA and the Third, Independent and Housing Sectors.

[38] www.ouraberdeenshire.org.uk/images/Garioch/mens_shed_conference_report.pdf, Accessed April 29, 2015.

[39] *Men's Sheds in the Scottish Borders: A Framework for Development*. Volunteer Centre Borders, February 2015.

[40] Myra Duncan, *Learning about Community Capacity Building from the Spread of Men's Sheds in Scotland*. Dunvegan: md consulting, February, 2015.

every week across the UK. The potential of Sheds has been recognized in a wide range of national media. Interest has been shown by public health organisations and charities, and the Government Minister for Health requested a meeting with Shed representatives. By May 2014 Shed development workers were employed in Wales, Scotland and England and moves were afoot to double the number of these workers within the year. Most importantly, the idea has been established in the public consciousness as to what is possible even in times of austerity, meeting both public and charitable objectives. With grassroots demand growing the outlook for the Movement looks very positive in all parts of the UK.

How the Shed Movement in the different parts of the UK beyond England resolves the complex peak body issues was unclear early in 2015. Men's Shed Movements and peak body organisations were forming in different parts of the UK, including Northern Ireland, Scotland and Wales. By late 2014 the Collingham Shed in Nottinghamshire was working with Jeanette Bates at ACRE (Action with Communities in Rural England) and with regional Age UK representatives to scope the opportunities and likely support for a new regional structure in the UK[41], which might include funding for a project development manager based at the ACRE office in Gloucestershire. The draft proposal acknowledged that 'There must remain a willingness to ensure the Shed system is ALWAYS bottom-up!'

ORIGIN AND DEVELOPMENT OF MEN'S SHEDS IN NEW ZEALAND

This section provides a history of the early development of Men's Sheds in New Zealand. Beginning in 2007, with the visit of two New Zealand delegates to the AMSA conference in Manly and the opening of the first 'Bloke's Shed' in the South Island near Dunedin. Men's Sheds subsequently opened in the North Island in Hamilton, Thames and West Franklin in 2008. By 2015 there was a robust New Zealand-wide Shed sector with a national association, MENZSHED NZ, formed in 2013. This section acknowledges the important role in the early development played by Dr Neil Bruce (in 2007 the Director of the Community Learning Centres, Melville and Cambridge High Schools in Hamilton) and by Peter McNeur (Director of Wairarapa REAP). It is also important to acknowledge the early supportive role of ACE Aotearoa[42], the bicultural peak national adult and community education (ACE) body in New Zealand. There has also been support for Men's Shed development from the Christchurch Men's Centre prior

---

[41] Men in Sheds: Outline Proposal, Jeanette Bates, ACRE, December 11, 2014.
[42] *Aotearoa* is the most widely accepted Maori name for the country of New Zealand.

to and particularly in the wake of the devastating September 2010 and February 22, 2012 Christchurch earthquakes.

It is important at the outset to stress that unlike in Australia, individual Men's Sheds in New Zealand up until early 2015 had developed relatively independently of other Sheds. No national guidelines or funding had been available in New Zealand to facilitate a common approach. However the conversations though New Zealand Shed Conferences (the first of which was held in April 2010) provided a forum for a wider exchange of ideas, closer cooperation and liaison with government and non-government organisations about possible support or funding of Men's Sheds in New Zealand.

Neil Bruce and Peter McNeur's account of their enlightening experiences at the 2007 Australian conference in Manly, optimistically headed 'Community Men's Sheds: A New Zealand Goal' was the lead article in the *ACE Aotearoa Newsletter* in December, 2007.[43]

> As observers, we mixed with many Australian shedders over the two days and were given warm welcomes by workshop presenters Drs Barry Golding and Mike Brown. Both had visited New Zealand earlier in the year and had given presentations in 2007 at the NZ Community Learning Association in Schools (CLASS) and Adult and Community Education (ACE) Aotearoa Conferences in March and June respectively. It was at these two conferences many Community Education personnel were introduced to the Australian Men's Shed phenomenon for the first time.

> On arrival [at Manly], Peter and I were impressed by the size of the conference with over 200 registered delegates and held in an imposing 1885 former St Patrick's Seminary building (now the International Institute of Management) high on the hill overlooking Manly Beach, Sydney. We noted the genuine enthusiasm of the shed representatives, the motivational stories from guest speakers and a comprehensive organisation that reflected a movement that was impressively grounded and enthusiastically promoted throughout each state in Australia.

Bruce and McNeur were so enthused that they committed themselves to publicly exploring the possibility of developing:

---

[43]Neil Bruce, *Adult and Community Education Newsletter*, December, 2007, http://www.aceaotearoa.org.nz/sites/aceaotearoa.org.nz/files/0712%20ACE%20Aotearoa %20Newsletter.pdf, Accessed December 11, 2014.

... at least two Community Men's Shed pilots in New Zealand in 2008. Presently we are anxious to make contact with any individuals, groups or organisations, which have men's health and welfare as a part of their brief. Clearly there are processes and procedures that need to be followed in developing any pilot. We know there are resources that are required. Obviously we are keen to ensure that any such shed movement be consistent with the needs of the communities they represent so this requires a comprehensive period of consultation, time commitment and most of all enthusiasm. We are presently developing a data base of interested people, organisations, potential sponsors and shedders, be they individuals keen to be involved with a specific shed or community groups, who can see that a men's shed in their environment would have positive benefits for their local community as a whole.

In June 2008, Barry Golding was supported by ACE Aotearoa to undertake a visit to New Zealand, as a follow up to the 2007 visits referred to above by Neil Bruce, specifically to talk about Men's Sheds. The 2008 visit included presentations and workshops about Men's Sheds to shedders, academics and adult educators in Wellington and Auckland, during which time he visited early Men's Sheds in both Hamilton and Thames. Bernard McMillan, independently corroborating Neil Bruce's account, reported on the development of early Men's Sheds in New Zealand to 2009 as follows:

> The concept of community men's sheds was brought back to New Zealand by Dr Neil Bruce ... and Peter McNeur. ... Starting with a community consultation process including public meetings, and a public launch in early December 2007, the Hamilton Men's shed was opened in March 2008. A men's shed was also established in Thames (Coromandel) in March 2008. A number of other community sheds have been established in Waiuku and Dunedin with plans for others in Newtown (Wellington), Wairarapa, Blenheim and Picton. I understand that other sheds around New Zealand are in various stages of development. There is also an emerging cluster of 11 community men's shed initiatives in Christchurch and rural Canterbury, some of which are likely to begin in 2009. Apart from the sheds in Hamilton and Thames, most others, and particularly those in Canterbury, are still in their

formative stages. In general New Zealand is over 7 years behind the Australian level of growth.[44]

Neil Bruce's first-hand account of the history of Men's Sheds in New Zealand between 2007-10, penned in April 2014, is complementary and comprehensive.

> One of the early articles I wrote, following both Barry Golding's visit to New Zealand [in March 2007] and my attendance at the 2nd AMSA conference in Sydney, spearheaded NZ awareness through the December 2007, *ACE Aotearoa Newsletter*. From this pioneering article others became more informed of shed interest and practice nationally (e.g. Donald Pettitt had recently been appointed as the CEO of Canterbury Men's Centre and was anxious to explore the potential for men's shed establishment in his region. I met with him on a couple of occasions en route through airports in 2008).
>
> From my involvement at that time, no community Sheds other than the [Devonport Clay Store Community Workshop, in a North Shore Auckland suburb] - non-aligned with any network of community facilities) existed in NZ. A "Blokes Shed" was operational in Mosgiel [Taieri] in 2007. Meanwhile, I was able to establish the Hamilton Community Men's Shed in the Waikato region from a [project] launch in December 2007 with a steering group of five and the physical opening of a shed on March 19, 2008.
>
> As Director of the Community Learning Centre of Melville High School at the time, I was able to give presentations about shed development at Adult Education conferences within NZ - one ACE conference in Auckland in 2008, and two Community Learning Association in Schools Conferences (representing 225 school districts around NZ) in Waiheke in 2008 and in Greymouth in 2009. Each of these presentations had 20-25 delegates from around NZ who were interested in fostering sheds in their regions.
>
> At this time the Waiuku region representative, Arthur Buckland also made contact with me in Hamilton. Their West Franklin Community Men's Shed began soon after Hamilton's in leased premises. Their

---

[44] Bernard McMillan, *Community Men's Sheds: A Commentary*, Report for Rowley Resource Centre, Christchurch, February, 2009.

former joinery facilities were comprehensive, with a huge array of woodworking gear and space for others to sublet and store projects on the go. Hamilton Shed members enjoyed a visit to their shed and acknowledged the enthusiasm of their members, the diversity of their projects, the wide range of specialist equipment and a significant focus on several nautical projects - repairing an historical hull and maintaining fleets of sailing boats for sea cadets. Following my Winston Churchill Fellowship to study Men's Sheds in Australia and Great Britain in May-June 2009, it was time for me to rekindle connections with members in Australian Sheds at their Hobart conference [in 2009]. At this conference I gave a presentation on my report 'Community Men's Sheds from NZ to Australia England and Scotland 2009' [45]. Personal reflections included:

> Ageing men in sheds are full of enthusiasm and vigour, quite the opposite of stereotypes for senior aged men and their abilities. Shed experiences appeared to have helped many to rediscover an active retirement life, wanting to make the very most of the life they were now living. Many were enthusiastic because they had survived bouts of depression, disappointment or lifetime partner loss and had got themselves back on a more even track. With new friends and projects to think about, their minds were alive and they were buzzing. ... When I heard the stories of those who had dealt with depression and fought back to health again or an incapacitated stroke victim now realising he was not a burden to society but an asset, passing knowledge and skills on to other. These realities had become life changing.

With such images in mind Arthur and I, together with Trevor Scott (Oxford Community Men's Shed) and Rural Education Activities Programme (REAP) Marlborough representative Ailsa Carey, attended the Hobart Australian [Men's Shed] Conference in 2009. Following the Conference, we four NZ delegates were determined to carry the national association goal forward. In conjunction with Peter McNeur, we were able to acknowledge his professional roles in the Rural Education

---

45

http://www.communitymatters.govt.nz/vwluresources/wcmfreport09bruce/$file/wcmfrepor t09bruce.pdf, Accessed February 24, 2015.

Activities Programme (REAP), Adult and Community Education Aotearoa programmes and his support for the establishment of the first New Zealand purpose-built, Henley Men's Shed [in Masterton], which became the preferred venue for a first New Zealand national conference.

In selecting the Masterton Shed [as the 2010 New Zealand conference venue], two specific goals were clear; to show what facilities and equipment a purpose-built shed could contain, and to invite shed representatives from around New Zealand to discuss the need and purposes for forming a national association.

With various sheds being established around the country, sometimes independent and not linked to specific providers, sustainability was an important factor to consider along with any support and guidance that could be given for new sheds. In at least one case, a shed had ceased operation before the two years were up. This was in part due to a lack of depth in personnel and funding. A change of Government and Community Education policy saw physical and personnel resources reduced by 80 per cent in December 2009 which did not help shed growth in many areas. The dissolution of 200 out of 220 community educational positions in schools (including my fulltime Directorship of Community Education at Melville High School) was a significant blow to a network that had begun to encourage shed growth in local communities. In such Spartan times, the idea of a shed being a community resource, springing from and addressing the needs of a community now required the work of volunteers who needed considerable tenacity and drive to continue any impetus. Such "dedicated drivers" enthusiastically motivated men and promoted the positive values of shed membership. ... Ailsa Carey, as a REAP Marlborough Community Education Organiser and woman, appreciated how valuable a men's shed could be and confirmed she was "very proud to be associated with this wonderful concept" and "have become an honorary Picton Men's Community Shed bloke". [Carey's] involvement behind the scenes reflected observations I had made overseas and at home, that many women are some of the staunchest supporters of men's sheds – not there to dominate or direct but to ably and tactically assist men in their communities to establish sheds using their networking skills and focusing on resource acquisition and facilitation.

From these 'bones' other sheds in New Zealand began to take root and a national awareness began to develop in response to the needs for further guidance and requests for assistance.

Neil Bruce continued to visit Sheds and meet with regional delegates to support local Shed development (in Te Awamutu, New Plymouth, Wanganui, Levin, Rotorua, Tauranga, Taupo, Auckland North Shore, Devonport, and Henderson), including presentations and visits to Morrinsville, Gisborne, Whakatane, Matamata, Wairoa, and Napier communities.

THE DEVELOPMENT OF MENZSHED NZ

In the six years from 2009 most Shed members in New Zealand have strongly embraced the formation of a national Men's Shed Association, called MENZSHED NZ in early 2015. The first Men's Shed Conference in New Zealand was held on April 9-11, 2010 in Masterton. [46] It was hosted by the recently completed Henley Men's Shed, the first purpose-built Shed in New Zealand. The conference steering group acknowledged that:[47]

> All sheds are uniquely different, but the issues are the same. We are facing them for the first time – target groups, diversity, money, coordination, programmes opening times, organisation, management, safety, registration, charitable status, insurance, and resources are some of the issues we face.

As an outcome from the 2010 Masterton conference, a small group of volunteer delegates was encouraged to advance a national association of Men's Sheds, *MENZSHED Aotearoa[48]*. (The 'Z' in the title was included to give the New Zealand Sheds a point of difference from other international Sheds). The association objective was to provide support for existing and prospective Men's Sheds in New Zealand.[49] Relying purely on volunteers, however, progress was quite slow and some Sheds chose not to affiliate.

Positive support, however, did come from the Canterbury Men's Centre[50], a venture unique at the time in New Zealand, that emerged from an August 2005

---

[46] http://nzmenssheds.wordpress.com/, Accessed February 24, 2015.

[47] http://nzmenssheds.wordpress.com/, Accessed February 24, 2015.

[48] *Aotearoa* is the Maori name for New Zealand.

[49] http://menzshed.org.nz/ MENZSHED New Zealand, Accessed March 13, 2014.

[50] http://canmen.org.nz/, Accessed February 24, 2015.

'Men's Issues Summit' and was officially opened in April 2008 at Christchurch Community House. In conjunction with his role as Centre manager, Donald Pettitt began to host New Zealand Shed contact details and addresses on the Men's Centre website.[51] This interim service remained until a national association was established and had its own website. However, it was hard for the steering group from the Masterton conference to make much headway towards a national association due to: a lack of resources in Sheds; no agency being prepared to offer functional or funding support; large distances between Sheds. The prime focus for most Sheds was, understandably, their own individual survival and sustainability.

By July 2012, little had been advanced and a further national conference was convened at the Wellington High School to which AMSA CEO, David Helmers, was invited. David Helmers's experience with forming a national association in Australia as well as his assistance with the national association being established in Ireland in 2011 was considered important to give strategic direction to the New Zealand Association. From this 2012 conference, a second steering group of volunteers was charged with specific tasks to prepare for the creation of a national association. This steering group was convened by a newly appointed Canterbury Men's Centre "Men's Shed Coordinator", Martin Cox (appointed on a six month contract position). Cox and the Canterbury Men's Centre at University of Canterbury facilitated a seminar on Men's Sheds titled 'Health by Stealth: Men's Sheds Supporting Men and Community' on September 5, 2012 the day after a launch in Christchurch of the book, *Gender, Masculinities and Lifelong Learning*. The book involved collaboration between a number of New Zealand adult education academics previously at University of Canterbury in Christchurch and included a Chapter by Barry Golding about 'Men's Sheds, Community Learning and Public Policy[52]. Barry Golding contributed to both events, which attracted a wide range of Canterbury Men's Shed practitioners and brought some of the issues associated with Men's Sheds to the attention of interested New Zealand academics.

A 3rd National New Zealand Shed Conference followed in February 2013 hosted by the Waimea Shed in Nelson. At this conference, held over three days, a constitution was drafted and eventually agreed upon. Fine-tuning of the constitution continued post-conference. MENZSHED NZ was granted registration as an incorporated society on September 3, 2013 with charitable status confirmed on October 17, 2013.

---

[51] http://nzmenssheds.wordpress.com, Accessed February 24, 2015.
[52] In Marion Bowl *et al.*, *Gender Masculinities and Lifelong Learning*. London: Routledge, 2012, 134-146.

For the new association, two issues became important. First, the national association would be an association of Shed organisations rather than of individual shedders. Only one Shed representative per shed (holding member status) could vote on association issues. Second, apart from the usual executive positions, a board of nine would include "regional representatives" to give regional support for existing and proposed Sheds. New Zealand would have thus five broadly defined Men's Shed Regions, three in the North Island and two in the South Island, as outlined in Chapter 1.

The next New Zealand Conference was hosted by Menzshed Kapiti at Waikanae on March 14-16, 2014, by which time the confirmed number of Men's Sheds operating in New Zealand was 39. Discussions at this conference revolved around the development of a national website, benefits of national membership, access to the existing Shed insurance scheme, and how to encourage non-member Sheds to join the national association. It was noted that those Sheds that resisted joining the national association (a minority of New Zealand Sheds overall) cited bureaucratic fears as a principal area of contention[53]. Other concerns related to expense and questions about the value of becoming part of an international association. Even though such networking would be of considerable benefit for members, there was broad agreement that the main focus for Men's Sheds in New Zealand would be for them to 'do their own thing'.

Such Shed members, it appears, had not balanced their concerns with the likely advantages a national association might provide. These advantages, subsequently realised, included: a national point of contact for funding, sponsorship, local and regional networks; a consistent web presence advocating for all Sheds (member or non-member Sheds); the ability to negotiate discounts (such as for insurance, materials and services); the publication of newsletters; hosting regional cluster meetings; the sharing of surplus resources; support for new Shed initiatives, as well as providing information about partnerships (with government and non-government departments), not to mention sharing highlights and successes of related projects and community links via regular newsletters.

By late 2014 the estimated number of Men's Sheds operating in New Zealand was 50. It was agreed that national conferences would be held bi-annually, occurring in the 'even' years immediately after each Australian national conference. This was planned to assist and encourage mutual membership, contact and communication between countries. Hence the next New Zealand conference was planned for 2016, in Christchurch.

---

[53] http://www.odt.co.nz/lifestyle/magazine/208800/clubbing-together-blokes-shed, Accessed February 24, 2015.

REFLECTIONS ON GROWTH OF NEW ZEALAND MEN'S SHEDS

Unlike in Australia, notwithstanding Bernard McMillan's comprehensive scoping study demonstrating the obvious need and potential for Shed establishment and benefit as early as February 2009, there had been relatively little empirical research into Men's Sheds in New Zealand to 2015. Nevertheless New Zealand Sheds have many anecdotal insights into the benefits occurring for members. Unlike in Australia, there has been very little published research and positive publicity about the benefits of Shed participation. Nor has there been national government support as developed in Australia, where the federal government has targeted the poorer health statistics of men and provided funding linked to men's health and wellbeing via the national Men's Shed association, AMSA. In addition, no organisation in New Zealand embraced the Men's Shed concept in New Zealand for men and took up the role of an auspice body, for example in the same way that UnitingCare did with early Sheds in Australia and Age UK did in Britain.

Research undertaken as part of the establishment of the Henley Men's Shed concluded that, in spite of reasonably good local coverage about the positive value of Shed participation, the Men's Shed Movement in New Zealand remained 'largely below the media and political radar at present'[54]. As a consequence, unlike the rapid growth seen in Australia and Ireland, New Zealand Sheds have developed more slowly. While diverse Shed start-ups have occurred in New Zealand, a consistent characteristic in New Zealand, as in other countries, has been the presence of at least one key person empowering others as a 'driver' of the Shed idea. The following Sheds are provided as examples from New Zealand.

Steering group members of the Northshore Men's Shed Trust under Ross McEwan took five years of fundraising and building before their Shed was opened publicly in 2013. Arthur Buckland had already leased a former joinery shop in 2007-8, and with the requisite equipment, attracted shed enthusiasts to the West Franklin Men's Shed. Dr Neil Bruce pioneered the Hamilton Men's Shed via his networking role in adult and community education. In less than three months from launching the Shed idea in December 2007, the Hamilton Shed was operational, albeit with no money but with rent-free accommodation for nine months.

Two 'Bloke's Sheds' evolved independently and slightly earlier near Dunedin in Otago on the south of the South Island at Mosgiel (Taieri) in 2007 and South Dunedin in 2008 with support from a local Dunedin Resident Naval

---

[54] http://henleymenzshed.kiwi.nz/data/documents/MS-research-Final-pub.pdf, Accessed February 24, 2015, 6.

Officer, Lieutenant Commander Phil Bradshaw. Peter McNeur assisted the development of the Henley Shed in Masterton, north of Wellington in the Wairarapa, in his role as Director of the Rural Education Activities Programme (REAP) from 2008. With a Shed initiative already partly underway and the first purpose-built Shed being planned and constructed, Peter McNeur assisted by encouraging community organisations to work together, including the local Henley Park Trust, the Rotary Club Chapter and as well as through the REAP. The Rowley Community Shed in Christchurch arose from a local Community Centre research initiative undertaken by Bernard McMillan, Coordinator of the Rowley Community Resource Centre.[55] Finally, MenzShed Kapiti was created by the enthusiasm of Nigel Clough and his involvement in the start-up of the Wellington Menz Shed. Clough's involvement in the first conference of Shed representatives in Masterton and his encouragement of colleagues to explore a possible Shed establishment in Waikanae on the Kapiti Coast resulted in the establishment of MenzShed Kapiti.

There are several factors that may have contributed to the slower growth of Men's Sheds in New Zealand. One of these is the fact that New Zealand/ Aotearoa has a significant bicultural dynamic, as well as a significant proportion of Pacifica people and recent immigrants from Asian and Middle Eastern backgrounds. Many Maori and Pasifica men already contribute to their own gender-specific, cultural practices and organisations. This effectively reduces the number of men in the overall population likely to become involved with Men's Sheds.

Maori culture has its own *Kaupapa* or "cultural mores and activities" such as the regionally unique traditional carving created for village *maraes* (meeting grounds) that reflect their history, stories and traditions: *kapa haka* (performing arts competitions); ceremonial *waka* and *pou* carving (traditional war canoes and pole and wall panels). Each physical activity (buoyed by comprehensive regional and national competitions) requires not only skilled artisans, but also the time required to practice, rehearse and create new works. Many of these traditional Maori activities are already gendered and conducted in shed-like workshops.

Other factors likely to have some influence in New Zealand include competition for time and involvement of men generally in a country where an extremely diverse range of outdoor, individual and team activities already occurs. There is extensive team involvement in summer and winter sports codes, music

[55]http://www.bing.com/search?q=rowley+shed+research&qs=n&form=QBRE&pq=rowley +shed+research&sc=0-0&sp=-1&sk=&cvid=22ce9442bbb54740ad5718d5e3310a52, Accessed February 24, 2015.

groups, orchestras, bands, choirs, dance, and theatre groups. Mountain biking, boating, swimming, tramping, hunting, mountaineering, gardening, fishing and duck shooting are very popular for men in New Zealand. So too are practical activities found in clubs, model and engineering groups, vehicle restoration, woodturning, computer support, St John's Ambulance, volunteer fire brigades, service clubs (Rotary, Lions, Jaycee), Age Concern and Grey Power. New Zealand's smaller population reduces the potential for total Shed numbers to expand at a rapid rate to the extent that they have done in other countries.

In spite of these differences and difficulties, the Men's Shed Movement is still expanding in New Zealand. As of February 2015, close to 60 Men's Sheds had registered with MENZSHEDS NZ (as mapped in previous Figure 4), with another 20 that had either opted not to join or else were in start-up mode.[56]

MEN'S SHEDS ELSEWHERE IN THE WORLD

Insights from International Exchanges

By the end of 2014, as documented in later in Chapter 10, the evidence base was growing, with over one hundred articles published about Men's Sheds across the world. All were published in English and most were readily available via the internet. All originated from six mainly Anglophone nations (including Canada and the US), most of them from Australia. Men's Sheds had begun to interest community workers and researchers in many other mainly non-Anglophone countries by 2014. This section summarises the value and impact of some of these international exchanges of information by researchers and Shed practitioners.

Men's Sheds to 2015 had spread and developed new national Movements on the Australian model in the UK, Ireland and New Zealand, in part because of reciprocal visits and presentations by Shed researchers and practitioners: including by Barry Golding and David Helmers (from Australia), John Evoy (from Ireland) and Neil Bruce (from New Zealand), particularly since 2007. Neil Bruce's world study tour in 2009 involved visits to many early Men's Sheds in Australia, the UK and Ireland. Barry Golding undertook many academic and community presentations about Australian Men's Sheds in other European nations between 2008 and 2011, including Sweden and Denmark (where the first *Mænds Mødesteder* ['Men's Venue'] opened in early 2015[57]), Finland, Germany,

---

[56] Roger Bowman (Secretary MENZSHED NZ), January 23, 2015.

[57] Mænds Mødesteder, https://www.evensi.com/maends-modesteder-blommevej-3-4671-stroby/148405801, Accessed June 1, 2015.

Portugal and Greece. More recently Barry Golding presented about Men's Sheds in China in 2012, the US in late 2013, as well as in Malta, Slovenia and France in October 2014.

Several nations in Europe participated in Grundtvig[58] Program-supported workshops, initiated by John Evoy in Ireland during 2013, exploring Men's Shed theory and practice. Researchers from Slovenia, Portugal, Malta and Estonia completed an OMAL (Older Men Adult Learning) European Union-funded program in 2014 focusing on education and learning of older men aged 60+ years who experienced deprivation and social exclusion. The focus of the research was on improving knowledge of organizations and programs at the community level, offering activities (social and educational) inclusive of older men. This learning-oriented research[59] provided evidence and insights about where older men from similar socioeconomic backgrounds currently meet and learn informally in nations without Men's Sheds.

The question why Men's Sheds (sometimes called 'man caves' or 'men's dens' in their personal manifestation in parts of North America) have not yet gained traction in community settings in the USA or Canada is difficult to answer simply. The author, in emails and research reconnaissance visits to Canada (Vancouver and Halifax, Nova Scotia) in 2007, encountered a general reluctance by academics to consider, acknowledge or address the possibility of some men's disadvantage. And yet in places such as Vancouver in Canada the presence of men of all ages 'living rough' on the streets was very obvious to Barry Golding, with mobile 'soup kitchens' being common for homeless men in several parts of the city in 2007.

Barry Golding undertook a research visit to Lexington, Kentucky in the USA in November 2013, where there was interest in Men's Sheds from academics in the adult education field. Golding observed a soup kitchen set up in downtown Lexington for homeless men of all ages next to the Vietnam Veterans' War memorial. With 20 war Veterans *a day* committing suicide on average in the US since 1999, widespread rural population aging and relatively high male unemployment in the US in 2015 of around six per cent, it is likely and highly desirable that Men's Sheds might at least be trialed in some parts of the US and Canada from 2015 onwards.

---

[58] The Grundtvig Program was a sub-program of the European Commission's Lifelong Learning Program 2007-13, related to adult learning.
[59] Marco Radovan and Sabina Jelenc Krasovek, *Older Men Learning in the Community: European Snapshots*. Tisk: Ljubljana, 2014.

On June 4, 2014 John Evoy from Ireland gave an invited presentation on 'Men's Sheds: A Mobilisation of Men in New Ways' at a Men's Health Week Conference in Copenhagen, Denmark, organised by Dr Svend Aage Madsen, President of Men's Health Society Denmark. John Evoy and IMSA convened a world-first 'International Men's Sheds Festival 2014' in Dublin, Ireland, on October 3-5, 2014. The Festival was attended by several people interested in Men's Sheds in Europe, including Dr Madsen, as well as several Australian, UK and Irish shedders. The Danish Sheds opened in early 2015 and discussed towards the end of this Chapter are one outcome of this activity and of information exchange between Ireland and Denmark.

An International Association

During both the 2011 (Brisbane) and 2013 (Ballarat) AMSA Conferences international delegates from Australia, Ireland, the UK, New Zealand and Canada met and developed plans for an International Alliance of Men's Sheds Associations (IAMSA), whose aim would be 'to support the development and sustainability of Men's Shed associations globally.' [60] Photograph 27 shows international Men's Shed delegates from Ireland, New Zealand, Australia, Canada and the UK.

---

[60] *Discussion Document: International Alliance of Men's Sheds Associations*, April 2, 2014, based on notes from a meeting during the October 27-29, 2013 AMSA Conference in Ballarat, Australia.

Photograph 27 International Men's Shed Delegates from Five Countries at the 2013 AMSA Conference in Brisbane. From left to right Sarah Evoy (IMSA), David Helmers (AMSA), Neil Bruce (NZ), Barry Golding, John Evoy (IMSA), Eric Laroche (Canada), Harvinder Channa (Age UK)

IAMSA's mission would be: to freely share information between national associations; seek financial support; and provide information, guidance and support for existing and emerging national associations. The common characteristics of IAMSA member organisations would be that they are representatives of each national Men's Sheds Movement, are not for profit, not connected to any political or religious grouping, and non-discriminatory.

Men's Sheds in Europe

During 2014 a number of other countries, particularly in Europe, continued to show interest in Men's Sheds, and John Evoy had set up a European Men's Shed's website[61] via IMSA. By February 2015 one of these initiatives had translated into a formal Shed opening in Malmo in Sweden on February 1, 2015, funded through crowd-funding pledges totaling SKR57,950 and explicitly based on the Australian model, though not a *Men's* Shed, as summarised in the group's statement of intent and rationale:

---

[61] http://menssheds.eu/, Accessed February 16, 2015.

[What we want to do] Rent out a local basement area in which to start a Swedish branch of the Men's Shed movement. (Note; ours will have a Swedish twist and will not be exclusively for men).

[Why we need to do this] What we are planning on creating here is a physical space dedicated to building stronger relationships between individuals and the wider community. Our vehicle for doing this is by providing the setting for people to come together and work hands-on. Creating, fixing, tinkering with practical items and problems. With the overarching theme being that general wellbeing stems heavily from connecting with other human beings and that that connection comes easier during a shared experience of creativity.

We think there is a substantial need in Swedish society to have more options and environments for people to connect with each other in meaningful ways. It's possible to see that this model has worked in other countries and we're asking for a chance to try it here![62]

Dr Svend Aage Madsen, leader of research into European fatherhood and male postnatal depression, based at Copenhagen University Hospital in Denmark, and Vice President of the European Men's Health Forum, reported that he expected three to five Sheds to emerge in Denmark in the 2015 European spring. Dr. Madsen is also President of Men's Health Society in Denmark [63] , a multidisciplinary organisation dedicated to the field of men's health in all its aspects in Denmark. The Society has coordinated Men's Health Week in Denmark since 2003, distributes publications and participates in national and international conferences and meetings. The Society is head of the Men's Health Forum, Denmark, representing 42 organisations from all areas of society dedicated to working to improve men's health. During 2014 the Forum received grants of around €1.4 million Euro for work with men's health in Denmark, including research, education for health professionals, development of male-friendly health information, as well as establishing Men's Sheds for being together and wellbeing.

---

[62] https://www.kickstarter.com/projects/155662736/shed-i-malmo, Accessed February 3, 2015.
[63] www.sundmand.dk, Accessed February 16, 2015.

Dr Madsen, whose work is focused 'on the practical questions on how to develop and implement male sensitive communication with fathers in health services'[64], noted that:

> We are very much inspired by the Australian and Irish work with Sheds. I heard about the Sheds in Ireland and Australia through contacts in the men's health movement. I invited John Evoy to Denmark in Men's Health Week in 2014 and was invited to Ireland for the Men's Sheds Festival in Dublin in October 2014. Since then we have been working to establish as many as 9-10 Sheds in Denmark and hope at least half of them will be running during April 2015.[65]

The only other countries in early 2015 aside from Australia, Ireland, the UK and New Zealand that had any community men's sheds (or equivalent) open, albeit in small numbers, were Canada, Sweden and Denmark, as summarised below.[66]

Men's Sheds in Canada

The first Men's Shed in Canada was started by Doug Mackie in the St James area of urban Winnipeg (population 800,000) in Manitoba. Mackie explained[67] that his daughter, then living in Saskatchewan, '… met a woman from Australia in June 2008 who told her about Men's Sheds'. Mackie then found the Mensheds Australia internet site[68]. The original Shed in St James was commenced in mid-2008 under the auspices of the St James Assiniboia Over 55s Centre that Mackie was a committee and Board member of. After 18 months there was a falling out and the Centre closed down the Shed, resulting in a group of men, including Doug Mackie, forming a private, non-profit organisation, 'Mensheds Manitoba Inc.'.

A new Shed, the Woodhaven Shed, was (in March 2014) located in the Woodhaven Community Club. Doug Mackie reported in March 2014 that:

---

[64] http://european-fatherhood.com/whoweare.php?mode=view&id=1, Accessed February 13, 2015.
[65] Svend Madsen, February 6, 2015.
[66] Since there is no national assocation to register Sheds, all seven community Men's Sheds open or forming to May 2015 in Canada, as well as those in Flagstaff (Arizona, USA), Malmo (Sweden) and Copehagen (Denmark), are included on the global map in Chapter 2.
[67] Doug Mackie, March 12, 2014.
[68] Mensheds Australia www.mensheds.org.au/, Accessed March 22, 2014.

Currently our membership varies from 34 to 88. We meet twice a week, Tuesday and Wednesday afternoons for card playing, woodcarving, bark carving, stained glass, Diamond Willow cane or walking sticks along with lots of camaraderie, raillery, socialization. About once a month we have a Men's Shed Café where men come and gain confidence in their cooking skills. We do volunteer work in the community as well.[69]

In early 2015 Gene Mitran[70] reported on advanced planning and some initial funding though the Northern Health Authority (NHA) Mental Health Unit for a 'Menshed' at Vanderhoof, a remote town of 4,500 people in central British Columbia, founded through the Nechako Valley Historical Society (NVHS). NVHS had the use of several historical buildings on a site along Highway 16 west of Vanderhoof. A small number of men were meeting socially as NVHS Menshed in late 2014 in the 'Smithers Building', an already heated temporary premises (a critical winter requirement in Canada), while planning for more permanent premises in 2015. Doug Mackie reported via the Shed's *Keeping Busy* Newsletter in January 5, 2015 that other Sheds in British Columbia were planned in the towns of Hope (150 kilometers east of Vancouver) and Pemberton (in British Colombia, north of Whistler).

The Okanagan Men's Shed Association was registered as a non-profit society in July 2013 with a plan to introduce the idea of Men's Sheds to the Okanagan Valley in southern British Columbia. A Canadian Parliamentary Secretary, Linda Larson posted a note on the web about this Association in May 2014 as below:

The Okanagan Men's Sheds Association does not currently have a permanent location where they meet or permanent equipment that they use for their projects and activities, but they are working to build local connections and opportunities in their communities. At the moment, the Okanagan Men's Shed is looking for volunteers to help establish the first permanent Men's Shed location in Kelowna. Several other communities

---

[69] Woodhaven Community Club site, http://woodhavencc.ca/programs/, Accessed March 22, 2014. The webisite defined 'A Men's Shed [as] any community based, non-commercial organization which is open to all men where the primary activity is the provision of a safe, friendly and inclusive environment where men are able to gather and/or work on meaningful projects at their own pace, in their own time and in the company of other men and where the primary objective is to advance the health and well-being of the participating men.'

[70] Gene Mitran email to Doug Mackie, December 28, 2014.

in British Columbia are also working to establish their own Men's Sheds.[71]

By January 2015 the Okanagan shedders had a temporary meeting area in Kelowna plus a woodwork shop at a seniors' residence complex, as a base for several community service projects, chat and coffee gatherings. They had established an informative and encouraging 'little brother' relationship with the Yass Valley Men's Shed in New South Wales, Australia. The Association was exploring funding options and planning to set up a 'come and see' Shed pilot to get the concept better understood and accepted by health, seniors' and government services providers as well as by the community.

While there were very few Sheds established in Canada to early 2015, researchers from University of British Columbia in Canada and University of Manitoba received a $3 million (Canadian) Movember[72] grant in October 2013 for five Mental Health research projects over three years. Project 3, led by Dr Corey Mackenzie and Dr Kerstin Roger at the University of Manitoba (in Winnipeg), was described in October 2014 by Movember Canada as being:

> ... aimed at older men, a vulnerable sub-group who experience depression and have high rates of suicide. This project will evaluate and extend on an existing program called Men's Sheds, which provides a masculine environment (woodworking, repairs etc.) for men who are socially isolated and/or experiencing illness challenges. A men's sheds tool-kit will be developed and made available to enable Men's Sheds to develop across Canada.[73]

Part of the funding was for a project aimed at researching and developing a plan 'to expand the Canadian Men's Shed community programs'. The project specifically aimed to both develop '... a toolkit for groups of men who wish to start a new Men's Shed, and [and create] a national Men's Shed network'[74] which

---

[71] http://osoyoosdailynews.com/2014/05/16/okanagan-mens-sheds-association/, Posted May 16, 2014.
[72] Movember is a now international annual event, originally begun in Adelaide, Australia in 1999, involving the growing of moustaches during November. The Founation aims to raise awareness of (and funds for) men's health issues, such as for prostate cancer, as well as for other male cancers and associated charities.
[73] Movember (Canada) News: Mental Health Funding, October 20, 2013, http://ca.movember.com/news/5705/mental-health-funding/?category=local, Accessed January 7, 2015.
[74] Men's Sheds: Project Profile http://menshealthresearch.ubc.ca/mens-sheds/, Accessed January 6, 2015.

included a website. In Year 2 of the project the researchers were working with four unidentified community groups in the process of setting up Men's Sheds: in Camrose (Alberta), Oxford (Ontario), Halifax (Nova Scotia) and Pemberton (British Columbia). It is ironic that under the conditions of the Movember funding none of these funds has flowed to the small number of existing, often struggling Sheds. The researchers, curiously, have 'intentionally attempted not to be heavily influenced by what's happening internationally'[75]. As a consequence it is very concerning that to early 2015 very little use had been made of the accumulated experience, research, expertise and resources generated from the 1,300 plus Men's Sheds in the four other countries with well-established Sheds and Shed Movements, including the Australian Men's Shed toolkit.

Men's Sheds in the US

To early 2015 no community Men's Shed was open in the US. In late 2012 Richard (Dick) Stockinger from Flagstaff in Arizona registered the Tinkers Den Inc.[76]. It was prompted by an article about Men's Sheds in *The Australian* newspaper in 2011[77]. During 2014 Stockinger circulated early plans for a 'Tinkers Den', to be set up on the Australian Men's Shed principles[78]. It aimed to:

> .... furnish an environment where older persons may gather to socialise, relax, exchange ideas, feelings, concerns and emotions, to both learn and teach new technical and social skills, and to provide a place promoting good health and productive work activities which benefit both the individual members, guest and the greater Flagstaff community.

---

[75] Corey Mackenzie, January 9, 2015.
[76] www.statelog.com/tinkers-den-inc-flagstaff-az, Accessed May 2, 2014.
[77] *The Australian*, June 25-26, 2011.
[78] Richard Stockinger email to David Helmers, September 13, 2014.

PART III

Men's Shed Innovation and Diversity

Part 3 examines a range of Men's Sheds that have been 'early', 'innovative', and 'remarkable' or 'new and cutting edge' across four countries with active Men's Sheds Movements to 2015. What becomes clear from the Men's Sheds used as case studies across Australia (Chapter 6), Ireland (Chapter 7), the UK (Chapter 8) and New Zealand (Chapter 9) is that all Sheds are different, in terms of their gendered dimension, their size, the way the Sheds are organised, who comes, and what does (and typically does not) occur in the Shed space. This examination of approximately 60 Sheds, with diverse shedders and Shed attributes, selected from the 920 plus Men's Sheds open in Australia, and the four hundred plus Men's Sheds open to 2015 across the UK, Ireland and New Zealand, seeks to illustrate and emphasise that Sheds are set up for and by different men, for different purposes, in very diverse contexts and communities. This Shed diversity is one of the key characteristics of this remarkable, grassroots Movement now extending to diverse communities within and beyond these four countries.

MEN'S SHED DIVERSITY ACROSS FOUR COUNTRIES

The Men's Shed early histories, from Australia in Chapter 3 and from Ireland, the UK and New Zealand in Chapter 5, identified a number of 'early pioneer' Sheds in each country. The term 'pioneer' is used in the general sense of 'one that goes before, preparing the way for others to follow'. Being early or first in some way, these early Sheds typically faced a number of common difficulties getting established and funded. These difficulties included becoming understood by service providers, governments and communities. They also involved getting men actively engaged and creating the enthusiasm, momentum and information base for other Sheds to form, get funding and become networked. Many of these early Men's Sheds had to be innovative, and several have since been very influential in each country.

Chapters 6 to 9 systematically examine around a dozen Men's Sheds from each country organised under four deliberately broad headings: 'Early pioneer'[1], 'Innovative', 'Remarkable' and 'New and Cutting Edge'. The following broad selection criteria were used for each country to create a small set of case studies of:

- *'Early pioneer'* Men's Sheds, which were historically early for that country.
- *'Innovative'* Men's Sheds, which at a relatively early stage, have broken 'new ground' and influenced Shed practice in each country, typically in terms of their innovative Shed programs, the groups of men they work with in the Shed and/or the groups they collaborate with in the wider community.
- *'Remarkable'* Men's Sheds, selected because of one or more remarkable aspects, including activities conducted in the Shed, the unusual venue in which the Shed is located and/or the remarkable ways in which the Shed has worked with the wider community or with other Sheds.
- *'New and cutting edge'* Men's Sheds, which have opened quite recently (after 2010) and done something that is different, new and innovative from most previous Men's Sheds, and which might be seen as setting possible trends for future Sheds.

It was difficult picking a small number of Men's Sheds in each of these four categories to illustrate the great diversity of Shed types across each country. It is not that those selected are the 'best' Sheds. It is simply that the Sheds and their Shed arrangements best suited the needs of the men and the communities that devised them. Indeed, the important message behind this part of the book about Shed innovation and diversity is that there is *no right answer*. All Shed organisations are and should be unique and different.

In that sense all Men's Sheds are in some way early, innovative, remarkable or new and cutting edge within the communities they have been set up in. Most will and should transform over time with changes in men's needs and interests, as well as changes in the communities in which they operate. Indeed some of the earliest Australian Men's Sheds featured in Chapter 2 'shone' more strongly early on than they do today, and a small number were closed by early 2015. In part this is because many of the men who created and needed a Shed in a community

---

[1] Chapter 6 does not include Australian 'early pioneer' shed case studies as they have already been documented in Chapter 3.

setting over a decade ago are no longer able to participate, and some have sadly passed away. In other cases the Shed organisation has been unable to become sustainable, gain the essential community support, adapt to changed circumstances and/or ensure succession from the original management team or leadership.

The selected 58 Shed case studies (10 early, 16 innovative, 16 remarkable, 16 new and cutting edge) in Chapters 6 to 9 were all opened in the decade after 2005. Indeed most (50) were opened within the past five years. There are around a dozen each from Australia (12), the Irish Republic (12), England (11) and New Zealand (15), with four from Northern Ireland and two each from Scotland and Wales.

The case studies range from large, specialised full production workshops to Sheds in small and remote communities that essentially serve as social gathering places. Some Sheds have auspice arrangements, including with local government, adult education and health centres. Other Sheds are fully independent and incorporated associations. Some Sheds are in aged care settings for mainly older men, while others are for a wide range of men and sometimes also include boys. Finally, some Sheds cater for 'all comers' while others are specifically for men who are refugees, War Veterans, with dementia or with a disability, or from diverse cultural, national, Indigenous or linguistic backgrounds.

Australian Men's Sheds

The history of early Men's Sheds in Australia has been comprehensively covered in earlier chapters. Chapter 6 therefore focuses on an examination of Australian Men's Sheds that have developed relatively recently, in the past decade to 2015. The aim is illustrate the remarkable diversity of Sheds developed in diverse locations for equally diverse purposes and participants, using case studies from all Australian states.

INNOVATIVE AUSTRALIAN MEN'S SHEDS

Three Men's Sheds included to illustrate this 'innovative' theme in Australia have all developed in rural and remote communities, emphasising the decentred nature of Men's Sheds innovation found in all countries. The case studies are of a Community Men's Shed in Traralgon South in rural Victoria, the Lightning Ridge Menshed Inc. in outback northern New South Wales, and the Quorn Men's Shed in the Flinders Ranges in rural inland South Australia.

The *TSDA (Traralgon South and District Association) Community/Men's Shed*, referred to locally in 2015 as the 'Community/Men's Shed'[1], serves a rural area in the La Trobe Valley in Gippsland around 175 kilometers east of Melbourne. It is innovative in several senses, particularly in the way it has reached out through its diverse programs and its umbrella organisation, the TSDA, to men, women and young people in the surrounding community. The Shed, like the surrounding and close knit rural community, had literally 'risen from the ashes' from an area severely affected by the devastating Black Saturday bushfires of February 7, 2009.

The shed building is situated behind the Traralgon South Fire Station 13 kilometers south of Traralgon. It is managed by a subcommittee of the Traralgon South and District Association (TSDA). TSDA and its Community/Men's Shed service the surrounding small towns of Balook, Callignee, Callignee North, Callignee South, Koornalla, Le Roy, Tarra-Bulga and Traralgon South. The

---

[1] http://www.tsda.org.au/index.php/tool-library-community-shed/, Accessed January 8, 2015.

TSDA Shed, formally opened on March 24, 2013, was by early 2015 fully operational over a total of four days (Monday, Tuesday and Thursday, 10am-2pm and Wednesday, 6.30pm-8.30pm), supported by a female paid Shed Coordinator and TSDA administrative assistant. The Shed promotes and manages numerous and very diverse programs, workgroups and fundraising events. It includes a fully equipped, multipurpose workshop area with tools purchased through the assistance of a Bushfire Relief Fund, in conjunction with several Victorian State Government Departments. The Shed has also relied on the generosity of donations from many local businesses and individuals.

The TSDA Community/Men's Shed opened its doors to welcome both male and female members of all ages across the community as well as providing facilities to members of the general public who want to use the facilities to complete their own personal project.[2] The TSDA provides many community engagement programs. A Youth Group uses the Shed for activities which support secondary school-aged young people every second Friday night. The Shed is also a community venue for a very wide range of structured programs for all ages, ranging from fitness classes to cup-cake making, as well as art and craft classes.

The Shed actively participates in community projects within the Traralgon South Kindergarten, holding Community Pizza Oven events. It aims to develop innovative programs including welding training, building boxed shelving, scrapbooking, wire working and furniture restoration. The Shed plans to expand the scope of its programs to include the provision of work-based, accredited qualifications including Safe Food Handling and Responsible Service of Alcohol Certificates through a local vocational education and training provider.

The evocatively named town of 'Lightning Ridge' is the location of the *Lightning Ridge Mensshed*. Located in remote, semi-desert country 700 kilometers inland in northern New South Wales, it is close to the Queensland border. The town would not be there but for the attraction to miners and tourists of the largest known deposits of black opals in the world. Its population, with disproportionately more males, has swollen in recent years to approach 5,000 people, ethnically very diverse and many of them transient. Close to one in five of its locals are from the local Yuwaalaraay Aboriginal Nation. Lightning Ridge Mensshed, which began organising in 2009 and officially opened on May 21, 2011, has provided a unique point of reference for many people and organisations across this very diverse outback community.

---

[2] Kerry Henry, July 24, 2014.

The Shed's Coordinator, Chuck Peters proudly presented about the Lightning Ridge Shed at the 2011 AMSA Men's Shed Conference in Brisbane. He stressed the innovative way the Shed had embraced the community and vice versa. The Shed is open five and a half days a week (and on Saturdays by appointment) and maintains an active Facebook Page[3]. In Chuck's words, the Shed deliberately aims:

> To involve men in the community, young and the elders alike, to get involved and to reintroduce skills that they have possibly forgotten. ... We have changed our shed with loving and dedicated care, with new paint and internal structural changes. .... We are not just about work. We all love our cuppa (playing cards, chess, reading or watching a movie, doing what men are generally good at). Our Shed is non-smoking and alcohol free. Being a mining town, when it gets hot most of the men go underground mining and often prefer that to coming to the Shed. We have a small number of men who have made the Shed their home: they come every day and are disappointed if it's not open. These guys are often single and live out in the [opal] fields. They are off the grid and the Shed provides a shower, power and computer access through the Broadband for Seniors programs. We are the first Shed to have a HAM [amateur] radio shack and hope many more will follow.

Quorn Men's Shed is in a similarly remote small township of Quorn (population around 1,200 people) in the central Flinders Ranges of South Australia 40 kilometers north of Port Augusta. Quorn's history for 100 years from 1878 was closely tied to its role as a major interstate railhead. All these railway lines are now closed or bypass the town, though the Pitchi Richi railway still operates a tourist service to Port Augusta and tourism is now one of the major industries.

Quorn's demographic, like that of many small rural towns in Australia is ageing. Around ten per cent of the local population is Aboriginal. The Men's Shed concept began after two well attended public meetings chaired by the local Mayor. From there a Shed planning team evolved. The abandonment by the local Youth Club of the former Scout Hall gave the team the opportunity to negotiate and secure a long-term lease. The local Lions Club provided the convenience of an auspice arrangement, avoiding the need for a complex incorporation process. The local government (Council) CEO encouraged the Men's Shed to take over

---

[3] Facebook Page https://www.facebook.com/pages/Lightning-Ridge-Mens-Shed-Incorporated, Accessed March 5, 2015.

the long-standing community Men's Breakfast on behalf of the Council in their newly leased Shed. The Shed opened in July 2012 with a Community Men's Breakfast, joined by a local Church Minister who blessed the Shed and its intended activities.

The Quorn Men's Shed actively publicises its Mission in order to increase membership within the Quorn community and surrounding rural townships. As newly appointed hosts for the community breakfasts, the Shed caters for men and other attendees from all walks of country and town life. The Shed's Management Team recognised that social contacts are major contributors to good health and wellbeing. As it remains a community program, Men's Shed membership is not essential for attendees. Its breakfast participants frequently include men from the elderly residential care facility in Quorn. Other sporting and service groups in Quorn are now involved. The Shed's efforts were formally recognised nationally when it became the proud recipient of a 2014 AMSA Innovation Award.

The Quorn Men's Shed, via its 'member speakers' program at the community breakfast, seeks to build or re-build men's confidence and give its diverse members a sense of purpose and a feeling of wellbeing. As the Shed's 2014 Secretary, Brian Walters summarised:

> Following the first member's presentations [at the breakfasts], we have not looked back. Team efforts become the norm and closer relationships are formed. One member spoke of his time in a boy's institution, never knowing his brother was deliberately kept in a separate building on the same site. Other presentations included a property owner who hosted Donald Campbell, his crew, support staff and *Bluebird*, the latter housed in a spare "Chook Shed" for a year awaiting suitable weather conditions until the final successful attempt at the world land speed record on nearby dry Lake Eyre. One man talked about outback-family relationships with the Flying Doctor Service. The presentations by Shed members are wide ranging, and typically cover reminiscences of their time at school, on the farm, their first job, service in the armed forces, family, travel, health and hobbies. Each one further develops that warm sense of wellbeing.[4]

---

[4] Brian Walters, August 10, 2014.

REMARKABLE AUSTRALIAN MEN'S SHEDS

Four Australian Men's Sheds in three states are included for illustration in this section. They are the huge Ballarat East Community Shed (BECS) in the city of Ballarat in Victoria; Sarina and District Community Men's Shed and Woodgate Men's Shed are both on the central Queensland coast, and Airds Bradbury Menshed is in southwestern Sydney in New South Wales.

Ballarat East Community Men's Shed[5] (best known locally as BECS) is a remarkable Men's Shed for a range of reasons. Its rambling complex of huge sheds on a large former factory site makes it one of the biggest Men's Sheds in the world by floor area and by the amount of land it sits on. Located just 2 kilometers east of the Eureka Stockade, where Australian democracy has its roots in the miners' rebellion against the British in 1853, it has perhaps soaked up some of the Eureka spirit with its strong and independent flair for innovation. BECS is one of very few Sheds where the men have optimistically and collectively bought the Shed outright, by borrowing the money, making it relatively independent of governments.

Photograph 28 Logo of Ballarat East Community Men's Shed, Victoria

---

[5] http://www.becs.shed.org.au/, Accessed January 31, 2015.

The Shed's logo in Photograph 28, above, says it all, featuring the BECS acronym, a handshake of friendship under a trussed roof, flanked by a hammer and a guitar. The range of activities and projects that the dozens of regular participants, all men, have undertaken over the years is remarkable. The Shed provides extensive workshop and storage space for diverse individual and group projects. BECS built the wooden seats for a paddle steamer on Ballarat's Lake Wendouree and conducts fund raising barbecues ('sausage sizzles') wherever and whenever they are allowed. BECS also fitted out and acts as a base for the 'Ballarat Soup Bus' that provides free meals for homeless people in Ballarat.

The rest of this story about BECS (set up in 2006) focuses on its unusually comprehensive and original vision and mission, including its intended use of the Shed space and the opportunities it has deliberately created for its members. Set up in 2006, BECS' Vision statement was clear, deliberate and expansive. BECS set out to:

> ... address the issues of men's health (physical, emotional and social well-being) in the community; to engage the elderly, differently-abled, youth, Veterans, Indigenous and other groups of men of the Ballarat and surrounding communities and to specifically address any issues of isolation, loneliness and depression; to support the social interaction of men in transitional periods (e.g. redundancy, bereavement, retirement, ill health, relocation, respite care), and to share, disseminate and preserve the skills, abilities and interests that are relevant to the community.[6]

Its Mission was similarly broad, explicit and empowering. BECS aimed to:

> ... facilitate links between men and health-related agencies, family organisations and specialist health professionals within the community; to work with Government agencies to assist ex prisoners returning to the community; to advocate the benefits of partnerships between men's sheds and community; to develop a men's shed, which can operate on a cost neutral basis, that is, its ongoing costs can be met or exceeded by its revenue; to initiate and continue activities of particular relevance to men, and to provide strong social fabric for men experiencing isolation.

---

[6] BECS http://www.becs.shed.org.au/index.php/about-mens-sheds/71-our-statement-of-purpose, Accessed April 15, 2014.

In pursuing its vision, BECS committed itself to the following set of values that are rarely made so clear, inclusive and explicit. Specifically, these values are:

> ... compassion and empathy in serving men in our community; sincerity and devotion to improving men's health; honesty and integrity in all our activities; to be open to all races, religions and socioeconomic groups; reliability and trustworthiness in delivering on our promises; responsiveness to the needs of men, their families and their community; wisdom in applying technology and innovation to the improvement of our shed; respect for the value added by teamwork and participation in lifelong learning; appreciation of the value of contributions by partners and sponsors, and responsibility and generosity in giving back to the community.

BECS was also very explicit about the Shed as a venue:

> ... where men of all ages can meet in a social non-threatening environment to share experiences and work together; a place where young men can learn from the experience and wisdom of older men in our community; where men will gain support in times of personal difficulty brought on by unemployment, idleness, loneliness, trauma and/or depression; a place of activity and purpose; a place of positive attitudes and caring; a daytime meeting place for men - an alternative to the pubs; a place of belonging leading to a reduction in social isolation to better address men's health issues, improving lifestyles leading to improved quality of life.

Finally BECS deliberately seeks to offer its members opportunities of:

> ... improving self-esteem with youth, unemployed, disabled and older men; developing self-worth through personal effort and community contribution; participate in community service; intergenerational mentoring; support for youth and their aspirations and motivation; helping men with their businesses, or to start a new business; promoting a good work ethic; respect for older people and their knowledge; recognising, regenerating and celebrating craftsmanship; sharing knowledge and skills; assistance to pass on knowledge and experiences; teaching and skills development; realising their potential; developing their hobbies and other interests, and simply someone to talk to.

Sarina and District Community Men's Shed is approximately 36 kilometers south of Mackay on the central coast in Queensland. It illustrates a common attribute of most successful Sheds: a strong connection to the community. Planning for the Men's Shed in Sarina was instigated by means of a public meeting in December 2011. Through the generosity of sponsors and benefactors, the shed was set up in makeshift premises with around 30 initial members only a few months later in May 2012.[7] Two years later in 2014, the Sarina-based Shed in this coastal town of around 6,000 people had attracted around 80 registered members. It negotiated an agreement with the Mackay Regional Council to lease a block of land with a shed building previously utilised by the local SES (State Emergency Services) that to 2015 acted as its temporary premises.

The group undertook extensive redevelopment of the existing shed building. This was fuelled by a proactive approach by the Shed's Planning and Grants sub-committee that raised a total of nearly A$50,000. Further fundraising and sponsorship was identified as crucial to the progression of planning and development of a new shed. As with BECS above, members actively contributed support by organising raffles, sausage sizzles and through the active sale of manufactured, restored and repaired items[8], donated by members and the community.

The Sarina and District Community Men's Shed made the decision, as a group, to actively ensure it would become 'self-supporting' financially. This involved taking on projects restoring or repairing furniture that the Shed sells in order to fund additional projects and programs. This approach serves the local community by providing work for men who otherwise would be unlikely to seek work, and by assisting the community in a voluntary capacity by offering to take on community services and projects. The Shed has been fortunate to have been donated a large range of woodworking and metalworking tools and equipment through the community and its members.

By early 2015 the extensions to the former SES shed building were complete and the workshop was being set up. The Sarina Shed offers its members a relaxed environment that fosters social relationships between members, who can either participate in structured daily events or help with daily Shed maintenance tasks. The Shed also sets itself apart by utilising a 'smoko meeting' and discussion on 'Open Shed' days that encourage conversation between members. On the first

---

[7] The Sarina and District Community Men's Shed, http://www.theshedonline.org.au/mens-sheds/profile/sarina-district-community-men%27s-shed-inc-, Accessed July 17, 2014.
[8] The Sarina and District Community Men's Shed, fhttp://www.theshedonline.org.au/mens-sheds/profile/sarina-district-community-men%27s-shed-inc-, Accessed July 17, 2014.

Saturday of every month a "knock off early BBQ" lunch is held. Importantly, the Shed also supports widows of former members and is committed to organizing grieving services for its members as they sense that 'little is done in this area'.[9]

Woodgate Men's Shed is included to illustrate how quite small Sheds that clearly identified their goals can very successfully and quickly engage with the local community. Woodgate is a small town of 1,000 people situated halfway between Bundaberg and Hervey Bay on Queensland's Burrum Coast. Woodgate Men's Shed is a community project originally sponsored by the Woodgate RSL (Returned Services League) Sub-Branch. Due to a large amount of public interest in a Shed project, a steering committee was elected in 2010 to investigate acquiring land for a shed, raising the necessary money and setting up a shed that incorporated meeting and social facilities as well as a workshop.

The Woodgate Men's Shed became incorporated in February 2012 with a constitution that identified the needs of their community and provided for the Shed's goals and objectives, which were agreed to, as below:

> The objects of the Shed are to advance the health and well-being of our members by providing a safe and happy environment where skilled and unskilled men can, in the company of other men:
> - pursue hobbies, pastimes and interests
> - learn new skills, practice and pass on old skills
> - learn about their own and other men's health and well-being
> - by their efforts, contribute to their families, their friends, the Shed and their community
> - mentor younger men.

Initially the Woodgate Men's Shed operated from a member's garage. With vigorous fundraising, generous community support and some grants, construction commenced in February 2014 on a new shed on public land leased through the Bundaberg Regional Council. The 20m X 12m shed was built with strong support from volunteer local tradesmen, local and district businesses and members. By late 2014 members were able to move into their new 'home' and complete the fit out. The grand opening by its 65 members took place on March 12, 2015.

Over the past two years the Shed has held a series of health talks from local health professionals representing health and wellbeing organizations, including Alzheimer's Australia, Stroke Foundation, Donate Life, Heart Foundation, Cancer Council, the Public Trustee and Hearing Australia. Three senior medical officers gave talks on arthritis, Metabolic syndrome and prostate disease. All

---

[9] Jon Eaton, January 13, 2015.

were open to the public with several partners attending. The Woodgate Shed also has a busy community fundraising program which involves 'sausage sizzles' at hardware stores and local fairs and events, as well as sales from their popular product stalls with items produced in the Shed and from members' gardens.

The *Airds Bradbury Menshed* is included in this section because it illustrates the diversity of its in-shed and community outreach activities and programs in a peri-urban setting, and also because of its huge contribution to many aspects of the local and regional community and the men involved. Initiated in 2009 by Housing New South Wales, is located in large suburban public housing estate. Airds and Bradbury are adjacent suburbs of Campbelltown in Sydney's outer southwest, with a combined population of approximately 15,000 people. Sydney's outer southwest has grown recently and rapidly, and the suburbs are relatively disadvantaged socioeconomically, with elevated unemployment.

By 2010 the Shed project was in an auspice arrangement with Macarthur Diversity Services Initiative (MDSI[10]). MDSI is a not-for-profit, non-government organisation which employs around 80 people, providing a wide range of services to the region including aged care programs, interpretation services, English lessons, Indigenous programs and various recreational programs which includes the Menshed. A newspaper article shown in Photograph 29 gives an account of its programs in 2013.

Photograph 29 'Men Behaving Grandly' Newspaper Article about the Airds Men's Shed, March 2013

---

[10] http://www.mdsi.org.au/what-we-do/mens-shed, Accessed January 8, 2015.

By 2015 the Men's Shed had around 60 active members with a coordinator paid to run it for ten hours per week. It was open five hours a day, four days per week, supported by a ten hour per week coordinator paid by MDSI. Having MDSI 'behind the Men's Shed' was an advantage, providing access to its professional grant writers who have been helpful in obtaining grants and financial support for the Shed, as well as advice and assistance with occupational health and safety, risk management and government compliance. Financial support was received for the Shed, its equipment and its adjacent community garden from Community Builders NSW, the Western Suburbs [Rugby] League Club, the IMB [Building Society] Community Foundation as well as from state and federal governments.

The 'hands-on' work associated with the Airds Bradbury Menshed included woodwork, artwork and sculpture, metal turning and welding, repairing trailers, lawn mowers and whipper snippers for the local community, cooking, computer work and a community garden. The Shed had a Barbecue Day on the last Friday of every month, typically with a guest speaker about various topics such as diet programs, use of fire extinguishers, scam information and computer training as well as healthy eating, including through salads, for example, from the community garden. One of its artists with a disability recently won a valuable regional art award.

The Shed is actively involved in a remarkable range of community outreach programs, including building a mobile cooking trailer for community use, creating metal sculptures for the Campbelltown Art Gallery and doing jobs for the local community. It has made urban search and rescue tunnels and cubby houses to educate children in fire safety, organised training programs at the Shed for the Campbelltown police, made target holders for a local archery group, repaired bicycles for Aboriginal children in foster care and arranged a free exercise course for men at the Shed run by exercise physiologists.

The Men's Shed also has a large, well-established community garden, started in 2011, to supply the men at the Shed with fresh produce that encourages healthy eating. It supplies produce to the MDSI Café Kulcha as well as the Airds Food Co-operative to local residents of Airds. The Men's Shed garden was featured on *Gardening Australia* on ABC TV in 2013. The Shed had many other jobs 'in the pipeline' in early 2015. In partnership with the Campbelltown Council, the Shed was building Indian Myna (a pest bird) traps to sell to the public. It had also secured a woodworking sculptor to work with the men and planned to commence leatherwork in the Shed.

NEW AND CUTTING EDGE AUSTRALIAN MEN'S SHEDS

Four diverse, 'new and cutting edge' Australian Men's Sheds are included as examples in this section. Two are at opposite ends (and socio-economic extremes) in the huge state of Western Australia. The Mosman Park Community Men's Shed is in a relatively affluent suburban Perth, the capital of Western Australia. The Fitzroy Valley Men's Shed, by contrast, is in one of the most disadvantaged and remote Indigenous communities in the far north of Western Australia. The Mount Pleasant Men's Shed and the Tintinara Community Men's Shed, both in rural South Australia, are included because they are typical of many new but small Sheds valiantly and creatively striving to use their small group's collective skills to provide premises for future use by the community.

Mosman Park Community Men's Shed, located between Perth and Fremantle, is a new purpose-built 'super-shed', claiming on their Shed web site to be the largest Men's Shed in Western Australia with over 200 members[11]. Officially opened at the Tom Perrot Reserve on December 15, 2012 by Colin Barnett, Premier of Western Australia, also Member for Cottlesloe in whose electorate the Shed is located, it was an initiative funded mainly by Mosman Park Rotary and Lottery West. The huge and striking new rectangular shed on two expansive levels was purpose-built for a range of activities on the edge of the Mosman Park football oval, allowing for a wide range of future activities, currently including woodwork, gardening, photography and amateur radio.

The story of how this 'super-shed' was established is carefully chronicled with words and photographs in a big, professional book titled *From Green Grass to Fabulous Facility: The Development of the Mosman Park Community Men's Shed*[12]. As the dedication in the book suggests, it was created by a 'hard working group of volunteers ... who took an ambitious idea and turned it into reality'. Their story starts, appropriately, with a visit and presentation in April 2009 to the Rotary Club of Mosman Park by the laidback but very persuasive Bill Johnstone and Alan Gowland from the nearby Fremantle Men's Shed. Fortuitously, 'The Mayor of Mosman Park and Councillors were present and they indicated some land could be available' on which to build a Men's Shed in Mosman Park.

In February 2010 (less than three years before the official Shed opening, on December 15, 2012) a public interest meeting was held that 40 local men attended and a steering committee was set up. Progress was swift: the committee met

---

[11] Mosman Park Men's Shed, www.mosmanparkmensshed.com, Accessed April 15, 2014.
[12] *From Green Grass to Fabulous Facility: The Development of the Mosman Park Community Men's Shed*. Produced by David Beckley, December 2012.

monthly during 2010, formally incorporated the Mosman Park Community Men's Shed, drew up draft building plans and was allocated a site for the shed on the side of a large sporting reserve. By early 2011 the Shed had joined the Western Australian Men's Shed Association (WAMSA), the site was pegged out and applications for funding had gone out. The Mosman Park Rotary Club generously gave A$30,000, but the biggest early funding windfall (in September 2011) was a LotteryWest Grant of A$723,000. The commitment of funds from the four neighbouring Councils for a full time Shed manager for the first two years of operation was 'icing' on the, by most Australian Men's Shed standards, already generous 'cake', While the shedders and the community fund-raised actively and very effectively, without an extra A$65,000 'tipped in' by the Mosman Park Rotary Club, the Shed's completion and extensive professional fit-out would not have been possible.

A huge Shed project on this scale is not for the faint-hearted and is unlikely to be often, if ever, replicated on that scale. For context, Western Australia generally had been booming economically to 2015 because of recent mining and gas field development. Mosman Park is a relatively advantaged Perth suburb adjacent to Peppermint Grove, one of the ten most advantaged suburbs in Australia. [13] The Shed's Steering Committee had access to very strong professional networks, people, skills and connections to bring to the project planning, management, fundraising and construction phases. Its Shed has been very ably led through the energy, networks and initiative of its Chair, Brett Pollock, since June 2010. How it functions as a Men's Shed in the medium and longer term will be interesting to watch and learn from, given its sheer size and the opportunities and expectations created by such a large and expensive, new multi-purpose space. As the last words of the Shed's book put it, 'Now that the shed is open for business, the first chapter in the history of MPCMS is complete and an exciting new era commences'.

Fitzroy Crossing is in the same state as The Mosman Park Shed above, but here the similarities drop away, despite its *Fitzroy Valley Men's Shed* also being new and cutting edge. Fitzroy Crossing is situated midway between Halls Creek and Broome, straddling the Fitzroy River 2,500 kilometers northeast of Perth and is surrounded by some of the most disadvantaged and remote Aboriginal

---

[13] Australian Bureau of Statistics, Media Release, 'ABS Releases Measures of Socio-economic Advantage and Disadvantage', March 26, 2008, http://www.abs.gov.au/ausstats/abs@.nsf/mediareleasesbyReleaseDate/AC5B967F97D490 2ECA257B3B001AF670, Accessed August 6, 2014.

communities in Australia. People from five nearby Aboriginal Nations live in 44 Aboriginal communities within 200 kilometers of Fitzroy Crossing in the broader Fitzroy Valley[14]. Around 80 per cent of the two thousand people who live in the Fitzroy Valley are Aboriginal, as are 60 per cent of those living in the 1,500 person community of Fitzroy Crossing. One of the town's main social imperatives is getting younger, local Indigenous people into paid work, a cause the Shed has deliberately embraced.

The Fitzroy Valley Men's Shed is similar to most other Sheds in that its stated concern is for *all* men, neatly encapsulated in a Bunaba Nation phrase, *Gurana Yani U ('For all Men')*, the name of its auspice organization, shortened to the acronym GYU. Where it differs is that the original and main aim of GYU was to train and employ local Indigenous people to work in the mining industry, with the broader aim of aiding in the prosperity of men by helping them to build a better future for themselves and their community. This unique Shed opened its doors to both Indigenous and non-Indigenous people in 2008, when Andrew ('Twiggy') Forrest (a Western Australian mining magnate) and The Australian Children's Trust met with the Fitzroy Crossing community to discuss the potential for employment and training for the wider community. The women of this community identified a specific lack of opportunities for men in the Fitzroy River region. With the support of the Australian Children's Trust, a facility was purchased including earth moving equipment, industrial tools and equipment. Through the instrumental use of this facility, the GYU Men's Group was able to facilitate training of male community members for the mining industry.

While the local community welcomed the facility itself, it was quickly realised that some essential social components were missing, and GYU sought to incorporate a Men's Shed community program as part of the holistic structure of the new facility. Community members and the Australian Children's Trust came to an agreement that the facility would operate under the direction of the GYU for two years, at which time the Men's Group would then purchase the shed, forming the Gurama Yani U Men's Group in May 2012[15].

The Men's Shed run by GYU is 'cutting edge' for several reasons. The GYU, in conjunction with community and supporting groups, responded to community concerns, specifically to the need for employment for men within the Fitzroy Crossing area. The Shed, which is capable of both earth moving and demolition

---

[14] 'Closing the Gap: Local Implementation Plan', Fitzroy Crossing. Version 2, September 15, 2010.
http://www.dss.gov.au/sites/default/files/documents/05_2012/fitzroy_crossing_lip.pdf, Accessed August 6, 2014.
[15] Gurama Yani U, http://www.fitzroyvalleymen.org.au/, Accessed July 31, 2014.

work, serves as a platform for creating and supporting ongoing employment within the local community. Through an arrangement with a mining company, the Shed supports local Indigenous employees who participate in fly-in-fly-out (FIFO) mining operations in the Pilbara. The Shed also supports and assists with industry qualifications. The GYU in 2014 employed six local people in a range of contracts in Fitzroy Crossing and surrounding communities.

The GYU has other community-based programs to complement the employment-based foundation of the Shed, including a small community nursery, small poultry farm and a number of family nights each year. This Shed, while uniting men together for a common purpose of mutual support, differs from other Men's Sheds in that it is premised on a broader community vision. It has not been easy, as projects like this with an enterprise focus need sound management. The CEO since April 2014, Alan Scott, summarised the situation to early 2015.

> Locally we have good working partnerships with Marra Worra Worra, Women's Resource Centre, Karriyili, Nindilingarri Health, Fitzroy Valley Police, Shire of Derby/West Kimberley, Fitzroy Valley District Hospital, Mangkaja Arts Kimberley Training Institute, Fitzroy Valley District High School, Muway Constructions and Downer EDI Mining. We also have support from Department of Housing, Department of Indigenous Affairs, Department of Prime Minister and Cabinet, Department of Community Health and Department of Justice. Our Men's Shed envisages not only a decent employment for locals as our crew, but also empowers them by training so that they can enter into business in their own right and we can support them to kick-start those businesses by offering administrative support. [16]

Mount Pleasant Men's Shed is in a small town of only 500 people in the northern Adelaide Hills, 55 kilometers from Adelaide in South Australia. It is included as an example of a new or emerging Shed typical and very much at the cutting edge of Men's Shed practice in Australia beyond the metropolis. It is important to again acknowledge that all new Sheds are cutting edge locally. Not all can tap into opportunities created by existing significant expertise and resources (as was the case in the two Sheds above). Nor do they all necessarily manifest the desperate community need (exemplified by the Men's Shed in the Fitzroy Valley)

---

[16] 'Fitzroy Valley Men', http://www.fitzroyvalleymen.org.au/category/messageboard/, Accessed August 6, 2014.

that can leverage significant external funding. While most Men's Sheds struggle in the establishment phase, it is this early struggle, exemplified by the Mount Pleasant Men's Shed case study that can create the critically important bonding between the members of the original committee. Not all Sheds make it through difficult early setbacks, and not all members of the original committee are involved (or alive) to see their vision finally realised.

The young Shed's history in Mount Pleasant goes back to 2012 when an interest was shown in the development of a Men's Shed. It was envisaged quite simply, as for most Sheds across Australia, as a place where people, older men in particular, could meet and socialise. With a fully equipped shed, it was hoped to be able to allow men to conduct hobbies such as woodworking. As with most Sheds this was a group effort, but the vision, leadership and drive typically comes from one person or a small number of people. In this case, it was from its Chairperson, Bob Long.

After discussion between the Shed Committee and the Barossa Council, a tentative site was identified. Work was then carried out clearing vegetation and assessing what the site might offer, but there were two major setbacks. The Barossa Council put a stop to the on-site work, and an application for funding in 2013 to the Australian Men's Shed Association was not successful. A separate funding application to a private company led to a small but important A$750 donation to allow the shedders to hire a portable timber sawmill to salvage pine logs in liaison with ForestrySA. By mid-2014 they had dismantled two existing sheds, harvested forest timber and milled over 3,000 metres into suitable sizes to build their 21m x 12m shed. To 'cool their heels' and raise money, the group cut firewood for sale to the public. To maintain a public presence, the men built a float featuring a shed in the Mount Pleasant Street Parade 2013, which they displayed afterwards at the local Agricultural Show.

Though the group is small, the accumulated knowledge and skills within groups like this is vast. Meantime they meet fortnightly at the Mount Pleasant Bakery, reaching out to any new members who might wish to join them in this endeavour. By late 2014 they sent out a call, as below:

> Your input is only as much as you are able to give, from moral support, to heavy physical work and anything in between. Those with computer skills will have a chance to use them, as will those who simply want to have a coffee, within a social atmosphere.

The group stressed that they were 'more than willing to consider any job: ... nothing is too big or too small'. The group's aim was to have a concrete foundation at Old Talunga Park by 2015, ready for the construction of a large shed for future use by the community. Having a proposed Shed only in the planning stage and a site for it yet to be approved doesn't stop a Shed and its shedders from working towards their goal! As with many other Men's Sheds, the journey is as important as the destination.

The *Tintinara Community Men's Shed*, like the Mount Pleasant Men's Shed, is included as a good example of a Shed 'feeling its way' early on, but making remarkable progress. Like many small Australian towns, Tintinara (a South Australian community of only 250 people) is enthusiastic about their 'Tinty' Men's Shed. From the first community meeting on October 31, 2013 to shed completion took only a year. As with most other Sheds, the group of interested potential members 'checked out' other Sheds nearby, in this case at Meningie, Murray Bridge and Strathalbyn, before going back to the Tintinara Development Group to take the typical next steps: getting community members to sign up to the idea, locating a potential site or existing shed, gaining the necessary permissions and funding, doing some plans and a budget, and adding services plus equipment.

A disused railway goods shed was seen as 'a standout location' and, through the intervention of the Coorong District Council, permission was obtained for the use of the state-owned building and its refurbishment as a Men's Shed. By February 2014 the initial steering committee had handed over Shed management to a Committee of elected members auspiced through the Council. At that time the shed consisted of a (leaky) corrugated iron shell covering a timber framework, with four sliding doors and a concrete and rubble floor. There was no power or water, and the total Shed finances stood at only A$3,300, raised via donations from the 27 members who had initially signed up.

The Committee established its five agreed 'core' activities: to provide: a venue where members of the local community could come together to work in groups or individually on DIY projects; a strong social fabric for people who may experience isolation; a partnership between the members of the Men's Shed and the local general and business community; links with health-related agencies and health professionals, plus sharing, dissemination and exchange of skills and abilities.

The Tintinara Community Men's Shed and the wider community were very clear about two overriding principles.

> The benefits of membership should not be restricted to men only, and the facilities should be available in full to any female members who may

wish to use them. Moreover, they do not wish to be perceived as an 'old man's' shed and younger participants will be actively encouraged (once the refurbishment is completed and the shed can be opened outside normal working hours).[17]

The first requirement of this fledgling organisation was to refurbish the shed to a state whereby these core activities could be achieved. Quotes from local tradesmen were obtained for: the supply of materials and labour to re-roof the shed; the supply and installation of power to the building; and the concreting of the entire floor area inside the shed. Design plans for the building were drawn up, and a proposed budget and time frame for refurbishment were determined, subject to suitable financing. The initial cost of the shed was estimated at around A\$55,000. At least half of this cost was met *gratis* by members and other community groups who offered their assistance. A grant proposal was submitted and accepted by Community Benefit South Australia for funds to cover these initial works. The main focus for Shed members therefore became the renovation of the fabric of the building.

From the first day that the building became available, the aim was to welcome all members to the Shed, though the committee was aware that the facilities offered were limited. With few facilities in the empty shed, the important, regular event for volunteers became the 'morning teas' when all work stopped on both weekdays the shed was open. There was one serendipitous outcome from the removal of the old iron on the shed. With the purchase of an iron guillotine and an iron roller, the shedders made raised garden beds for sale from the recycled roofing iron, with more than 20 immediate orders. Further funding came from the Coorong District Council for the purchase of tools, and a grant of A\$5,000 was received from the Australian Men's Shed Association.

The power connection and cabling were in place by February 2015, the first anniversary of the Men's Shed. The floor had been concreted, the roof repaired and the inner walls painted. A long workbench with insets for various drills and saws had been installed along the length of one wall. With power, tools and a working area, the next step was to open the shed on weekends to allow access for those members of the community who work during the week. If the Tintinara community can create a viable Shed in a year, many other new and cutting edge possibilities are likely only just around the corner in many other communities.

---

[17] 'Tintinara Community Men's Shed', John Benyon, August 12, 2014.

Irish Men's Sheds

John Evoy, Anne McDonnell & Barry Golding

Chapter 7 includes four case study examples in each category of 'early', 'innovative', 'remarkable' and 'new and cutting edge' Irish Men's Sheds. They include examples from diverse Counties and locations across both the Republic of Ireland (12 case studies) and Northern Ireland (4 case studies). Again, both Irish jurisdictions on the Island of Ireland are interchangeably referred to in this Chapter as 'Ireland' and 'Irish'.

EARLY PIONEER IRISH MEN'S SHEDS

The inspiration for the earliest Men's Sheds in Ireland came from previous Australian Men's Sheds and its national Association. Four 'early pioneer' Men's Sheds (including groups of Sheds) from different Irish Counties are included below as case studies at Tipperary, Arklow, in Meath and at Killarney. All have, from early beginnings in Tipperary in late 2009, helped inspire, support and encourage the growth of a strong and distinctive Men's Shed Movement on the Island of Ireland, with 240 Men's Sheds open across Ireland within five years, supported by a secure Irish Men's Sheds Association (IMSA)[1].

The earliest Men's Sheds in Ireland were created through collaboration between service providers and communities. Social inclusion, community development and family support agencies played a significant role in setting up Men's Sheds during these first five years. Dr Lucia Carragher's research report, *Men's Sheds in Ireland: Learning through Community Contexts* summarised the nature of the support for and development of Men's Sheds across Ireland to 2013.

> Some of the Irish sheds have developed with support from local Family Resource Centres (FRCs). These are state-funded organisations designed

---

[1] John Evoy confirmed there were 270 Sheds registered with IMSA to May 11, 2014.

to 'combat disadvantaged communities and improve the functioning of the family' through a 'bottom-up' approach that involves local communities tackling the problems they face, thus creating partnerships between voluntary and statutory agencies. ... Other sheds are developing with the support of Local Development Companies (LDCs). ... While many sheds have clearly received support to help them get started, many others have not and have been set up by groups of men who do not have any agency connections.[2]

Tipperary Men's Shed was the first Men's Shed to open on the Island of Ireland. 'Tipp Men's Shed' was founded in August 2009, directly inspired by the Men's Shed Movement in Australia. At a Men's Development Network (MDN) health training day held in Knockanrawley Resource Centre, a video clip was shown of Barry Golding speaking about Men's Sheds in Australia. True to the wider mission of Knockanrawley Resource Centre ('to encourage, foster and empower people, groups and the community as a whole to identify and make changes that enhance their lives'[3]), a Men's Shed became part of the Centre's community development plan. It was something that men in the community themselves wanted. In describing Tipperary Men's Shed, Ruth Smith, its Project Coordinator, observed in 2014 that 'The group continues to fluctuate and change like any group, but the support it has given to Tipperary Town men is always solid and non judgmental.'[4] In late 2010, Tipperary Men's Shed hosted the first meeting of the Irish Men's Shed Forum, attended by 85 men from across Ireland.

Knockanrawley Resource Centre, together with the local community, originally started Tipperary Men's Shed as an organic garden, with members later meeting weekly and working together, mainly through woodwork and metalwork. Insurance for activities became a challenge in the early days of the Shed. The men overcame this challenge by building a shelter for themselves. The new shelter became a space to carry out car mechanics, potter with seeds and plants, and undertake other activities. The Shed members grow their own food and are involved with a local free food project with supermarkets in the town. Other activities of the Shed to 2015 included local historical explorations in conjunction with the local community bus, learning about life coaching and other aspects of personal development, Do-It-Yourself (DIY) and welding. In 2015 the Shed

---

[2] Lucia Carragher, *Men's Sheds in Ireland: Learning through Community Contexts*. Dundalk: The Netwell Centre, 2013, 16-17.
[3] 'Knockanrawley Resource Centre – Mission Statement', http://knockanrawley.ie/about-us/mission/, Accessed October 7, 2014.
[4] Ruth Smith, Project Coordinator, Knockanrawley Resource Centre, Tipperary Town.

continued to network with other local Men's Sheds, sharing ideas and experiences to help them develop their own Sheds.[5]

Soon after the meeting of the Irish Men's Sheds Forum in Tipperary Men's Shed in late 2010, the first meeting of representatives of each Men's Shed from across Ireland took place in Arklow, a coastal town in County Wicklow on the east of Ireland on March 14, 2011. The meeting was hosted by *Arklow Men's Shed*, by which time the Irish Men's Sheds Association (IMSA) had been formed. Part of this meeting marked an important step in the early life of IMSA as summarized below in *EXPLORE,* the quarterly magazine of AONTAS (the peak national Irish adult and community education body) in May 2011.

> The first part of the meeting allowed Sheds to share information about work they are undertaking as well as those new to the idea of Sheds to ask questions. After this part of the meeting, Shed members were taken to see the new boat-building project being undertaken by the Arklow Men's Shed which will build a boat over the course of the next 14 weeks. The second part of the meeting saw the representatives from the Men's Sheds come together to decide on operational structures for the organisation and key tasks for the IMSA over the course of the year. Key developments were that the IMSA have decided to ask members to participate in a competition to design a logo for the organisation and that the steering group decided to ask for a voluntary contribution from each Shed towards the costs of moving IMSA forward and that a submission made on behalf of the IMSA has made it to the shortlist of 42 entries for the Social Entrepreneur's Bootcamp 2011[6].

The media excerpt below describes the launch of the boat, a 20-foot (6 metre) timber dory named *An Bád Inbhear Mór,* shown in Photograph 30.

---

[5] Ruth Smith, January 31, 2015.
[6] AONTAS, May 2011, *EXPLORE,* No.18, Dublin, 5.

Photograph 30 Arklow Men's Shed Dory, *An Bád Inbhear Mór*, 2015

> This [boat building] project has brought about a great sense of hope and pride not only to the men involved, but also to the whole town. The boat was paraded through the centre of the town with a pipe band on the day of its launch and there was a great buzz. There was such great excitement when it finally took to water and it did exactly what it was supposed to do.[7]

This project captured the tradition of boat building within Arklow Town. Men taking part ranged from 30 to 60 years of age. Thirteen weeks were spent building the boat at Arklow Men's Shed's rented workshop space. On completion of the project, in the spirit of community, the Shed donated the boat to a local voluntary group, the Arklow Sea Scouts.

As an early Irish pioneer, Arklow Men's Shed has been generous in sharing its experience and knowledge with others. Indeed, in 2012 the Arklow Men's Shed welcomed delegates from all over Europe, as one of a number of Men's

---

[7] Alan Jacques, December 5, 2011, 'Arklow: Men Leave their Shed in a Boat', in *Changing Ireland*, http://changingireland.blogspot.ie/2011/12/arklow-men-leave-their-shed-in-boat.html, Accessed October 7, 2014.

Shed tours to take place nationwide to allow visitors to assess the Men's Shed model in Ireland for possible replication across Europe.

> A total of 16 visitors from countries including France and Wales attended the local workshop. "We showed them the work we do at the shed including the construction of dog boxes and chairs as well as the boats we made. We showed them around the workshop and showed them the tools that have been donated by the local community," said Mr. Ryan [the Men's Shed Chairman]. He also outlined that Arklow Men's Shed is of great benefit to men who are retired or unemployed or who cannot work full time due to disability.[8]

As for many other early Irish Sheds, community development organisations have been crucial in the setting-up of the *Meath Men's Sheds* in County Meath. Considering the social inclusion, community support and community development remit which many local organisations have in the Republic of Ireland, it is not surprising that Men's Sheds projects have been supported by such organisations. In the words of the Meath Men's Sheds coordinator, Kay O'Connor's 2014 description below, there is evidence of what can be achieved for the development of Men's Sheds, with a community development approach on behalf of agencies and workers.

> There are now six Men's Sheds in County Meath operating under the LCDP programme of Meath Partnership. Each of the Men's Sheds are different as the participants decide their own programme of activities; examples include woodturning, art, playing bowls, cards, photography and most importantly drinking tea! Because the projects are funded, fortunately the participants do not pay membership fees or cover the costs of insurance or rent. This mitigates the financial barrier of members joining and ensures all men who would like to participate can do so. Meetings are held weekly in Men's Sheds in Athboy, Broomfield, Dunshaughlin, Moynalty, Navan and Summerhill. The men themselves, the members of the Shed, have ownership of the project and they engage in a wide range of activities. The pastimes and hobbies are too numerous

---

[8] 'Arklow Men's Shed Welcomes Visitors from all over Europe', in *Wicklow People* newspaper, June 27, 2012,
http://www.independent.ie/regionals/wicklowpeople/lifestyle/arklow-mens-shed-welcomes-visitors-from-all-over-europe-27871387.html#sthash.9KVlVDIo.dpuf, Accessed October 2014.

to mention, but to mention a few, since Men's Sheds began, members have been playing bowls, cards and chess; they've been practicing archery, painting, taking part in computer classes; there's been much activity around restoring a variety of old transport and farm equipment and furniture, and trips are organised and other Sheds are visited. Occasionally members take a break and just read the paper or share stories over cups of tea. There is no charge for becoming a member or participating in the Men's Shed and no prior notice is required for interested participants to attend; just drop in, see what's on offer, meet the members and share a cuppa and a yarn.[9]

The Meath Men's Sheds story is both early and innovative. A self-description from one of the six Meath Men's Sheds is illustrative as to why the innovation works.

We live in a rural community where there is a lot of social isolation. ... The Men's Shed (Moynalty Men's Shed, Meath) provides a means for men to get out and about during the day, meet other men of similar age and interests and there is something for everyone to do - that's what makes it interesting.[10]

Service providers in many places across Ireland have recognized a general lack of involvement of men within community learning, adult education and other community development activities. In describing the start of its first two Men's Sheds, Kay O'Connor identified how a lack of men within community groups prompted local action.

In September 2010 the Men's Shed project was introduced to County Meath by Meath Partnership. Through our community-based activities, we became aware that community groups were predominantly comprised of women and that there was a significant lack of social outlets in which older men could engage, particularly for those men living alone in rural areas. Subsequent examinations of projects and best practice models acknowledged as successful in engaging older men, encountered the Men's Shed movement in Australia. Recognizing the

---

[9] Kay O'Connor, Local Community Development Projects Officer, Meath Partnership.
[10] http://www.meathpartnership.ie/about-us/newsletter/meath-mens-sheds/, Accessed October 7, 2014.

potential of the Sheds in an Irish context, in 2010 Meath Partnership[11], in collaboration with the Third Age Foundation, secured limited funding for a pilot project from Age and Opportunity through their Get Vocal Initiative and thus the Shed concept was introduced in two locations in Meath. This pilot funding was aimed at specifically targeting older men, but following this initial pilot phase, funding has been secured through the Local Community Development Programme [LCDP], and since 2011 the membership has been open to all men.[12]

The start of many other early Irish sheds occurred very informally and in quite informal settings. *Killarney Men's Shed* self-describes its early but quite recent beginnings below.

> Killarney Men's Shed began life in November 2011. A group of men met in a hotel in Killarney and started the ball rolling. Premises were donated by the Kerry Mental Health Association with a grant from South Kerry Partnership Development and the assistance of TUS [a community work placement scheme] and RSS [Really Simple Syndication] workers associated with RTE [Ireland's national television and radio broadcaster]. With the goodwill from a lot of Killarney Businesses, the shed conversion got underway. A step-by step start up guide was downloaded from the Australian Men's Shed Association, and working on this as the 'bible', a small steering committee was assembled.[13]

Killarney Men's Shed opened its doors on March 20, 2012, with an official opening on June 20 in the same year. David Helmers, AMSA Executive Officer, officially cut the ribbon. Since then, the activity of the Shed has grown significantly. Killarney Men's Shed makes it clear that 'New members are always welcome and can be assured that there is something of interest for everyone, as the men have ownership of the projects and decide their own programme of events.'[14] It's hard to imagine not being able to find something of interest in Killarney Men's Shed. The list of activities includes a Tool Museum, gardening,

---

[11] http://www.meathpartnership.ie/social-development/mens-sheds, Accessed January 8, 2015.
[12] Kay O'Connor, 'Men's Sheds, How Men's Sheds were Introduced to Meath', http://www.meathpartnership.ie/social-development/mens-sheds, Accessed October 7, 2014.
[13] http://killarneymensshed.weebly.com/history.html, Accessed October 7, 2014.
[14] http://killarneymensshed.weebly.com/mission-statement.html Accessed October 7, 2014.

art, vintage stonework, cards, darts, chess, and computers. A member of Killarney Men's Shed describes his experience in the excerpt below.

> As well as meeting new people, we have great banter and a sharing of stories. People also have the chance to learn new skills in a relaxed, informal way. ... It's important for men to have somewhere to go for company.[15]

The Irish Men's Sheds Association held its 2012 Annual General Meeting in partnership with Killarney Men's Shed, hosting over 200 attendees. Killarney Men's Shed has devoted time and energy to supporting other Shed start-ups in County Kerry and beyond, emulating the kind friendship, support, advice and information it had received while setting up in on-line conversations with the Bateau Bay Men's Shed, in the central coast of New South Wales in Australia. Photograph 29 shows its Worldwide 'Shed Brothers Certificate' acknowledging its Shed brotherhood with Bateau Bay.

---

[15] Donal Hickey, 'Forget the Chat at the Pub, now it's Down to the Shed', *Irish Examiner*, June 21, 2012.

Photograph 31 Worldwide 'Shed Brother's Certificate' with Bateau Bay
(Australia), Killarney Men's Shed, November 11, 2014

In March 2014, in the local St. Patrick's Day parade in Killarney, County Kerry, the Killarney Men's Shed was named the 'top community support group', an honour well deserved by a Shed that has worked hard to provide opportunities for men in the area.

INNOVATIVE IRISH MEN'S SHEDS

The Men's Sheds introduced in this section as innovative Irish Men's Shed case studies include two Sheds in Northern Ireland and two in the Republic of Ireland. They include the Ennis Men's Shed and a group of Men's Sheds in Louth (Louth

Community Men's Sheds) in the Republic of Ireland, as well as Action Mental Health Sheds and the North Belfast Men's Shed in Northern Ireland.

The *Louth Community Men's Shed* project was designed to address the high levels of social isolation experienced by many older, retired men across the northeast of Ireland. Three Community Men's Sheds (Dundalk Community Men's Shed, Cooley Men's Shed and Drogheda Community Men's Shed) are now strategically located across the northeast, covering Seatown (Dundalk), Drogheda and the Cooley Peninsula area. These sheds provide opportunities that are closely matched to the needs and skills of older men and the communities in which they live. The skills learnt and shared among the men in these Sheds include woodwork, woodturning, woodcarving, art, computers, ceramics, cooking, horticulture and photography. Through the provision of activities which promote a sense of belonging, the Louth Community Men's Shed projects aims to achieve outcomes of positive ageing and wellbeing for those men who participate, as well as their partners, families and communities.[16]

All three Men's Sheds in County Louth work together and cross-border with other Sheds, creating an atmosphere of solidarity and community for all involved. As the Louth Community Men's Shed's *Winter Newsletter* summarised in 2013:

> During 2014 we will continue to network and work with other men's groups and organisations on both sides of the border, in communities that still suffer from disadvantage and from the legacy of the conflict. We know that Men's Sheds can play a significant and practical role in fostering more cohesive communities. Men's Sheds can help connect men with their communities and mainstream society and at the same time act as a catalyst in stimulating community economic activities. We have achieved a lot over this past two years and we are grateful to the International Fund for Ireland for their financial support. Without this funding we could not have completed much of the cross-border work that we have[17].

---

[16] 'Official opening of Drogheda Men's Shed Project'.
http://www.internationalfundforireland.com/component/content/article?id=482:official-opening-of-drogheda-mens-shed-project, Accessed October 7, 2014.
[17] Louth Community Men's Sheds, *Winter Newsletter* 2013,
http://agefriendly.ie/louthagefriendly/wp-content/uploads/Mens-Sheds-Winter-2013.pdf, Accessed October 7, 2014.

Louth Men's Sheds project 'has one criteria, men'[18]. Started by the Netwell Centre (Dundalk Institute of Technology) and the Louth County Council as part of the Louth Age Friendly County Initiative, this innovative Men's Shed project was first funded by the International Fund for Ireland (IFI) under the *Building Foundations Programme for Community Based Economic and Social Regeneration*. In 2011 Eva Beirne, Men's Shed Coordinator with the Netwell Centre, emphasized the role of Louth Community Men's Shed project in having a positive impact on men's wellbeing and mental health through all-important social connection.

> The primary focus of the project is on older men but younger men will play an important role too. Younger men can support the development of projects in the sheds and they can learn and share in the wisdom and experience of older men. There is very strong evidence pointing to the vulnerability of older men to isolation and loneliness as they age and experience difficulties adjusting to changes in role identity associated with retirement (farmers retiring, in particular may find this transition difficult), as well as to changes in social networks, especially widowhood. We also know that increasing people's social interaction can have a positive impact on well-being and mental health. ... Ultimately this can only be a positive thing not just for improving the quality of life of older men in County Louth but also for our society and the social connectedness of our community.[19]

Photograph 32 shows the official launch of Louth Community Men's Shed in September 2011, attended by 150 guests.

---

[18] 'Mens Sheds', http://agefriendly.ie/louthagefriendly/mens-sheds/, Accessed October 7, 2014.
[19] 'Mens Sheds', see http://agefriendly.ie/louthagefriendly/mens-sheds/, Accessed October 7, 2014.

Photograph 32 Launch of the Louth Community Men's Shed, Seatown, September 2011 (centre: Eva Beirne, Shed Coordinator; at right: Dr Lucia Carragher)

Dundalk was the first of three Men's Sheds to be opened in Louth. A press release from the launch records that:

> ... cutting the ribbon at the official opening event were special guests, Barry Golding, [from] Australia and Michael O' Muircheartaigh, recently retired GAA [Gaelic Athletics Association] commentator for RTE [Ireland's national TV and radio broadcaster][20].

Also at the launch, International Fund for Ireland Board member, Rose-Mary Farrell, said:

> We believe that the Men's Sheds project will have a very positive impact for reconciliation in County Louth. It will bring men from the two communities together, in a safe, shared space. It will help them to see the

---

[20] 'Ribbon cut on first of three Men's Sheds for Louth',
http://www.internationalfundforireland.com/media-centre/93-press-releases-2011/417-ribbon-cut-on-first-of-three-mens-sheds-for-louth-14, Accessed October 7, 2014.

myriad of things which unite us, which far outweighs that which divides. And it will bring together young and older men, to share their stories, skills and knowledge[21].

Louth Community Men's Shed project is innovative in many ways. Watching its video clip[22], it is impossible not to be struck by the level of transformation that has taken place, in terms of buildings, communities, and men's personal lives. One shedder smiles, saying: "As far as I'm concerned, it's magic."[23]

The *North Belfast Men's Shed* also provides much needed, innovative opportunities for men whose communities and lives had been impacted by the conflict in Northern Ireland. Alexey James, North Belfast Men's Shed Coordinator, described the roots of North Belfast Men's Shed.

> In 2011, the North Belfast Partnership coordinated research into the needs of older men living within their catchment. Many of the local neighbourhood areas within North Belfast were amongst the most deeply impacted during the period of the Northern Ireland conflict and continue to experience high levels of division, deprivation and need. The research concluded that a combination of social, economic and historical factors meant that older men living across the North Belfast "Neighborhood Renewal" areas were more likely to experience isolation and loneliness. As a result, an initiative called the Rejuvenate Programme was put in place to promote and provide activities for men 55 and over. Funded by the Big Lottery Fund and supported by a range of local organisations and agencies, the centrepiece of the Rejuvenate programme is the North Belfast Men's Shed, shown in Photograph 33.

---

[21] 'Official Opening of Drogheda Men's Shed Project', http://www.internationalfundforireland.com/component/content/article?id=482:official-opening-of-drogheda-mens-shed-project, Accessed October 7, 2014.
[22] https://www.youtube.com/watch?v=1nGMro2Vtrw, Accessed October 7, 2014.
[23] 'Louth Community Men's Shed', Video, https://www.youtube.com/watch?v=1nGMro2Vtrw, Accessed October 7, 2014.

Photograph 33 North Belfast Men's Shed, March 2, 2014 (Shedders, Barry Golding at right)

The biggest challenge for the Shed is to achieve sustainability beyond the current funding. With this in mind a Shed Management Group of members has been formed and members have taken on a volunteer role to oversee the day to day running of the Shed. Health and safety has been a top priority from the start and a two-day training course for men wanting to use Shed workshop machinery is one of the measures that has been put in place. Links with other community organisations and services have enabled a range of health and wellbeing programmes to be run through the Shed.

From the start, links with other Men's Sheds helped to shape the development of the North Belfast Shed. Visits to Sheds in Armagh and Louth were particularly influential. One of the biggest challenges in setting up the Shed was not only finding a suitable building but also finding one that men from different community backgrounds would feel comfortable and safe coming to. Having found such a location, one of the biggest successes to date has been the renovation and redecoration work carried out by members to get the Shed up and running. Equally, if not more importantly is the warm and welcoming atmosphere that has been created by the men, which is often commented upon by new members and visitors alike.[24]

A shedder from the North Belfast Men's Shed explains how it works at a personal level.

It's saved me from day time TV, got me back making things in my own shed and gave me the opportunity to share some of my skills with other men. ... I've made new friends and really enjoy the *craic* when we're working away or just having a cup of tea.[25]

During the opening ceremony of North Belfast Men's Shed in 2012, North Belfast Partnership CEO, John McCorry, said:

I am so pleased that with the support of the Big Lottery Fund and others, a group of local men have been able to meet together since November last year to get the Shed up and running. As part of our "Rejuvenate Programme" the men have redecorated and refurbished the new Shed venue on Duncairn Gardens, as well as having the opportunity to try their hand at wood carving, wood turning, copper art work, willow weaving, digital photography and water colour painting[26].

A two-year Shed evaluation included three separate, insightful shedder quotes that confirm the innovative cross-community element of the North Belfast Men's Shed:

- "There are people here from all backgrounds and areas: the Shed has given me the opportunity to meet and mix with them regardless of where they come from and which I otherwise would not have had."
- "Through the Men's Shed it has brought me into contact with others' whom I would not have otherwise met. I so look forward to the activities, but most of all the camaraderie. Friendships formed in the Shed are developing outside the shed in other fields."

---

[24] Alexey Janes, North Belfast Men's Shed.
[25] North Belfast Men's Shed Opens, http://www.northbelfastpartnership.com/north-belfast-mens-shed-opens, Accessed October 7, 2014.
[26] As above.

- "We've never had any problems in the Shed with people not respecting others point of view: it's like being at work, you leave your stuff at the door and show respect to other people and they show you respect."

Concerns about mental health for men not in paid work is a common theme across many innovative Irish Sheds, as exemplified by the *Action Mental Health (AMH) Men's Sheds* set up at several sites in Northern Ireland, including in Downpatrick, Steeple Antrim and Fermanagh[27] in 2013. AMH Men's Sheds aim to:

> ... bring together men aged over 60 to share their skills and socialise, while working on practical activities of their choice - joinery, gardening, art, photography and computers. Described as a place for men to be themselves, to work at their own pace, to exchange ideas and learn, members support each other, forming friendships and membership is free.[28]

Gaby Murphy of Action Mental Health's Fermanagh Men's Shed provided the following description of a typical day in an AMH Men's Shed.

> The P.A. [public address] system has just announced that the daily walk is about to begin. You can ignore it or join in. There's nothing compulsory in the Men's Shed, although a gentle walk to the shore at Derrygore can set you up for the day. The picture framers are already in the joinery shop producing works of art, or so they tell us. Still it's always a good sign that they're making progress when they still have all their fingers at the end of the day! Meantime in the shed quite a crowd have gathered and absolute silence prevails. The game of draughts that started the day before has reached a critical stage as spectators watch every move with bated breath.

> Meanwhile in a corner of the room two new members were wrestling with the complexities of their computers. When I asked them how they were getting on, one replied that he eventually hoped to write his life story. ... A small group of 'retired' athletes had slowly climbed the stairs to the gym ... Whilst [their] class continues, three keen swimmers leave

---

[27] http://www.amh.org.uk/services/mens-shed, Accessed January 8, 2015.
[28] Eoin McAnuff, Action Mental Health Men's Sheds, January 21, 2015.

... for their weekly swim. ... Did I mention the keen gardeners who are heading for vegetable tunnel? They hope to exhibit their efforts at the next County Show ... Yes! You can try anything you like in the Shed even cooking, but you've got to be prepared to take the 'slagging' [mocking comments] if your efforts prove disastrous. Other more enriching events that one can attend include talks on men's' health; the importance of exercise and the excessive use of 'the demon drink' and 'how to grow old gracefully'....[29]

Fermanagh Men's Shed came into being in April 2013 and was given shelter from the elements by Action Mental Health's (AMH) New Horizons Service in their attractive building at Drumcroo. New Horizons had been in existence for over twenty years and was equipped with every piece of equipment that a new Shed could possibly require. AMH has provided life-changing services across Northern Ireland since 1963 and was awarded a grant of £380,823 from the Big Lottery Fund's "Reaching Out: Connecting Older People" programme. It used the grant to establish Men's Sheds projects in Downpatrick, Antrim and Enniskillen to target hard-to-reach and at-risk men who are socially isolated due to bereavement, retirement, or who live alone or in institutional care. The project is planned and managed by the men themselves. AMH work in partnership with Age NI [Northern Ireland], Volunteer Now and local Health and Social Care Trusts. As Eoin McAnuff summarized:

> We were welcomed with open arms from a humble beginning with four members. We now have over fifty keen members with various talents and experience of the trials and tribulations of everyday life. With the building open to shedders four days a week we soon made ourselves at home, and became part of the furniture. 'Why do men join the Men's Shed?' is a question we are often asked. Firstly to enjoy the company of men of a similar age, and then when we get to know each other the "craic" begins. Tall yarns are spun over the 10 o'clock break when far off school days are remembered and before the tea break is over, old fellas of 60 plus become school boys again.[30]

Men's Sheds gatherings and conferences have been an important way of Shed organisations innovatively sharing their ideas and expertise. *Ennis Men's Shed* in

---

[29] Gaby Murphy, Action Mental Health Men's Sheds, January 21, 2015.
[30] Eoin McAnuff, Action Mental Health, Fermanagh Men's Shed.

County Clare was the first Shed in Ireland to organise a major conference, called *No Man is an Island*, held over two days in April 2014. The conference invited men to examine issues affecting men and their mental and physical wellbeing.

> We, at Ennis Men's Shed, have decided that it's time these issues are highlighted, locally and nationally, and time to let men understand that 'it's ok, to be not ok'. We sincerely hope that you will consider joining us for the conference and help to support us in raising much needed awareness on these issues.[31]

Ennis Men's Shed also broke new ground in the Republic of Ireland by being the first Men's Shed to support a Women's Shed running it using the same facilities.

> The aim is to promote social interaction and aim to increase the quality of life and help out in the Community ... run on the same principles as the Men's Sheds as non-profit organisations, to advise and improve the overall well being of all women.[32]

REMARKABLE IRISH MEN'S SHEDS

Four Men's Sheds in: Dungarvan (Dungarvan Men's Shed, Waterford), Gorey (Gorey Men's Shed, Wexford), Galway (Cumann na bhFear [Men's Shed]) and Holywood (Holywood Men's Shed, Down) have been selected for close examination because of the remarkable ways each Shed engages and contributes to the wider community. The particular emphasis in each of these sheds is about empowering the men as participants to take action themselves.

Dungarvan Men's Shed opened in May 2012[33]. Its origins go back to 2011 when three men, two of whom had recently 'experienced the life changing experience of redundancy'[34], decided to use the 'skills, knowledge and experience in business and community' to take action themselves. The Shed's Facebook page gives an insight into the level of activity happening within the shed by 2014.

---

[31] Frank McNamara, January 11, 2015.
[32] http://www.clarefocus.ie/index.php/component/option,com_jcalpro/Itemid,1/extmode,vie w/extid,20817/, Accessed January 21, 2015.
[33] Michael Cass, January 11, 2015.
[34] 'Reflections on the Founders of the Dungarven Men's Shed'.

News from the Shed: Another cracking start to the week in the Shed, with gardening and maintenance getting Monday off to a great start! [Others] get stuck into the guttering on the lower workshop roof! Plenty going on in the woodwork department as well, with Jim renovating some chairs and stools, while [other men] started making a crib for one of the local churches.

Also on the woodwork front, the [Shed] is running a FETAC [national awarding body for further education and training awards] Level 3 Woodwork course … teaching a range of cutting techniques, basic woodwork joints and the design, building and decoration of a number of small projects. The Shed wishes all those participating good luck, and we hope you have great fun while at the same time learning something new to add to your CV!"[35]

What is truly remarkable about Dungarvan Men's Shed is the level of energy within the Shed for involving the wider community and for ensuring its sustainability. Shedders are not afraid to get involved in any project, from homemade raft races at the Marine Festival, to painting walls for the Tidy Towns community project, visiting the local community hospitals once a month to chat to the patients or having a 'sing song'. Dungarvan Men's shedders help the community as much as they can, and also take great pride and pleasure in helping themselves.

In direct response to a lack of places for men to meet, Dungarvan Men's Shed was started as a place where men could really talk to each other and share their knowledge and experience and just 'be themselves'. The Shed featured on the Irish TV show *The Secret Millionaire*, in which businessman Vincent Cleary went undercover in the community and, on visiting Dungarvan Men's Shed, donated €7000 for workshop roof repair. Dungarvan Men's Shed has since raised funds through self-organised fundraising events, and has gained sponsorship from a supermarket chain, which:

… agreed to support us by supplying us with all our requirements on the catering front, such as tea, coffee, bread, milk, biscuits etc., as well as donating a microwave oven. As if this wasn't enough, they have also offered to supply us with a range of equipment, such as power tools, carpentry and metalwork tools, gardening supplies and so on, when they

---

[35] https://www.facebook.com/DungarvanMensShed, Accessed January 23, 2015.

have them in stock. This unsolicited offer came completely out of the blue and means so much to us as a voluntary organisation with no revenue, as we don't charge any fees to anybody (of the male gender!) who wishes to join the Men's Shed, and therefore rely on help from external sources.[36]

The Shed also receives ongoing assistance from the local statutory community education provider and the Town Council. Dungarvan Men's Shed prides itself on its sustainability and strength within and for the community, and regards itself as being 'a classless shed'. As Steve Wallace reported in behalf of the Shed in early 2015:

In our brief time we have been in Wolfe Tone Road, we have turned a collection of derelict and dilapidated buildings into a working, thriving, integral part of the community.[37]

County Wexford VEC [Vocational Education Centre] started *Gorey Men's Shed* in 2010. The aim from the outset was to provide an opportunity for men from the local community to be part of the growth of a Men's Shed. This Shed is often referred to as a model for other men's sheds in Ireland, mainly in terms of its journey to sustainability. The Shed's early emphasis was on programs that would be both interesting for local men to take part in and that which would support group development. In time, through a community development ethos, the group became self-sustaining and moved to independent premises. The group has been pro-active in fundraising, seeking and securing small grants for activities such as woodturning.

Gorey Men's Shed has also been very active in the local community, working with several community and voluntary groups, including being part of the National Sheepshearing Competition held in Gorey. In its early days, Gorey Men's Shed also provided much needed support to the local Girl Guides. Some of its recent (2014/15) projects included building a fashion stage and ramp funded by packing bags in Gorey supermarkets and building a model lighthouse as well horticultural work and courses on the Shed's allotment area.

---

[36] 'Dungarvan Men's Shed', http://www.theview.ie/dungarvan-mens-shed/, Accessed January 23, 2015.
[37] Steve Wallace, January 23, 2015.

The *Cumann na bhFear* ('Men's Shed' in Gaelic) volunteer group in Galway is modeled on the Australian Men's Shed Movement with the addition of female members. In addition, it embodies a very strong community, social inclusion and heritage ethos. The Shed's 2015 website boasted a powerful and inclusive aim: 'Empowering men & women to learn & mentor skills that can promote self worth, contribute to preserving Irish heritage, protect the environment and improve the quality of life of local communities'[38]. On an individual level, a participant recently noted, "I would be lost without the place."[39]

The primary role of the Shed is to encourage retired, working and unemployed men and women of all ages to help each other develop, learn and/or teach skills and crafts that can benefit themselves and the wider community. There is a focus on the provision of practical skills whose existence is seen to be endangered by a modern society, where the ability to make or repair everyday items has been devalued. Hence the members provide courses and workshops on traditional Irish heritage crafts such as woodturning, woodcarving, basket making, blacksmithing, drystone walling, beekeeping as well as other areas of benefit including cycle maintenance, electronics, soldering, panel beating, metal fabrication and furniture restoration. There are parallels here with the role of Gal Gael in conserving Scottish craft skills in Glasgow, mentioned earlier. The Shed's story is summarized below in their own words.

> We set up the usual committee, started looking for a place to start up, and we were very lucky. A plumber left a premises belonging to Galway City Council and we asked officials for it. We made a good arrangement with city officials. We started working in the premises and the word spread about us! A lot of men came on board; a lot of the men are very talented. We make beehives, we also do wood turning. We have blacksmithing days, and old Raleigh bicycles are a special feature of our Shed! We repair old shovels, spades and forks, welding courses as well. We do some general engineering and we make iron gates. Some of the ladies run a tile mosaic course on a Friday night. The place has a kitchen and the laughter emanating from it tells its own story. ... God bless Men's Sheds.[40]

---

[38] http://cumannnabhfear.blogspot.com.au, Accessed January 8, 2015.
[39] Michael Tiernan, Cumann na bhFear.
[40] As above.

The Holywood Men's Shed, in Holywood, County Down, is just ten minutes from central Belfast in Northern Ireland. A group of men have come together very recently and set up a remarkable Men's Shed. This case study illustrates that the Men's Shed model is not necessarily about a building or 'shed' as such: it is about the men. In their own words:

> [The Men's Shed] ... is a place for men to meet, have fun and do practical things. It can be any sort of a building, perhaps a disused/little used one, or it may not be a building, it could be boat or some other sort of venue. In Holywood we have met in a number of places, such as Redburn Community Centre and the South Eastern Regional Campus. We are currently looking for a permanent place to meet.[41]

The Shed's 2015 (Facebook) website proclaims that 'Holywood Shed is for all men. It brings men together to do practical projects for the good of the community and promotes well being of participants'[42]. The Shed has gone from strength to strength, despite not having permanent premises to operate from. By late 2014, Holywood Men's Shed had been donated a small shed and were delighted with this generosity. The Shed was operating under the auspices of the Holywood Shared Town Consortium and had already taken part in projects such as the building of a community fruit press, a local oral history project and a community photographic competition. In early 2015 the Shed reported that recent projects had included 'building a Tardis (video booth) to consult young people about their views of the town and building a 3D printer for model making'[43]. From their Facebook page, it is clear that community involvement is strong, with a sense of fun and a concern for sustainability.

> Residents of Holywood have been very generous with donations towards the Men's Shed. Not only have we recently been donated a [small] shed but we have also been given an excellent aluminium ladder. Remember, if you know anyone moving house or clearing out their garage, encourage them to think of donating tools and equipment to Holywood

---

[41] http://www.globaldistrict.com/holywood/profile.asp?CID=1262, Accessed January 8, 2015.

[42] web https://www.facebook.com/pages/Holywood-Mens-Shed/171042426256664,, Accessed January 8, 2015.

[43] Bill Lockhart, February 21, 2015.

Men's Shed. They will be put to really good use for the benefit of the community. It also helps us keep to our low cost sustainable model![44]

NEW AND CUTTING EDGE IRISH MEN'S SHEDS

Four Men's Sheds have been selected from across the many possibilities across Ireland that are, in different ways, illustrative of being 'new and cutting edge'. They include sheds in both urban Dublin (Clondalkin Traveller Men's Shed) and Belfast (Greater Shankhill Men's Shed) and as well as from rural Donegal (Ardara Men's Shed) and Limerick (Limerick Men's Shed Network).

Clondalkin Traveller Men's Shed (Dublin) is new and cutting edge in the way it works with Traveller Men in Ireland. "Travellers" refers to a nomadic Irish ethnic group. Irish Travellers are a people with a separate identity, culture and history, although they are as fully Irish as the majority population[45]. However as a community and as individuals, Travellers in Ireland face many challenges on a daily basis including higher unemployment, discrimination, lower education attainment and poorer health outcomes.

The Irish Men's Sheds Association, Irish Traveller Movement and Clondalkin Traveller's Development Group worked together to realise Clondalkin Traveller Men's Shed as a way to create spaces for Traveller men in the community of Clondalkin, in District Dublin 22[46]. Being open to all men in the area, Travellers and non-Travellers, is a cutting edge approach to community development. In addition, the Shed is involving a lot of younger men from the local area, something that many Men's Sheds often struggle to achieve.

Clondalkin Traveller Men's Shed centres around building and repairing bicycles. This project provides a sense of pride for the men involved, as individuals can complete projects themselves, learning along the way and gaining confidence in a comfortable, fun space. The Bike Project has a high involvement of young Traveller men who enjoy the relaxed atmosphere and opportunity for practical learning. Minister for Justice and Equality, Frances Fitzgerald spoke in 2012 when she visited Clondalkin Traveller Men's Shed.

---

[44] https://www.facebook.com/pages/Holywood-Mens-Shed/171042426256664, Accessed February 21, 2015.
[45] http://www.paveepoint.ie/question/who-are-the-travellers/, Accessed May 12, 2015.
[46] A separate Clondalkin Men's Shed was forming in January 2015 for retired older men as well as younger, unemployed men: Tom Lennon, January 23, 2015.

> It's great also to see so many men using the Bike Project. This is a concept that came from Australia and I've seen how well it works in towns throughout Ireland. … I've never seen so many people so enthusiastic about the project. I really do hope it continues to flourish and that some of you guys can go on to be instructors in courses that bring bike making skills to other communities.[47]

The Bike Project has been the focus of a radio show, *Grassroots*[48], looking at 'community action projects where people are making a positive difference'. In the radio show one young man, aged 17, explained his experience of Clondalkin Traveller Men's Shed as follows:

> We learn how to take bikes apart and put them back together again. Basically we learn things that we never knew before. I get an achievement out of it; I get to say "I done that"[49].

Ardara Men's Shed, in the small town of Ardara in southwest Donegal, is new and cutting edge in the way it specializes in keeping traditional skills alive. On one level, it has similar aims to most Irish Sheds when it self-describes as meeting:

> … from 7pm to 10pm on Wednesday and Thursday evenings, and everyone is very welcome regardless of background or experience. We are always looking for new members and new project activities. Just call in to say "Hello" and have a cuppa and a chat.[50]

The Ardara Men's Shed has made huge strides in keeping traditional skills of the local area alive. At the Irish Men's Sheds Association National Conference held in Castlebar, County Mayo, Ardara Men's Shed won the "Best Project" award, recognizing the significance of the Shed's loom and hand weaving project.

---

[47] 'Minister Pays Tribute to Achievements of Clondalkin Traveller Development Group', http://www.francesfitzgerald.ie/2012/06/minister-pays-tribute-to-achievements.html, Accessed February 21, 2015.
[48] https://audioboom.com/boos/1118276-grassroots-episode-7-travellers-men-s-shed, Accessed February 21, 2015.
[49] As above.
[50] 'Adara Men's Shed wins Award at National Conference', http://www.ardara.ie/Article_Details.aspx?article_id=1982&tscategory_id=43, Accessed February 21, 2015.

"This is great recognition for the Ardara Men's Shed," said Colm Sweeney, who has been a weaver all his life. "It also recognises the importance of maintaining traditional crafts such as spinning and weaving, which are so much part of the culture and history of Donegal and of Ardara in particular. At one time, almost every family in this area would have had a loom, either in a shed or a room in the house, and the sound of the loom would have been part of everyday life. The Men's Shed is an ideal way to keep these kinds of skills alive and make sure they are passed on from one generation to the next.[51]"

Two members of Ardara Men's Shed, including Sweeney, traveled to the IMSA National Conference with one of the Ardara Men's Shed looms carefully in tow, so that it could be demonstrated to those in attendance at the conference, including *Taoiseach* (Republic of Ireland Prime Minister) Enda Kenny. The men demonstrated the process of spinning and weaving wool. Ardara Men's Shed (which had three looms at the time) also undertook an exciting project bringing together local craftsmen to build a new loom from start to finish within the Shed. The loom itself is a replica of a Donegal traditional loom used for hand-weaving wool 150 years ago. Wood turning, woodwork, carpentry, building a wind turbine and art are among the other activities of the dynamic Ardara Men's Shed.

The *Limerick Men's Sheds Network* is itself new and cutting edge. It comprises 'a network of agencies and community groups whose aim is to actively support the engagement of men at a community level'[52]. There are at least seven Men's Sheds across Limerick City, the third largest city in the Republic of Ireland (population 90,000), including the world-first 'Wheelchair Association Men's Shed' who extend their Shed beyond wheelchair-users to include people with a physical disability or mobility impairment. The network is vibrant and the connection that it provides for Men's Sheds from different communities is powerful. The Sheds learn from each other, and the men themselves are making connections across communities. As one example, in 2013 the Limerick Men's Sheds Network hosted a workshop on wellbeing, called 'Mind Your Self', which involved inputs from men involved in Sheds across Limerick City.

The network provides an extra layer of support and camaraderie and gets Sheds in its network talking to each other about what's working for them. The descriptions below, specifically about St Munchin's Men's Shed and St Mary's

---

[51] As above.
[52] *Limerick Men's Shed Network*, leaflet, 2015.

Men's Shed, are taken from the Limerick Men's Shed Facebook page, which includes numerous photos of events at which the sheds of Limerick have come together, other

> *St. Munchin's Men's Shed* meets every Wednesday afternoon from 2-3pm. We meet in the Ballynanty Hall for a hot dinner and a catch up. Our shed is up and running for the last two and a half years. Our group is made up of men from St. Munchin's parish and beyond. We regularly enjoy a game of pitch and putt. We hope to get out for a few games in the coming weeks, weather permitting. In the past we have also enjoyed going for swimming lessons that was very popular. We have participated in educational classes, such as cooking, furniture restoration, photography and guitar lessons.[53]

> *St. Mary's Men's Shed.* What do we do? To date we have built a traditional local boat called an Angling Cot with the support of the AK Illen boat building school in Southill. The AK Illen is like a second home to us at this stage and we are presently undertaking a 10-week tool maintenance course facilitated by the school instructors. We are also participating in a metal work class on Wednesday evenings from 7.00pm to 8.30pm at St. Mary's Adult Education Centre on the Island Road, the class being provided by City of Limerick Adult Education Services. Our group sees the importance of linking with other Men's Sheds in the City, and to date we have linked into the Irish Wheelchair Association Men's Shed and Southill Men's Shed who have hosted a number of 'come dine' events and boy are they good cooks!"[54]

The Greater Shankill Men's Shed (in Belfast, Northern Ireland), the final new and cutting edge Irish exemplar, opened quite recently on January 8, 2013 is illustrative of the value of nurturing a shed 'space' in a way that projects and activities are free to evolve and take shape, and not forced. Rev. Tony Meehan, Chairman of the Board of Trustees of Greater Shankill Men's Shed, explained that the Shed was started 'after a lot of thought and discussion among a number of men in the Shankill Road areas of Belfast'. He continued.

---

[53] https://www.facebook.com/Thelimerickmensshedsnetwork, Accessed February 21, 2015.
[54] As above.

We had at that stage NO idea what it was going to take but decided it was to organically grow. Men are harder to motivate to get out of the house to get involved in activities but we all, or most like to build or tinker or fix things. Our first premises was an unused Snooker Hall on the Shankill Road complete with eight full-size snooker tables; that was our first activity sorted! As a Pastor working across the communities of the Falls and Shankill roads I had little enough time to be chairing other meetings and organising more activities. However I saw the vision and benefit of "Men's Sheds" on men's health in general, wellbeing and mental health. We started to meet on Monday mornings for some "craic" (local saying for fun) snooker and coffees. Initially I was tea boy, key holder, fundraiser, secretary as well as chairman of the board.[55]

Tony Meehan's insightful description describes how the Shed evolved. In Meehan's words, "We can see the magic that happens".

Slowly but surely men crawled out of the woodwork and we started to get things done. At one stage we had 18 men from 18 to 64 years of age coming regularly. We started a carpenter on a Jobstart Scheme to start to get a workshop established. I successfully applied for and received a startup grant from the Big Lottery for tools and equipment. The workshop was open Monday to Friday. We were also networking with other men's groups and Sheds in Belfast. We started to help a local women's group fixing furniture that they were up-cycling for charity. Things were starting to take shape until we found out that our insurance company would not cover us to use power tools because the electrical circuits in the premises we rented needed work done to bring it up to specs. We had to have our carpenter relocated to another project. As the saying goes, the path of love never runs smooth![56]

On St Patrick's Day 2014 the Greater Shankill Men's Shed ran a cross-community event that involved an Irish music group, 'Celtic Cross' and Scottish dancers. This type of activity can seem simple in description. In reality, it is a powerful event for communities that once faced what seemed like an insurmountable divide. Communities in Belfast are now looking forward together with optimism to what the future holds.

---

[55] Tony Meehan, Greater Shankill Men's Shed.
[56] As above.

CHAPTER 8

UK Men's Sheds

Barry Golding & Mike Jenn

Chapter 8 includes 15 case studies of 'early', 'innovative', 'remarkable' and 'new and cutting edge' Men's Sheds in the United Kingdom. Case study Sheds include examples from diverse locations across England (11), Scotland (2) and Wales (2). Two Northern Ireland Men's Sheds examples were included in the 'Irish' Chapter 7.

EARLY PIONEER UK MEN'S SHEDS

Chapter 5 has already explored the two models of early Men's Shed development in mainland UK. The 'Age UK' model with its brand name 'Men in Sheds' operated first from 2009, and the 'grassroots' community model, some of whose Sheds also adopted the 'Men in Sheds' words in their Shed name, has continued to grow rapidly alongside the Age UK model since 2010. 'Men in Sheds' in Hartford (15 minutes drive west of Chester) which officially opened the first 'Men in Sheds' in the UK in 2009 has already been briefly introduced because of its role in the UK Men's Shed early history. So too has the Camden Town Shed (in London), the earliest Shed set up using the *grassroots* model in England. The Westhill Men's Shed in Aberdeenshire, Scotland, and the Squirrel's Nest Men's Shed in Bridgend, Wales are included as the first to be established via the grassroots Men's Shed model, in Scotland and Wales respectively. All four Sheds, with Men in Sheds Hartford, have been influential early pioneers in the UK, shaping how the Men's Shed Movement developed first in England, and since 2013 in Scotland and Wales.

The Camden Town Shed 'is a club offering a workspace where older people can work on practical project with others'[1]. It hires a room in a community centre a

---

[1] http://www.camdentownshed.org, Accessed January 8, 2015.

mile north of Kings Cross in Camden, London. It opened on April 26, 2011 just three months from being first envisaged, through local fundraising, the donation of most of the equipment and bargaining for three months free rent on the basis that the Shed would improve the community centre's program and pay later. Photograph 34 shows its workshop in full swing in early 2015.

Photograph 34 Camden Town Shed, London, with Workshop in Full Swing, 2015

Mike Jenn, who initiated the Shed, wrote in 2014 that:

> Although it's just 70 square metres it is a good venue for a small Shed but in a poor location at the end of a cul-de-sac on a little-known Council estate. The maximum number that can work indoors is about nine people, although we do sometimes work outside, especially on anything large or that creates a lot of dust or fumes. Sadly, no one attends from the estate in which it is located, but as we are not publicly funded, people can attend from anywhere, and some travel up to an hour to get to us from other parts of London. Woodworking is the main activity of the Shed but we have recently acquired a kiln for clay firing.
>
> One of the first people to come had such low income and prospects that he had become suicidal. Since then it has always been free to attend the Shed although people are asked individually to contribute as much as they can. This individual approach avoids the 'lowest common

denominator' effect of a group discussion on 'subs' [subscriptions] and has resulted in some people paying by standing order much more than could be expected. Others still contribute by cash on the day, often only after being asked. People come in just to use the facility (but not to profit) and others because they want to be part of the group. The latter are more willing to engage in community projects or making stuff for sale. We negotiate charges for community projects individually and enjoy seeing our products in use. The best example was the archery club that asked us to produce a de-mountable castle that disabled children would be motivated to fire at. We painted it with dragons and ghouls as specific targets (people and animals were out) and through the smallest slits in the walls an arrow would hit a bell.

One aim was [for the Shed] to become self-sufficient within three years, a target we missed by just five per cent. Our basic running costs of around £5000 per year were met principally by member contributions (55%) and training courses in woodturning (30%). Sales of made items account for about 12% of net costs, mainly due to the difficulty of 'getting to market'. Local 'fairs' do not work well for us but we are beginning to have some success on national websites. We will also take commissioned work but are conscious we only have a volunteer workforce. We open two days per week but would open more if there were more willing and suitable supervisors. One day is men only and the other mixed because we wanted to see if it made a difference. Few women have attended, on average about one a week. One who has attended most is skilled and says she likes 'the lack of fuss'. There is no real difference in the behaviour of the guys when a woman is present, though some things might not be said and on one or two might be more ready to help a woman. We are all retired guys.[2]

Mike Jenn was also the driving force behind the UK Men's Sheds Association, quietly championing and supporting the bottom-up development of independent, grassroots sheds in the UK as Age UK were rolling out a mainly top-down pilot. Jenn added that:

> One aspect that gives me great satisfaction is how our Shed has served as a living example to many dozens of visitors enquiring about setting up

---

[2] Mike Jenn, March 25, 2015.

one of their own. Helping to get this movement going has been very rewarding.

With the slogan 'Make friends, share interests and help our community'[3] the *Westhill Men's Shed* was the first Men's Shed established in Scotland. It was set up in a renovated former library in Westhill, leased at a 'peppercorn rent' from the Aberdeenshire Council, beginning operation on February 4, 2013. Its origin goes back several years to 2009 when Jason Schroeder, then Community and Development Worker in Westhill (population 10,000, 12 kilometers west of Aberdeen), attended a presentation in Aberdeenshire about the Men's Shed movement by Neil Bruce from New Zealand. Around the same time the Aberdeenshire Council's Community Plan (2010-14) recognized the common problem (and opportunity) of men living longer after retirement and needing to stay social and engaged in the community. The experience of the Men's Sheds in Australia was seen as interesting.

In the summer of 2010, Jill Sowden, employed as a Community Planning Officer by the Aberdeenshire Council, visited Men's in Sheds in Cheshire in England. While many of the men she spoke with were there for company, some were passing on skills, and others had been sent by their family doctor, it was clear that the Men's Shed had made a huge difference to the lives of the men who participated. Evidence gathered through a community-wide consultation in the Garioch (one of six areas of Aberdeenshire), combined with reports from Westhill doctors in Aberdeenshire, indicated a growing concern for retired men's mental health and wellbeing.

Sowden decided to see whether the men in Westhill had any interest in the concept of a Men's Shed, She therefore wrote a series of articles in the *Westhill Bulletin* asking for people interested in forming a Men's Shed to attend meetings over the winter of 2010-11. Jason Schroeder created a video presentation to stimulate interest and awareness to local groups, including the 50+ Club, Rotary, Lions and Adult Education Evenings. A Blog site was created on the local community website as a permanent, updated page. A small group of men started up the Westhill and District Men's Shed, meeting privately from June 2011 with continued support from service professionals. After several months the group was strong enough to break away from the 'professional umbilical' and, by late 2012, had created an independent committee, logo and identity. They secured the first Community Asset Transfer by the Aberdeenshire Council of the former Westhill Library and began renovation. The Westhill Men's Shed, shown in Photograph 35

---

[3] http://www.westhillmensshed.co.uk, Accessed January 8, 2015.

in 2015, opened three days a week from February 4, 2013, though the final fit out was not completed until July 2013.

Photograph 35 Westhill Men's Shed, Aberdeenshire, April 2015

In the first year the Shed had three thousand individual visits, which grew to five thousand within 18 months of opening.[4]

The *Squirrel's Nest Men's Shed* in Bridgend, Wales was the first Welsh Men's Shed to open. The Squirrel's Nest wood workshop on which it is based goes back over a decade before the first Men's Sheds were established in the UK. In 2002 a small group of men from the Welsh town of Bridgend (population 140,000, 30 kilometers west of Cardiff) acknowledged that they shared common mental health issues. They had each been referred to the ARC (Assisted Recovery Centre) day centre where they found themselves together turning wood on lathes, an experience they found relaxing. They also learnt something new, and more importantly, formed friendships and shared stories, 'shoulder to shoulder'[5]. At that stage the group did not have a name, and in 2008 had to relocate again when the ARC moved, this time as part of an outdoor education project called EcoDysgu in Bridgend, located in a disused garage which they renovated and

---

[4] Jason Schroeder, January 29, 2015.
[5] The Australian Men's Shed Association adopted its 'Shoulder to Shoulder' slogan after Barry Golding used the term during his presentation to its 2007 Manly Conference, shortened from the original "Men don't talk face to face, they talk shoulder to shoulder".

continued their woodturning. In July 2102 they had to relocate yet again to Unit 38 in an enterprise park in Tondu (a village 5 kilometers north of Bridgend), becoming a formally constituted group called 'The Squirrel's Nest', which in their own words, 'helped them just by being there, doing what they do'.

Photograph 36 shows 'The Squirrel's Nest' poster. Photograph 37 shows woodturning underway in the Squirrels Nest Men's Shed.

Photograph 36 'The Squirrel's Nest' Poster, Wales, November 2014

Photograph 37 Woodturning in The Squirrel's Nest Men's Shed, Wales,
November 2014

The men from the Squirrel's Nest Men's Shed recounted the rest of the story in
late 2014. In early 2013:

> ... one of the men came across a newspaper article about a group of men
> in Carmarthenshire (West Wales) who were trying to form a Men's Shed
> Association for Wales and were going to hold a conference about it. He
> had also heard about Men's Sheds in Australia and so with a few men
> from The Squirrel's Nest decided go to the conference in Carmarthen. At
> the conference they ... invited John Evoy from Ireland to speak, and
> learnt about Men's Sheds. The Squirrel's Nest soon realised that what
> they had been doing for all these years, and the benefits they were seeing
> had also been discovered by the Men's Shed Movement in Australia and

Ireland. ...Who'd have thought that there was already a Men's Shed in Wales!

The Squirrel's Nest men decided that they would sign up to be members of a Men's Shed Association for Wales: there was an obvious and mutual benefit and they were keen to see the idea grow. The Squirrel's Nest became known as 'The Squirrel's Nest – A Men's Shed in Bridgend' and also as the first working Men's Shed in Wales. Soon groups of men from around Wales, all interested in the idea of Men's Sheds, came visiting The Squirrel's Nest and they were inspired to go away and set up their own Sheds.

Late in 2013 [we were] approached by the Prostate Cancer UK (PCUK) [who] had heard about the Men's Shed Movement and thought that the ethos would be of benefit to the men they supported. They asked The Squirrel's Nest to put to them a proposal to open the Shed for men with prostate cancer; they wanted to try a new way of supporting their men through the Shed. So the proposal was made and accepted and The Squirrel's Nest started to open on Fridays also, specifically for men with or who are undergoing diagnosis of prostate cancer.

Since working with PCUK and through the networking ... news of The Squirrel's Nest Men's Shed is spreading. In the autumn of 2014 the Shed had two separate visitors all the way from Australia. David Helmers, CEO of Australian Men's Shed Association, came with his [IMSA] counterpart from Ireland, John Evoy. One week later, Paul Villanti, Board Member of the Movember Foundation in Australia also visited. The BBC has also been filming at The Squirrel's Nest Men's Shed for a programme about communities and more recently [some of the men] were interviewed and aired on BBC for a programme about Men's Sheds, isolation and loneliness.[6]

INNOVATIVE UK MEN'S SHEDS

Three individual UK Men's Sheds are examined as case studies in this section to illustrate the theme of Shed innovation in the UK. One Shed is from Milton Keynes in Buckinghamshire, another is from Durham in England, and the other

---

[6] 'The Story of Squirrel's Nest', 'Rob V.', November 12, 2014.

from Rhyl in Wales. An innovative group of twelve Sheds from Kent in England is also included.

Men in Sheds MK (Milton Keynes) in Buckinghamshire, England has been consistently innovative by virtue of its focus on practical construction projects for other community groups including with younger men. The Shed is located in a unit within an industrial park in Kiln Farm in the outer western suburbs of Milton Keynes, 60 kilometers northwest of London in Buckinghamshire. Photograph 38 shows the Shed entrance.

Photograph 38 MK Men in Sheds Entrance, February 2014, Buckinghamshire, England (Peter Gallagher, Chair, at left)

The Shed was founded in March 2012 after 80 men responded to a press article by one of its founder members inviting men to attend a public meeting, with 50 actually attending. The meeting was co-hosted by Age UK Milton Keynes and Milton Keynes Christian Foundation. Age UK were instrumental in subsequently helping the Shed move into its first permanent facilities, an industrial unit of over 4,000 square foot (370 square metres). The Shed now thrives as an independent operation but continues to be nurtured in the background by these and other founding organisations.

Men in Sheds MK in 2014 had over 60 active members and attracted 20 to 30 men on each of the three days a week it opened. Activities were as diverse as model train and plane making, photography, computing, electronics, sculpture, plus wood and metal working and turning[7], as well as the Shed's critically important social space. Its members were responsible for the operation and fund raising. Established as a Charitable Incorporated Organisation (CIO), perhaps the first CIO Shed in England, it is managed through a set of Trustees and an elected Management Committee. Members, through the respect of their peers and background experience, manage the various areas of the Shed. Unlike other Sheds associated with Age UK, it has no paid supervision. Membership is open to men over 18 years, and all participants are regarded as equals, not as clients.

The MK Shed has offered inspiration and assistance for other communities who want to set up Men's Sheds. National and local TV, radio and press make frequent calls to their Shed to gain an insight into 'what goes on' in Sheds. It is well regarded by members of the local council and its Parliamentary members. It is also grateful for essential 'set-up' monies from the local Council, on-going funding from Milton Keynes Community Foundation and support from a number of trade suppliers. With a large and growing older population, the hope is that more Sheds will be established locally.

Whilst offering the 'traditional activities' of a Men's Shed, the MK Shed also seeks to be radical and forward-looking. In 2014 it had an e-commerce site about to be launched, was developing an electronic product to monitor Shed access and machine usage and had built an electric roadworthy car as part of one of the participants' PhD. The MK Shed story clearly won't end here.

Rhyl Men's Shed is a good example of several Sheds across the UK that have been innovative in encouraging traditional crafts, in this case including construction of some traditional Welsh structures. Located on the north coast of Wales, an hour west of Liverpool, some of the organisations that have brought the Shed to fruition have existed informally since at least 2009. Parts of Rhyl (population 25,000) are amongst the ten most deprived areas in Wales. Denbighshire County Council provided six months funding for a development worker in October 2013 and the Rhyl Men's Shed opened in January 2014. The small shed structure, comprising a workshop and outside compound with a 'poly-tunnel' for plant propagation, is open to adults over 18 years. Simon Poole, then

---

[7] http://www.meninshedsmk.biz/dotorguk/, Accessed January 8, 2015.

the Shed coordinator, wrote enthusiastically in 2014 about a small but engaging enterprise.

> We're finding we're regularly getting 12 to 15 guys in the Shed on both Mondays and Tuesdays: in fact last week we had around twenty each day! We've still not "made" a lot of stuff, some boxes, like bird boxes and planters as acquiring kit [basic equipment] has been a priority but we've already finished one community project.

> Our next project will be in conjunction with the local Communities First team, the local youth team and some residents. We're going to build some Roundhouses! There are about three sites identified across Rhyl (one in an adventure playground) where permission has been granted, and this has also entailed a couple of visits to get ideas. First to Llynon on Anglesey to see the Iron Age houses erected at an historical visitor centre, and then to Nefyn on the Lleyn Peninsula ... where the local community has erected less traditional structures. They also have the most wonderful wooden workshop-cum-boathouse where some local old boat builders are renovating some clinker boats. These visits have also led to an involvement with local Iron Age technology specialists with the potential of some workshops, and maybe some woodland training courses. Being in the current facilities, with its raised planters, produce being grown and having a cross section of generations chatting happily round a table in such a welcoming environment, eating cake that [one man] has brought in, whilst a couple of others are either pottering round outside or sanding one of the boats.[8]

In early 2015, Poole, now North Wales Advocate for the newly formed Men's Sheds Cymru Association (MSCA), reported that:

> ... the funding to support this initiative (four positions for three years) has come via a National Lottery bid by Rhodri Walters (MSCA project manager) who was a Hafan Cymru employee at the time of application and needed a 'host' organisation to support the bid. Hafan Cymru was initially established to support, in the first instance, female victims of domestic abuse. However it now includes male victims too, and is expanding in its role of combating social isolation in various forms. ...

---

[8] Simon Poole, June 19, 2014.

Since January 2015 I have been asked to talk to a number of interested parties across North Wales, and can feel the beginnings of a groundswell of interest. We have quite a bit to do to catch up with Ireland and the rest of the UK. However, the examples are out there and we're very much hoping to emulate the Irish Men's Shed model.[9]

The Cree project in East Durham, England has creatively linked the Australian Men's Shed name with the name for a traditional local variant of a shed, called a *'cree.'* A 'cree' is described in the *New Geordie Dictionary,* in the dialect from the north east of England, as a small hut or pen. Originating in the coal pits of the north of England, a cree is effectively a Geordie slang word for 'shed'. Many 'Crees' have been set up very recently (in the two years to 2014), initially in the East of County Durham, and subsequently in many other places in the UK. By August 2014 at least ten Crees were operating in East Durham[10]. Malcolm Fallow, of the East Durham Community Development Trust (EDT)[11], tells the story.

> The East Durham Trust (EDT) serves an area of Northern England previously dominated by the mining industry. Since the last colliery closed in 1993 the area has experienced some of the worst levels of social and economic deprivation in the UK. In 2012 a number of key staff in the local Health Authority were inspired by the Australian Men's Shed movement and mindful of the effects of the pit closures approached EDT with a proposal to utilise the organisation's deep-rooted community links and start some *'Crees'* in the area. A significant sum was invested from the National Health Service {NHS} budgets, primarily as a suicide prevention measure. EDT started by employing a coordinator, part of whose role was to engage and train two volunteer "Cree Champions" per community to promote and support Cree development. Each Champion was given Mental Health First Aid training as well as Applied Suicide Intervention Skills Training (ASIST) from specialist providers. Each community could also draw on a central funding 'pot' to help kick-start activities.

---

[9] Simon, February 18, 2015.
[10] 'Cree Quarterly Report', August 2014, East Durham Trust, Durham.
[11]

http://www.eastdurhamtrust.org.uk/index.php?option=com_content&view=category&id=73&Itemid=119, Accessed January 8, 2015.

The idea proved very popular and soon many of EDT's partner organisations were hosting Cree groups. Significantly, each Cree developed a specific focus of attention depending on its member's interests, ranging from growing vegetables to stonemasonry, and each had a place for the men to talk and have a cuppa. As the project progressed evidence of improvements in the mental wellbeing of participants was collected using the WEMWS [Warwick Edinburgh Mental Wellbeing Scale] questionnaire. This justified further investments allowing for extended geographic spread, noticeably into challenging areas such as Teesdale, where hill farmers live in isolated and often inaccessible areas.

The Crees spread quickly because the Champions were empowered by their training; they were people of their community, they knew who needed a Cree, they would challenge and cajole, they were constant reminders and they had access to existing partners and a common fund. The focus of the activity was often of secondary importance to the coming together of men in general. One of the earlier groups we developed agreed to come together to refurbish kids bikes: very few bikes actually got refurbished, but a lot of men established some vital social networks. Activities like this also helped many men escape the 'drinking group'. You would make yourself an outcast if you just stopped drinking, but the social 'rules' did allow you to leave that kind of group to do something worthwhile like joining a Cree.[12]

Like AMSA in Australia, *Kent Sheds* in the County of Kent in England have innovatively adopted part of an ex-services motto of working 'Shoulder to shoulder' [to all who have served][13]. The Kent Sheds idea received a huge boost in January 2012 when Groundwork South won a Kent County Council tender to help develop twelve Sheds across the County of Kent, approximately 40 kilometers east of central London. The joint funding came from Kent County Council Public Health Department and the Armed Forces Covenant (Libor) Fund for ex-servicemen. Thanet Shed, one of the Kent Sheds, proposed a small 'mobile shed' mounted on a trailer, the first in the UK. Thanet were concerned that operating from a fixed location might limit the number of people they can assist.

---

[12] Malcolm Fallow, January 23, 2015.
[13] Kent Sheds http://www.kentsheds.org.uk/index.html, Accessed September 5, 2014.

Julie Cowdry, Kent Sheds coordinator in 2014, explained how it would work and what was innovative:

> We saw that a mobile workshop could reach people in rural and isolated communities that typically have less engagement with outside groups and poorer mental health and wellbeing in our region. The volunteer-run Mobile Shed will now cover the whole county, benefitting the most isolated people and recruiting people from groups that can be difficult to engage in static health and wellbeing initiatives. The mobile shed will also enable us to assist and support Sheds across the county and act as a mobile advertising placard for the concept. Kent Sheds will build on this by training and supporting 'Shed Champions' within the local community and providing specifically developed materials related to the people we seek to engage. We aim to bring communities together to work shoulder to shoulder.

REMARKABLE UK MEN'S SHEDS

Four recently established UK Sheds are included in this section to illustrate how they aim to cater, in remarkable and different ways, for men and their communities in very diverse contexts across four English counties, including Dartford in Kent, Norwich in Norfolk, Swindon in Wiltshire and Wincanton in Somerset. Three of the Sheds deal mainly with specific groups of men including armed forces Veterans (Dartford), fathers and boys (Norwich) and stroke survivors (Swindon) while the fourth involves men generally (Wincanton). While all four Sheds are clearly relatively young and 'works in progress', they have each been creatively grafted onto pre-existing community organisations.

Dartford is a city of over 100,000 approximately 30 kilometers miles east of central London in Kent. *The Dartford Men's Shed* was officially launched in April 2014 by a group of armed forces Veterans, whose policy was to equally involve those who had never served. Daren Riley, founder of the Shed explained their aims.

> The Armed Forces are mixed gender and we know the different contribution women can make, and believe they will help us reach a greater number of people. We aim to work with other organisations to serve the community. One early project was to create a green play area for a children's nursery. Another was to work with the British Legion

[whose motto is "Shoulder to all who served"] in sowing 20m poppy seeds around Dartford to commemorate the 100th anniversary of the start of WW1. We have also raised a flag for each of the three Armed Services at Ebbsfleet International Train Station. We have a contract with a Government Department to deliver a five week certificated course in community work for people claiming unemployment benefit.[14]

The Shed has a motto 'Putting the pride back into Dartford'[15] and is particularly reaching out to men who are lonely, isolated or bored. The 13 shedders involved in 2014 were offering gardening, decorating and general maintenance services, to stress that 'Many men have shedloads of adversity over the years' and need the activity '... as part of their rehabilitation and confidence building'.

The Norwich Men's Shed, located in the County of Norfolk, 2.5 hours drive north east of London, is a good example of how a Men's Shed can be grafted onto or embedded within an existing organisation to increase its appeal and reach. MensCraft, whose slogan is 'Working for men's development and wellbeing'[16], was originally established in 2007:

> ... by professionals working with men in different ways throughout the County, following a public meeting to address the lack of an organisation that specifically focused on supporting the development and wellbeing of men, boys and fathers. We're part of the movement that is responding positively to the challenges that feminism has set us, and also work in partnership with a local Women's Centre. Some of our work is inspired by the 'mytho-poets', but our 'bread and butter' is stuff like the Shed, and working with fathers through the local Children's Centres. We have also run young men's rites of passage and mentoring programs ('Journey into Manhood') as well as retreats that focus on issues around modern day masculinity and manhood.[17]

The 'mythopoetic model' focuses on psychological self-help and 'male rites of passage' in the context of concerns about boys and men's wellbeing. The mythopoetic men's movement sprang up in many places including the UK,

---

[14] Darren Riley, January 6, 2015.
[15] Dartford Men's Shed http://www.dartfordshed.moonfruit.com/home/4582447652, Accessed September 5, 2014.
[16] http://menscraft.org.uk, Accessed September 5, 2014.
[17] Andy Wood, February 18, 2015.

largely as a reaction to the feminist movement. MensCraft still hold regular Men's Lodges.

The Norwich Men's Shed opens three days and one evening a week mainly for woodwork. Andy Wood, MensCraft director, outlined its early aims.

> We aim to bring a 'bigger picture' to the Shed's context by being a wider resource for men and by linking strongly to the community. It is early days yet but we are already offering taster sessions to other agencies for their male clients: people recovering from mental and physical health problems in particular, but also to drug/alcohol recovery groups and a local asylum seeker/refugee organisations. We have drawn down specific funding to pay a sessional facilitator to run fairly basic woodworking projects so that these men with additional needs can 'feel their way 'into the shedding environment. Shedders get involved in these sessions, by showing people around, introducing them to other shedders, explaining how the Shed works and generally encouraging them to feel confident to return without their support worker or group.[18]

Wood explained in early 2015 that 'the Shed's aims are similar to those of most Sheds: to provide activity, identity and meaning for their members, by providing a safe and supportive environment to do practical activities'[19]. In addition shedders take on a wide range of jobs for community organisations on a donations basis, which helps fund the Shed.[20] In early 2015 Norwich Men's Shed moved into new premises (in Pitt Street) and was considering how older men might support the younger men in the Shed, exploring holding women's sessions in the Shed and partnering with complementary organisations such as Kitchen Kings (cooking groups for older men), Drub (a no-alcohol night club) and the local Women's Centre.

Swindon is a local government area of around 200,000 people one hour east of Bristol in the County of Wiltshire. The philosophy *of Men's Shed Swindon* sits very comfortably with the purpose and values of SEQOL, the local social enterprise that has supported the development of a Men's Shed project. SEQOL is an employee-owned community interest company 'supporting people to make the

---

[18] Andy Wood, as above.
[19] Andy Wood, as above.
[20] http://meninshedsnorwich.wordpress.com, Accessed January 8, 2015.

most of their lives', and the Men's Shed comes under the charitable arm of SEQOL Charity.[21]

Men's Shed Swindon, with its optimistic slogan 'There is life after a stroke', is essentially a men's social group for stroke survivors. Although members are recommended through SEQOL's stroke therapy services, the Shed does not provide a therapy service. It is a facility for men who have suffered a stroke to meet, socialise and carry out 'hands-on' practical activities decided by the group. Chris Chidsey and Mick Condon, two of the volunteers now involved in the program, eloquently told the story of how it works in the Shed[22].

> It had been noticed that men were reluctant to partake in day care services and many of the social activities that appeal more to women, and were at greater risk of psychological difficulties and depression. Following a stroke, the men would often speak about a loss of identity and low self-worth because they felt they could no longer do some of the things they enjoyed like 'do-it-yourself'. This was true even if they had a place to work at home. They joined somewhat dubious about what a shed could offer, but found that they were able to achieve more than they thought, by discovering new ways to work that could be shared by men in similar positions to themselves.

> Joining the group is by invitation only. Several men use wheelchairs and others have weakness to other limbs, more often than not to the side they used to naturally favour. The volunteers are an essential part of the group, to assist the members with some of the tasks they struggle with due to their impairments, which range from weakness or poor coordination, to communication and speech difficulties. It's surprising the things we take for granted, like putting a drill into a keyless chuck, can seem almost impossible if you all but loose the use of one of your arms. The volunteers are there to assist with this, but not surprisingly members have learnt to adapt. You may see one member holding the back of the chuck whilst the other turns the front. As time has gone on, members have identified, brought in and shared solutions to problems. These have ranged from a different quick-release drill chuck to magnetic hexagon socket drives with hexagon-shaft drill bits.

---

[21] www.seqol.org, Accessed September 4, 2014.
[22] Mick Condon, SEQOL, January 20, 2015.

As the confidence of the group has grown we have introduced more power tools beyond battery-operated drills and screwdrivers. Each tool is assessed and discussed and a safe system of work is written up for its use by those identified as capable. This has opened up the range of tasks we can now undertake. These days we research projects or design our own as a group. We are limited to the two hour window we have to work in each week, lifting and handling larger projects and our own, imaginations and experience… and sufficient tea and biscuits.

We believe that as a group we have had a positive effect on the individuals within the group. Spirits have been lifted and through the making of some of our garden accessories; bird tables, hedgehog homes, benches and planters, which we donate to local charitable organisations, the members feel like valued members of their own communities. Attending the shed also has benefits for their family and friends. Without the group, many would have risked becoming very socially isolated and possibly developing depression and even more health problems. This would have impacted on their carers and wider family and friends, and possibly caused them to experience similar mental and physical health problems. A wife of one of the group member's, whose husband was left wheel chair bound following his stroke, said:

> "This has made such a difference to him. The group meets on a Wednesday but he starts to get ready for it on a Monday. Although it is only two hours, it is two hours that I get to spend on my own doing whatever I want, which is invaluable to me."

The Men's Shed in Swindon expects to expand and support many more people to get together in a safe and controlled environment, encouraging social exchanges, enjoying creating things, mostly through working with wood and growing in confidence and self-esteem, whilst developing team-working skills, with anticipated benefits to the men's partners, families and carers.

Wincanton is the site of the *Touch Wood Men's Shed* project. Wincanton is a town of around 5,000 people in South Somerset, one hour south of Bristol. The Balsam Centre, a 'Healthy living and family centre' managed by the Wincanton community since 1999[23], obtained Big Lottery Funding in 2014 to run a Men's

---

[23] Balsam Centre, http://balsamcentre.org.uk/, Accessed September 5, 2014.

Shed project called *Touch Wood.* Annette Yoosefinejad, volunteer coordinator for the project explained what had happened.

> The Shed has been working with the Owl and Hawk Trust that has given the shedders money to cover the material costs for building Barn and Little Owl boxes. One of the boxes is now up in a primary school in Dorset. And of course the shedders have been repairing odd things, building planters and tap boxes for the charity that runs the Men's Shed. Lads from the local secondary school are also working with the shedders one afternoon. The idea is to give them father figures/mentors outside of the education system, where there are no tests or exams but a place where they can work and build a relationship with other adults who are not family/carers or teachers. Obviously, the shedders have had DBS [Disclosure and Barring Services, UK] checks.

Future plans for the Shed which is currently located in a former hospital mortuary, include working collaboratively with the local Forest School, Job Done and Growing Space programs.

NEW AND CUTTING EDGE UK MEN'S SHEDS

Four different, very young UK Sheds are included in this 'new and cutting edge' section: from Broadstairs in Kent, Collingham in Nottinghamshire, West Lancashire and Fife in Scotland. It is of interest that two of these Sheds (in West Lancashire and Fife), while seen as new cutting edge, are effectively rebadged 'Tool Sheds', set up through previously networked organisations, TotalReuse and Tools for Self Reliance (TFSR), both committed to recycling and sustainability.

Broadstairs Town Shed was the first Shed to open in the County of Kent. Broadstairs is a coastal town of around 25,000 facing the English Channel in East Kent on the Isle of Thanet, around two hours by car east of London. Broadstairs Town Team, a local community-led group, conceived the Shed in March 2013[24]. They got off to a 'flying start' in November 2013 when they actively campaigned for, and won, £50,000 funding to create the Shed from the 'People's Millions' Big Lottery Fund. This funding enabled recruitment of a part-time project co-

---

[24] Broadstairs Town Team, http://www.broadstairstownteam.org.uk/town-shed.php, Accessed September 5, 2014.

ordinator, the workshops to be equipped to a high standard and the Shed to open three days a week. Claire Shelton, the Shed coordinator wrote in early 2015 that:

> It also means that we can offer sessions for free. The first three months of the project saw a complete refurbishment of the building that we leased from the Thanet District Council. The win enabled the purchase of woodworking equipment, but a lot was donated and volunteers did all the work, bar the rewiring and flooring. We officially opened on May 9, 2014, and held our first induction sessions at the beginning of June. Since then we have inducted over 65 new Shedders, mostly men of all ages but a few ladies too, and have a core team of nine 'Shedheads' who run the sessions.
>
> We have been involved in several community projects already, including an art project making windmills for the 'Turner Contemporary Summer of Colour' events in nearby Margate. We have recently built a replica of a 25-foot (7.6m) Viking boat for the Ramsgate Summer Squall event. This happened in a commercial boat-building shed, which we have been promised the use of in the future for future large projects. Our boat was burnt on the beach as the grand finale of the Summer Squall of this multi-arts festival. We have also received a number of commissions, including for local signage and play equipment. We have developed a line of products for sale, and our programme of training on tablet computing and health and wellbeing sessions are up and running. We have been overwhelmed by local support and are incredibly proud that the Shed is a community-run-and-led organisation, delivering community projects and connecting people across Thanet.
>
> Many friendships and connections have been made and The Shed is now very well known locally as a place to meet, make things and share. Our plans for 2015-16 include cookery classes linked to a local restaurant and we are searching for a larger building. Our ideal is to be open five day a week and sustainable in the longer term.[25]

Collingham is a small village (of around 3,000 people) in Nottinghamshire, just north of Newark on Trent. *Collingham and District Men in Sheds* aims to support '... the needs of local men by providing friendship and skill sharing in our new

---

[25] Claire Shelton, January 9, 2015.

Shed'[26]. The Collingham and District Men in Sheds Chair, John Leigh, explained how their Shed started, how it progressed and where it was up to after around a year of investigation and a year of operation to late 2014. The account below, contributed by the Shed with all of its original exclamation marks,[27] neatly summarises how Sheds often get established in new sites. It also documents enthusiasm for all of the important investigative and consultative stages, with both the men and the community.

> We first got the 'Shed' bug, having attended a presentation in Leicester, in September 2011. But with a lot else going on in the village, it wasn't until early 2013, that we started to research seriously the local potential. We visited the Age UK Shed at Blidworth, a former mining area near Mansfield and one of three pilot projects. We were both moved and impressed by what we learned there, what the 'Shedders' had to say about the benefits it had brought them. Age UK typically had a lower age limit of 50-55 for attendance, but we decided that we'd be open to any man, from age 18 to 108, three days a week at present, but soon to extend to Saturdays too! And perhaps a 'Ladies' day in the future: and why not?
>
> Subsequently we held meetings in Collingham, to establish levels of local interest and support, and poll opinion as to the type of activities that would be welcomed! A questionnaire was used as an effective method to do this – and it worked! Seeking premises, the word went out. We advertised locally and walked the streets to see what we could find, at the same time putting together a Business Plan to provide a framework to ensure that we stayed on track, compiling 'evidence' of the need and potential benefits through a series of relevant Appendices. And that worked too! We found premises ... at a reasonable rent, but once the owner saw our Plan, he identified immediately with our aims and objectives. Consequently, with great generosity, he offered the units, rent-free!
>
> We obtained initially, from a village-based organisation, funding to establish two areas: one for woodworking, and one social/kitchen space. Then from our District Council, a grant to convert/extend the toilet

---

[26] http://www.newark-sherwooddc.gov.uk/meninsheds/, Accessed January 8, 2015.
[27] 'Collingham & District Men in Sheds', John Leigh, Chair, October 3, 2014.

facility, making it suitable for wheelchair users. And more recently, from our County Council, a further grant, enabling us to extend into a third area, to be used for art, pyrography [decorating wood with burn marks], computers/internet and model making – whatever our Shedders want! And still all RENT FREE!

Our official, well-publicised launch took place in September 2013, with support from local BBC Radio, newspapers, councillors, doctors and our Member of Parliament – but overwhelmingly from local people, and the 'Shedders' themselves. After the launch, we started work, decorating, building benches/shelving – sorting through, the huge quantity of tools/equipment/machinery that was so generously donated to us, from so many individuals – and that will never be forgotten! The Constitution and business format for our organisation was established in consultation with a local agency, which also supported our grant applications – and of course, a Committee was elected! We developed a Health and Safety Policy, covering both equipment and people, obtained appropriate insurance and took advice on security from our local Police. Two Coordinators attend each session we are open, with First Aid training undertaken at regular intervals.

So what's next? We take every opportunity to publicise what we do, what the potential benefits are, by maintaining contact with our funders and supporters, with local agencies whose service users we may be able to help, and by getting involved in the wider debate at County and National levels. Where we identify the demand, we may invite visiting speakers, and/or plan visits to places of interest – and learn from one another, of course! Our organisation is run entirely by volunteers – and what a range of backgrounds, skills, experiences and personalities there is. For the 'Shedders', it's the friendship and contact that's so important, as well as what we actually do! And we must never forget that! They must always be involved and listened to as we develop what the Shed provides. The ever-present challenge for ALL Sheds is to maintain momentum, attract more members by identifying interest in fresh projects and activities in order to achieve long-term, financial sustainability![28]

---

[28] John Leigh, January 12, 2015.

The Total Reuse organisation encourages alternative uses for reusable things that people and organisations throw away. *Total Reuse Men's Sheds* in Lancashire, England went from zero to the three Sheds in just four years. The first such Shed was launched in October 2010 with one member, a grant from the National Lottery, and a plan to repair, restore and make things that could generate income to sustain a Shed and the idea. In the first year it engaged 175 individuals aged from 9 to 71 years and gained a reputation for making bespoke furniture such as Victorian pine farmhouse tables from salvaged timbers. Martin Gamester eloquently told the story in early 2015. From the start:

> We quickly realised that it wasn't just older men who wanted to get involved. Male and female, young and old, able and not quite so able were motivated by the idea of 'making stuff' and diverting items from landfill. The core function of a Shed remained, in that we provided a place where people felt valued and could make a contribution as part of a team. The Shed was sustainable within 12 months because everything we made was a 'limited edition', based on the unique sourcing of the materials, and each piece prolonged a bit of the social history attached to the building from where the materials came.

> We also realised that not all older men are practical. Whilst they enjoyed the Shed environment, they didn't all have the skills to make stuff. This led to the development of other activities under the Total Reuse banner that would keep them fully engaged. Glass Works provided creative opportunities to recycle glass. Total Clearance, an ethical domestic and commercial clearance service, provided work, an additional income stream and a source of materials. A computer reuse project has been added in Preston, a paint mixing station in Bootle, and the original Shed in Skelmersdale launched a hand tool refurbishment project aimed at supporting people suffering from early stage dementia under the Tools for Self Reliance scheme.

> Four years later we have three Tool Sheds (in 2015, the 'West Lancs Tool Shed' in Skelmersdale, West Lancashire; 'Leyland Tool Shed' in Leyland and 'Sefton Tool Shed' in Bootle[29]) that have a very clear vision of why they exist. Firstly, it is to facilitate activities that improve

---

[29] http://www.totalreuse.co.uk/index.php/departments/the-tool-shed, Accessed January 8, 2015.

the health and wellbeing of older men. Secondly, to achieve this by the repair, restoration, manufacture or creation of 'stuff', thereby diverting it from landfill, and thirdly to produce bespoke items from salvaged materials that have a story. Having spread the message that 'If it's reused it doesn't need recycling', the Total Reuse Team have recently designed and installed a 50 seat cinema, decorated a cafe commemorating 60 years of live music, and come up with ideas for a retro nightclub, all using only reclaimed, reused and up-cycled materials. They are also now being asked if they can 'do anything' with stuff i.e. they are creating unique products from the floor tiles from Manchester Cathedral, parquetry flooring from the Royal Liverpool Infirmary and cast iron radiators from the former White Star Line offices. The 'Sheds' have a regular flow of visitors and Total Reuse is happy to help anyone looking to establish a new Shed. If they like and want to copy what the Tool Shed does they can set up under the Tool Shed banner. If they want to keep it simpler, Total Reuse will still help them to get established. After all, a Shed is what its members want it to be.[30]

The Ecology Centre in Scotland, within which the *Kinghorn Loch Workshop* (also called 'The Tool Shed') is located, self-describes its setting '... in the stunning grounds by Kinghorn Loch in Fife, where we actively use nature and the environment as a tool to improve the quality of life'[31], for young people and adults of all ages and abilities, as well as providing work experience and training opportunities for unemployed adults.

'The Tool Shed' was previously part of the broader Tools for Self Reliance (TFSR) network, established in the UK in 1980, with more than 50 other groups across the UK now doing similarly. The new 'Tool Shed', which started in March 2011[32], is a good example of both old, new and cutting edge. It is about thinking globally and acting locally, collecting and refurbishing tools, consistent with TFSR's broader, global aim of relieving poverty in Africa. Aside from building partnerships with many local and regional organisations to collect and refurbish tools and renew its volunteer mentors, the Shed is actively working with young people (under 21 years) to learn new skills from experienced shedders. Jo Hobbett, the Tool Shed Coordinator, noted in early 2015 that the Workshop's

---

[30] Martin Gamester, January 6, 2015.
[3131] 'Welcome to the Ecology Centre', www.theecologycentre.org, Accessed September 5, 2014.
[32] http://theecologycentre.org/333_The+Tool+Shed+-
+Part+of+the+UK+Men's+Sheds+Network.html, Accessed January 8, 2015.

outcomes were clear, extensive and positive, for both the older mentors and young volunteers. Hobbett tells her personal version of how and when the Shed opened.

> Maybe it began 25 years ago, when I moved to a new city for a couple of years, and found myself spending every Thursday evening making new friends and sharpening rusty old saws with the local Tools for Self Reliance (TFSR) group. Or maybe it began one *dreich* [an Old Scottish term for 'dull, overcast, drizzly, cold, misty and miserable weather'] back in January 2011, when one of the (highly valued but on this particular day, very grumpy) older volunteers at the social enterprise I am lucky enough to work with declared that there was nothing he could do as his knees were playing up. None of the usual volunteers tasks appealed to him that day. I turned to him and asked what he liked to do. [He said], "I just like pottering about in my Shed ... but it gets a bit lonely."

> Or maybe it began when we heard about the Men's Shed movement in Australia, a few months after opening our Shed once a week at the beginning of March 2011, and we secured funding through the Change Fund, supporting active and healthy retirement. This allowed us to open three times a week, in a proper workshop, with some staff support to do the less interesting jobs.

> When our Shed, one of the early ones in Scotland, actually started isn't important. What *is* important are the friendships built up along the way, the stories told and worries shared as well as the thousands of refurbished tools sent out via TFSR to African craftsmen and the local schools and community groups that we have donated hundreds of gardening tools to over the last few years. To 'Give something back' is the most common reason Shedders give for how they came to join either of the local Sheds. The reason they stay, however, well, it's down to the cups of tea and the *craic* [gossip and fun] really.

> At the end of 2014, our Shed moved out of its barn/ shed as The Ecology Centre's 15-year lease at the farm came to an end. The well-established Shed played a significant role in securing funding to buy land on an adjacent site beside the loch (Scottish Land Fund) and further funding to build a new Centre (Big Lottery) that will be ready for the organisation

to move into by mid-2015. Meanwhile, a new permanent, rent-free home has been created for and by the Shedders on the new site by welding together three large recycled shipping containers. Many and varied skills have been crucial in the creation of a now fully operational, fully serviced (with a composting toilet) warm and welcoming space to work together. Work has now resumed to refurbish tools for groups in Africa as well as gardening tools for our local community. Our improved workshop facilities have meant a fourth weekly workshop session to meet a local demand for activities for men living with early stage dementia. This is what makes us 'innovative': like most voluntary organisations, we can 'spin on a sixpence', and because we have particularly close links with our community, we can listen to and respond to local needs quickly.[33]

---

[33] Jo Hobbett, January 6, 2015.

New Zealand Men's Sheds

Barry Golding & Neil Bruce

Chapter 9 includes case studies of 'early', 'innovative', 'remarkable' and 'new and cutting edge' New Zealand Men's Sheds. They include examples from diverse locations across most New Zealand regions, from both the North and South Islands.

EARLY PIONEER MEN'S SHEDS IN NEW ZEALAND

Three very widely spread 'early pioneer' Men's Sheds in New Zealand, in South Dunedin, Hamilton and Picton, all began operation or officially opened between 2007-9. These and later sheds in this chapter illustrate the struggle from the outset in 2007 to gain traction and make appropriate adaptations of the already established Australian model to the earliest Men's Sheds in New Zealand. While the South Dunedin 'Bloke's Shed' and the Hamilton Men Community Men's Shed were set up around the same time (in 2007-8), they were 1,300 kilometers apart and were developed totally independently. The inspiration for both will be shown to derive from knowledge of the Australian Men's Shed model.

The *Taieri Bloke's Shed* and the *South Dunedin Bloke's Shed* opened in the far south of New Zealand near Dunedin in 2007. Photograph 39 is a newspaper article about meeting planned to establish a Shed in Dunedin from September 2007.

More than a garden shed

Photograph 39 Newspaper Article about a Meeting to set up the 'South Dunedin Bloke's Shed', September 2007

They operated slightly earlier and semi-independently of the later established national association until relatively recently. Both resulted mainly from the impetus of Phil Bradshaw, a former Lieutenant Commander in the Royal New Zealand Navy. Bradshaw based the Bloke's Shed concept on an article he had read about a Men's Shed in Australia. Bradshaw recounted the story in early 2015.

> I was the Royal New Zealand Navy's Resident Naval Officer (RNO) in Dunedin for four years between 2006-2009. I am a Marine Engineering Officer and was in charge of Navy Recruiting prior to moving to Dunedin. Around 2000 I bought a Triton Work Centre as we were finishing off a house build, and received a copy of the *Triton Times* newsletter that mentioned that Triton (a tool manufacturer) had donated some work centres to a 'Men's Shed' in Australia[1]. It had a brief article on the purpose of the sheds, which struck me as a great idea.

> During my initial introduction to Dunedin I met with Des Adamson, the Dunedin City Council Business Development Manager that led to my introduction to some Otago/Southland High School Technical

---

[1] Ted Donnelly suspects was Shed was the Hills District Triton Users in Thornleigh, NSW, Australia, known in 2015 as the Hornsby Berowra Shed.

Department Heads and the Southern Group Training Trust. We shared a common concern over the relatively low number of students entering technical and engineering careers, and developed the 'Otago/Southland Grass Kart Challenge' (whereby school student teams build a [downhill] 'grass kart' to comply with a range of criteria during the school year and compete against the other schools in the final term) as a means of enticing students into technical classes, producing something tangible as a team, and igniting the passion for engineering. It became apparent that some of the teams would benefit from additional mentoring and guidance with their builds.

One of my responsibilities as a former RNO was to engage with the community and I became a member of the Otago Officer's Club, whose membership was primarily former military officers. One Friday night I ended up talking to an elderly member whose wife had recently passed away after a long illness that had required him to spend the majority of his time caring for her. He was in good health and was suddenly at a bit of a loose end as he now had time on his hands, but had became isolated and many of his friends had also passed away. It was his situation (coupled with my background involving mentorship for young adults and my awareness of the Men's Sheds) that was the final trigger for the idea that a community Shed, predominantly but not exclusively for retirees might provide a venue for fellowship and companionship, whilst enabling them to 'give something back' in the process. One of my contacts suggested I should talk to Age Concern about the concept, which I did. They thought the idea had merit and that it was worth calling a public meeting to gauge the interest. We were unaware of any Men's Sheds operating in NZ at the time. The local community paper ran a story that promoted the public meeting held on October 26, 2007[2]. We were staggered when fifty people turned up. Clearly there was a need for a communal shed.

Finding a venue for the first shed became a challenge, but as word got out (helped by more articles in the newspaper) we were contacted by the Otago Aero Club who had some spare hangar space that was a little run down but with potential. This became the inaugural home of the Taieri Blokes Shed, with the Kings High School Tractor Shed (once

---

[2] 'More than a garden shed'. *The Star*, September 27, 2007.

refurbished) becoming the second. Initially we assumed that the Shed would appeal to predominantly retired men who may have downsized or moved into a retirement village and lost their shed in the process, lost access to the facilities they may have had when they were working, had become more ambitious in their projects and needed access to larger equipment, or were now at a stage where they would like to learn to use their hands to build things; we envisaged the Blokes' Shed would provide this support.

We expected that the blokes would want to utilize the Shed primarily for their own projects, and that the 'price of admission' would be to contribute some time to work on a community project of some kind to be built in the shed. As it turned out, the appeal to the majority of blokes was to help with building a community project. Most did not have any personal projects they wished to undertake, and embraced the concept of being able to give something back to the community. As time has shown, the majority of projects undertaken by the Sheds have been for community groups that otherwise could not have afforded to have the work done commercially.

Given that the Sheds tend to primarily undertake community projects, the community support for the Blokes' Shed in return has been significant, with people offering surplus tools, equipment and materials. As such the Bloke's Sheds have come into existence via this 'bottom-up' approach, in a very organic way. The sheds have been recipients of some community grants, but in general the vast majority of equipment and materials has been donated. As much as the community benefits from the items produced by the Blokes' Sheds, the members benefit from the fellowship, camaraderie and social interaction the Sheds provide.[3]

The October 2007 meeting mentioned by Phil Bradshaw resulted in the formation of a Dunedin Bloke's Shed Steering Committee. Bradshaw was clearly thinking ahead: a newspaper article that followed the meeting records that 'Lt Cmdr. Bradshaw believes the idea could go national. Each Shed, catering for around 50 would have is own flavour but comply with [the same] general principles'[4]. James Sunderland recorded the brief history of this Shed's development in his 2013

---

[3] Philip Bradshaw, January 12, 2015.
[4] 'Men say 'Honorary Blokes' are Welcome in their Shed', undated newspaper article.

Masters thesis based on the Taieri Bloke's Shed[5]. Early support for the Shed steering Committee came from the Royal New Zealand Navy, St Johns Ambulance, The Methodist Mission, Age Concern, Dunedin City Council and Dunedin Returned Servicemen's Association with a grant from the Lotteries Commission. Local hardware stores and the Mosgiel Probus Club (a fellowship group for retired persons) also assisted. The Taieri Bloke's Shed began operation at Taieri Airfield in 2007 and officially opened in July 2008. The South Dunedin Bloke's Shed officially opened in September 2009 with help from the King's High School that allowed the use of their subsequently re-clad corrugated iron tractor sheds.

While the South Dunedin 'Kings' Shed retained a steady and committed membership, the Taieri Shed experienced rapid growth. Taieri moved in July 2014 to a larger workshop to cope with membership numbers and the demands of community projects. Both Sheds are well known in their communities as a result of very diverse project work for local non-profit groups. Examples include building picnic tables at the Orokonui Eco-sanctuary, lanterns for Naseby township, planter boxes for the main street in Mosgiel, raised garden beds for the Hospital stroke recovery ward and local kindergartens, a puppet stage for a kindergarten, room dividers for kindergartens, children's clothes lines, installing hand rails for the elderly, repairing wooden bicycles for kindergartens, and building animal shelters and lecture seating for the S.P.C.A. (Society for the Prevention of Cruelty to Animals).

Although both Sheds purposefully chose the term 'Bloke's Shed' to prevent overt exclusion of female membership, both had wholly male membership at the time of writing and were developed independently from other Men's Sheds in New Zealand. Neither of these Dunedin Sheds was a member of MENZHED New Zealand prior to 2014, but by 2015 had 'Complementary hosting' status on the MENZHED NZ web site. As in Australia, a major incentive for joining the national association in New Zealand has been the competitive national insurance arrangements negotiated by the national peak body.

The establishment of the *Hamilton Community Men's Shed* in the city of Hamilton in the central region of the North Island, New Zealand occurred around the same time as the earliest Sheds, above, were developed around Dunedin on the far south of the South Island. The Hamilton Shed had more first hand associations with the already established Australian Men's Shed Movement. It

---

[5] James Sunderland, *The Taieri Blokes Shed: An Ethnographic Study*, Master of Occupational Therapy thesis. Dunedin: Otago Polytechnic, 2013.

followed a presentation in early 2007 about Men's Sheds and learning in New Zealand by Barry Golding, which included promotion of the AMSA September 2007 Conference in Sydney. Dr Neil Bruce from Hamilton, then a community educator in a local high school, subsequently attended the Sydney conference with Peter McNeur and came back inspired. Bruce organized three community meetings in Hamilton (a regional North Island city of around 140,000 people) to discuss the idea in late 2007. Data from a Methodist City Action survey had confirmed that a Men's Shed would be a good idea in theory. At that stage, apart from the Bloke's Shed activity in Dunedin mentioned above, 1,300 kilometers to the south, there were no other Men's Shed organisations in New Zealand to use as a template, no venue, core activity or purpose, members or equipment and no obvious community agency to provide start-up funds. The idea for a Hamilton Community Men's Shed was launched publicly by Neil Bruce in the *Waikato Times* on December 13, 2007, but the Shed was not formally opened until March 19, 2008[6].

As the account that follows explains, being one of the earliest attempts to set up a Shed in New Zealand made it far from 'plain sailing'. These difficulties (and successes) are important to hear, as many (but not all) are common to other Shed startups. One unexpected, early administrative hurdle in 2008 involved obtaining 'Charitable Status'. Before granting this status, the Charities Commission required the committee to remove references to men "meeting for socialisation" (even though its benefits for positive physical mental wellbeing are well known). Socialisation was not deemed to be a valid measure of 'charitable purpose' [7], and as a consequence, the goals needed to be more aligned with 'educational purpose'.

In spite of the word 'Community' being included within the Shed name, 'Hamilton Community Men's Shed', the idea of a shed for men, being unfamiliar then in New Zealand, made it a target for denigration by some female journalists.[8] This has occurred sporadically in Australia[9] and England[10]. Even after three years

---

[6] http://ketehamilton.peoplesnetworknz.info/hamilton_community_men_s_shed, Accessed January 8, 2015.

[7] http://www.hayesknight.co.nz/home/news/news-items/2012/4/26/is-the-definition-of-charitable-purpose-relevant-to-nz-society-in-2012.aspx?tag=1402, Accessed September 18, 2014.

[8] http://www.stuff.co.nz/taranaki-daily-news/opinion/6748348/Worthier-ways-for-Mens-Shed-to-assist, Accessed September 18, 2014.

[9] http://blogs.abc.net.au/queensland/2011/08/sunshin e-valley-mens-shed-to-close.html, Accessed September 18, 2014.

[10] http://www.theguardian.com/lifeandstyle/shortcuts/2011/nov/30/women-need-sheds-more-men, Accessed September 18, 2014.

of Shed activity, with a high community profile and regular articles in community newspapers, a syndicated opinion piece for the *Waikato Times* remarked, 'Is it the outdated, laughable sexism [of a Men's Shed] that bothers me or the sheer effrontery' that a group of 'stale pale males' had the gall to apply for council funding, 'something for nothing' in support of their man cave activities?' Without reference to knowledge of Men's Shed community benefits elsewhere, it prompted some vigorous and sometimes reactionary discussions and responses[11]. Nevertheless many positive reactions came, including from supportive women[12], and the debate does have to be had. It is also important to acknowledge, as with many Sheds, that the Hamilton Shed would not have survived without the contributions of many women who in early 2014 comprised half of the Men's Shed Trust Board (associate) members.

Engaging a coordinator in a series of temporary premises with a small number of volunteers proved extremely difficult in the early days of the Hamilton Shed. Finding funds to pay the rent, fit out the shed, engage new members, ensure workshop safety and to open regularly, was a drain on the Shed's very limited early funds and morale. At one stage four of the Men's Shed Trust Board members agreed to contribute NZ$200 just to ensure the coordinator was reimbursed before Christmas in 2008. Membership waned and the Shed effectively went into recess for several months until a suitable City Council facility (now a fully equipped 10m x 12m workshop) eventually became available.

Beyond these early difficulties, in its six years of operation to 2014 Shed members had completed many valuable projects for a diverse range of community groups including: the local animal welfare group (SPCA), Hospice, St John's Ambulance, Women's Refuge, the Waikato Hospital, Cancer Society, local schools, children's play centres, the Salvation Army and the Waikato Potters' Society. Being an 'early pioneer' Shed in New Zealand, it has helped advise many surrounding community representatives from Te Awamutu, Rotorua, Tauranga, and Taumarunui about Shed start-ups. It has also run user-pays children's classes, made musical instruments and run women's workshop sessions. In 2009 Neil Bruce was awarded a Winston Churchill Fellowship to study Men's Sheds in Australia and Britain and also received a Paul Harris Rotary award for Men's Shed community work. This has given Shed members a high level of engagement nationally and internationally.

---

[11] http://www.stuff.co.nz/waikato-times/opinion/6770097/Mens-sheds-where-real-magic-does-happen, Accessed September 18, 2014.
[12] As above.

The Hamilton Community Men's Shed also pioneered a New Zealand Men's Shed insurance scheme in contact with AMSA representatives. While the New Zealand Government had established an Accident Compensation Scheme (ACS) with compulsory contributions based on workplace and personal risk forty years ago, Shed members needed a greater range of cover while operating at the Shed. The Hamilton Shed's 2010 policy became the de facto foundation 'Shed insurance policy' in New Zealand. With six more Sheds added in 2011, a significant drop in premiums occurred, which continued to remained competitive to 2015 in spite of the impact of the 2011 Canterbury Earthquakes on insurance premiums nationally.

Hamilton Community Men's Shed, like many other Men's Sheds, had to grapple with how to safely operate an 'open door' policy with limited resources, volunteers and space. During 2008-9, trusts advocating for men with mostly intellectual (but some physical) disabilities effectively 'swamped' the Shed, impacting negatively both on shed membership and the community perception of what a Men's Shed stood for. The Shed acted to clarify its membership policy: the Shed was 'not a service provider' and it was requisite that members be 'independent men' (with or without support) because of the need for 'safety in the shed'. Photograph 40 shows a community pipe-making course underway in the Shed in September 2013.

Photograph 40 Community Pipe-making Course in the Hamilton Community Men's Shed, New Zealand, September 21, 2013

In 2015 the Hamilton Shed was open on Wednesdays from 10 am to 12 midday, Wednesday evening from 7-9pm and Saturday mornings, It has a welcoming on-line invitation, stressing that 'no skills/tools/materials are necessary. Bring a positive outlook and a willingness to be part of a group of friendly people.'[13]

It is important to observe here, that compared with recent Men's Shed start-ups in Australia, many Sheds in New Zealand, without the strong national or state representation through governments available in Australia, have struggled to get traction and have also faced a significant number of compliance issues.

The *Picton Men's Community Shed*, like many early Sheds in New Zealand, drew some of its early inspiration from the Hamilton Shed. The ferry port of Picton / Waikawa (population 4,000) in the Marlborough region south of the Cook Strait established their Men's Community Shed in a former Sea Scout building in 2009[14]. The Shed idea had strong support from REAP (Rural Activities Education Program) and Marlborough's community education organizer, Ailsa Carey. Carey acknowledged that her enthusiasm stemmed from Neil Bruce's *ACE Aotearoa Newsletter* article (in December 2007) about Men's Sheds, affirming that:

> It would be a great thing to offer men in Picton as we have an ageing community (and I have been vocal in my sexist view about this!) ... REAP's philosophy is to support a project to get underway and then "spin it off" and let the community/members fend for themselves whilst maintaining support as required.[15]

By early 2015 the Picton Men's Community Shed was open in the morning on Wednesdays and Saturdays, operating as a stand-alone entity, neither legally constituted nor as an incorporated society or a trust. While the Picton Shed is primarily woodwork-based, it caters also for metalwork, with a metal lathe and welding equipment. The Shed also has a successful garden operation involving propagation and sale of plants. A pioneering project, due for completion by mid-2015, was the restoration of a 27-foot Montague (Clinker-built) Whaler that will become a static display at the Picton Seaport Trust Maritime Heritage Reserve. As with many small but active Sheds (in this case with 20 financial members,

---

[13] Kete Hamilton: Hamilton Community Men's Shed, www.ketehamilton.peoplesnetworknz.info/hamilton_community_men_s shed, Accessed January 8, 2015.

[14] http://pictonpowerhouse.blogspot.co.nz/p/picton-mens-community-shed.html, Accessed January 8, 2015.

[15] Ailsa Carey email to Neil Bruce, June 2, 2014.

only half of whom were regularly active), a key operational concern of the Picton
Shed was the raising of funds (NZ$3,000 to $5,000 per year) to meet fixed
running costs. The income from plant sales, paying jobs and donations was not
regular or reliable. Concern was also held for succession planning if any of the
office bearers wished to step down.

INNOVATIVE NEW ZEALAND MEN'S SHEDS

Four New Zealand Sheds, two from both Islands, are examined as case studies in
this section to illustrate the theme of innovation. They include Sheds in Masterton
(Henley Men's Shed), Te Awamutu (Te Awamutu Men's Shed), Christchurch
(Redcliffs Community Shed) and Wellington (Eastbourne & Bays Menzshed).

Masterton (population 25,000) is one of the oldest inland towns in New Zealand's
North Island. Situated on the Henley Lake Leisureland on the eastern edge of
Masterton, the *Henley Men's Shed* was created through a close partnership
arrangement between the Henley Men's Shed, the Henley Trust, the local Rotary
Chapter and the Wairarapa Branch of the Rural Education Activities Program
(REAP)[16]. As New Zealand's first purpose-built, community Men's Shed, its
motto is "The place where blokes can be blokes together". A part-time
coordinator was funded for 20 hours per week and the Shed opened on June 22,
2009. With the venue completed, the Henley Men's Shed became the ideal venue
to host the first Conference of New Zealand Men's Sheds in April 2010.
Photograph 41 shows Men's Shed delegates meeting outside the Henley Men's
Shed during the Conference.

---

[16] http://www.nzherald.co.nz/wairarapa-times-
age/news/article.cfm?c_id=1503414&objectid=10995723,
 Accessed January 16, 2015.

Photograph 41 Men's Shed Delegates Meeting Outside the Henley Men's Shed during the first New Zealand Conference, April 10, 2010

By early 2015, Henley Men's Shed had around 120 mainly older men involved in a diverse range of innovative activities. Although from the start a relatively large shed with a floor area of 450 square metres, further expansion had already occurred. Shed activities included woodwork, metalwork, horticulture, garden tool maintenance, cooking (in the kitchen or outdoor pizza oven), storytelling, themed tutorials and specially focused men's health information sessions. The Shed's ethos and focus were self-described by its coordinator, John Bush.

> The concept of what a man does in his shed in the backyard is brought into a community setting, adding the atmosphere of 'blokeship' and forming new friendships. Those who join the Henley Men's Shed can share and develop skills, make or repair things, relate experiences, discuss health and other issues, talk about anything while enjoying a cuppa and biscuit or even another bloke's scones. Aimed mainly at retired men in the community, the Henley Men's Shed has proven to be a great place to break the boredom that is often associated with extra spare time resulting from major life changes, such as downsizing the family home, loss of a partner or retirement.

The Henley Men's Shed is run in a relaxed manner, where men can just call in when they want, stay as long as they want and do something or nothing. You will see blokes repairing things for home, or making a new item or a toy for the grandkids, sitting in on a talk over an issue important to men, or joining a small team doing a community project. So many things to do at the Men's Shed – no wonder it's so popular. New blokes are always welcome to call in and check the place out during regular hours: Monday to Friday between 9am and 2.30pm excluding public holidays.[17]

Henley Men's Shed prides itself on a secure financial base and strong management. It is an incorporated society in its own right and a registered charity and is actively involved in community fundraising, illustrated in Photograph 42.

Photograph 42 Shedders in the Henley Men's Shed Working on a Community Helicopter Fundraising Project, April 2013

A Henley Men's Shed evaluation project was undertaken with support from a Tertiary Education Commission research grant[18]. The shed structure includes a mezzanine floor for model making and craft-type activities as well as a library.

---

[17] John Bush, January 19. 2015.
[18] http://menzshed.org.nz/wp-content/uploads/2014/06/Report-on-Henley-mens-shed-June-2010.pdf, Accessed September 18, 2014.

There is also a fully equipped kitchen where members can explore cooking skills and which also provides a 'cozy venue' for chats. In the workshop area, dedicated specialist areas exist for woodwork, metal-based activities and a multimedia room for tutorials. Several members enhance the woodwork activities with expertise in fine wood working and turning. The Shed runs regular holiday programs for children making trolley carts, rafts and creating musical instruments. John Bush (also a MENZSHED NZ Board member) has initiated a safety management training program for the Henley Men's Shed and other Sheds nationally, as well as establishing a Men's Shed first aid course in conjunction with St John's Ambulance.

Three locals from the regional town of Te Awamutu (population 13,500), south of Hamilton, established the *Te Awamutu Men's Shed* in March 2011, following an exploratory visit to the Hamilton Shed, about 25 minutes away. The rural Shed still receives solid community support to 2015. The Te Awamutu Men's Shed comprises a three-bedroom cottage with a detached single garage, which was custom "refurbished" for shedder use. In addition, Shed members created a new 6m x 9m workshop close to the house with a covered area between, sheltered from the prevailing winds, to increase the useable work areas outside. The Shed's funding officer sourced grant applications to purchase new trade quality machines to fully equip the Shed. In 2013, the Shed was runner-up in the local Community 'Health and Wellbeing' Award. Of particular interest has been the transformation of the rear section into a bountiful community garden under the guidance of a former market gardener and Shed member.

While woodworking activity predominates, specific community projects include new playschool furniture and toys, Christmas parade float displays, repairs and renovations for the Te Awamutu Museum, the Maori Women's Community Trust, and local school and community boards. One innovative feature of the shed is a machine that "brands" completed Shed projects and doubles as an advertising sign. The Shed chairperson, a local technical school teacher, has also implemented an innovative, graduated membership system, with colour-coded name badges which denote that Shed induction has been completed, particular safety levels reached and abilities to use designated equipment. As at many other Sheds, there are, at the Te Awamutu Shed, operational concerns regarding member involvement and succession in particular, especially when members' health levels vary and their ability to be actively involved decreases.

The *Redcliffs Community Shed* in Christchurch evolved in 2011 through an arrangement with the owner to rebuild his shed to specific requirements in return for favorable lease conditions upon completion. Using predominantly volunteer labour, support came from interested locals and the owner, and local businesses donated materials and grants. Several local women quickly became interested in shed space for craftwork and negotiated to use half of the shed for their activities. The Shed operated in 2014 under the umbrella of the Sumner Bays Union [charitable] Trust. Auspice arrangements like this one are not common in New Zealand Men's Sheds, as most Shed organizations have sought the freedom of retaining full management control. Advantages of working under the auspices of an organization include Shed members not having to become too involved in administration, financial accountabilities, insurance and applications for funding grants.

In 2014 the Redcliffs Shed was open from 10am to 3pm on three days a week, with a dedicated 'Men's Night' where the main project involved building a dinghy. The shed was open for a 'tea/coffee and chat' for anyone who drops in, as well as for both a special-needs craft group and ladies craft group. The Shed also exhibits, promotes and sells work by local artists and craftspeople in return for a donation based on the cash value of sales and shed usage. Its 2015 intentions included seeking funding for a part-time Coordinator/Promoter to oversee Shed activities, to encourage membership and develop closer ties with community members through the provision of stimulating activities.

The *Eastbourne & Bays Menzshed* is located in Williams Park, Days Bay, Lower Hutt (Wellington) on the seaward edge of the East Harbour Regional Park. It is a beautiful area of native bush subject to problems with introduced pests. The Shed in 2015 was involved in practical conservation to control these pests in collaboration with the Mainland Island Restoration Organisation (MIRO) which had 450 traps, 80 kilometers of trap lines and 40 trappers, by making up bait 'orders' from the bulk stock held in a secure bunker. The Shed also had a group of special needs young men who came each week and enjoyed working in 'a man's environment'.

Opened in March 2011[19] and operating as a Charitable Trust from a former City Council owned Fire Engine Shed on Council Land, the Shed is not charged for rent or electricity. Photograph 43 shows Men's Shed delegates from around New Zealand outside of the Shed on 20 June 2012.

---

[19] http://menzshed.org.nz/lower-ni-a-to-m/eastbourne-and-bays-menzshed/, Accessed January 8, 2015.

Photograph 43 New Zealand Men's Shed Conference delegates outside Eastbourne & Bays Menzshed, Wellington, New Zealand, June 20, 2012 (David Helmers from AMSA in Australia is towards the front on the left; Neil Bruce is squatting in the centre)

Though small, the Shed is innovative in the way it has cultivated very good relationships with local schools, kindergartens and preschools as well as the way it has become involved in the enhancement of surrounding native vegetation and bird life. Intergenerational mentoring with local school children has resulted in significant and reciprocal community benefits from shedder involvement.

REMARKABLE NEW ZEALAND MEN'S SHEDS

Four Men's Sheds are included in this section as remarkable New Zealand Men's Shed case studies. Two are on the North Island, at Rotorua (Rotorua Community Menz Shed) and on the Kapiti Coast (MenzShed Kapiti). Two other Sheds (McIver's Oxford Community Men's Shed in Oxford and the New Brighton Menz Shed in Canterbury) are on the South Island. Each one will be shown to be remarkable in a different way, with quite different histories in very diverse community settings.

Rotorua is a North Island city of around 70,000. *Rotorua Community Menz Shed* members have shown remarkable resilience by regrouping and reinventing their

Shed after a slow and difficult start. Initially the Shed was a foundation partner in a newly established local Community Centre Trust at a former bowling club. The Shed members, however, could not get assurances from the Board that their Shed organization could operate independently. Further difficulties arose with ownership and use of facilities and tools with significant implications for safety. Following a delegation to the Mayor, a city council-owned building was offered at a not-for-profit rental, on the proviso that unused rooms were to be made available, as a Community Centre, to other groups who would pay rent to cover the basic expenses. Two months after converting surplus rooms into spaces acceptable to other groups, the Shed officially reopened on March 15, 2014, with nine members who swelled to fifty members five months later.

By late 2014 the Rotorua Shed had acquired a grant to cover the services of a Funding and Finance Officer as an administrator of the front office, the Shed itself and five other charitable groups using the Community Centre four hours per day for five days per week. With the open area nearly all taken up with community groups, Shed members constructed walls to create more rooms and secured triple the original machinery from a local high school. Shed expansion was aided by three personal non-interest bearing loans of NZ$5,000 provided by members to help pay for the setting up costs and initial running of the Shed.

Along with several other Sheds nationally, the Rotorua Shed completed memorial crosses for the Returned Services Association's World War I remembrance project. The Shed maintains good relationships with local businesses that make surplus or reject materials available to other Sheds. Official Shed days were Tuesday to Thursday, with Friday being an 'extra' day for work on the building or to raise money for the Shed.

MenzShed Kapiti, at Waikanae on the Kapiti Coast north of Wellington, started from a casual and unremarkable "How about we …?" conversation among three enthusiastic local men in 2009. The idea of establishing a place for "men to do what men do" and to increase engagement of older retired men on the Kapiti Coast also generated interest and support from important Kapiti women (a lawyer, a local councilor, and the mayor). By June 2010 MenzShed Kapiti was registered as an Incorporated Society and Charitable Entity with 25 members. With an inclusive "Members are the Shed" motto and a unique NZ brand logo (since adopted by the National Association and other New Zealand Sheds) the Kapiti Shed has developed considerable member diversity and strength. The enthusiasm of members, who represent a wide range of Wellington professionals, civil servants, engineers and tradesmen, facilitated the initial acquisition of a previously council-owned 40m² shed on a disused Council works depot at a 'peppercorn' rental. Tapping into its diverse range of shedder skills and backgrounds, members worked tirelessly to reconfigure it as workshop with an official opening on September 9, 2010 (Photograph 44).

Photograph 44 MenzShed Kapiti Official Opening, September 9, 2010

With rapid growth and generous support including tools and materials from the community and local businesses, members have completed multiple projects for kindergartens, schools, volunteer firefighters, the Department of Conservation, and various other groups and individuals in the community. Pressure on cramped facilities led to a major extension and renovation with the acquisition of an adjoining 90m² shed. The labeled additions to the Shed are shown in Photograph 45.

Photograph 45 Labeled Additions to MenzShed Kapiti to June 2014

By early 2015 MenzShed Kapiti had over 75 financial members, regular Shed attendances of 20 to 30 men and had established a website[20]. MenzShed Kapiti had also hosted the 4th National Conference for Men's Sheds in New Zealand in March 2014, and had given solid support for emerging Sheds and the National Association, MENZSHED New Zealand. Shed member Peter Blackler in 2013 undertook Treasurer roles for both organisations. MenzShed Kapiti has been acknowledged for its remarkable progress and achievements, by winning local, regional and supreme community awards for Health and Wellbeing for the Wellington Region. As at other successful New Zealand sheds, further extension and construction work was ongoing. Photograph 47 provides an illustration of the important social function of Men's Sheds, in this case an evening function at MenzShed Kapiti.

Photograph 46 Evening Social Function during the MENZHED NZ Conference at MenzShed Kapiti, March 14, 2014

Situated near Christchurch in the Waimakariri River area of Canterbury on the South Island, the Men's Shed in Oxford operated as a 'Shed without a shed' from 2010. During that period it was mainly involved in fundraising and assisting the start up of other local sheds. Two years later, in October 2012, a purpose-built 20m x 9m *McIver's Oxford Community Men's Shed* was officially opened on part of a local recreational reserve. Named after the sponsor who provided the building, the shed is fully lined, has an office and recreation room, a wide range of woodworking equipment and some metal working equipment. A Trust and members, all of whom are voluntary, run the Shed.

---

[20] http://menzshedkapiti.org.nz/, Accessed January 8, 2015.

In early 2015 McIver's Community Men's Shed was open three days a week, servicing the districts around Oxford[21]. Its past activities have included a holiday and mentoring program for young people run by senior Shed members. Local rest-home residents attend on a regular basis. The Shed had been linked with the local community gardens, now given over to the Enviro Oxford Group, but establishment of the gardens remained an ongoing responsibility of the Men's Shed. Community projects in Oxford have included building new Cemetery Gates, a pergola at the police station, and repairs to children's toys from the local Playcentre. As with many Sheds, ongoing funding is one of the key challenges.

A steering group to establish a Men's Shed in New Brighton, a coastal suburb of Christchurch, was formed in 2009. However a number of factors typical of many other Shed start-ups delayed establishment. These factors included a lack of council support, no suitable locations (before and after the earthquakes), objections by neighbors to the building of a shed and wavering support from some community groups. It wasn't until September 27, 2013 that the *New Brighton Menz Shed*, was finally opened in a 6m x 6m double garage, on the grounds of St. Faith's Church, New Brighton[22]. The availability of the kitchen and toilet facilities in the nearby church hall was a great advantage when planning such a small shed.

In its protracted, four-year start up phase, the New Brighton Menz Shed group contributed to a regional Canterbury Men's Shed Hub, a regional Shed network, a first for New Zealand but similar to several Australian Shed 'Clusters'. Promoted and facilitated by the Canterbury Men's Centre, a dedicated men-focused health initiative, the Men's Shed Hub encouraged the establishment of new Sheds within the Canterbury region. This post-earthquake period in Christchurch required citizens and Shed members to show a remarkable tenacity and persistence under duress.

Now a registered charity, a Trust runs the Shed independently. Decisions on its activities are largely arrived at by the membership of the Shed, which includes all of the trustees. The Shed is open to women becoming members and can run mixed or women only sessions subject to the availability of suitable supervisors. The New Brighton Shed Secretary, Ray Hall was elected Chair of MENZSHED NZ in late 2014. Hall has since contributed his knowledge and skills in website design to both organisations.

---

[21] http://oxfordcommunitymensshed.webs.com/what%20we%20do.htm, Accessed January 8, 2015.
[22] https://sites.google.com/site/newbrightonmenzshed, Accessed January 8, 2015.

NEW AND CUTTING EDGE NEW ZEALAND MEN'S SHEDS

Four diverse, New Zealand Men's Sheds are introduced as 'new and cutting edge' case studies in this section, including one on the North Island and three on the South Island. They include one rural Shed in the small town of Alexandra (Alexandra Men's Shed), as well as Sheds in Rolleston near Christchurch (Rolleston Men's Shed) and in Nelson (Men's Shed Waimea). Auckland's first purpose-built Men's Shed, North Shore Men's Shed, is also included.

Alexandra is a rural town of around 5,000 people one hour east of the iconic tourist town of Queenstown. Locating a suitable venue and premises was one of the *Alexandra Men's Shed*'s early frustrations. Central Otago District Council property officer, Brian Taylor noted during this searching process that "We've explored every option for the Men's Shed, and in every other option, there's been something wrong". This site selection process took two years. After several false starts, the Vincent Community Board offered the steering group a five-year lease on a site at the bicycle park in Alexandra's Molyneux Park for a peppercorn rental. Following a meeting of prospective shed members in October 2010, the first Shed opened in April 2011, later moving to its current (2015) site in March 2012. The Alexandra Men's Shed is registered as a Charitable Trust with members being mainly retired men with a principal focus on woodworking.

Now owning their own, former Ministry of Works office block created for the Roxburgh Dam hydroelectric project in the 1950s, Shed members in late 2014 were negotiating with the Alexandra Blossom Festival Committee to build an additional space to house a joinery shop, engineering shop and float storage area. Meanwhile they continue to make ride-on toys and rocking horses to sell at pre-Christmas craft sale days. Shed members had made connection with the nearby independent Dunedin Bloke's Sheds as the Alexandra Shed's chair, Neil McArthur, is the southernmost Regional Representative for MENZSHED NZ. The Alexandra Men's Shed recently won a local Heritage and Environment Award for its valuable contribution to the local community.

Rolleston is a 'new' Canterbury town of 10,000 people southwest of Christchurch. With earthquakes devastating much of central Christchurch in 2010 and 2011, many residents moved further out, making Rolleston one of the fastest growing towns in New Zealand. Because it is a 'new' community there were no existing buildings for a Shed, so the *Rolleston Men's Shed* physically started from scratch. Meeting for the first time in December 2012, members formed a Charitable Trust. It began with the purchase of a woodworking workshop in a temporary building.

The local council donated some land for their use. A temporary shed was planned for the site late in 2014. The facilities will include an engineering workshop, a committee room for computer training, plus toilets and a kitchen, making it available also for external hire.

Money remained a concern, as most of the shedders acknowledged they are more "hands on than fund raisers", and there was the hope that management would locate someone with specific funding skills. In the meantime, Shed members had contributed community work for a local playcentre, schools and local clubs. They found that by charging for materials at retail price and asking for a donation, everyone could benefit.

Men's Shed Waimea was the Nelson region's first Men's Shed. As a city of 43,000 people, Nelson, in the north of the South Island, has a relatively mild climate and is a popular place for coastal retirement. Shed membership to 2014 had been healthy and donations of surplus machinery and tools had been bountiful. Two regional councils supported the Shed with grants early on, and the Canterbury Community Trust had given further support. Following meetings in 2010 and 2011, Shed members took possession of the former Nelson District Kennel Club rooms and leased the surrounding grounds from the Nelson Harness Racing Club at Richmond Park. Their facilities include a meeting room, 'smoko room' and a museum for the vintage tools that they acquired. Topsoil excavated for the car park was set aside for the Shed's vegetable garden. A small building was earmarked for arts and crafts and a large metalworking and engineering garage had been constructed.

The large physical site and equipment gave members the opportunity to undertake woodwork, metalwork, engineering and horticultural projects. The Shed aims to put men in Tasman Bay, Richmond and Nelson in contact with each other, sharing their 'skills, knowledge and fellowship', where 'Older men can catch up, younger men can learn [and] all can learn new skills and hone old ones'[23]. The members' collective enthusiasm included the hosting of a third national Men's Shed conference in New Zealand in February 2013, which resulted in the establishment of the National Association. The Shed has the space, facilities and numbers to be a multifaceted shed complete with an adjacent motor home park for visitors.

Following a trip to Australia visiting a Men's Shed during 2006, Northcote Birkenhead Community Coordinator Jill Nerheny was so impressed with the

---

[23] WEB http://www.menzshed-waimea.kiwi.nz/, Accessed January 8, 2015.

Men's Shed concept that she wanted to establish a similar Shed on the North Shore of Auckland. Though it took almost seven years before opening, *Men's Shed North Shore* became the first purpose-built Men's Shed in Auckland, New Zealand's largest city when it officially opened in April 2013. A steering committee was formed at a public meeting in Northcote in September 2007. Many vacant buildings were inspected for over two years without success before a piece of recreational land in Elliott Reserve in Glenfield was found and leased from the Auckland Council on May 1, 2010. Fundraising and design centered on the preferred activities of woodwork, model making, engineering and electronics. On December 13, 2009, a Deed of Trust was signed and a Certificate of Incorporation was received on March 19, 2010. A contract was signed for a 300m² building and construction commenced, with building completion on May 23, 2012.

Shed members continued with the internal framing for toilets, a kitchen, office and the electronic workshop, as well as the installation of wiring, plumbing, insulation and cladding. The single level shed, ideal for men who could not negotiate stairs, includes shelving at a level suitable for people to reach anything from the floor. Good lighting was a priority and fibre-optic broadband cabling was installed for fast internet connection. Equipment donated during the build was positioned for the opening on April 7, 2013[24] when the Chair of the Kaipatiki Local Board, Lindsay Waugh (a woman), cut a timber "ribbon" with a chainsaw. With the Shed open three days a week between 9am and 4pm, membership during the first year grew from 20 to 120 men. Over that time, members clocked up 9,000 hours in the shed of which 5,000 hours were for a variety of community projects. Membership was still growing in late 2014 and a 100m² extension was on the drawing board for 2015.

The North Shore Men's Shed demonstrated a thorough attention to detail to achieve the best possible facility. Time was not an issue for the committee. Their clear vision was to have a purpose-built facility paid off before encouraging members to join. The facility is a credit to the Auckland community, and being in the largest New Zealand city, it benefits from high profile exposure in local and national media.

---

[24] http://mensshednorthshore.org.nz, Accessed January 8, 2015.

PART IV

Conclusions after Two Decades of Men's Sheds

Part 4 summarises and critically analyses the evidence after two decades of Men's Sheds experimentation and practice. Chapter 10 provides a synthesis of the available international research and evidence. Chapter 11 identifies important theory and practice implications of Men's Sheds. Chapter 12 contains a critical discussion of some emerging Men's Shed issues as well as trends and possibilities for the Men's Shed Movement. It includes consideration of how the principles behind Men's Sheds might shape other fields of men's practice, including in nations and fields of male-gendered theory and practice in which Men's Sheds (or a local cultural equivalent) might be anticipated to gain future traction.

CHAPTER 10

Research Evidence from Men's Sheds

> *'We believe in a particular order not because it is objectively true, but because believing in it enables us to cooperate effectively and forge a better society .... The real test of 'knowledge' is not whether it is true, but when it empowers us. ... [T]ruth is a poor test of knowledge. The real test is utility. A theory that enables us to do new things constitutes knowledge'.* Yuval Noah Hariri, *Sapiens*, 2014[1]

This Chapter provides a summary of all research available on Men's Sheds in community settings internationally to 2015.

WHAT RESEARCH IS AVAILABLE?

Appendix 3 contains a list of all articles in the two decades, 1995 to 2014 which focus on, or which are inclusive of Men's Sheds in community settings. What follows is a broad overview of these 103 articles published in these two decades. The numbers in brackets are the number of published articles.

- Of all 103 articles, around 84 per cent (87) originate from Australia.
- The 16 articles originating from outside of Australia are from the UK (4), New Zealand (4), Ireland (3), Canada (3) and the US (2).
- Only five articles were published before 2005: in effect 95 per cent were published in the decade from 2005, and one half (50) were published in the three years 2012 to 2014.
- Around one half of all articles (49) were published in either journals or professional magazines.
- Around one in three articles (23) were peer reviewed journal articles or conference papers.
- Around one quarter of all articles (22) were in academic reports, program evaluations or book chapters. The remaining one quarter of

---

[1] Yuval Noah Harari, *Sapiens: A Brief History of Humankind*. London: Harvill Secker, 2014, 110 and 259.

articles appeared as either published conference papers (13), evaluations of Sheds or programs (7) or in other sources (8).

- One third were either authored (19) or co-authored (14) by myself, Barry Golding. Jillian Cavanagh as well as Nathan Wilson, both from Australia and with colleagues, each contributed seven papers since 2012 and 2013 respectively. The most prolific research outside of Australia has been by Christine Milligan and colleagues in the UK (3 articles). In effect around one half of all publications have included one of these four named researchers as contributors.

Of the 49 journal articles, 20 articles (41%) were peer refereed. Of all journal articles in the two decades:

- 25 were mainly about learning through Men's Sheds, most of which included Barry Golding as one of the authors.
- 11 were mainly about Men's Sheds and health.
- 4 articles focused on Indigenous spaces for men, including Men's Sheds, with Cavanagh as one of the authors for each article.
- 9 other articles adopted a broadly critical perspective towards various aspects of Men's Sheds.

Most of the research publications summarised in this chapter, though not accessible or of direct interest to all shedders, have been important for many others involved in or supportive of the Movement, including Men's Shed coordinators, organisations with auspice arrangements with Men's Sheds, Men's Shed peak bodies, academics, policy makers, government and non-government organisations. The research has also provided evidence for prospective Shed auspice and funding bodies. Aside from the obvious success measured by the number of Sheds that have been opened and communities that have 'come on board' globally, it is now possible to make a case that Men's Sheds are a good thing for a range of reasons, with measurable, positive outcomes.

While Appendix 3 focuses on articles related to community Men's Sheds[2], several popular and influential books about personal sheds from the past two decades are included at the end of Appendix 3. These non-research publications

---

[2] The exception is Leon Earle's 'Sheds and Male Retirement' paper, published with colleagues in 1995. It is included because of both its academic interest and relevance to some very early Men's Shed proposals, despite being based on inferences about men's backyard shed experiences.

are provided as a reminder that they were much more likely to have been accessible to and have motivated individual men's shedders than relatively recent, sometimes obscure, peer refereed, academic journal articles and book chapters.

Despite the limitations of the data and the research methods employed to date, identified later, there is a growing body of evidence from Australia, and more recently from Ireland, on who participates and what benefits there are from shedder participation. There have been four comprehensive and well-documented[3] major surveys of Men's Sheds in Australia:

- The learning-focused survey in late 2005 of 22 Men's Sheds in the state of Victoria, Australia, published in March 2006 by Barry Golding and Jack Harvey[4].
- The learning-focused study by Barry Golding and colleagues, involving surveys and interviews in 2006, inclusive of 24 Men's Sheds in five Australian states, published by NCVER in 2007[5].
- The health and wellbeing-focused beyondblue study by Paul Flood and Sharon Blair, using a quasi-experimental design comparing Australian shedders (1,436 survey respondents) with a control group of non-shedders (1,200 survey respondents). Backed up by qualitative data from 27 interviews, it was published by beyondblue in 2013[6].
- AMSA's *Survey of Australian Men's Sheds, 2013,* with survey returns from 287 Australian Men's Sheds in 2013, analysed by Barry Golding and Jack Harvey in February 2014[7].

The only comprehensive and rigorous Men's Shed survey undertaken outside of Australia was by Lucia Carragher in Ireland[8]. It involved surveys and interviews

---

[3] Rick Hayes and Michelle Williamson's 'best-practice' guidelines published in 2006-7 based on early Victorian Men's Sheds were useful, influential and accessible scoping studies, limited by lack of clarity in their methods and sample selection. The La Trobe University evaluation for AMSA in 2012, despite its large sample size (209 Australian sheds), is not sufficiently rigorous methodologically to be included.

[4] Rick Hayes and Michelle Williamson's research on Victorian Men's Sheds published in 2006 included some excellent case studies, but the methodology, sample size and available data were not clearly identified.

[5] Barry Golding *et al., Men's Sheds in Australia: Learning through Community Contexts.* Adelaide: NCVER, 2007.

[6] Paul Flood and Sharon Blair, *Men's Sheds in Australia: Effects on Physical Health and Mental Well-being.* Ultrafeedback Report to beondblue, Melbourne, 2013.

[7] Barry Golding and Jack Harvey, *Survey of Australian Men's Sheds*, Report to Australian Men's Shed Association, Tertiary Tracks and Federation University Australia, Ballarat, February, 2013.

(297 survey respondents from 30 of the 55 Irish Men's Sheds open in May 2012) and was completed in February 2013. The research method and instruments for Carragher's Irish research were adapted from the 2007 NCVER Australian Men's Sheds study undertaken nationally in Australia by Barry Golding and colleagues, providing the first opportunity to compare some aspects of Irish and Australian Sheds at approximately the same level of development, albeit six years later in Ireland. All five major surveys combined provide a reasonably good profile of the demographics and perceptions of shedders in Australia (in 2006 and 2012) and Ireland (in 2012).

Systematic Reviews of Men's Shed Literature

While most academic studies of Men's Sheds include literature reviews relevant to the specific theme of the particular study, three articles are essentially major systematic reviews of the Men's Shed literature.

- Gary Misan's *Men's Sheds: A Strategy to Improve Men's Health*[9] for Mensheds Australia in 2008, through the University of South Australia in Whyalla.
- Nathan Wilson and Reinie Cordier's *Narrative Review of Men's Shed Literature*[10] in 2013, through the University of Sydney.
- Christine Milligan and colleagues' *Men's Sheds and other Gendered Interventions for Older Men: Improving Health and Wellbeing through Social Activity: A Systematic Review and Scoping of the Evidence-base*[11] undertaken in 2013 through the University of Lancaster in the UK.

Both major, recent narrative reviews of the available research evidence, by Wilson and Cordier in Australia, and by Milligan and colleagues in the UK were undertaken more or less in parallel. Both preceded the new Australian data available in 2013 from the beyondblue study by Flood and Blair, the new Irish

---

[8] Lucia Carragher, *Men's Sheds in Ireland: Learning through Community Contexts*. Dundalk: Dundalk Institute of Technology, 2013.
[9] Gary Misan, *Men's Sheds: A Strategy to Improve Men's Health*, Report for Mensheds Australia Ltd. Whyalla: University of South Australia, August, 2008.
[10] Nathan Wilson and Reinie Cordier, 'A Narrative Review of Men's Sheds Literature: Reducing Social Isolation and Promoting Men's Health and Well-being', *Health and Social Care in the Community*, 21 (5), 451-463, 2013.
[11] Christine Milligan *et al.*, *Men's Sheds and other Gendered Interventions for Older Men: Improving Health and Wellbeing through Social Activity: A Systematic Review of the Evidence*, Report for the Liverpool-Lancaster Collaborative (LiLaC) and Age UK. Lancaster: Lancaster University, April, 2013.

data from Carragher's *Men's Sheds in Ireland* 2013 study and the new Australian data that became available from Golding and Harvey's analysis of the 2013 AMSA data. Much of this new data underpins the rest of this chapter.

Limitations of the Data and Research Methods

While much of this Chapter is an overview and synthesis of all data and research to early 2015, the evidence is necessarily early and partial, given that the Men's Shed Movement is so recent. It is only around 22 years since the first ever community Shed, only 17 years since the first 'Men's Shed' in Australia, and only six years since the first Sheds opened in Ireland, the UK and New Zealand. It is only a decade since the first research presentations at a Men's Shed-specific conference in Australia in 2005. While it is less than five years since the first Men's Shed-specific gatherings or conferences in New Zealand (Masterton, 2010), Ireland (Moynalty, 2010) and the UK (Leicester, England, 2011), it is remarkable that more than 30 per cent of (over 400) Men's Sheds in the world were open outside of Australia by early 2015.

Both Wilson and Cordier's and Milligan and colleagues' narrative reviews were critical of the small sample sizes and the lack of validated measures in previously published studies, deeming them to be inadequate to definitively assess the impact of Men's Sheds on health and wellbeing as an intervention. While the beyondblue study was rigorous in terms of its experimental design and use of validated research instruments, its comparisons of shedders with non-shedders involves a number of assumptions that arguably limit the validity of some of its conclusions. I agree with Wilson and Cordier's broad conclusion, in their 2013 narrative review, that 'The range of variables that might contribute towards best practice in Men's Sheds has not yet been adequately conceptually measured, tested and understood'[12].

My first point of departure from Wilson and Cordier's contention is that the positivist research paradigm is not the only 'gold standard' for evaluating research in this field. My second concern is with their suggestion, returned to later, that the potential health benefits of Men's Sheds should be the sole or principal concern. I have recently suggested, with John McDonald, that:

> ... because men's sheds are community-based and very diverse in terms of their location, context, organisation, purposes, participants and outcomes across four nations, 'gold standard' research designs to

---

[12] Nathan Wilson and Reinie Cordier, 2013, as above, 458.

measure men's health outcomes are unlikely to produce generalizable findings. The expansion of the grassroots men's shed movement can be understood precisely because each shed emerges and takes shape in response to community needs. No two sheds are the same. Sheds defy engineering by central bureaucracies. Therefore imposing a positivist research paradigm to define universal 'best practice' seems futile, as does subjecting sheds to an evaluative regime designed to measure shedders health outcomes.[13]

Both narrative reviews of the Men's Shed literature identify a number of significant limitations posed by the relatively small amount of available data and the limited scope of the research methods employed to 2013. Aside from the Australian and Irish data identified above, no similar or comparable data were available from Men's Sheds in either New Zealand or the UK to early 2013.

As alluded to above, unlike many other forms of professional, clinical and therapeutic practice, Men's Sheds are not a professional, top-down service that lend themselves to simple 'cause and effect' evaluation. Men's Sheds instead exhibit many of the characteristics of a new grassroots social movement. Like other new, reformist social movements, Men's Sheds are not amenable to simple, 'single-order' systems of explanation [14] which assume a single purpose and standard operating procedures. As Chapter 11 will emphasise, Men's Sheds do not come out of one theory or field of practice: nor are they exclusive to one academic field (health, welfare, gender studies, gerontology, adult education, for example). While it is possible to use a number of existing theories to identify factors and preconditions that led to Men's Sheds as an innovation and which encouraged their recent adoption and proliferation, Men's Sheds practice has in several senses run ahead of traditional models of professional practice, policy and research.

While this chapter is an attempt to 'stand back' and 'make sense of' the evidence from Men's Sheds as a new grassroots social movement to early 2015, the movement has far from run its course in any country and has so far only affected some men's practice in only four countries. Men's Shed activity as a social movement is qualitatively distinct from (and arguably often in opposition to) normal or institutionalized action and thus tends to be non-logical or pre-

---

[13] Barry Golding and John McDonald, 'Researching Older Men's Self-directed Learning in Australian Community Contexts: Methods, Frameworks and Results', Paper to Symposium of Self-Directed Learning, Strasbourg, France, October 29-31, 2014, 5-6.

[14] Alan Scott, 'Ideology and the New Social Movements', in Chapter 24, *Controversies in Sociology*, Tom Bottomore and Michael Mulkay (Eds.). London: Unwin Hyman, 1990, 4.

rational.[15] Any empirical evidence collected from Men's Sheds is necessarily secondary and, while it may suggest some possible 'causes', it will be unable to 'explain' this grassroots Movement from a purely positivist[16] perspective. Given the many social and cultural variables at play in Men's Sheds, neither the research nor this book will be able to accurately predict the Movement's future.

Issues Posed by Men's Shed Diversity

Part 1 began by distilling and defining the common or shared attributes of Men's Sheds in a community setting. It stressed that all Sheds are different and therefore difficult to simply define. Part 2 searched for and identified an underlying and now broadly agreed central ethos about what a community Men's Shed is and how it relates to and identifies with other Sheds and the wider Movement. Part 3 illustrated the diversity of Men's Shed innovation, at an individual Shed level, beyond these common generalities across four nations. This huge diversity of Men's Sheds organisation types and purposes is very relevant when attempting to answer even a simple research question about what a 'Men's Shed' *is*, or what it *should* be. Given this diversity the rest of this chapter explores some '*What is ... ?*' questions with research evidence of diversity and possible commonalities. Chapter 11 proceeds to explore some closely related and difficult '*What should ... ?*' questions, typically referred to by researchers as 'normative' (involving a value judgment).

It is common, despite this huge Shed diversity to 2015, for researchers to select one case study or a small number of case studies to answer an often very specific research question. Unless the rationale for such a sample selection is carefully explained, there is a danger that both a convenient or purposeful sampling technique will produce a result that says more about the sample chosen and much less (or nothing) about how representative the sample is of the field of Men's Sheds.

There are now sufficient Men's Sheds in any of the four countries with at least 50 Men's Sheds to legitimately use surveys or interviews conducted across many Men's Sheds and shedders. Such research is more likely to come up with data that are more representative and therefore explanatory of Men's Sheds and shedder diversity than studies that analyse just one Shed, one type of Shed, or one thread of particular interest to particular researchers in a very specific field. Such

---

[15] These ideas are discussed in similar terms in Scott, 1990, p. 6, above.
[16] Positivism only recognises scientifically verified proof.

data, as well as being capable of defining what is 'typical' or 'average', are able to identify ranges in the spread of data as well as outliers.

These data, including the summaries that follow, are subject to a range of limitations. These limitations include not only how and why the Shed case studies and samples have been chosen but also what theoretical perspective or academic discipline a researcher 'brings to' the shed, the objectives of the research project, as well as which government or other agency funded the research. If I am from an adult learning research background for example (which I am), I will take a very broad definition of a Men's Shed, and tend to look for, see and report mainly learning outcomes from the Shed. If, however, I am a men's health academic, a psychologist, occupational therapist, disability advocate, Indigenous researcher, or a men's suicide or substance abuse expert, I will define and value a Men's Shed differently. Diverse researcher will therefore look for, find, ask questions about and report on quite different outcomes using different data.

To take an example, the *Men's Sheds in Australia: Effects on Physical Health and Mental Well-being* study in 2013 [17] for beyondblue (a national, depression initiative) deliberately defined, examined, studied (and valued) Men's Sheds for the roles and outcomes of interest to beyondblue, made explicit in its report title. While such studies often collect valuable data of interest to Sheds and shedders about other aspects and outcomes of Men's Sheds 'along the way', they will always be limited by the factors mentioned above: the definition of what a Men's Shed *is* (or *should be*, as teased out later in Chapter 11), the purposes of the study, as well as the interests and disciplines of the researcher and/or the research funder. The final, obvious limitation of the answers to the questions that follow is that they mostly derive from the most recent Australian data and research, the only country with a relatively mature Men's Shed sector with a sufficient range of research already completed.

The Evidence

The available body of research and data identified above, particularly from Australia, and to some extent from Ireland, provides a reasonable source of information on which to base the seven subsections that follow, arranged around each of the following research questions as they apply to Men's Sheds.

- Who takes part?

---

[17] Paul Flood and Sharon Blair, *Men's Sheds in Australia: Effects on Physical Health and Mental Well-being*, Ultrafeedback Report for beyondblue, 2013.

- What are the outcomes for men?
- Why do Men's Sheds work, and for which men?
- Who else benefits from Men's Sheds and how?
- What do men do in the Shed?
- What have Men's Sheds got to do with men's health and wellbeing?
- What is the role of women in Men's Sheds?

The most recent (mainly 2013) Australian data summarised below come mainly from the *Men's Sheds in Australia* study for beyondblue[18], as well as from the *Survey of Australian Men's Sheds 2013*[19]. The Irish data come mainly from Carragher's *Men's Sheds in Ireland* study from 2013[20]. Some inter-country and longitudinal comparisons are possible with data from the 2007 *Men's Sheds in Australia* study[21] that used many similar questions and methods.

Who Takes Part?

The first community Men's Sheds in Australia developed during the late 1990s were deliberately designed for and oriented towards the needs of mainly older men, many of whom are retired or unemployed, War Veterans, as well as men with problems with physical or mental health. While the scope of Men's Sheds has changed and broadened over time in other countries and contexts, it is clear that Men's Sheds have been most attractive to older men who are not in paid work for a range of reasons[22]. It is important, before looking first at the Australian data on who takes part, to acknowledge that some Sheds have catered for and been set up specifically for boys or younger men. In countries like Ireland with relatively high unemployment younger men tend to be more involved in Men's Sheds but participation is still skewed towards older men.

The median age (age of the middle person, if participants are placed in a line from youngest to oldest) of shedders in Australian Men's Sheds is approximately 70 years (mean or average 69 years). Around eight out of ten men (78%) who participate are between 60 and 79 years of age, with many still involved well

---

[18] Flood and Blair, 2013 as above.
[19] Barry Golding and Jack Harvey, *Survey of Australian Men's Sheds* 2013, Report to Australian Men's Sheds Assocation, Tertiary Tracks and Federation University Australia.
[20] Lucia Carragher, *Men's Sheds in Ireland: Learning through Community Contexts*. Dundalk: Dundalk Institute of Technology, 2013.
[21] Barry Golding *et al.*, *Men's Sheds in Australia: Learning through Community Contexts*. Adelaide: NCVER, 2007.
[22] Barry Golding *et al.* (Eds.), *Men Learning through Life*. Leicester, NIACE, 2014.

beyond the age of 80 years and some well into their 90s[23]. Relatively few men participate in Australia with an age of less than 50 years. This median age has increased by five years (from around 65 years) in Australia in a decade[24]. While it is true that more older men are participating on average, it is also likely that many of the same men who signed up to the earlier Australian Sheds are now older but still healthy enough to participate and be involved.

While around one half of shedders (49%) across Ireland are relatively old (age 60-79 years), the shedder median age of around 60 years means that a much higher proportion than in Australia is of working age. Indeed, around one in five men (19%) involved in Ireland are age less than 40 years and three out of ten are between 40-59 years[25]. Relatively fewer (only 2% of) Irish shedders are older than 80 years and only around one half (53%) are retired from paid work. The relative youth of many Irish shedders is likely to be related to the elevated, much higher levels of unemployment post the Global Financial Crisis. On average, shedders who *would* work if they could get a job are around three times as numerous in an average Irish Men's Shed as in Australian Sheds. One third (33%) of Irish shedders agreed that they expected to get more work as a result of participating in the Shed. For this reason, the prospect of the Shed being part of an important pathway back to work is more likely in Irish Men's Sheds.

Shedders are much more likely than all other men not to be in paid work for some reason. This is unsurprising given that most Sheds are only open during weekday work times. Typically, older men come to Men's Sheds during age retirement. Younger men tend to come because of disability, unemployment, caring responsibilities or early withdrawal from the paid workforce. In Australia around eight out of ten shedders (80%) are retired from paid work, with around one in ten (11%) still in the paid workforce, with the balance either unemployed or not in paid work because of a disability or a caring role.

Men who participate in Men's Sheds are, on average, around twice as likely to live outside of the major cities. Men's Sheds in both Australia and Ireland, while found in very diverse locations, including in capital cities, are disproportionately located in areas further away from the major cities, particularly in smaller and regional towns. While around seven out of ten Australians (69%) live in major cities, only around four out of ten Shed participants (42%) live in major cities[26]. Australian shedders are, on average, around twice as likely as all

---

[23] Paul Flood and Sharon Blair, 2013, as above, 7.
[24] Barry Golding *et al.*, 2007, as above.
[25] Lucia Carragher, 2013, as above
[26] Paul Flood and Sharon Blair, 2013, as above, 7.

Australian men to live in inner regional, outer regional and remote locations. Shedders in Ireland are similarly around twice as likely as other men in Ireland to live in Counties beyond the large capital cities of Dublin (in the Irish Republic) and Belfast (in Northern Ireland).

The other background worthy of note is that shedders' previous paid work backgrounds tend to be more trade-related. In Australia, around four out of ten (41% of) shedders are current or former tradesmen; in Ireland it is similar (45%). While some men participate from professional backgrounds, including with completed university education, only one quarter (25%) of Australian shedders and one third of Irish shedders (33%) agree that they 'really enjoyed learning at school'. Older shedders, by virtue of their age, are much more likely to have very limited completed formal education levels, typical of the era during their childhood when school-based brutalisation was much more common. Shed practitioners are also, on average, much more likely to experience lower functional literacies and less likely than younger men to use a computer or have access to the internet at home.

What Are the Outcomes for Men?

The most strikingly consistent agreement from Men's Sheds research, in both Ireland and Australia, is that virtually all men who participate feel *at home* in and enjoy participating in the Men's Shed. It is a powerful multiple benefit. Men overwhelmingly 'really enjoy' what they are doing, meeting and making good friends in the Shed, while giving something positive back to the community and feeling better about themselves. What men mainly get from a Men's Shed is the social and community identification as a valued member of the Shed organisation. The many other benefits that accrue to most (over three quarters of) men, which includes access to health information, feeling better at home and improved communication skills, wellbeing, confidence and social skills, are valuable 'icing on the cake'.

Consistent with the above, the beyondblue research in Australia in 2013 identified social interaction as the main reason that men join and participate in a Shed, and also the greatest benefit to men who participate. While the essentially personal and social desire 'to meet new friends', 'to keep busy' and 'to learn new skills' were amongst the main reason for joining (for 27%, 17% and 10% of shedders respectively), the more reciprocally-oriented opportunities 'to give back to the community' and 'to share knowledge and expertise' (22% and 12% respectively) were close behind. While significant benefits (for example to identity, happiness, wellbeing and health) can be anticipated to accrue as a *consequence* of increased men's social connection through Shed membership, it is important to note that only one in twenty men (5%) *mainly* joined the Men's Shed '*for* their health'.

These reported 'main reasons' for participation were validated by men's responses in the beyondblue Men's Shed research in Australia by means of a follow up question about the 'greatest benefits' of participating, a question that accepted multiple responses. Three fundamentally social benefits, 'socialising or getting out', 'making friends' and 'talking about issues', were regarded as the greatest benefits of participation, by 45 per cent, 41 per cent and seven per cent of shedders respectively. The reciprocal benefits of 'learning or passing on skills' and 'for the community' were of lower order importance (20% and 13%). It is significant that 'for health' was perceived as a greatest benefit by only three per cent of all shedders: a statistically and conspicuously 'minor benefit'.

It is remarkable that these diverse social and community outcomes are consistently and widely achieved across diverse grassroots Men's Sheds on opposite sides of the globe in Australia and Ireland. The fact that they are achieved without the need for formal 'programs' and service delivery models, largely through the agency of mainly older men beyond paid work, and supported mainly by volunteers and informal mentoring, is astounding, and leads to the 'Why does it work?' question below.

Why Do Men's Sheds Work, and for Which Men?

While some Shed organisations include men who have been referred to them by welfare, health, aged care or disability professionals, most men who participate in Men's Sheds are primarily self-selecting. Almost no one is compelled to come to the Shed[27]. Ironically, this element of non-compulsion leads men to commit to come whenever they can, to support the Shed and other men. As evidence, almost all shedders (97% in Australia, 99% in Ireland) agree that they enjoy being able to participate when they want to.

The idea that the Shed is their own, mainly or totally *men's* space, about which they are consulted and have a say, is vitally important. Indeed eight out of ten (80% of) Australian shedders and nine out of ten (91% of) Irish shedders agree that they 'have some say over how the organisation is run'. However it is not a *laissez faire* place where anything goes. Almost all men who participate in Men's Sheds acknowledge the importance of someone being responsible at all

---

[27] Exceptions might include the very small number of men who attend some Sheds as part of a community-based corrections order or as part of a community obligation to an unemployment program.

times, and overwhelmingly agree that the role of the Shed organisation leader is critically important.

The research evidence confirms the importance of the Men's Shed, in both Australia and Ireland, as a welcoming and relatively comfortable place in the community to practice existing skills and to learn new skills. Around eight out of ten men find that their skills are already good enough for them to take an active part in the organisation. That nineteen out of 20 shedders in both Australia and Ireland acknowledge that they would like to improve their skills puts paid to the widespread, erroneous idea that men not in work, including those that are older and retired, don't want to learn. That the same very high proportion of Men's Shed participants simultaneously see the Shed as a place to learn new skills, be with other men, 'get out of the house', meet new friends and keep them healthy confirms the power of the bottom-up Men's Shed model and ethos.

The relatively younger shedders in Ireland, who are also more likely to seek future paid work, are generally more positive about the hypothetical prospect of learning through the Shed if future opportunities were to become available. Three quarters of Irish shedders (75%) answered 'yes' to this hypothetical learning prospect and another 20 per cent answered 'maybe' (compared to 62% and 13% in Australian Sheds). Shedders from both nations indicated they would be much more interested in 'hands-on' learning (77% Australia, 71% Ireland), with most men (58% Australia, 56% Ireland) also interested in social learning, which allowed them to 'meet other people', with around one half of shedders in both countries opting for learning, should it become available, through special interest courses, in small groups or through field days or demonstrations.

Who Else Benefits from Men's Sheds, and How?

Hard evidence about the benefits of Men's Sheds beyond participant benefits is relatively limited. However, the downstream benefits to men's partners, families, children and grandchildren beyond the Shed are likely to be significant, based on what is known. Almost all men agree that as a result of participating they feel better about themselves: around 17 out of 20 shedders in both Australia and Ireland feel more accepted in the community and three quarters of men report that they feel happier at home. Given that in Ireland 58 per cent of shedders currently live with a wife or partner, 72 per cent are fathers and 45 per cent are grandfathers, feeling more accepted in the community as well as feeling happier at home are significant wellbeing outcomes that are presumably positive and transferable.

Given the economic rationalist, neo-liberal context typical of most Western nations, it is surprising that so few analyses have been undertaken of the social return on investment in Men's Sheds, including for stakeholders other than shedders themselves. The only such analysis available to early 2015 is Australian (and from only one Shed, Lane Cove Men's Shed in Sydney)[28]. It identified a very positive overall social return on investment of 6:1. That is for every one dollar invested by the auspice agency in the Shed, there were six dollars of value in outcomes. The breakdown of who benefits is of particular note. Most of the apportioned outcome value (46%) represented savings to government health services. While the benefit to shedders was significant (38%), respite for family and relatives accounted for nine per cent, and value to the community for seven per cent of the total benefit.

The 2013 Australian (AMSA) survey was able to delve more deeply in a qualitative manner into the multiple community benefits as perceived by those responding on behalf of each Shed organisation[29]. The multiple responses were coded and allocated to the most frequent response categories. 'Fixing or making items or providing a handyman service' (34% of Sheds), 'undertaking community renovation, refurbishment, maintenance, construction or repair projects' (26% of Sheds) and 'making products for distribution or sale' (21% of Sheds) were predictably important community benefits reported by Men's Sheds organisations. However the most commonly reported community benefit (from 38% of Sheds) was 'assisting, supporting or liaising with activities conducted by other local organisations, service clubs, charities or fund raising events'. In addition some Sheds (6%) reported on the benefits of community engagement, via 'recruiting and retaining members, including promoting the Shed by newsletter and contributing items to the local media'.

This high level of community engagement and outreach is unsurprising when the fact that only one in ten Australian Men's Sheds have any paid employees is factored in. Australian Sheds are heavily dependent on contributions from the local community, including essential support from volunteers and fundraising through other community organisations, Positive and active community liaison is essential for the success of most Men's Sheds. Shed organisations are also expected to reciprocate and generously give back, either in kind or through fundraising, via the sale of products, donations or provision of services. Whether this high level of dependence in Australia on unpaid volunteers and reciprocity through local community organisations is reflected in Ireland, the UK or New

---

[28] Matthew Bevan, *Social Return on Investment: Lane Cove Men's Shed*, UnitingCare Ageing, Sydney, 2012, 38.
[29] Free text responses from 246 Men's Sheds identified a total of 562 different ways in which men's sheds engaged and contributed to the community. These responses were assigned and then sorted into ten broad categories.

Zealand is thus far much less well research or understood. However it is anticipated, based on the case studies presented in Part 3, to be somewhat similar.

A number of other qualitatively important, but less highly ranked community contributions were observed in the 2013 Australian research for AMSA.

- Around one in six (17% of) Australian Sheds reported activities categorised as 'engaging and contributing to the community through youth mentoring or youth at risk programs including working through schools'.
- Around one quarter of Australian Sheds acknowledged that their Shed's contribution to the community was related to the benefits to the men: including 'providing a safe space in the Shed for men to drop in, socialise, chat, gather or do stuff' (13% of Sheds), or 'providing mental or physical health information to shedders, encouraging or referring men to doctors and social workers; assist men with a disability' (11% of Sheds).
- Other community contributions reported in the Australian research included 'undertaking visits from and to local aged care facilities' (6% of Sheds).

What Do Men Do in the Shed?

Interestingly, the question of how Sheds are structured and what men actually *do* in the Men's Shed is amongst the most poorly researched aspect of Men's Sheds. It is for this reason that the diversity of Men's Sheds, richly illustrated in Part 3 with national case studies, is important. The 2013 AMSA study in Australia and Carragher's Irish study are again useful in identifying some general trends.

In Australia, one third of all Men's Sheds are in some type of auspice arrangement. Depending on how closely or loosely coupled that auspice arrangement is, most such Sheds are more likely to be involved in one or more activities which complement or reinforce that parent organisation's values and activities. For example, a Men's Shed auspiced, funded, staffed, promoted by or formally reporting to a War Veterans, health, adult education, local government or church organisation is likely to pay more attention to the mission statement, aims, expectations and anticipated outcomes of its relevant parent organisation, than an independent Shed is to its own mission statement and member expectations.

Unsurprisingly, fundraising for the Shed is one of the major activities. Most funding for Sheds, from whatever source (and most Shed organisations have multiple though small sources of external funding), comes with some expectations and accountabilities, even if they are informal. Seven out of ten Australian Sheds in the AMSA research report 'an effective fund raising program'.

The hands-on activity in most Australian Sheds is typically informally organised, though two thirds of Sheds have a volunteer Shed manager and only one in ten Men's Sheds have any paid employees. Around one half of Men's Sheds in Australia have 30 or fewer members and only around one half of Sheds receive support from an actual sponsor organisation or partner. Six out of ten Sheds in Australia have participated in male health programs and three out of ten Sheds actively participate in either a State Men's Shed association or a youth mentoring program. When combined, these statistics and the wide distribution of Sheds across Australia paint a picture of the 'average' Australian Shed, if there is one, as being relatively small, loosely coupled, only partly funded, with few or no paid staff, supported and run by volunteers, and potentially insecure.

This picture of Shed organisation in Australia appears to be somewhat different from the situation in Irish Men's Sheds, though the data are early and limited. Carragher's study (with Shed survey returns from 30 Sheds) confirmed that close to one in four (23% of) Irish Sheds relied on full time paid staff and 37 per cent relied on government funding. Despite this, two thirds of Irish Sheds were open all year round, half of them in a stand-alone facility. Ninety per cent of Sheds in Ireland provided 'diverse activities' (rather than being focused on one activity). Participants decided on the nature of the activities in 90 per cent of Irish Sheds. Only one in five Irish Sheds (18%) rated the future of their organisation as 'very secure'.

Compounding their inherent vulnerability, many Sheds in all countries dream and fight to remain fiercely independent and 'stand alone', to keep it sustainable and grassroots and to keep the Shed organisation from becoming too bureaucratic. While many Sheds appreciate the benefits of belonging to a peak Men's Shed Association, the general preference is to operate the Shed organisation independently. There is a general desire to manage each Shed collaboratively, as cheaply and as simply as possible, to ensure the Shed is as grassroots, accessible and cheap to attend as possible. Only two thirds of Australian Sheds, mainly recent and developing Sheds, have a risk management plan or formal induction process for new members. In the case of Irish Sheds, only ten per cent reported that they had 'no rules'. The role of a national (and or state/cluster) Shed association is nevertheless very important, not only because it increases the ability of Sheds to get information from other Sheds on 'how to' options, including the provision, when required, of simple, standard or relatively inexpensive occupational health and safety, insurance and Shed management options, but also because it increases credibility and bargaining power with governments and community organisations.

What Have Men's Sheds Got to Do with Men's Health and Wellbeing?

While the role of health and wellbeing in Men's Sheds is becoming an increasing focus from a research perspective, the evidence base is still relatively limited. From a Shed organisation perspective, it is perhaps the most overemphasised area. The Australian Men's Shed survey from the AMSA 2013 survey ranked the provision of physical and mental health as only ninth out of 11 factors, with only 11 per cent of all Sheds specifying it as one of their four most important points of engagement with, and contribution to their communities.

Nevertheless, feeling good, staying as healthy and as well as possible, for as long as possible, in order to contribute positively to the Shed, to other men and the community, are all very important to most shedders. Beyond this, there is less agreement about what is appropriate in terms of health and wellbeing advice and services being made available to shedders through Sheds. The best data on the question about the 'contribution of the Shed to the health and wellbeing of its members' again comes from the 2013 Australian AMSA survey and Carragher's 2013 Irish study.

Seven broad categories summarising the way Australian Sheds make a significant difference were identified amongst the responses from 245 Sheds in the AMSA study. These responses were sorted from the most frequently to the least frequently reported way, summarised below.

1. Providing a safe space in the Shed to meet, make friends, relax or socially engage and be with other men in the Shed. (58% of Sheds)
2. Providing access via the Shed to health information, including via Shed visits, talks, support groups or programs. (22% of Sheds)
3. Encouraging talk and informal discussion of issues men are facing, including with health and wellbeing. (21% of Sheds)
4. Giving opportunities for men to actively participate in the Shed or a Shed activity or project and give meaning or purpose to men's lives. (16% of Sheds)
5. Providing group and other support for men with existing mental or physical heath problems. (16% of Sheds)

6. Encouraging men to connect with, belong to, give back or contribute to the wider community, by doing or achieving something of value to or for others or learning a new skill. (13% of Sheds)
7. Encouraging referral through health monitoring. (7% of Sheds)

In summary, most Australian Sheds report that they make a significant difference to health and wellbeing of men *informally*: by providing a safe space in the Shed to be with other men. This clearly encourages and provides men with a chance to talk informally about their health and wellbeing while simultaneously and actively participating in the Shed, giving back to the community and giving purpose and meaning to their lives. While access to health information as well as group support for men perceived to need it are important, informal approaches are regarded as being much more appropriate than formal approaches, as seen from the perspective of the Men's Shed organization.

This data is suggestive of a real danger in any Shed, and in the Movement more broadly, that an overemphasis on men's health, and in particular on the way in which health might be *done to* men without their being consulted, will be counterproductive and risk turning men away. Health and the research associated with it can and do become contentious issues in some Men's Sheds and in the sector when their importance is overplayed.

From a shedder perspective, the evidence is clear that participation is regarded as being inherently *salutogenic* (health giving). Nine out of ten Irish shedders (91%) in Lucia Carragher's Irish study agreed that their wellbeing had improved as a result of participating in the Shed; one third (31%) agreed strongly. While 95 per cent of Irish shedders regarded the Shed as a place 'to be keep them healthy', an identical percentage also agreed it was about 'being with other men', 'meeting new friends', 'getting out of the house', 'learning new skills' and 'giving back to the community', with 56 per cent of shedders registering 'meeting new friends' as their strongest agreement.

From a government point of view, if Men's Sheds are going to be supported: by the health sector, locally, through states, Counties or nationally; through the provision of services, funding, premises or staff; through Shed auspice arrangements or support of individual Sheds or the peak men's Shed bodies, these various agencies will want evidence of impact and outcomes to justify their investment. If Sheds or peak bodies take money from any source aside from untied donations, it is very likely that the funding body will require collection of that evidence, through Shed program evaluations, reports, Shed data, or though commissioned or independent external research. In particular, funding bodies will want to know that men targeted with preventative health funds form part of their target group, and that there is evidence that some intended health and wellbeing outcomes are being achieved.

Complicating the measurement of outcomes is evidence from Ireland and Australia that many men who participate in Sheds are already physically or mentally unwell and/or have been affected by recent and difficult changes in their lives. Indeed some Sheds are organised around catering specifically for such men. Of Irish shedders, three out of ten (31%) self-assessed their health as below 'good' (with 25% self-assessing their health as 'fair', 4% 'bad' and 2% 'very bad'). 'Physical health issues' had interfered with Irish shedders' social activities for 38 per cent of men in the most recent month, and 'emotional health issues' for 38 per cent.

For Australian shedders, the only comparable data are from the 2007 *Men's Sheds in Australia* study. Men who participated in Men's Sheds:

> ... provided considerable evidence of recent, significant and difficult changes in health, relationships and employment. 'Within the past five years' 55% had experienced retirement, 45% had experienced 'a major health crisis', 30% 'a new impairment or disability', 27% 'an inability to get paid work', 25% 'a significant loss in my life', 19% 'separation from a partner' and 19% 'a financial crisis'. Eleven per cent of men had experienced 'separation from a family home' in the past five years and 10% 'separation from children'.[30]

It is difficult to objectively determine the overall or longitudinal health impact of a Shed or on an individual because of this evidence of pre-existing health and wellbeing issues. In essence, some shedders are less well than other men when they present at a Shed. This raises the question as to whether it is unreasonable to expect the Men's Shed to provide proof that it will not only improve the health of shedders, but also produce evidence that they will be healthier than men who are *not* shedders. It is important to observe here that this arguably *unreasonable* expectation was embedded in the rationale for the beyondblue study.

These difficulties complicate longitudinal measurement of the health and wellbeing characteristics of shedders compared to non-shedders. In addition, it will always be difficult to separate the likely longer-term health benefits to shedders as a consequence of participating from the normal changes in health as they age. What is certain is that, as a consequence of participating in Australian or

---

[30] Barry Golding, *et al.*, 2007, as above, 32.

Irish Men's Sheds, almost all men (more than 90 per cent) feel better about themselves, feel like they belong, are doing what they really enjoy and can give back to the community. In addition around eight out of ten men agree that they get access to men's health information and feel happier at home. This evidence combined is highly suggestive of significant benefit in terms of men's self-perceived health and broader wellbeing, in the Shed, in the community and at home.

Interestingly, Ireland and Australia are the only countries in the world to have national men's health policies (developed in December 2008[31] and May 2010[32] respectively) and are also the main sites in which Men's Sheds have so far taken firm root and spread very widely. The Australian peak body, AMSA, received most of its initial funding (2009-2011) through the Australian men's health strategy. As part of its service agreement, put in place in order to secure that funding, AMSA is required to not only implement health-related programs, but also to supply evidence of impact and cooperate with related research and evaluation. For this reason, AMSA includes men's health-related material on its website and in its newsletter. It also actively collaborates with developing and distributing many male-specific health programs, information and materials, and includes health messages and presenters in its national biennial conferences. Separately, it works with and benefits from funding, programs and research oriented to men's mental wellbeing through bodies such as the Australian depression initiative, beyondblue, including programs such as the Australian *Shed On Line* initiative discussed at the end of Chapter 11.

Limited again by assumptions about what is 'normal' from a typical Australian shedder perspective, men mainly participate for the friendship, companionship and giving back to the Shed, other men and the community, though hands-on activity and not specifically for its likely health benefits. It may be that men in Australia see posters advertising the Shed On Line in some public male urinals in Australia. Some would get information via health promotion messages, posters and kits distributed into all Men's Sheds organisations registered though AMSA, which may or may not get traction in the Shed they are participating in. One third of all Australian Sheds have had a member attend a previous national conference held every two years in Australia at which health messages would have been obvious. Through any or all of these experiences,

---

[31] *National Men's Health Policy 2008-2013*, Ireland,
http://www.mhfi.org/menshealthpolicy.pdf, Accessed March 2, 2015.
[32] *National Male Health Policy*, Australia,
http://www.health.gov.au/internet/main/publishing.nsf/Content/male-policy, Accessed March 2, 2015.

most Australian shedders would be aware of a wide range of subtle (or unsubtle) health-oriented messages, presentations, advertising, badging and other health-oriented collateral, but all this would typically lie outside of and beyond their day-to-day experience in the Shed.

Some men would understand and strongly support these developments and the associations between their Men's Shed and men's health, as well as interventions designed to inform and address their own health from outside of the Shed. However there is an undercurrent of concern amongst *some* Sheds and shedders that Sheds are not and should not be only or mainly for men who are problematized from a health deficit model. In particular, many men do not want their Shed targeted by intervention programs, professional service providers or research that presupposes that they are in some way helpless or need outside help. Shedders and Men's Shed organisations therefore need to be consulted over the design or application in the Shed of externally sourced health programs, services and research, however well meaning they may be from a government or service provider point of view.

That said, Australian men's shedders are generally much more comfortable about health and wellbeing programs that are locally initiated, led, controlled and conducted in or through the Shed. AMSA research shows that around one third of all Australian Sheds (34%) hosted presentations in the Shed by guest speakers including local health professionals. Around one quarter of Sheds used the *Spanner in the Works* [33], a male-oriented health program developed and distributed through AMSA. One in five Sheds: conducted health-related and wellbeing awareness events, days, seminars or breakfasts (19%); provided information or support programs related to male health issues (19%); or participated in male health week (18%). Other Australian Sheds participated in regular health check-ups and referral programs (12%); cooperated with Pit Stop[34] or health van initiatives (6%), engaged with DIY [35] ('Do-It-Yourself') or conducted first aid training programs (5%). Around three in ten Sheds (29%) conducted other (otherwise unclassified) health programs and most Sheds undertook several of these initiatives.

---

[33] 'Spanner in the Works' is a health promotion initiative under the male health policy that is directed at Australian males of all ages.

[34] 'Pit Stop' is a flexible Australian health program, originally designed in Western Australia specifically for men, encouraging them to be more proactive about their health and have fun while they do so, using the analogy of vehicle maintenance.

[35] 'DIY Health' is a men-friendly health screening and information project and associated resources run by AMSA in Australia.

Some health researchers have recently and erroneously claimed that *the* answer (including *my* answer as a fellow researcher) to legitimate resistance to overt health interventions in Men's Sheds is via a 'health by stealth' model. While health for men is highly desirable, the characteristics of this model, which presumably implies covert work by health workers in men's best interests, is teased out and firmly rejected below as both patronising and duplicitous. For most shedders, the many intrinsic aspects of the Shed activity itself are seen as making a difference to their health and wellbeing informally, not covertly or by 'stealth'. Professor John Macdonald, a highly respected Professor of Men's Health at University of Western Sydney and a fellow AMSA Patron, uses the term *salutogenic* ('health giving') to stress and reinforce the positive aspects of health *through* sheds, without necessarily having to 'tack on' health professionals or programs. As Macdonald has often acknowledged, Men's Sheds already 'tick' several of the key World Health Organisation Social Determinants of Health. In Macdonald's words, Men's Sheds are *inherently* salutogenic.

Evidence confirming the importance of informality in approaching men's health comes from the 2013 Australian research through AMSA. Men's Sheds organisations were asked 'In what ways does your Shed make a significant difference to the health and wellbeing of its members?' The data summarised below were categorised from multiple responses from 245 Australian Sheds. They are presented from the most frequent to the least frequent response categories.

- The most frequent (and most often cited) response to this question about making a significant difference to the health and wellbeing of shedders, by six out of ten Sheds (58%), was about 'providing a safe space in the Shed to meet, make friends, relax or socially engage and be with other men in the Shed'.
- While overtly (or perhaps more subtly) 'providing access via the Shed to health information, via Shed visits, talks, support groups or programs' was cited by one in five (22% of) Sheds, most of the other categories of responses, were, like the main 'safe place' response, essentially about the value of Shed informality.
- Being a safe place to talk, specifically 'being a place that encouraged talk and informally discuss issues men are facing, including with health and wellbeing' was cited by one in five (21% of) Sheds.

- Informally providing '... opportunities for men to actively participate in the Shed or a Shed activity or project and give meaning and purpose to men's lives' was mentioned by 16 per cent of Sheds.
- Informally 'providing group and other support for men with existing mental or physical health problems', and 'encouraging men to connect with, belong to, give back or contribute to the wider community, by doing or achieving something of value for others or learning a new skill' were also regularly cited (by 16% and 13% of Sheds respectively).

Despite this clear and unequivocal evidence from both shedders and Men's Shed organisations of the powerful impact of *Shed participation itself* on men, men's lives, and their health and wellbeing, some health academics are still arguing for more proof from a positivist,[36] health intervention paradigm. From a program intervention and evaluation perspective, they presumably need proof that the cost of a Shed intervention or particular program undertaken through Sheds is 'good value for money' and that it makes men healthier. Unsurprisingly, since the national Movement in Australia is already linked through its funding agreement to the Australian men's health policy and its implementation, peak Men's Shed bodies have to be careful not to be unwittingly dragged into the same problematic, deficit-based, top-down, 'professionals know best' and 'older men don't care about their health' mantras that Men's Sheds were, in part, set up to extricate and liberate men from. To go back to the wise, powerful and early words, penned in 1996 by Maxine Kitto about the perceived early success of The Shed in Goolwa.

> The Shed Project is a strategic health promoting resource to ensure older, retired men retain the role of productive and valued community member, preventing taking on the role of sick "person". This strategy has been very successful, regardless of the fact that we have no funding for the program. ... The Shed project worked because the men were empowered. I had no idea what men did in the shed but I knew they were healthier with a shed than without a shed. ... The Shed Project should be recognised as a health promotion resource and funding should

---

[36] Positivism is the philosophy of science that information, derived from logical and mathematical treatments and reports of sensory experience, is the exclusive source of all authoritative knowledge, and that there is valid knowledge (truth) only in this derived knowledge.

be made available. Most important as health professionals, we should be constantly aware of a valued social role in the health of older men. [37]

Whatever future research is undertaken 'to prove' the link between Men's Sheds and health, it needs to be based on men's empowerment and agency, underpinned by an acceptance and understanding that this is about men, typically older and not in paid work, being, getting and staying well. It is also about being empowered through their social participation and agency in the Shed. Men's health *through* Sheds, from this perspective, is both simple but fragile, as Maxine Kitto alluded to two decades ago. It is more about staying well and encouraging other men to do similarly, than it is about 'slick' health messages through expensive posters, advertising or websites and kits sent to all Men's Sheds, which tends to be the way beyondblue and Movember operate in Australia as advocates of men's mental health.

It need not be either/or, but a 'line needs to be drawn, at the Shed door', to ensure that shedders are properly consulted about any intervention by health professionals and academics, for whatever good reasons, and that existing shedders are not disempowered or de-motivated by an inappropriate intervention leading them to walk away. Given that 90 per cent of Australian Sheds have no paid workers, and that most are totally dependent on volunteers, the veiled argument in some health research articles, that the approximately one million Australian dollars going to AMSA each year, is not good value without this evidence needs briefly deconstructing.

This funding to early 2015 has helped organise a voluntary sector with around 930 active Men's Sheds, with around 50,000 active, weekly participants. The national subsidy for shedder participation in Australia of no more than 25 cents a week per participant in a sector almost totally dependent on volunteers is miniscule when compared with a combined national health, ageing and disability budget in the tens of billions of dollars. The value of Men's Sheds is therefore significant, without even considering the benefits to men's partners, extended families and the community and the positive return on the minimal government. When one factors in the particular value in likely cost savings to governments from the healthy participation and community contribution of men not in paid work, including men who are older, War Veterans, Indigenous, rural, migrants,

---

[37] *Goolwa Heritage Club: The Shed*, Maxine Kitto, Co-ordinator, The Heritage Club, District Council of Port Elliot and Goolwa, no date, faxed to Alison Herron, Manningham Community Health, July 5, 1996, 2-3.

with dementia, carers, with a disability, or at risk of suicide, arguments that Men's Sheds are a folly without more evidence verge on the absurd.

What is the Role of Women in Men's Sheds?

Publicly naming a shed as a *Men's Shed* from July 1998 was identified in Chapter 1 and teased out in Chapter 3 as something of a 'watershed'. For much of the next ten years, until the national Men's Shed Movement began to be acknowledged in Australia, most new Sheds faced many of the same issues naming the Shed as a *Men's* space[38]. Surveys about the gendered nature of Sheds as part of the 2007 NCVER Australian Men's Sheds research[39] confirmed three broad categories of attitudes towards women in Men's Sheds. Around one third of men came to Sheds with agendas that completely precluded the idea of interacting with or being inclusive of women in the Shed. Around one third of men tolerated women as part of the Shed organisation, on condition that the men could still behave 'like blokes' (men). The remaining one third of men suggested that they would and should be equally accommodating of both men and women in the Shed, though most acknowledged that this was to keep women, the community and funding bodies 'on side'. However other findings in the same study about Shed effectiveness confirmed that for men with the most difficult lives, health and family circumstances, being in a *men's only* space in the Shed itself was an important attraction for many men and part of the Shed's 'recipe' for success.

Despite common (and continuing) concerns from a small minority of shedders about the involvement of any women in Men's Sheds, most men acknowledge that participating with women's (typically their partner's, carer's or daughter's) active support and encouragement is in the men's best interests. While Men's Sheds typically make a local decision *whether* to include women as participants (or not), and if so *how* to include them, it is widely acknowledged that women have played major roles in developing and championing many Sheds, the Movement, and national and state Shed associations. While most or all in-shed participants are men, almost all major media stories about Men's Sheds have been researched and reported by women. One in three of the approximately two hundred acknowledged contributors to this book were women. Women have been behind many Shed startups and the procurement of funds, and some Sheds have a female coordinator, whose key role is to know when to step forward (and back).

---

[38] Globally, around five Sheds registered with national Men's Sheds associations in Appendix 2 are primarily or solely for women.
[39] Golding *et al., Men's Sheds in Australia,* 2007.

Data from the 2013 Irish Men's Sheds study by Lucia Carragher[40] confirm that while nearly three-quarters of male participants (72%) reported feeling comfortable with women hypothetically participating in Men's Sheds, *in practice* just seven per cent of Sheds actually catered for both men and women. Those that did tended to cater for women on different days or separately from the men. The Ennis Men's Shed, for example, in celebrating the 2014 opening of the Ennis Women's Shed in Ireland, announced that 'the Women's Shed would be using the same facilities as the Ennis Men's Shed [but] at different days and times'. Nevertheless most Men's Sheds in Ireland and Australia have decided to remain largely or totally male-gendered spaces in the Shed itself, and have received general and widespread community and government support and understanding for this decision.

In Australia and Ireland, government support for Men's Sheds has been strong, politically bipartisan and at all levels. In 2008, the former President of Ireland, Mary McAleese, called for more social activities geared towards older men in Ireland when she noted:

> I often attend senior citizens' events and one of the things that would perplex me would be the vast number of women and the small number of men at these events. I would ask 'Where are all the men?' They are just not as good at social engagements as women.

McAleese's observations are confirmed by evidence of the strong community networks forged by Irish women, something which is in no small part attributable to the decades of struggle for gender equality, which can also be seen in other developed countries for many the same reasons. In October 2014 Michael D. Higgins, President of the Republic of Ireland and IMSA Patron since April 2013, spoke passionately in support of the Men's Shed Movement at the first International Men's Shed Festival convened by IMSA in Dublin[41]. Photograph 47 shows President Higgins at the Armagh Men's Shed display at the Festival.

---

[40] Lucia Carragher, *Men's Sheds in Ireland: Learning through Community Contexts*. Dundalk: Dundalk Institute of Technology, 2013.
[41] www.youtube.com/watch?v=4QdknYCbStU, Accessed May 4, 2015.

Photograph 47 Irish President, Michael Higgins Viewing the Armagh Men's Shed
Display at the International Men's Shed Festival, Dublin, April 2014

In Australia during Julia Gillard's three year term as Prime Minister (2010-13)
there was particularly strong knowledge of and support for the movement 'from
the top'. Gillard's partner, Tim Mathieson was at that time a Patron of the
national organisation, AMSA. Whilst Deputy Prime Minister, in 2009, Gillard
offically opened the Melton Men's Shed in her Federal electorate in outer
suburban Melbourne.

In Irish Men's Sheds, Lucia Carragher's research found that most men who
participated experienced a sense of belonging (95%) and felt valued and
productive, fostering a healthy openness between them. For an overwhelming
proportion of men, the Shed was a place where men felt comfortable in accessing
male health information (88%), where they could make good friends (99%), and
give back to the community (97%), making them feel valued and productive. The
majority reported feeling better about themselves (97%), more confident (89%)
and more healthy (95%). These important social and self-esteem effects were not
lost on the women in their lives. Women are often the ones who made the first
contact with Men's Sheds on behalf of their husbands, fathers or partners,
encouraging them to take the first step to attend. As one Irish shedder said:

> Well I must say I look forward to it for a very social reason. For me,
> [Number one], it's great to come over, talk to people, discuss about
> nothing or something important. Number two, my wife is glad to see me

out of the house but she's interested in what I'm doing too, but it's conversation and she loves to see me in it. Number three, I love the joinery and all that.

Thus, while women's role in Men's Sheds in Ireland superficially appears insignificant, it is anything but. Carragher found that nearly one quarter (23%) of Men's Sheds were managed by female coordinators. In addition, while participants' preferences for learning opportunities in the Irish study were first and foremost that another Shed member with the appropriate skills would teach them, when an outside tutor was sought, there was no necessary preference for male tutors.

In summary, these community places and spaces work very effectively as mainly or wholly male-gendered spaces, for men to gather, do and learn things together informally and 'hands on', interacting socially and giving back to the community. It is men who are experiencing particular difficulties in their lives, families, communities and identities beyond paid work that are most attracted to, and benefit most from male gendering of the Shed space or organisation. It is nevertheless important to acknowledge the subtle but critically important role of women in the creation and support of Men's Sheds and in the support of the men who participate, both as partners and professionals. This includes acknowledgement of some important aspects of women's active involvement in the invention of several of the first Sheds in Australia for men in a community setting after 1993. While Men's Sheds are in some ways a grassroots response by some men alienated (from as early as the 1980s) by the predominantly female-staffed and female-focused character of many community services (as documented at the start of the book), Men's Sheds have clearly been widely understood and strongly supported and valued by many women.

CHAPTER 11

Men's Shed Theory and Practice

Men's Sheds practice is not rocket science. The original vision of Men's Sheds was to give older men permission to go somewhere in a community setting, separate from their home, work voluntarily alongside and be together with other men, do things and talk. Beyond this simple idea, Men's Sheds do not lend themselves neatly to study by just one academic field and exhibit a number of tensions and paradoxes between theory and practice.

Practitioners and theorists from a number of fields have shown interest in Men's Sheds. Given that the earliest Sheds and Men's Sheds were developed in aged care settings, gerontologists (those who study the science of ageing), and more recently occupational scientists (an interdisciplinary field dedicated to the study of humans as 'occupational beings') have shown some interest. Men's health workers and researchers are particularly interested in how Men's Sheds affect older men's health and wellbeing as a therapeutic intervention, an interest that is subjected to some critical unpacking in the '*Is the Men's Shed's primary purpose men's health and wellbeing?*' discussion that follows later in this chapter.

WHAT ARE THE TENSIONS AND PARADOXES?

Men's Sheds can be seen, simultaneously and paradoxically, as both radical and conservative. On the one hand they are part of a transformational, radical, 'bottom-up' movement. On the other hand, they are conservative in that they reinforce some traditional gendered stereotypes about 'places for men'. This section deals critically with five key tensions and paradoxes.

- Should Men's Sheds be grassroots (bottom-up)?
- How should Men's Sheds be governed?
- Should women be involved?
- Is the Men's Shed's primary purpose men's health and wellbeing?
- Should it be for all men?

Should Men's Sheds be Grassroots (Bottom-up)?

The original rationale for Sheds, and later Men's Sheds, comprehensively documented in the history in Part 2, was about empowering mainly older men to create a place and space in a community setting where the provision of professional services, often but not always by women, is deliberately removed, other than with the agreement and the invitation of the shedders. This approach is based around copious evidence from Shed participants of a general scepticism towards and aversion of formal service delivery, based on previous negative experiences of top-down, often inappropriate, patronising, deficit-based, female-gendered and ageist delivery of services.

Much of my own (Barry Golding's) research has championed and highlighted the value of a bottom-up, grassroots, informal approach, in particular to learning informally *through* Men's Sheds. I have rigorously and consistently avoided positioning and naming Sheds as formal learning centres. This approach is based on copious evidence from Shed participants of a general scepticism and aversion towards formal learning, based on men's previous negative experiences of top-down, formal education, including school education in past eras. If a Men's Shed was instead called a 'Men's Education Shed', a 'Men's Health Shed' or a 'Men's Anti-Suicide Workshop', few men would take part. None of these putative set-ups, while possibly laudable, is what men not in paid work would necessarily choose to attend of their own free will, let alone spend an extended time at.

K. C. Glover and Gary Misan, in their 2012 critical examination of men's *experiences* in Australian Men's Sheds, suggest that it is:

> The change of experience in the world and a sense of purpose in the sheds along with mutual validation of males [that] may be the greatest benefits men's sheds provide. ... [since] socialisation was perhaps the most consistent reason voiced why men attended a shed. [The] most valuable part of this socialisation is the ability to maintain an experience of the world with other men that is more in harmony with how they feel, [rather than being] about having to play roles, such as "Employee", or "Boss" or "Father."[1]

---

[1] K. Glover and G. Misan, 'Men Together: Questions of Men's Experience in Sheds', *New Male Studies*, 2012, 1 (2), 63-73, cited from 70.

In addition to a reluctance to play these 'top-down' roles identified by Glover and Misan, I would add a reluctance to play the role of compliant customer, client, patient, or student. These patronised roles are often imposed on older men in health, welfare, aged care and adult education settings by both male and female professionals and para-professionals. There is sometimes a tendency to act top-down, without proper consultation or men's permission. Many professional experts and service providers in conventional health, aged care and occupational therapy settings arguably operate from a 'gender blind' perspective, which purports to treat men and women equally but which can be blind to men's different and diverse masculinities, needs and experiences. Many service providers wrongly perceive older men from negative, patronising or deficit models, sometimes associated with unfair, inaccurate, negative and stereotypical views of older men exhibiting and practicing negative and hegemonic masculinities[2]. The bottom-up Men's Shed, from this perspective, is both a shelter and welcome relief for such men where they can be empowered and encouraged to experience and express themselves, *with other men, as men.*

It is unsurprising why this subjectively positive experience of being an older man, actively participating as an equal partner in a bottom-up Men's Shed organisation, can be both powerful and transformational. Men's Sheds challenge older men's multiple marginalisations and myths about being old, male, lonely, alienated, unloving and not caring about themselves or their health and wellbeing. As Glover and Misan put it, 'men come together in men's sheds not to be corrected or fixed, but to be able to express themselves to other men while not having to fear being judged'[3]. For this reason, it is a serious mistake for Men's Sheds to start up and advertise themselves as being specifically or mostly for old, lonely, depressed and unwell men (as some Sheds have done), since most men understandably will 'run a mile' and stay away in droves.

From this perspective, the short answer to the question posed is that it *should* be grassroots and bottom-up, run by the men themselves, wherever and whenever possible. For many men with limited health prospects and life spans, the journey

---

[2] Hegemonic masculinity is a concept, popularized by Australian sociologist R. Connell, about practices that promote the dominant social position of men, and the subordinate social position of women. One of the problems of the concept is its negativity. For example the concept has been used to simplistically suggest that all men avoid talking about health problems or consulting health care when it is needed. Hegemonic masculinity has been criticised because it tends to solely be associated with negative characteristics, that tend to unfairly depict *all* men as unemotional, aggressive, independent, and non-nurturing, without recognizing positive behaviours such as bringing home a wage, being a loving husband and father and contributing to the community.

[3] K. Glover & Gary Misan, 2012, as above, 71.

with others creating the Men's Shed is more important than the destination. For this reason, Men's Sheds that are created for and 'handed on a platter' to men or a particular Shed with all the requisite funds without them being consulted and involved can be a serious mistake.

That said, community organisations in 2015 are subject to risk management and occupational health and safety hurdles that were much lower or non-existent in the 1990s when Men's Sheds in community settings were invented. In the case of men with cognitive impairment including dementia, there is a case for ensuring all men are empowered to experience the Shed as much as possible bottom-up in 2015. There typically need to be systems and people in place to make it safe and as risk free for all men and staff as possible. This may require sensible and negotiated modification of the Shed environment, tools and activities, hand in hand with appropriate shedder and staff training.

How Should Men's Sheds be Governed?

Almost two decades on from the first Men's Shed in Tongala, the fundamental unit of governance of the Men's Shed is the still The Company of Men, the collective group of male co-participants in the Shed. Nevertheless, all research confirms that one person, respected and chosen by the men, formally or informally, has to be vigilant and responsible at all times *in the Shed* whenever it is open. There have to be rules agreed to by the men about the safe operation of machinery, safe working practices and behavior respectful of all shedders. These things cannot be left to chance or to an anarchic collective. In order to formalise shedder participation and be covered by insurance, most shedders are required to join the Shed organisation, and by doing so subscribe to the existing, jointly negotiated Shed rules. Most shedders meet regularly, typically socially and informally, to ensure that there is appropriate consultation including regular review of mutually agreed operating procedures and Shed rules.

As an important and fascinating aside, many Men's Shed organisations have elements of a standard uniform for members, sometimes with a cap, logo, name-tag, shirt or overalls, which not only confirm Shed membership, but bestow a sense of collective identity when participating in, as well as beyond the Shed in meetings, community settings and Shed conferences. In this sense, Shed membership goes well beyond governance and is a critical part of many men's identity and pride in their own Shed and collectively as shedders. It is about *their* organisation, their Shed, where they come from, where they are free to exercise agency, and most importantly, where they feel happy and at home in the company of other men.

If the Shed is independently incorporated (that is, it is not in an auspice arrangement or responsible for part of government or a non-government organisation's services), the Shed's only other essential obligation is to the community in which it is embedded. That said, there is arguably a moral obligation, if a Shed is to operate in the community as a Men's Shed, to at least acknowledge the community cultural capital on which it is 'trading'. All new Men's Sheds in community settings are developed, to a greater or lesser extent, on principles and practices now well established, typically hard won and developed by trial and error, by previous and existing Men's Sheds. Typically, for its own benefit and the benefit of other Sheds in the state or County, region or nation, the Shed organisation affiliates with one or more peak body Men's Shed organisations.

This affiliation not only provides the community and other Sheds with evidence, displayed on peak body websites and their searchable Shed Locators, that they are open and operating. It also encourages the mutual, open and free exchange of information between other Men's Sheds and their members. In countries in which the national peak body has negotiated a discounted group insurance scheme, there is also a significant financial incentive to join.

Sheds in auspice or service provider arrangements clearly have other obligations. While an auspice arrangement is often simpler and provides a quicker Shed opening, there is an argument that being nested within an existing organisation bypasses the essential part of the 'journey'. In addition, relationships between the Men's Shed and the auspice body can sometime sour with time for a wide range of reasons, to do with misunderstandings about: governance, policies, funding and resources, venue, safety, insurances and operating procedures, as well as with changing participants, Shed coordinators, auspice organisation managers and personalities.

These problems with governance also occur within the peak bodies. Part 2 provided information about the history of individual state and national associations. Much of this history predates some significant, very recent and emerging governance issues peak Men's Shed organisations were experiencing by early 2015. In Australia there have been recent significant (but arguably healthy) disagreements about demarcation of roles between AMSA and some states. In the UK in 2015 a fracturing was occurring of the UK association. This is likely to result is a number of new regional peak bodies, such as Welsh, Scottish and Northern Ireland Associations, with implications also for the innovative 'Island of Ireland' Shed strategy initially adopted by IMSA.

These governance issues highlight questions that are common to all grassroots organisations, about who can and should speak and at what levels of government on behalf of Shed organisations, and at what levels Sheds might be most effectively resourced and coordinated. One argument would be that in large countries like Australia, as well as in populous and culturally diverse nations such as the UK, with four historically different states, it will be difficult for one national organisation to properly service and support the diverse needs of all Sheds across all constituent states. The other argument might be that a national Men's Shed organisation has more influence over national government health, aged care, unemployment and welfare policy and funding. National bodies typically have more research capacity and data to support proposals for funding, as well as capacities and efficiencies of scale to support a national Men's Shed sector. There is likely room and benefit for both national and state or regional peak bodies, as long as there is broad agreement about which body is best placed to undertake particular functions.

Should Women be Involved?

Before beginning to address this slippery, normative ("should") question, it is timely to reflect on the wide range of approaches to women's participation informed by research data earlier in the 'What *is* the role of women in Men's Sheds?' section. It is also useful to reflect on debates, begun several decades ago in Australia, teased out at the start of this book, about whether and why *some* services for *some* men might be gendered. The reason for re-examining this question is that many of the same debates, about the extent to which Sheds should be just for men, and whether and how women might be involved, occur whenever a new Men's Shed plans to set up in any new place, town, community or country. For some women, pro-feminist men and communities, the call for male gendering of *some* places to provide *some* services for and by *some* men feels like giving up some hard won gains for women's equality.

Being a *Men's* Shed (or not) therefore remains a 'big deal' for many communities, service practitioners and governments[4]. Research into fatherhood and family services in the UK in 2000 discussed in Chapter 1 provides a neat and

---

[4] Lucia Carragher is acknowledged for her advice and contributions to this section: see Barry Golding and Lucia Carragher, 'Community Men's Sheds and Informal Learning: An Exploration of their Gendered Roles', in J. Oustrouch-Kaminska and C. Vieira (Eds.), *Private Worlds(s) Gender and Informal Learning of Adults*, ESREA Series: Research on the Education and Learning of Adults (ELOA). Rotterdam: Sense Publishers, 2015.

relatively simple way of explaining this difficulty. Sandy Ruxton[5] acknowledged that the majority of Age Concern's service users at that time over a decade ago tended to be older women. Ruxton suggested that there was a need 'to develop more clearly gendered approaches to outreach, particularly with older men who are socially isolated'[6]. Ruxton adopted a stance, taken in much of this book, by acknowledging that:

> Although men-only groups are not attractive to all men, they have a place in a menu of options. For some men they provide vital encouragement, support and friendship in a safe environment. Having the space and autonomy to initiate their own activities is crucially important for some older men.[7]

It has been difficult for many service providers to accept men's agency, particularly in a wide range of areas of comprehensively feminised theory and service provision (such as in adult education, health, aged care and welfare). Their previous approach has been to treat all men and women in the same way (using Ruxton's 'gender-blindness' strategies), alongside the provision of compensatory services mainly for and by women (effectively providing 'gender-differentiated' services only for women). Maxine Kitto's story about the health of the men in the car park at Goolwa in 1993 in Chapter 2 is particularly illustrative here. Gender equity strategies in any field that discount men as gendered beings and having gendered needs are always going to be problematic. Men's Sheds are becoming widely acknowledged as being about *men themselves* dealing positively and daily with critical 'life and death' issues. It is about staying happy and healthy and making sense of being a man in later life.

Is the Men's Shed's Primary Purpose Men's Health and Wellbeing?

While my own research in the past decade has focused on how learning occurs in community settings *through* men's sheds, I am the first to acknowledge that this is but one thread of many purposes. My 2014 book with others, *Men Learning through Life*[8] comprehensively analysed how much important learning occurs informally for men, through hands-on communities of practice, including through

---

[5] Sandy Ruxton, *Working with Older Men: A Review of Age Concern Services*. London: Age Concern, 2006.
[6] As above, 25.
[7] As above, 3.
[8] Barry Golding *et al.* (2014). *Men Learning through Life*. Leicester: NIACE, 2014.

informal mentoring. The book's Chapter 8, 'Men's Sheds: A New Movement for Change' examined learning through Men's Sheds in some detail and linked some of this informal learning to learning about health and wellbeing. Wilson and Cordier baldly concluded, after a narrative review of my work, based around their belief in logical positivism as a 'gold standard' of proof, that, while my research associates 'learning with greater well-being' ... 'this association appears untested and therefore cannot be substantiated.'[9] The academic argument aside, this contention effectively dismisses all of what shedders say about their subjective experiences of Men's Sheds. Listening to shedders would appear to be timely and sensible and, in my opinion, offers a very high standard of proof.

Glover and Misan point to my paper with others, titled 'Let the Men's Speak' from 2008[10] as 'a good place to start to read about men's experience in Men's Sheds', with 'shedders speaking for themselves'. I have argued recently in an international forum that:

> .... amongst the wide range of available research methodologies [to be applied to Men's Sheds], one of the most insightful and powerful is the raw and only minimally mediated, published stories (narratives) of men who participate. ... Men's sheds provide an informal environment where men can let down their (hegemonic and hetero-normative) guard, feel safe to expose some of the fragilities and vulnerabilities of their past and present without feeling judged as a weak or 'lesser' male, and to gather resources and capabilities for individual agency ... What men share and learn from each other in a social, local and situated context ... is precisely why sheds work and why qualitative methodologies are particularly relevant to this field.[11]

As an example, no one can read about Men's Shed experiences in Creswick Men's Friendship Shed's *Tales from the Shed*[12] or Dubbo Community Men's

---

[9] N. Wilson and R. Cordier, 'A Narrative Review of Men's Sheds Literature: Reducing Social Isolation and Promoting Men's Health and Wellbeing', *Health and Social Care in the Community*, 21 (5), 451-463, 2013.

[10] Barry Golding, Annette Foley and Mike Brown, 'Let the Men's Speak: Health, Friendship, Community and Shed Therapy', Paper to AVETRA Conference, Adelaide, 3-4 April, 2008.

[11] Barry Golding and John McDonald, 'Researching Older Men's Self-directed Learning in Australian Community Contexts: Methods, Frameworks and Results', Paper to Symposium of Self-Directed Learning, Strasbourg, France, October 29-31, 2014, 9-10.

[12] Jackie Slade, *Tales from the Shed: Collected Wit, Wisdom and Tales from the Creswick Men's Friendship Shed*. Creswick: Hepburn Health Services, 2007.

Shed's *A Shed Load of Stories*[13] and not be moved by the transformational nature of their experiences. It is a very high level of proof to be convinced of and transformed by the positive effect on their own lives, health and wellbeing, expressed *in their own words*.

To return to the academic argument, Wilson and Cordier take one extract from my 'Shedding Ideas about Older Men's Learning' paper, published in 2011[14], to exemplify their interpretation of my approach to health that I would argue is addressed and acquired informally *through* Men's Sheds participation and experience. The extract that they selected from my paper read that:

> ... while older men have much that they need to learn to maintain their health and wellbeing and cope with radical changes as they age, they are much less likely to participate or be engaged if education, learning, health or wellbeing are fore-grounded and named as the activity or within the program or the organisation.[15]

Largely on the basis of this quote, Cordier and Wilson label me as an 'health by stealth' advocate, by claiming that:

> ... the learning and 'health by stealth' approach advocated suggests that any overt focus on learning and health makes it harder to access men. This creates a conceptual problem as health initiatives and funding bodies are unlikely to accede to such a covert approach. That is, how can policy makers and researchers measure or evaluate such initiatives using such an indirect approach?

While I welcome independent critiques of my research, I am offended that Men's Sheds should be inaccurately positioned in this way. My response on behalf of shedders is that there is nothing covert about men exercising agency. What I have done consistently, at least since 2009, is acknowledge that the fundamental Social Determinants of Health *are already embedded* in the bottom-up, grassroots Men's Shed model. While I acknowledge the reality that 'tacking on' health services to some Men's Sheds, top-down, with 'strings attached' will always occur, it is totally inappropriate for Men's Sheds to sign up to positivist research and

---

[13] *A Shed Load of Stories: From the Dubbo Community Men's Shed*. Dubbo: Dubbo Community Men's Shed, 2012.

[14] Barry Golding, 'Shedding Ideas about Older Men's Learning'. *Lifelong Learning in Europe*, 2, 119-124, 2011.

[15] Barry Golding, 2011, as above, 122.

evaluation agendas tied to health program funding. This is particularly the case if it obligates shedders to participate in external research agendas that are effectively covert and that fundamentally violate the independence of Men's Sheds.

Recognition that Men's Sheds might have traction as well as health and wellbeing benefits via programs for other groups of men (with a disability, unemployed, Indigenous, experiencing health and wellbeing issues) as well as for boys has considerably broadened interest in Men's Sheds, and has been like 'a moth to a flame' for some men's health professionals or academics. As Derryn Porat identified in 2013, there has been a recent, strident call from some academics in health disciplines, particularly from Wilson and Cordier:

> ... for so-called 'evidence-based' research in the pursuit of further funding options [that] has come to dominate many discourses in social policy, social programs, ageing, health and others, with an overwhelming emphasis on judging the 'performance', quality and effectiveness of services according to and in relation to 'health outcomes.'[16]

Derryn Porat summarised the nub of Wilson and Cordier's conclusions. In their narrative 2013 review of Men's Sheds literature, Wilson and Cordier arguably seek to reposition and reinvent Men's Sheds for their purposes as a 'health promotion service'. As Porat put it:

> The basis of [Wilson and Cordier's] arguments is that Men's Sheds should be recognised as a male health initiative and that they must highlight the health-work involved in the sheds. ... [T]hey propose that reinventing the Men's Shed as part of a future male health picture is an 'untapped potential', distinguishing 'health-focus' sheds from other sheds that offer *'no health promotion'*, - just *'woodwork'.*[17]

Porat concluded that inherent to the Men's Shed framework:

> ... is the rejection of typical top-down service delivery approaches, which encourage social and personal assimilation based on predictable

---

[16] D. Porat, 'Redefining a Grassroots Indicator of Success among Community Men's Shed in Australia: An Exploration'. *New Community: A Quarterly Journal*, 11 (4), no page numbers, 2013.

[17] Porat's original italics.

and predetermined outcomes. ... The rise of the Men's Sheds movement represents something of far greater significance ... [It is] an innovative response by a disenfranchised group vis-á-vis a despondent and retracting welfare state. ... The success of a Men's Shed is measured by the 'heart and soul' that has been generated in the shed. ... It seems only fitting that the Men's Shed movement adopts a humanistic indicator of success, measurable for future research and evaluation and accountable and answerable to its own community.

There is much evidence in Parts 1 to 3 in this book that supports Porat's contention.

Should It Be for All Men?

While the short answer to this question is definitely 'Yes', the reality is that some Men's Sheds have made some men less welcome than others. The best way to begin to address the question is not to blame *all* Men's Sheds for this reality, but to again begin to tease out the issues indirectly. Most communities and community organisations, wrongly (and legally in some countries) practice some form of overt or covert exclusion or discrimination, on the basis of gender, age, sexual orientation, race, class, language, disability and behaviour. It is important to acknowledge that most Men's Sheds deliberately admit men (and some deliberately exclude women) because of the perceived, multiple benefits to men and the community of men doing things together, cooperating and communicating in a mainly or wholly male-gendered community place and space.

Research shows that most 'generic' Men's Sheds, *not* set up for particular groups of men, are typically less inclusive of men in some minority groups than the wider population. In Australia and New Zealand, for example, the proportion of shedders who are Indigenous (Aboriginal or Maori) is less than in the wider national populations. Similarly, Men's Sheds in the four Anglophone countries in which they have had most traction to 2015, tend, on average, to attract fewer men from culturally diverse, non-Anglophone groups. There are disturbing individual instances of behavior that I have been made aware of in a handful of Australian Sheds, typically expressed in derogatory terms: for example about admitting Indigenous men, men who use a wheelchair, from Moslem religious backgrounds or who are gay, bisexual or transgender.

The argument peak Men's Shed bodies advance to shedders in these few instances is to point out that excluding any of these groups from a community organisation such as a sporting club is unfair, discriminatory and illegal in most

Western countries. For the same reasons, arbitrarily excluding any group of men from a Men's Shed is not acceptable, including by law in many countries. That said, a small number of communities and Men's Sheds have chosen to encourage and include particular groups of excluded or objectively disadvantaged men, including Travellers in Ireland, Aboriginal and Torres Strait Islander men in Australia, War Veterans (including from civil wars) and men with dementia, on the grounds that a Shed specific to any of these groups is more effective and more desirable. In practice most Men's Sheds welcome and admit men of any age or background with a range of disabilities, through many are reluctant to take men as regular workshop participants if they require a high level of care without the support of an appropriate carer.

Common Perceptions (and Misconceptions) about Men's Sheds

Part 3 provided copious evidence that Men's Sheds organisations and shedders are often very passionate about doing things hands-on. Because as many as one half of all Men's Sheds have some woodworking equipment in the Shed, there is a mistaken perception in the community that being skilled, particularly at doing woodwork, is all that Men's Sheds organisations are about. This mistaken perception leads some men to avoid Men's Sheds because they sense they don't have the necessary skills to participate.

Other Men's Sheds do other, quite different and diverse things. In some cases, very little hands-on activity occurs in the Shed aside from 'having a cuppa' (tea or coffee). Those Sheds that do have woodworking equipment often have access to other activities separately or in parallel, sometimes including metalwork, gardening, cooking, craft, and art or hobby activities. Some Sheds only conduct regular community outings mainly or solely for men, without a physical Shed, and still call it a Men's Shed. Some Sheds, like the Killorglan Men's Shed in Ireland, photographed during the Shed's second Birthday celebration evening on November 4, 2014, have excellent choirs (Photograph 48).

Photograph 48 Killorglan Men's Shed Choir, Celebrating the Shed's Second
Birthday at the Canberra Hotel, Kerry, Ireland, November 4, 2014

In essence, anything is theoretically possible, depending on the interests of the
men and the capacity of the shed space to house and support the activity. This can
and does include fixing machinery or engines, setting up train model sets, model
making and computer repair, but extends to re-use, recycling, repair and
renovation, including of the Shed premises.

Men's Sheds have also tried to avoid formality. While it is essential that they
are safe, accessible and adapted to the needs and possible physical limitations of
the men who participate, Men's Sheds work best when they are informal,
voluntary and without obligation to attend or participate in any or all of the
activities. This freedom that shedders have to come (or not), and to voluntarily
and safely participate (or not) is in contrast to the stress, pressure, obligation and
risk that has sometimes been associated with men's paid work. Ironically, *not*
having to come to a Shed often frees up men to commit voluntarily as equal
participants in a shared activity, and to enthusiastically support 'their Shed' as
well as other men.

While Men's Sheds are fundamentally about keeping men active, social,
connected, contributing to the community and to other men, and in the process
staying as healthy, happy and as well as possible, most Men's Sheds have also

resisted becoming an outreach of health services, professionals and programs. The Men's Shed is typically (but not always) the 'men's turf', and men generally want to be able to decide which programs and professionals they invite or admit into the Shed. There have been times when the association of health providers with Men's Shed forums, conferences and associations has been actively queried and resisted by some shedders. While shedders have come to acknowledge the risks of depression, suicide and inevitable ailments associated with ageing, both for themselves and for the men in their midst, they strongly resist their Shed being just or mainly about 'doing health programs' or being a conduit for health information, or an alternative office for paid health workers.

This resistance sometimes causes dilemmas for Shed organisations supported by or in auspice arrangements with health organisations. It is rare for organisations that donate funds, particularly governments, to provide money without some 'strings' attached. Since they can't 'bite the hand that feeds them', sometimes Men's Sheds organisations have to compromise. For example, a health service or program providing funding for a Men's Sheds organisation will likely want some evidence that its funds are achieving the result they were provided for. This may mean that the men will be asked to participate in a survey, or the Men's Shed organisation will be asked to complete a report or participate in an evaluation or audit. For example, if the Department of Veterans' Affairs in Australia gives money for a Men's Shed, it will understandably want evidence that it is being used for the benefit of at least some war Veterans, and that the outcomes are positive.

When the peak Men's Shed body in Australia, AMSA, accepted significant federal government funding it came out of the national men's health budget, with 'strings attached' in the form of its men's health-related program and reporting requirements to government. Men's Sheds are not and should not primarily be about health programs or services. However the Men's Shed can and does provide a 'safe place' in which men's health and wellbeing can be informally enhanced, and to which professionals can be *invited* to assist and contribute, where appropriate and useful.

For many of the same reasons, Men's Sheds are not necessarily open or welcoming to all forms of research. Some Sheds actively resist or refuse to participate in some forms of research, usually for very good reasons. While most Sheds and shedders willingly participate, since they recognise that the data and insights generated by research have the capacity to benefit Sheds generally and the movement more broadly, some Shed organisations have indicated that they have had enough of being asked to respond to research surveys or participate in interviews, including from national and state Shed associations. Specifically, there is resistance to being constantly 'poked and prodded' by researchers, including being asked to complete surveys, if they are deemed to be unnecessary, too obtuse, academic or invasive, or if the results of the research will not be fed back in a form that is accessible to the Sheds and shedders that generously and voluntarily gave of their time and ideas to participate.

As discussed in Chapter 10, Men's Sheds have been linked, through the 100 plus items of published research to early 2015, to many academic and professional fields. For example through my own research as an adult learning academic, I have tended to focus on the learning that takes place informally, primarily by sharing of skills and informal mentoring. However most Men's Sheds (with some exceptions) are understandably wary of becoming sites for the uninvited imposition of formal learning or training programs. While Australian research suggests that around one in five men who participate in Men's Sheds *would* take up paid work if they could get it, Sheds would likely be less effective if they were rebadged as places just to train men obliged to enter or re-enter the workforce.

While this means that the scope for regularly 'tacking on' formal learning or vocational training to Men's Sheds is somewhat limited, some sheds do include younger people who have benefited greatly from being informally exposed to trade skills as a kind of pre-apprenticeship, and others have achieved an accredited certificate directly through the Shed. Other Sheds have incorporated non-formal (non-accredited but organised) training programs into the other Shed activities. While a Men's Shed is not a formal training program, many men will informally gain new knowledge and skills. As a result some men will indeed use the Men's Shed as a first step back to health and happiness, and perhaps also develop or redevelop skills and confidence required for paid work.

Finally but most importantly, while Men's Sheds organisations are not a service *for* men, they can and do provide activities and services organised and decided upon *by* men. This idea of men freely deciding and acting to help themselves and others is broadly defined by sociologists as *agency*. The related idea, that because any individual or group, in this case men, is experiencing difficulty, they therefore need be 'treated' as if they have something *wrong* with them is referred to as a *deficit* model of provision. Shedders are often very resistant to deficit models of provision, particularly when they are linked to the 'modern' and sometimes patronising notion of professionals 'treating' them as if they, professionals, always know best, and as if men have no agency or voice.

Some professional service providers, including some women, who tend to dominate community health, welfare, adult education and aged care provision in the countries where Sheds have so far spread, can have an unintentional tendency to make some men feel inadequate, small and powerless. The story of how the first Shed started in South Australia in 1993, and how the first *Men's* Shed started in Tongala in Victoria in July 1998, illustrate how the first Shed-based organisations for and increasingly *by* men were created, through men's perceived powerlessness in aged care settings. The perception that some services for men were inappropriate or not reaching men most in need was one of the first threads of this story discussed in Part 2.

When all the above is linked to *ageism*: that is the idea that simply because people (in this case, older *men*, are older they are necessarily less able), it is unsurprising that some older men resist professional service provider interventions, however well intentioned. These resistances can extend to medical check ups, interventions by health, social welfare and aged care workers. It can also include interviews and work suitability tests by employment agencies and job service providers. Some older men in community settings have reported extreme distress when they generously volunteered to 'give back' to the community. Particularly in contexts where they might interact with young people, both the older men and their motives are prone to be treated suspiciously. At worst they may be perceived as 'dirty, old men', and put through 'working with children' checks. These checks are now routinely required for good reasons because of past, often dreadful but rare instances of child sexual abuse by adults, including by a very small number of older men in positions of authority. However the way the checking process is actually carried out needs to be free of gender or age stereotypes.

SETTING UP A MEN'S SHED: SOME PRACTICAL ISSUES

Four related practical issues are teased out in this in this section:

- Getting funds and getting started
- Shed space
- Shed purpose
- Shed renewal and sustainability.

This list of issues was complied from analysis of over 300 extensive text responses to a question 'What do you think are the four major issues facing your Shed?' that formed part of AMSA's 2013 survey of all Australian Men's Sheds.

This evidence, plus similar narrative evidence from non-Australian sources, including this book's case studies, suggests that these four issues are widely regarded as the main practical issues facing *most* Men's Sheds in Australia, Ireland, the UK and New Zealand.

Getting Funds and Getting Started

Getting started as a Men's Shed is the most significant hurdle in many communities, despite the availability in Australia of the AMSA *How to Start/Run a Men's Shed* on-line manual. The most important issue facing most (58% of) Australian Men's Sheds, at start up and once established, is the availability of funds to set up and remain viable. While the Australian manual is widely used for many Australian and overseas Men's Shed commencements, it is impossible to create 'a one size fits all' manual for the wide range of dreams and expectations that men have for their 'ideal' Men's Shed across all countries, communities and governance arrangements. Ted Donnelly, who wrote the first manual for AMSA, recently moved into a retirement home in Sydney and immediately became aware that his manual was of limited usefulness in this very specific residential setting.

Most new Sheds start with a community meeting, leading to the setting up of an interim committee, whose task it is to seek funds and make plans for a Shed. In the absence of a Shed space or a cohesive group of men, and if setting up the Shed takes a number of years (as sometimes happens), it can be very difficult to maintain momentum and enthusiasm. Many Sheds start in temporary premises with limited facilities simply to hold the group together.

The funds necessary for a Men's Shed start up vary considerably. Some well-known and very successful sheds have started with very little, if any, external funding. Many have set up and renovated existing Sheds with very low or zero rent, with donated equipment and/or generous financial donations and labour from members. While these Sheds have often 'done it the hard way', and may be more limited in terms of the activities they are able to run, they typically have a strong sense of ownership and are generally more sustainable than Shed organisations saddled with high recurrent running costs. Other communities have gone 'all out' for a big, new stand-alone, 'super-shed' with all new equipment, enabling them to offer a range of community activities, typically obtaining funding from a range of external sources. The highest ongoing costs, and the biggest risks in terms of sustainability, as teased out in a later section, are experienced by Shed organisations that rely on paid staff and/or need to enter into expensive long-term rental agreements for the shed building or space.

Shed Space

Getting more or more appropriate shed space, including getting the Shed's own, permanent purpose-built shed or facility, is the second most important issue reported by Australian Men's Sheds, affecting close to one half (49%) of all Sheds that responded to the 2013 AMSA survey. Setting up a safe workshop that also combines a need for social exchange is always going to be a difficult balancing act. Most Men's Sheds acknowledge the critical importance of a separate, connected or adjacent space for men to socialise. Typically this will include at least basic tea and coffee making facilities, a refrigerator and a sink but some Sheds have a comprehensive, separate kitchen.

While a very small number of Sheds have no or few tools and equipment, *if* hands-on activity including the use of power tools are to be part of the Shed activity, there needs to be sufficient space for safe operation of the equipment. The space and occupational health and safety requirements (including safe storage of materials) are different for woodwork and for metal work and not necessarily complementary. Typically a Shed organisation seeks to safely compartmentalise different activities in particular zones within the shed. The frustrations about sufficient or appropriate space evident from the research are typically about trying to accommodate a range of uses in a relatively small shed space that, unless purpose-built, may not safely accommodate all the activities shedders might choose to engage in.

Shed Purpose

The AMSA survey in Australia in 2013 asked Shed organisations 'In what ways does your Shed engage with and contribute to its community?'[18] The response data give a comprehensive snapshot of the multiple purposes of a Men's Shed. Eleven different mechanisms for a Men's Shed's engagement with and contribution to its community were identified in the multiple responses, ranked below by the percentage of Sheds including a response in that category.

1. Assist, support or liaise with activities conducted by other local organisations, service clubs, charities or community fund raising events. (38% of Sheds)
2. Fix or make items including handyman service. (34% of Sheds)

---

[18] From 246 sheds (562 total responses), categorised and coded.

3. Undertake   community   renovation,   refurbishment,   maintenance, construction or repair projects. (26% of Sheds)
4. Make products for community distribution or sale. (21% of Sheds)
5. Conduct fundraising or other events for the Shed. (21% of Sheds)
6. Other ways, not categorised. (21% of Sheds)
7. Youth mentoring, youth at risk programs, including working through schools. (17% of Sheds)
8. Provide a safe space in the Shed for men to meet, drop in, socialise, chat, gather or 'do stuff'. (13% of Sheds)
9. Provide mental or physical health information to shedders, encourage or refer men to doctors and social workers; assist people with a disability. (11% of Sheds)
10. Undertake visits from and to local aged care facilities. (6% of Sheds)
11. Recruit and retain members, including promoting the Shed by newsletter and contributing items to the local media. (6% of Sheds).

In summary, while fixing and making items or products are very important aspects of a Men's Shed's contribution to the community, assisting, supporting or liaising with activities conducted by other local organisations, service clubs, charities or community fundraising events, when combined, are the most reported Shed engagement or community contributions, at least in Australia.

Shed Renewal and Sustainability

The third most important issue (facing 40% of Australian sheds) is related to Shed renewal: attracting, engaging or retaining Shed members, including ensuring training and succession planning with ageing members. With a median shedder age of 70 years in Australia and 60 years in Ireland, one half of shedders are older than 70 and 60 respectively. Many older men have experienced significant and debilitating early lives, working and non-working lives and life changes. The older they are, the more likely it is that they will experience medical and mental health conditions that limit their ability to participate as they approach the Fourth Age of dependency. The first ever Men's Shed officially was opened in 1998 with its instigator and name sake, Dick McGowan too unwell to participate in the opening. McGowan died the following year. Many Sheds since have had some men die before the Shed they were helping to create was opened. Some Men's Sheds have conducted wakes and funerals for fellow shedders.

Aside from illness and death, many other circumstances can arise that cause men to stop participating. These can include the need to adopt a caring role for a wife or partner, relocation, loss of mobility or change in interests. Not all Sheds cope well with changes in key leadership positions. Some Shed organisations can become cliques for groups of men or individuals who effectively turn other men away. One of the interesting outcomes of increased Shed densities in cities like Ballarat, in Victoria, with at least eight Sheds within 50 kilometers, is that men who are mobile have choices, and can (and do) 'shop around' for a Shed organisation that best suits their needs and interests.

Aside from the social and interpersonal issues, some Shed organisations can 'lose their way' by becoming over-committed and financially dependent on revenue, not only from declining membership and donations, but also from the pressure and obligation to undertake more outside work, or produce more goods for sale simply to 'stay afloat'. Sheds developed quickly in new premises that are subject to high initial or recurrent cost, including for paid staff and rental of Shed premises, are particularly vulnerable and potentially unsustainable. While Sheds that develop slowly, cheaply and with a large commitment from volunteers and from the community are desirable and more sustainable in the longer term, the time it can take to get established also risks losing interest, momentum and membership.

It is inevitable, for all of the above reasons, in a grassroots movement with more than one thousand very different Sheds across four countries, that longer-term Men's Shed sustainability cannot be guaranteed at a Shed organisation, peak body or Movement level. The best available data on Shed sustainability from the Australian 2013 AMSA survey[19] confirm that, despite the many individual and community benefits, many Shed organisations in Australia struggle with a range of issues related to sustainability. Of the Sheds that responded to the 2013 Australian survey, six per cent were not yet open. Of those Sheds that were open:

- around one third (32%) were located in a temporary or less than optimal building as a shed space.
- almost one half (45%) were struggling with one or more uncertainties that were impacting on their longer term sustainability, including: keeping or attracting members, maintaining Shed harmony, getting men to be fully involved, renewing Shed membership or the Shed committee, attracting community support or defining the Shed's role.
- Less than one in ten Sheds (8%) reported few or no significant sustainability problems.

---

[19] The overall 'health of the shed' was ascribed to each of the 263 Sheds that responded to the 2013 survey.

- Less than one in ten Sheds (7%) were 'bursting at the seams', with a mismatch between the limited space, limited funding resources and excessively high demand on its services from men and the community.

Do Men's Sheds Problems Change with Age?

This section moves away from the specifics to home in on the way problems in the Shed tend to change with the time since the Shed opened. In the early stages for most Men's Sheds, based on the Australian data, the main issue is how to get sufficient community support, funding and resources to create the shed space to meet the anticipated demand.

The most comprehensive data supporting the way problems tend to change with the age of the Shed organization come from the 2013 Australian AMSA survey. Earlier established, more mature Sheds (at least five years old, commenced before 2009) understandably agreed that they had many more of the 'basics' in place, such as a dedicated shed place (96% agreement), risk management and induction strategies (79%), and the lowest ongoing contact with AMSA. One quarter of these older Sheds (25%) had at least some paid employees. By contrast only two thirds of recent Australian Men's Sheds (registered in the past year) had a dedicated shed space and none had paid employees. In between these 'old' and 'young' Sheds, Shed organisations registered between 2-3 years ago had the most ongoing contact with the national organisation (AMSA) and the highest proportion (88%) of Sheds that had opted for AMSA's insurance cover.

Once a Shed is established, keeping it sustainable becomes the key issue, a phenomenon identified by experienced shedders as 'the five year itch'. This is unsurprising, given the high dependence on a volunteer base, the very low level of ongoing Shed funding, the difficulties of meeting expressed demand from men and the community, together with safety, 'red tape', management and succession problems. There issues are difficult for all Sheds and can put many Shed organisations under significant stress. Very few Sheds in Australia are coasting without some problems, even once the issues of establishment are largely behind them. For this reason, the support and advice from a peak Men's Shed body or regional Shed network or cluster can be very important.

What about Men's Sheds On-line?

Many community Men's Shed organisations have an active web presence. A typical Men's Shed website includes contact details and a profile of the Shed's activities as well as its forthcoming events. Many Shed organisations also (or instead) have a Facebook page. While many older shedders are reluctant users of some new information and communication technologies (ICTs), most Sheds have some shedders with recent professional, industry or trade backgrounds and relatively good ICT skills, who proudly create and maintain the Shed website.

State and national associations in Australia, Ireland, the UK and New Zealand depend heavily on their web sites for keeping member Sheds and a wide range of stakeholders informed and interactively connected. There is a 'Shed Locator' function on each national website that enables prospective shedders, partners and families to locate and contact Sheds as well as determine when they are open. There are links to forthcoming events, conferences, resources and research as well as to other national and lower-order peak body associations including states, networks and clusters.

A 'virtual' men's shed, Men's Shed Online[20] has been developed in Australia linked to AMSA's web site. The Shed Online self-defines as:

> ... an online social community for men, founded by beyondblue, The Movember Foundation and the Australian Men's Shed Association. Like the original Men's Sheds, The Shed Online is a place for men to socialise, network, make friends and share skills. It aims to recreate the atmosphere of "real life" Men Sheds – a safe space where men can feel confident to discuss and exchange information. The Shed Online aims to foster a sense of community and build men's social networks. In addition to being a place for men to interact with other men, The Shed Online also provides men with information on health and well-being. ... Becoming a member of The Shed Online gives men a safe environment where they can find many of these things in the spirit of "old-fashioned mateship".

There is a page on the Shed Online website that enables physical Men's Sheds organisations to register and post an online profile. Approximately one quarter of Australian Men's Sheds[21] had posted a profile on the site by early 2015. Despite a relatively positive evaluation of the program to late 2012[22], the Shed Online has

---

[20] www.theshedonline.org.au, Accessed February 6, 2015.
[21] 224 sheds, 24.4 per cent of all 920 men's sheds open had posted a profile to February 6, 2015.
[22] https://www.beyondblue.org.au/docs/default-source/research-project-files/bw0148-evaluation-of-the-shed-online---summary-report.pdf?sfvrsn=2, *Evaluation of the Shed Online*, December 2012, Accessed March 2, 2015.

been unable to create or re-create many essential attributes of a physical and social Men's Shed organisation. It is also dependent on men having access to the internet as well as the skills and confidence to actively participate in and contribute to the discussions.

CHAPTER 12

Men's Shed Issues, Trends, and Possibilities

WHAT IMPLICATIONS DOES MEN'S SHED PRACTICE HAVE FOR OTHER SERVICES?

The principles behind Men's Shed practice have the potential to be adapted to fit, and in turn be influenced by, a wide range of practical services and theoretical fields. This potential is greatest in practice for services to do with men not in paid work, including in adult and community education, health and wellbeing, aged care, welfare, gerontology, community development and occupational therapy. This section investigates and summarises this potential for two-way adaptation and diffusion. In doing so, it turns to some of the conclusions from the *Men's Sheds in Australia 2013* report for beyondblue[1], that have wider implications for other services for men, particularly for men beyond paid work. One of these conclusions is that 'men's sheds are a positive experience overall for members'. A second conclusion stresses the opportunity Men's Sheds present to men 'for an ongoing commitment over time'. A third conclusion is about the 'self-directed nature of sheds [that] appeals to members'.

Each of these conclusions would appear to apply to many other community places and spaces that men already feel at home in and exercise agency over, for their own good as well as the good of the wider community. Fire and emergency services organisations as well as a wide range of sporting clubs in Australia, New Zealand, Ireland and the UK all embody some (but not all) of the same principles as Men's Sheds. The fact that these organisation and community places already reach diverse groups of men opens up new ways of incorporating men's agency into thinking about informal learning and information exchange on place of some professional service provision. These include health and wellbeing for men of diverse ages and cultural and linguistic backgrounds, as summarised below. Other organisations have set up Sheds specifically for young people in mentoring relationships with older men as a way of entering 'the boy's space'.

---

[1] Paul Flood and Sharon Blair, *Men's Sheds in Australia: Effects on Physical Health and Mental Well-being*, Full report. Melbourne: UltraFeedback for beyondblue, 2013.

Age Diversity

The second beyondblue *Men's Sheds in Australia* report's conclusion, that Men's Sheds are ideally placed to reach some otherwise hard to reach demographic groups, suggests that it may be possible to make Sheds more diverse in terms of their membership, including by age, language, cultural and Indigenous status. While the median age of shedders in Australia is close to 70 years in Australia, the median age of 60 years in Ireland raises the possibility that younger men and boys might also benefit from the inter-generational nature of Shed practice. Some Shed organisations in urban areas in Australia have deliberately created two groups of shedders, younger and older than 50 years, in recognition that some younger men might be more comfortable in a Shed with men of a similar age.

Indigenous, Cultural and Linguistic Diversity

The small amount of data on the cultural and linguistic diversity and Indigenous status of shedders is far from consistent or conclusive. Australian Shed research from the 2013 AMSA survey suggests that Indigenous Australians as well as immigrants from non-English backgrounds are under-represented in Men's Sheds, comprising only one per cent and 6.3 per cent respectively of shedders. This compares to an overall representation of around 3 per cent and 25 per cent respectively in the wider Australian community. There are anecdotal indications from New Zealand that Pakeha (non-Maori New Zealanders with European backgrounds) are similarly over-represented compared to Maori and Pasifica in Men's Sheds. By contrast, the 2013 Irish research confirmed that nine per cent of Irish shedders speak a language other than English at home. Given that Irish is the main community and household language of three per cent of the population of the Republic of Ireland, and that only a very small proportion of older men speak languages other than Irish or English, it appears likely that there is a reasonable representation of Irish-speaking shedders in *Gaeltacht* (Gaelic-speaking) areas in parts of Ireland, where in fact Men's Sheds are particularly popular.

A small number of Men's Sheds in urban Australia, including Brimbank Men's Shed in Melbourne, have successfully involved groups of refugee and immigrant men with considerable success over many years. Other Sheds including Darebin in inner-suburban Melbourne have had successful Indigenous programs on particular days each week in 'mainstream' Sheds. Some Men's Sheds in Ireland have made themselves specific to Traveller men and some communities in Ireland dedicated to strengthening Irish language and cultural craft traditions.

While some Australian Men's Sheds have been set up as Indigenous-specific, there are only a small number of research articles specific to Indigenous participation in Men's Sheds in Australia. Some are based on poorly identified samples of sheds (and non-men's Shed 'groups') and very few are properly located [2] . There is arguably an untapped potential for more Indigenous involvement in Men's Sheds generally, as well as in Indigenous-specific Men's Sheds in some instances, as explored and agreed at a national 'Indigenous Men's Sheds Gathering' held on August 15-16, 2012 in Australia's Parliament House. While there has been some promising action research on Indigenous-specific men's spaces,[3] research is inconclusive in regard to the long-term success of Men's Sheds so far as Australian Indigenous men are concerned.

WHERE ELSE MIGHT MEN'S SHEDS WORK?

It is likely that some Men's Shed principles will be applied in other sites in which men enjoy gathering in other nations and cultures. Some already operate under different organisational names to 'Men's Sheds', and in different languages, including in some Indigenous cultural contexts. This section seeks to identify some places and spaces for future research and application.

The question of where else in the world Men's Sheds might have future traction remains open. Canada and the US, as Anglophone nations with many cultural and historical connections to the UK, Ireland, New Zealand and Australia, have so far been either slow or reluctant to take up Men's Sheds as a form of men's practice. To 2015 the next most likely places for Men's Sheds, or a cultural equivalent, to take hold is in Europe and Canada.

Some nations exhibit concerning statistics in terms of men's health and wellbeing. These statistics, particularly where there are big gaps between male and female life expectancy and elevated risk of suicide for men, suggest that some sort of Men's Shed-type intervention, perhaps by another name, might work elsewhere. Several highly industrialised Asian countries with a strong work ethic, including Japan and Korea, as well as some eastern European nations, including Slovenia and Lithuania, are characterised by relatively high suicide rates amongst older men beyond paid work. Estonia has one of the highest national longevity

---

[2] Cavanagh's research with others, as well as Jack Bulman's research with Rick Hayes, are good examples.
[3] Jack Bulman and Rick Hayes,'Mibbinbah and Spirit Healing: Fostering Safe, Friendly Spaces for Indigenous Males in Australia', *International Journal of Men's Health*, 10 (1), 6-26, 2011.

disparities between men and women in the world, ten years less than men. These may all be fertile sites for future Men's Shed development.

The recent growth of Sheds in the UK is particularly interesting, in that several very recent community workshop spaces, while registered with the UK Men's Sheds Association, are choosing not to be called *Men's* sheds or *Sheds*, and a small number are operating as Women's Sheds. Several are being set us as extensions of existing tool reuse and recycling cooperatives. Others are being set up on quite recent and relatively radical Makerspace[4] or Dutch Repair Café[5] models. Both these entrepreneurial, workshop-based models have histories not directly related to the origins of Australian Men's Sheds. Both models originated in Europe, in Berlin (in 1995) and in the Netherlands (in 2008) respectively. Both are premised on 'free' meeting places dedicated to people (men and women) repairing and recycling things together in community settings. Several of these models, being more radical, spontaneous and environmentally motivated, are more attractive to younger men *and women,* whose motives, though workshop-oriented, are more likely to be related to new technologies and materials and the use of ICT. Early indications from Sheds being planned during early 2015 in Sweden and Demark are suggestive of significant accommodation of the Australian Men's Shed model to fit local cultural imperatives.

DID THE MEN'S SHED MOVEMENT COME OUT OF PREVIOUS MEN'S MOVEMENTS?

The answer to this interesting question, with some qualification, is that "It did not". Men's Shed history in Part 2 shows that the Men's Shed Movement originated from and for men otherwise previously poorly connected and organised. There are two minor exceptions in Australia. One exception is the grassroots movement of male War Veterans, particularly some Vietnam War Veterans in South Australia who were self-organising in the late 1990s. The other

---

[4] Wikipedia noted, in February 6, 2015, that a makerspace (also referred to as a hackerspace, hacklab, or hackspace) is a community-operated workspace where people with common interests, often in computers, machining, technology, science, digital art or electronic art, can meet, socialize and collaborate. Hackerspaces have also been compared to other community-operated spaces with similar aims and mechanisms such as Fab Lab, Men's Sheds, and to commercial "for profit" companies such as TechShop.

[5] See http://repaircafe.org/about-repair-cafe/, Accessed February 6, 2015. 'The Repair Café was initiated by Martine Postma. ... [the first Repair Café opened] in Amsterdam, on October 18, 2009. ... [prompting] Martine to start the Repair Café Foundation [registered] on March 2, 2010. ... Since 2011, the foundation has provided professional support to local groups in the Netherlands and other countries wishing to start their own Repair Café.'

exception is the very small and loosely connected community of men's health workers and academics in Australia. Biennial National Men's Health Gatherings in Australia have provided an important point of contact between men's health workers and those working in the growing Men's Shed space for almost two decades. Organised by the Australian Men's Health Forum, which deliberately promotes 'a social approach to men's health and wellbeing' consistent with the Men's Shed ethos, these men's health gatherings have run parallel to Indigenous Men's Health Gatherings.

In 2007, Dr Spase Karoski completed his Australian PhD, *Men on the Move: The Politics of the Men's Movement,* through the University of Wollongong in NSW. His thesis is particularly informative about what the relationships might be between the development of Men's Sheds and Men's Movements in the same era. While Karoski's thesis included a thorough empirical study and analysis of several strands of the men's movement in Australia to that date (the same year the decision to form the national Men's Shed association was made) Men's Sheds were not mentioned at all. Karoski identified three main 'Men's Movements' in the era to 2007 in Australia: Mythopoetic, Profeminist and Father's Rights. None of these three Australian Men's Movements appears to have played any obvious role in the genesis or spread of the Men's Shed Movement in Australia. Other evidence suggests that while most men's health workers and academics quickly 'climbed aboard', the rapid success of the movement surprised and in many cases overtook some of those involved in these other Men's Movements, several of whom had previously been working in the field of men's health or working with men and boys.

Karoski identified a fourth, emerging 'Inclusive Men's Movement' category that is perhaps more relevant here. Karoski's overwhelming finding that the feminist movement had been 'the main catalyst for men joining the men's movement either in support of or as a reaction to its impact on the lives of men'[6] is of particular interest. Karoski saw the 'Inclusive' men's movement as playing a 'go-between [role] for the different men's movement ideologies', not only supporting women in their struggle for justice, but also 'working together with women to address the concerns that are specific to men'[7]. It is in this inclusive spirit, which involves putting aside an adversarial stance including confrontation with women that apply to the overwhelming majority of men involved in and participating in Men's Sheds. While it is about being separate for some of the time in the shed with men and separate from women, most men involved are

---

[6] Cited from Karoski, xii.
[7] Cited from Karoski, 280.

respectful of women, supportive of women's rights and critical of the very small number of men who come to the Men's Shed as misogynists.

The more complex answer, beyond the scope of this book, is that the Men's Shed and previous Men's Movements, while effectively separate, are arguably both reactions to the second wave of the Women's Movement, with all that Movement's repercussions.

WHAT ARE THE CURRENT TRENDS?

Most of the growth in Men's Sheds to 2015 in the four countries with national Shed Movements to early 2015 has been concentrated beyond the metropolis. Despite the large absolute number of Men's Sheds in all four countries featured in this book, Sheds have proved to be most attractive in smaller rural towns, communities, states, counties and regions. As an example, Irish and English Sheds are disproportionately located in smaller rural Counties. While 77 per cent of New Zealand's population lives on the relatively densely settled North Island, it has only 52 per cent of all New Zealand Men's Sheds. Similarly, Tasmania, the smallest state in Australia, with the highest proportion of the population living outside of the main capital city (Hobart), has almost twice the density of Men's Sheds as any other state in Australia.

In general, Men's Sheds in these smaller rural and regional communities reach out to and are more strongly supported than urban Sheds by a wider range of organisations across the community. They also tend to tap into an older demographic of men who have been displaced from paid work in hands-on industries and trades, such as farming, mining, manufacturing, retail or service industries. Many shedders in Australia have retired for a rural 'sea change' or 'tree change'. Others have moved 'off the land' into small rural and regional towns characterised by an ageing demographic.

Like many sporting teams and volunteer fire and emergency services organisations, Men's Sheds in smaller rural towns tend to involve a higher proportion of men. In many country towns across Ireland and Australia, Men's Sheds now take a prominent leadership role in the life of the community and are actively promoted in the local media. As a consequence, rural shedders and the scope of their activities in a particular Men's Shed tend to be very diverse. By contrast, while some suburban Sheds are also for 'all comers', many specifically target particular user groups or offer specific activities for more specialized purposes and 'target groups'.

While Men's Sheds, being a relatively new concept are usually retrofitted to existing communities, there are indications that some new suburbs are acknowledging the value and attraction of building a Men's Shed into communities during the planning phase. As an example, Armstrong Villawood, a new property development between Torquay and Waurn Ponds near Geelong in Victoria, opened the Armstrong Men's Shed in 2013 even before the houses on the site had been built.[8] The property developer advertised the fact as part of its marketing to new residents, who in that area would tend to include a significant proportion of older retirees seeking a 'sea-change'.

WHAT ARE THE FUTURE POSSIBILITIES?

This section reflects and builds on the two decades of experience in community Men's Shed, to come to some tentative conclusions about where Men's Sheds might be headed and how they might look and function in the medium and longer term.

It is useful before proceeding to turn to what some of those currently leading the Men's Shed Movement have to say. David Helmers, AMSA CEO in Australia was asked, in March 2014, what the future for Men's Sheds might look like. Helmers replied that:

> It is difficult to say. There has been considerable work done with strategic planning and developing a vision for the Association to service Men's Sheds, but very little has been done in thinking about what the Sheds might look like in the longer term. As AMSA and Men's Sheds themselves are relatively new, most of our resources have gone into addressing the current needs of Sheds. From an AMSA perspective, the next stage of Shed evolution will be about the governance of Sheds, about further exploring the definition of a Men's Shed, and working out what qualifies an incorporated entity to call itself as such. Because the Shed movement has grown organically, to plan what Sheds *should* look like in the future could be counter productive by predetermining the outcomes.[9]

As with all grassroots social movements, Men's Sheds are not completely new and will not 'shine brightly' forever. Stabilisation of Shed organisation and shedder numbers is already occurring in areas where Sheds have been established for several years, as some of the initial fascination inevitably wears off, and as

---

[8] The Shed held an information session about the Shed at the Armstrong Sales Centre on May 29, 2013.
[9] David Helmers, March 20, 2014.

post-World War 2 'baby boomers' go beyond the Third Age of retirement into the Fourth Age of dependency. It is likely that Men's Sheds, as a Movement, will follow some previous well-documented trajectories of other social movement as men's needs and societies change. Whether men the same age as my two sons, now in their 30s, will need or seek the company of other men in Men's Sheds is an interesting and open question.

Some lessons might be drawn from the history of two other popular, community-based learning movements for 'working men', which operated in all four countries where Men's Sheds have recently flourished to 2015. The best-known example is the Mechanics Institutes, started in Scotland in the 1820s but which began to wane after approximately a century of expansion. Mechanic's Institutes focused on the provision of libraries and courses. They rapidly spread to become a powerful and popular movement, mainly for 'working men' across the UK, Australia, New Zealand and Canada. At one point in the late 1800s there were more than 1,200 Mechanics Institutes in the Australian state of Victoria alone, five times the number of Men's Sheds (249) in Victoria to January 2015. By 2015 only a handful of Mechanics Institutes were open.

Though smaller in terms of its impact, the WEA (Workers Education Australia), also originating in Scotland, had spread to Northern Ireland, Australia and New Zealand within a decade of the first WEA in 1909. Most disappeared with or before the advent of government-supported vocational education and training colleges institutes as well as adult and community education providers since the 1970s.

More recent movements in informal adult education since the 1970s, including neighbourhood houses and community centres in Australia, have tended to be focused on the practical interests and social needs of women, particularly women not in paid work or seeking to return to the workforce. The U3A movement, started in France, with an academic emphasis in 1973, morphed into a quite different, community-based, self-help organisation in the UK and Australia within the decade. While U3A provides an important 'community connection through learning' for many older people in the 'Third Age' in the four countries to which Men's Sheds have spread to 2015, it tends to attract mainly older women who are already relatively well educated. U3As in most countries 'have a positive women to men ratio of 3:1' and tend to 'anchor female members in gender expectations about women's traditional roles'[10]. In effect, U3As tend not to be as attractive or welcoming to most men, particularly 'working class' men.

---

[10] Marvin Formosa, 'Four Decades of Universities of the Third Age: Past Present and Future', *Ageing and Society*, 1-25, 2012.

It is important to place the very recent growth of community Men's Sheds in all four countries with Men's Shed Movements in the context of the parallel demise of many community-based adult and education centres. Increasingly neo-liberal governments have progressively withdrawn government funding from providers and programs that are not overtly vocational or that were unable to demonstrate 'hard' or 'durable' health or other outcomes.

The social movement literature provides evidence from past movements of potential pitfalls for the Men's Shed Movement, including from past movements that have 'gone wrong', in the sense of not realising 'the hopes and aspirations of [their] participants or [not being able] to solve the problems that moved them to action in the first place'.[11] Four of these potential pitfalls have already been observed at a range of levels, from individual Sheds and clusters to state and national associations, as discussed below as possibilities.

The first possibility is the likelihood of the Shed Movement fracturing or splitting. As already discussed, this is already occurring to some extent between the national peak body organisation in Australia and some state peak body Men's Shed associations, as well as in the UK, in relation to some of its component national parts. The second possibility is 'fadeout' of the movement due to changed conditions or circumstances resulting in less interest in or perceived need for sheds. Some Men's Sheds in some communities are already closed because the early interest or fascination waned, because the people who set it up have 'moved on', or because it all became 'too hard'.

The third possibility is that Men's Shed organisations and shedders will become frustrated with lack of funding and longer-term sustainability. In some senses, many Men's Sheds have enjoyed a 'honeymoon period' with many auspice bodies, governments, communities and the media by being the 'flavour of the month'. Shed organisations beyond this period will increasingly compete for attention, resources and membership, sometimes in small and declining rural communities. They will also be pressured to produce more 'hard evidence' of impact in order to justify any or further external funding.

The fourth and final possibility is for a crisis to develop in the Men's Shed movement and peak body leadership, including a possible leadership vacuum developing with a lack of succession. There is evidence in all four countries with well-developed Shed Movements that the task of managing and juggling the common difficulties above is becoming more complex and increasing the risk of leadership burning out as a consequence.

---

[11] J. Brecher, P. Costello and B. Smith, *Globalization from Below: The Power of Solidarity*, (2nd Edn.). Cambridge Massachusetts: South End Press, 2002, 29.

Perhaps the most obvious future risk for the Shed Movement is what movement theorists call *cooptation*. This is a mechanism by which a 'movement may gain substantial benefits for its constituency, its members or its leaders, but [does] so in such a way that it ceases to be an independent force and instead comes under the control of sections of the elite'.[12] The history of other successful grassroots movements that governments have supported and thereby institutionalised is very long. By accepting men's health funds to organise the national Men's Shed Movement in Australia from 2009, AMSA arguably lost some of its independence. Similarly, taking funds for Men's Shed-related initiatives from non-government organisations like beyondblue and Movember in Australia is not without its risks. Indeed when any Men's Shed accepts money from another organisation, there are invariably some 'strings attached' in terms of expectations, accountability and/or outcomes.

There are several other ways that radical social movements can lose their way. One is by a 'leadership sell-out', that can occur if movement leaders are effectively 'bought out': with money, perks, flattery, opportunities for career advancement or other enticements, including from government or non-government organisations. Another is by 'sectarian disruption' where movements can fall prey to sects within or beyond them that attempt either to capture or destroy them. Mensheds Australia arguably posed such a sectarian risk in Australia as AMSA was forming in 2007. A possible future falling out between AMSA and several state associations in Australia or between the UK Men's Sheds association and regional Men's Shed associations in the UK might be an other example.

THE FINAL 'BIG PICTURE'

Steven Biddulph's *Manhood*[13] published in 2004 starts with an explosive opening: 'Most men don't have a life'. He was only partly correct. All men *do* have lives, but there is evidence a decade later of a general reduction in some men's worlds through midlife and some loneliness in older age beyond paid work.

The *Men's Social Connectedness* report for beyondblue in 2014 confirms the nature and extent of this loneliness, as well as its impact on men's mental health, particularly for 'men who have low levels of social support [and who are more likely to be] experiencing high levels of psychological distress'[14]. This loneliness

---

[12] Brecher, Costello and Smith, 2002, as above, 30-31.
[13] S. Biddulph, *Manhood*. London: Vermilion, 2004.
[14] beyondblue Media Release, December 11, 2014, 'Loneliness a Major Mental Health Risk for Australian Men. Research finds'.

and sense of isolation can occur both in work and beyond it. The value to all humans of having caring friends, family and community is not rocket science: it is now known to be a protective factor against depression, anxiety and suicide.

It does not have to be in a Men's Shed, but for *some* men, as this book confirms, it is a very valuable place, and for many men has become both a life changer and a lifesaver. For some men, Men's Sheds are not appropriate or comfortable. Some men and boys have had very negative experiences and socialisation as males throughout life and have come, for a range of reasons, to conform to a bleak stereotype of negative and hegemonic masculinity. Men who adopt aggressive, confrontational, disrespectful or adversarial stances in relation to women in their personal and community lives will not necessarily feel at home with all other men in a Shed. Managing and softening these stances and broadening the range of masculinities celebrated within the Shed will be an important future imperative. The final Photograph 49, of a father and son in the 'Tree of Life' Men's Shed in Belfast, is a reminder of what is possible, including between grandfathers, fathers and sons in some Sheds.

Photograph 49 Crann go Beatha ('Tree of Life') Men 's Shed, Belfast
(Geordie Murtagh with son Oisin), March 2, 2014

Perhaps a new and important frontier in Men's Shed practice might be to ask about and address the masculinities and wellbeing of boys. As I argued in 2008:

The drought of young men undertaking learning post-school is likely to persist until all post-compulsory education sectors, fields of study and professions recognize the extent of the ... change required. ... There is significant gender segmentation and gender blindness in pedagogy and practice in both work and education.[15]

It is of interest that some of the leadership for creating the first Men's Sheds (or their equivalent) in Denmark in 2015 is coming from a researcher with a focus on fatherhood in Europe.[16] Nathan Wilson, with others, have recently suggested, albeit on the basis of a very limited case study, that Men's Sheds appear to offer 'boys something different to the traditional classroom: a male-friendly environment that suits their needs, based on collaborative learning, engagement in meaningful occupations, and community service'[17]. While Australia was 'the first nation of its type to have a federal policy on the education of boys'[18], in Australia and elsewhere, most moves to 'make things right' for boys have since stalled. This is despite Marcus Weaver-Hightower's conclusion that intervention in boy's educational issues need not be either conservative or inherently dangerous, 'and can serve the interests of both boys and the society'.[19]

In conclusion, Men's Sheds are not *the* answer to everything for all men everywhere. They are a unique window into an enhanced acknowledgement of the agency and capacity of men, particularly of older men, in the company of other men. Men's Sheds allow men of all ages to celebrate and share their experiences, diverse masculinities, wisdom and experiences. In contrast, the bleak alternative is 'being a forgotten minority ... accorded a second order of importance, and, as a consequence, being misunderstood and underserved.'[20].

This book, in the wise and powerful words of adult education colleagues and friends, Antonio Fragoso from Portugal and Marvin Formosa from Malta, identifies Men's Sheds as one of:

---

[15] Barry Golding, 'Men, Boys and School: A Shed-based Learning Perspective', Paper to National Boys' Education Conference K-12, Sydney, October 12-14, 2008, 15.
[16] Dr Svend Aage Madsen.
[17] Nathan Wilson, Renie Cordier and S. Wiles-Gillan, 'Men's Sheds and Mentoring Programs: Supporting Teenage Boys' Connection with School', *International Journal of Men's Health*, 2014, 13 (2), 92-100, cited from 98.
[18] Marcus Weaver-Hightower, *The Politics of Boys' Education: Getting Boys Right*. New York: Palgrave McMillan, 2008.
[19] Cited in Foreword (by Michael Apple) to Marcus Weaver-Hightower, *The Politics of Boys' Education: Getting Boys Right*. New York: Palgrave McMillan, 2008, p. xiii.
[20] M. Formosa, A. Fragoso, S. Krasovec and T. Tambaum, Introduction, in M. Radovan & S. Krasovec (Eds.) *Older Men Learning in the Community: European Snapshots*. Ljubljana: Tisk, 2014, 9-13, cited from p. 11.

> ... an astonishing diversity of informal, non-structured spaces where older men feel secure and where various activities happen that can have a direct and indirect influence on their well-being. This obscure world has been mistreated and judged as unimportant both by research and policy, largely because [of] its unstructured character. ... [It] bluntly reminds us that community is mostly characterized by this unstructured character and diversity. ... Accepting the diverse, heterogeneous, informal spaces around us functions as a means of opening the doors to an educational vision of community.[21]

I have recently suggested that Men's Sheds are distinctive enough to constitute an alternative pedagogy[22] that I have playfully but purposefully called *shedagogy*.[23] Mark Thomson playfully but presciently created the 'Institute of Shed Science' almost two decades ago. Both of us, I would argue, are about radical educational liberation, as conceived by Ivan Illich in 1971[24]. I have recently suggested that:

> ... men's sheds are in part about older men working to build a more human and democratic society without exploitation and exclusions; ... affirming older men as learners and active beings in the process of becoming; ... bringing together existing knowledge and creating new knowledge; creating spaces of dialogue and participation and the construction of popular power through democratic organisations and coalition.[25]

As Fragoso and Formosa put it, Men's Sheds are one of many valuable and fascinating spaces, places, pedagogies and practices that remain embedded in very diverse community interstices:

---

[21] Envisaged by Freire, P., *Pedagogia del Oprimido* (*Pedagogy of the Oppressed.*) Madrid: Siglo XX1, 1985, see Fragoso, A. & Formosa, M. 'Discussion and conclusion', in M. Radovan and S. Krasovek (Eds.) *Older Men Learning in the Community*, 2014, 99-107, cited from 99-100;

[22] Pedagogy is the art or science of teaching.

[23] Barry Golding, 'Men Learning through Life: Floating the Idea of *Shedagogy*', Paper to ESREA Older Learners Network Conference, Valetta, Malta, October 23, 2014.

[24] Ivan Illich, *Deschooling Society*. Harmondsworth: Penguin Books, 1971. Based, on thinking by Freire (see D. Schugurensky, *Paulo Freire*. London: Continuum, 2011.

[25] Barry Golding, 'Older Men's Learning and Conviviality', in B. Schmidt-Hertha, S. Krasovek and M. Formosa (Eds.) *Learning across Generations in Europe*. Rotterdam: Sense.

... symbolic spaces that frame people's sense of belonging ... built from symbols that have powerful meaning in the community.[26]

Extending on the work and wise words of Bob/Raewyn Connell[27] and Marcus Weaver-Hightower, academic experts respectively in men and boys, this book provides evidence that, aside from the benefits of Men's Sheds to men's health and wellbeing, there are numerous social justice benefits of working with men *and* boys, exposing boys and men to traditionally masculine *and* non-masculine knowledges, improving their relationships with other humans, including women and other men, and thereby establishing a more just society.

POSTSCRIPT

As I completed the manuscript for this book in March 2015, I was reminded that some shedders would find this book a difficult and complex read. It is important to keep all this real. On one of my regular 100 kilometer Saturday morning bicycle rides with male friends north of where I live in rural Victoria, Australia, we by chance came across two men sitting outside the Newstead Men's Shed in a small rural town of only 500 people. The men eagerly and proudly showed us their Shed. We came away with a simple leaflet[28] about their Shed including 'What we do' and 'Why we do it' on the six days a week the Shed is open. Their logo is a shed with a hammer and nails above the door and there was a warm 'welcoming cuppa' inside. On the front of their leaflet is the slogan that greatly simplifies this book and the final big picture: "Having fun, making stuff, fixing stuff, talking about stuff, or doing nothing. Together". It's about enjoying and benefiting from the Company of Men. It's what Dick McGowan envisaged and it's that simple.

---

[26] Antonio Fragoso and Marvin Formosa, 2014, *as above,* 100.
[27] Robert W. Connell, 'Teaching the Boys: New Research on Masculinity, and Gender Strategies for Schools', *Teachers College Record*, 98 (2): 206-235, 1996.
[28] 'Newstead Men's Shed' Leaflet, November 2014, Victoria. Australia.

Appendices

APPENDIX 1 INDIVIDUAL ACKNOWLEDGEMENTS

My sincere thanks to all who assisted with advice, contributions and checking of the manuscript, listed by name by country.

For advice about Men's Shed development nationally, I am indebted to the following people from the national associations in *Australia* (AMSA): David Helmers, Gary Green, Liz MacDonald, Mel White; *Ireland* (IMSA): Anne McDonnell, John Evoy, Veronica Banville; the *UK* (UKMSA): Mike Jenn (England), Jason Schroeder (Scotland), Rhodri Walters (Wales); *New Zealand* (MENZSHED NZ): Neil Bruce, Ray Hall, Roger Bowman, Peter Blackler.

The following people provided essential information about the history of Men's Sheds in Part 2 from: **Australia:** *South Australia*: Helen and Peter Barclay, Dawn Juers, Robyn Lockwood, Alison Herron, Maxine Chaseling (Kitto), Heather Eglinton, Alli Pollard, Anthony Eyre, Mark Thomson, Jean Link, Leon Earle, Gary Misan, Brian Fenton, Bruce Lindqvist, Rob Jervois, Sharon Zacher, Jim Forbes, John Lambert, Keith Bettany, Jeff Whitbread, Allen Robins, Jayne Lane, Andrew Keightley, Jo Smith, Peter Cordaro, Karen Zacher-Partington, Ken Brown, Barry Heffernan, Russell Vine, Patch Campbell, Denise Fairbairn, John Monten, Tanya Short, Barry Fowler, Heather Hewitt, Bronwyn Filsell, Leanne Tripodi, Neil Edwards, Anne O'Reilly, Mervyn Chilcott, Karen Wright, Bryce Routley, Evan Reay; *New South Wales*: David Helmers, Ted Donnelly, Ruth van Herk, Bob Nelson, John Kent, Kimberley Glavas, Hugh Wright, Stuart Holmes, Jill Stowe, Anthony Brown, John Macdonald, Ray Cawthorne, Philip Diprose, Peter Torenbeek; *Victoria*: Gary Green, Ruth McGowan, Jean Courtney, David Reid, Neil Wakeman, Ric Blackburn, Paul Sladdin, Jackie Slade, John Quinlan, Brian Ward, Anthony Lai, Lyn Kinder, Barry Sproull, David Atkinson: *Western Australia*: Damien Dixon, Bill Johnstone, Brett Pollock, John Putland, Peter Robinson, Anne Brandis, Jeff Seaby, Clare Smith; *Tasmania*: John Waters, Jonathon Bedlow, Peter Shelley, Lester Jones, Helen Manser, Eleanor Taylor, Trish O'Duffy, Kate Beer, Allister Martin. *Queensland:* Graeme Curnow, John Bruggerman, John Murdoch, Don Scott, David Agnew, Marjorie McNamara. **UK:** *England*: Mike Jenn, John Harris, David George; *Scotland*: Jason Schroeder; *Wales*: Rhodri Walters, Robert Narayan-Taylor; **Ireland:** John Evoy, Anne McDonnell; **New Zealand:** Neil

Bruce, Ray Hall, Bernard McMillan, Roger Bowman; **Canada:** Doug Mackie, Gene Mitran, Arthur Post, Corey Mackenzie. **Denmark:** Svend Aage Madsen.

The following people provided valuable information, photographs and advice for the Men's Shed case studies in Part 3, from: **Australia:** David Helmers, Liz MacDonald, Roger Greenan, Kerry Henry, Monica Chisholm, Chuck Peters, Brian Walters, Doug Jenkins, Jon Eaton, Colin Heath, Andrew McGlinchy, Brett Pollock, Alan Scott, Bob Long, John Benyon, Rob and Olya Willis; **Ireland:** John Evoy, Anne McDonnell, Lucia Carragher, Veronica Banville, Ruth Smith, Andrew Kinsella, Kay O'Connor, George Kelly, Eva Beirne, Alexey Janes, Eoin McAnuff, Frank McNamara, Michael Cass, Stephen Wallace, Gerry McParland, Michael Tiernan, John Rogers, Bill Lockhart, Tom Lennon, Barry Semple, John Molloy; **UK:** Mike Jenn, Jason Schroeder, Debbie Chegwen, Luke Conlon, Peter Gallagher, Simon Poole, Lyndsey Wood, Malcolm Fallow, Julie Cowdry, Darren Riley, Andy Wood, Mick Condon, Christopher Chidsey, Annette Yoosefinejad, Claire Shelton, John Leigh, Martin Gamester, Jo Hobbett, Chris Lee; **New Zealand:** Neil Bruce, Ray Hall, James Sunderland, Bernard McMillan, John Hesketh, Dave Ryder, Philip Bradshaw, Bill Rogers, John Bush, Colin Hall, Lorraine Hamilton, Neville Dell, Wendy Rendle, Mike Parker, Peter Lewis, Peter Blackler, Bob Norrish, Trevor Scott, Neil McArthur, Neil Bennett, Alan Kisell, Ross McEwan, Ian Cameron, Archie Kerr.

I gratefully acknowledge the support and ideas from the following colleagues and friends who were helpful in 'carving out' this area of research, some going back almost two decades: from **Australia:** Dr Eric McClellan, Dr Annette Foley, Dr Mike Brown, Dr Jack Harvey, Adele Echter, Dr Helen Kimberley, Christine Hayes, Kevin Vallence, Soapy Vallance, Prof Lawrie Angus, Prof John McDonald, Prof Erica Smith, Dr Rick Hayes, Dr Anthony Brown, Prof John Macdonald, Dr Peter Willis, Tass Mousaferiades, Gib Wettenhall, Sally Thompson; **Ireland:** Dr Rob Mark, Dr Lucia Carragher, Dr Ted Fleming; **UK:** Dr Peter Lavender, Dr Allan Tuckett, Dr Veronica McGivney, Jim Soulsby, Prof Peter Jarvis, Dr Brendan Hoare, Prof Sue Jackson; **New Zealand:** Prof Brian Findsen; **Portugal:** Dr António Fragoso; **Slovenia:** Dr Sabina Jelenc Krašovec; **Finland**: Arja Mielonen-Walker.

My particular thanks to Chris Bettle for a thorough edit of the draft manuscript, and well as to Patrick Hope and Professor John McDonald for critical comments. Those who helped prepare the global Men's Shed data for mapping included Gavin Myers and Dajarra Golding. Robert Milne and Andrew MacLeod (CeRDI: Centre for eResearch and Digital Innovation, Federation University Australia) generously created all maps used in this book.

APPENDIX 2 GLOBAL MEN'S SHED LIST

This list includes the names of all Men's Sheds globally to May 2015 (total 1,416). The lists are sorted alphabetically by the registered Shed name: in Australia (933), the Island of Ireland (273: Republic of Ireland and Northern Ireland), the United Kingdom (16 in Northern Ireland, 148 elsewhere in the UK) and New Zealand (57). A locality has been added in brackets for Sheds where this is not clear in the registered Shed name or where there is more than one Shed either by that name or in that locality. The five Men's Sheds that were open to May 2015 in Canada, Sweden and Denmark are also listed. The 16 Sheds in Northern Ireland that are duplicated in the UK list are *italicised* on the UK list.

Australia: 2322 Men's Shed (Thornton), Aberdeen Men's Shed, Access Men's Shed (Woodridge), ACT Model Railway Society Inc. (Macquarie), Adelong Men's Shed, AFS Men's Shed (Rockhampton), Agnes Water / 1770 Dinky Di Community Men's Shed, Airds/Bradbury Men's Shed, Akoonah Park Men's Shed (Berwick), Alamein Men's Shed, Albany Men's Shed, Albion Park Men's Shed Inc., Aldgate Men's Shed Inc., Aldinga Bay Community Shed (Aldinga Beach), Alexandra Community Shed, Alexandra Hills Men's Shed (Capalaba), Allora Men's Shed, Altona Men's Shed Inc., Andy's Community Shed (Kingston, 5275, SA), Anglesea & Districts Men's Shed, Appin Men's Shed, Arana Hills Men's Shed, Ararat Men's Shed Inc., Ardlethan Men's Shed, Armadale Community Men's Shed Inc., (Kelmscott) Armadale Home Help (Men in Shed Program), Armfield Slip and Boatshed - Armfield Wooden Boats Inc. (Goolwa), Armidale Men's Shed Inc., Arncliffe Men's Shed, Arrunga Community Men's Shed, Artistic Blacksmiths (Blackwood), Ashgrove Men's Shed, Auburn City Men's Shed Inc. (Granville), Augusta Men's Shed, Avoca Men's Shed, Babana Aboriginal Men's Group Shed (Redfern), Babinda Men's Shed Inc., Badger Creek and District Men's Shed Inc., Bairnsdale Men's Shed, Balaklava Neighbourhood Shed, Ballan Community Shed, Ballarat Community Men's Shed, Ballarat East Community Men's Shed, Ballina Community Men's Shed, Balmoral Men's Shed, Balranald Men's Shed Inc., Bangalow Lions Men's Shed, Banksia Villages Men's Shed (Broulee), Bankstown Men's Shed, Bannockburn & District Men's Shed, Banyule Men's Shed (Heidelberg Heights), Baranduda Men's Shed, Barcaldine Men's Shed Inc., Barcoo Retirement Village Inc. Men's Shed (Blackall), Bargara Men's Shed Inc. (Kalkie), Bargumar Men's Shed (Caboolture), Barham Koondrook Men's Shed, Barmera Community Men's Shed, Barossa Men's Shed (Kapunda), Barossa Valley Tinkers Shed (Nurioopta), Barraba Men's Shed Inc., Bateau Bay Men's Shed, Batemans Bay Men's Shed, Bathurst Men's Shed Inc., Bauple Community Shed Inc., Bay & Basin Men's

Shed (Sanctuary Point), Bayside Men's Shed Group (Beaumauris), Bayside Men's Shed Inc. (Beaumaris), Bayside Uniting Church Men's Shed (Wynnum Plaza), Beaufort Men's Shed, Beechworth Men's Shed, Bega Men's Shed Inc., Belconnen Community Men's Shed, Bellingen Men's Shed, Belmont Men's Shed & Community Garden, Ben's Shed Inc. (Yarra Junction), Benalla Aviation Museum and Men's Shed Inc., Benalla Men's Shed Inc., Bendigo Men in Sheds, Bentmoor Community Men's Shed Inc. (Bentleigh), Berrigan Menshed Inc., Berry Men's Shed Inc., Berwick District Woodworkers Club Inc., Bicton Men's Shed (Palmyra), BIG4 Casino Resort, Biggenden Men's Shed Inc., Bindoon Men's Shed Inc., Bingara Men's Shed, Binnaway Men's Shed Inc., Birchip Men's Shed, Bisdee Men's Shed (Glenorchy), Blackheath Area Men's Shed Inc., Blayney Shire Community Men's Shed, Blokes Shed Hallidays Point, Blue Gum Hills Men's Shed Inc. (Wallsend), Boddington Community Resource Centre Men's Shed, Bombala Platypus Men's Shed, Bonnells Bay Salvation Army Men's Shed, Boolarra Men's Shed, Boort Men's Shed, Borenore/Nashdale Community Men's Shed (West Orange), Bouldercombe & District Men's Shed Inc., Bourke Men's Shed, Bowden Brompton Community Shed, Bowen Men's Shed Inc., Bowral Men's Shed Inc., Boyne - Tannum Men's Shed, Boyup Brook Men's Shed Inc., BP Men's Shed (Breakfast Point), Braidwood Men's Shed, Branxton-Greta Men's Shed Inc., Braybrook Men's Shed Inc., Break O'Day Woodcraft Guild and Men's Shed (St Mary's), Break the Cycle Glenquarie Men's Shed (Macquarie Fields), Bridgetown's Men in Sheds, Bridport Community Men's Shed, Bright United Men's Shed, Brimbank Men's Shed, Broadford Men's Shed, Brookton Men's Shed Inc., Broome Men's Shed (Sunshine), Bruce Rock Men's Shed Inc., Bruny Island Men's Shed (Alonnah), Bruthen Men's Shed, Bu Di Men's Shed (Beswick), Buderim Men's Shed, Bulahdelah War Memorial Hall Men's Shed, Bulli Woonona Men's Shed, Bunbury Men's Shed, Bundaberg Central Men's Shed Assoc. Inc., Bundanoon Men's Shed Inc., Bundeena Mensshed Inc., Buninyong Men's Shed, Bunurong Men's Shed Pakenham Inc., Burdekin Men's Shed Association Inc., Burleigh Community Men's Shed, Burnie Tool Shed, Busselton Men's Shed, Cairns Men's Shed Inc., Caloundra Men's Shed, Camden Community Centre Men's Shed (Camden Park), Camden Men's Shed (Harrington Park), Campbell Town & Districts Men's Shed, Camperdown Men's Shed, Canning Community Men's Shed (Shelley), Canowindra Men's Shed Inc., Capel Men's Shed (Ger0lup), Capricorn Coast Men's Shed @ carv (Yeppoon), Cardiff District Men's Shed, Cardinia Men's Shed, Cargo Men's Shed Inc., Carlton Men's Shed, Carnarvon Community Men's Group, Carrum Downs Men's Shed Inc., Casino Community Men's Shed Inc., Castlemaine Men's Shed, Ceduna and

Districts Men's Shed Inc., Central Coast Community Shed (Ulverstone), Central Highlands Community Men's Shed (Franklin), Central West Men's Shed Cevantes Inc., Cessnock Men's Shed & Community Garden Inc., Chadstone Indoor Aviation Group, Channel Men's Shed (Margate), Chapman Valley Menshed (Nabawa), Charleville Community Men's Shed Association, Charlton Men's Shed Inc., Charters Towers Regional Men's Shed, Chelsea Men's Shed Inc., Childers District Men's Shed Association Inc., Chiltern & District Men's Shed, Chinchilla Men's Shed Inc., Christmas Island Men's Shed, City of Canada Bay Men's Shed Inc. (Concord), City Side Men's Shed (New Farm), Clare Men's Shed, Clarence River U3A Men's Shed (Maclean), Clem's Shed (Minlaton), Clermont Men's Shed Inc., Cleveland Uniting Church Men's Shed, Clifton Springs Community Men's Shed Inc., Clontarf Community Men's Shed, Club Shed Cooktown, Clunes Men's Shed, Cobbers from the Creek (Cabbage Tree Creek), Cobden Men's Shed, Cobram Men's Shed, Cockburn Community Men's Shed, Coffs Harbour Men's Shed Inc., Colac Men's Shed, Coleambally Men's Shed Inc., Coleraine Men's Shed, Coles Bay Men's Shed Inc., Colo Vale Men's Shed, Community Men's Shed Oatlands, Community Workshed Inc. (Moruya), Coniston Men's Shed, Coolah Men's Shed, Coolamon Men's Shed Inc., Coolum Men's Shed Inc., Cooma Men's Shed, Coomba Men's Shed, Coonamble Community Shed, Coorong Men's Shed (Meningie), Copper City Men's Shed - Cobar, Copper Coast Community Shed (Kadina), Coral Coast Men's Shed (Bagara), Corinella District Men's Shed & Woodies Group, Corio Model Railway Club Men's Shed, Corner Inlet Men's Shed (Foster), Corrimal Community Men's Shed Inc., Corryong Men's Shed Inc., Cowan Men's Shed Inc., Cowra Men's Shed Inc., Cranbourne Community House Men's Shed, Cranbrook Community Men's Shed Inc., Creswick Men's Shed, Crookwell Community Men's Shed Inc., Crowley Men's Shed (Ballina), Croydon Hills Men's Shed, Croydon Men's Shed, Cudal & District Men's Shed, Culburra Beach Orient Point Men's Shed, Culcairn Men's Shed, Cunderdin Men's Shed Inc., Cunnamulla Community Men's Shed Inc., CY O'Connor Men's Shed (Boulder), Dahlsford Grove Lifestyle Village (Port Macquarie), Dalyellup Seasons Shed Inc., Dandenong Men's Shed, Darebin Men's Shed, Darlington Point Men's Shed Inc., Darwin Men's Shed (Nightcliff), Day Centre Men's Shed (Port Lincoln), Dayboro Men's Shed Inc., Daylesford Men's Shed, Deception Bay Men's Shed (Burpengary), Deniliquin Menshed Inc., Denman & District Men's Shed Inc. (Sandy Hollow), Derby Men's Shed, Dereel and Surrounding Communities Men's Shed, Derwent Valley Men's Shed Inc. (New Norfolk), Diamond Creek Men's Shed, Dimboola Men's Outdoor Group, Dingley Village Men's Shed, Dog House (Geeveston), Donald Men's Shed,

Dongara Men In Sheds Inc., Donnybrook RSL Men's Shed Inc., Dookie Men's Shed, Dorrigo Men's Shed, Doutta Galla Aged Services (Footscray), Doveton Men's Shed, Drouin Men's Shed Inc., Dubbo Community Men's Shed Inc., Dumbleyung and District Men's Shed, Dungog Menshed Inc., Dunoon Men's Shed, Dunsborough Community Men's Shed, Dural Men's Shed, East Hills District Men's Shed Assoc. Inc. (Panania), East Tamar Men's Shed (Mowbray), Echuca Moama Men's Shed Inc., Eden Men's Shed Inc., Edenhope Men's Shed Inc., Edgewater Village Men's Shed (Bli Bli), Elermore Vale Men's Shed, Elizabeth House - Shed Program (Noarlunga Centre), Ellenbrook & Districts Men's Shed, Elliston Men's Shed, Eltham Men's Shed Inc., Emu Park & District Men's Activity Shed, Erina Community Men's Shed, Eudunda Street Stafford Community Men's Shed, Euroa Men's Shed Inc., Evans Head RSL & Community Men's Shed, Exeter Men's Shed, Fassifern Community Men's Shed (Kalbar), Fiddlers Men's Shed Inc. (Mosman), Finley Menshed Inc., Fish Creek RSL Men's Shed, Flowerdale Men's Shed, Foothills Men's Shed Inc. (Forrestfield), Forbes Community Menshed Inc., Forestville Community Shed, Forrest Men's Shed (Manuka), Forrest Men's Shed Inc., Frankston Men's Shed, Fremanshed Inc. (White Gum Valley), Furlough House Men's Shed Inc. (Narrabeen), Furneaux Islands Community Shed (Flinders Island), Ganmain & District Men's Shed, Geelong Community Men's Shed, Geelong East Men's Shed (Norlane), George Cross Falcons Club (Cringila), George's Shed (Mount Isa), Gilbert Valley Men's Shed Inc. (Riverton), Gilgandra Men's Shed, Gin Gin Menshed Inc., Gingin Men's Shed Inc. (Gin Gin), Giralang-Kaleen Men's Shed, Gisborne Men's Shed, Gladstone Men's Shed Assoc., Glasshouse Country Menshed Inc. (Beerwah), Glen Innes Men's Shed, Glenroy Men's Shed, Gloucester Men's Shed, Goodwin Ainslie Men's Shed, Goodwin Monash Men's Shed, Goolawah Men's Shed (Crescent Head), Goomalling Men's Shed & Prostate Group Inc., Goroke Men's Shed, Gosford City Model Railroad Club Inc., Gosford Community Men's Shed, Gosnells Community Men's Shed Inc. (Thornlie), Goulburn Men's Shed Inc., Gracemere Men's Shed, Grafton U3A Men's Shed, Granville Men's Shed, Grawin-Glengarry- Sheepyards Opal Fields Men's Shed, Green Head Mensshed Inc., Greenbank RSL Men's Shed, Greenvale Men's Shed Inc., Grenfell Men's Shed Inc., Griffith Shed for Men, Gulgong Men's Shed Inc., Gundagai Men's Shed, Gundy Men's Shed Inc. (Goondiwindi), Gungahlin Men's Group (Ngunnawal), Gurama Yani U Inc. For All Men (Fitzroy Crossing), GV'S Men's Shed (Port Macquarie), Gympie Men's Shed, Hamilton Men's Shed, Hampstead Mule Shed (Northfield), Harrington Men's Shed Inc., Harrow & District Men's Shed, Harvey Men's Shed, Hastings Men's Shed, Hawkins Masonic Village Men's

Shed (Edgeworth), Heart & Soul Menshed (Forrestdale), Henty Men's Shed Inc., Herbert River Men's Shed Inc. (Allingham), Herberton Men's Shed, Hervey Bay Men's Shed, Heywood Men's Shed Inc., Hibbard Maritime Men's Shed (Port Macquarie), High Country Men's Shed (Omeo), Highfields Men's Shed, Hills Men's Shed (Cockatoo), Hillston Men's Shed Assoc., Hillview Bunyip Men's Shed, Hobsons Bay Men's Shed (Altona), Hocky's Community Shed (Snowtown), Hopetoun & District Men's Shed (Vic.), Hopetoun Men in Shed's Inc. (WA), Hornsby Berowra Men's Shed, Horsham Men's Shed, Howlong Men's Shed, Howrah Men's Shed Inc., Hume Men's Shed (Craigieburn), Hume Men's Shed (Sunbury) Inc., Hunters Hill Ryde Men's Shed, Iluka-Woombah Men's Shed, Inala PCYC Men's Shed, Indooroopilly Men's Shed Inc., Ingkintja Male Health Men's Shed (Alice Springs), Innisfail & District Men's Shed Inc., Inverell Community Shed Inc., Inverloch Men's Shed, Iona West Men's Shed, Ipswich Men's Shed Inc., Ipswich Young Men's Shed, Jamestown Men's Shed Inc., Jerilderie Men's Shed Inc., Jettys By The Lake Men's Shed (Windang), JewishCare Men's Shed (Dianella), Joondalup Men's Shed, Julatten Men's Shed, Junee Men's Shed Inc., Jurien Bay Community Men's Shed, Kalamunda Men's Shed, Kanahooka Men's Shed, Kandos/Rylstone Men's Shed Inc., Kangaroo Flat Men's Shed, Kaniva Men's Shed, Karingal Men's' Shed (Devonport), Karuah River Men's Shed, Katanning Men's Shed Inc., Katoomba Men's Shed, Kellerberrin Community Men's Shed, Ken's Shed (Heyfield), Kendall Men's Shed, Kenthurst Community Men's Shed Inc., Kentish Community Men's Shed (Sheffield), Kew Neighbourhood Learning Centre Men's Shed, Keysmen Shed (Keysborough), Kiama Uniting Church Men's Shed, Kilmore Men's Shed, Kim's Toy Boys Inc. (Erskine), Kincumber Men's Shed, King Island Men's Shed (Currie), King Valley Community Men's Shed (Moyhu), Kinglake Ranges Men's Shed (Kinglake), Kondinin Men's Shed Inc., Kooweerup Men's Shed, KTY Men's Shed (Kununoppin), Ku-ring-gai Community Workshop "The Shed" Inc. (Gordon), Kulin Men's Shed Inc., Kuranda Men's Shed Inc., Kurri Kurri Community Centre Inc., Kwinana Community Group, Kyabram District Men's Shed Inc., Kyneton Men's Shed Inc., Kyogle District Men's Shed, Labertouche & District Men's Shed, Lake Boga Men's Shed, Lake Cargelligo & District Men's Shed Inc., Lake George Men's Shed (Bungendore), Lake Grace Community Men's Shed, Lake Macquarie Heritage Boatshed (Toronto), Lakes Entrance Men's Shed, Lakeview Men's Shed Assoc. Inc. (Thornlands), Lalor and District Men's Shed Inc., Lancefield Men's Shed, Lane Cove Men's Shed, Lang Lang Men's Shed, Langwarrin Men's Shed Inc., Lara & District Men's Shed, Laurieton Men's Shed Inc., Laverton Men's Shed Incorporated, Leeton Shire Men's Shed,

Leichhardt-One Mile-Wulkuraka Men's Shed (West Ipswich), Leongatha Men's Shed, Leopold Men's Shed Inc., Leschenault & District Men's Shed (Australind), Lightning Ridge Men's Shed, Lismore Community Shed (NSW), Lismore Men's Shed Inc. (Vic.), Lithgow District Men's Shed Association Inc., Liverpool District Men's Shed (Greenfields Park). Lockhart Men's Shed Inc., Lockridge Community Garden and Shed, Lockyer Valley Community Activities Shed Inc. (Gatton), Logan City Community Menshed Inc. (Slacks Creek), Logan Village Men's Shed, Longford Men's Shed, Longreach Mensshed Inc., Lorne and District Men's Shed Inc., Loxton Community Men's Shed, Macarthur Men's Shed, Magnetic Island Men's Shed Inc., Maitland Men's Shed Inc., Majura Men's Shed (Dixon), Maldon Men's Shed, Maleny and District Men's Shed, Manildra Men's Shed Inc., Manilla Men's Shed Inc., Manji Men's Shed (Manjimup), Manning Men's Shed Inc., Manningham Men's Shed (Doncaster East), Manno Men's Shed (Mannering Park), Mannum Community Men's Shed, Mansfield Community Men's Shed, Mapleton Men's Shed, Marlin Coast Men's Shed (Smithfield), Maroochy Men's Shed (Maroochydore), Marrickville Men's Shed, Mary MacKillop Outreach Men's Shed (Haberfield), Mary Valley Men's Shed (Kandanga), Maryborough Men's Shed, Marysville Triangle Community Men's Shed Inc., McIvor Neighbourhood House (Heathcote), Meadowlands Men's Shed (Carindale), Meeniyan and District RSL Men's Shed, Melba Men's Shed Inc., Melbourne Men's Shed, Melton Men's Shed, Men In The Tin Shed (Kingaroy), Men-in-dee Shed (Menindee), Men's Shed Merimbula Inc., Men's Shed @ Moree, Men's Shed 100 Inc. (Middle Park), Men's Shed Airlie Beach Inc., Men's Shed at St. Andrews, Men's Shed Carina Inc., Men's Shed Dalby, Men's Shed Junction Village, Men's Shed Labrador Inc., Men's Shed Numurkah Inc., Men's Shed Pomona, Men's Shed Taree Showground, Men's Shed West Leederville, Men's Shed West Wyalong, Menai Men's Shed, Men's Bizz (Mowbray), Men's Shed All Saints Selby Inc., Men's Shed Edmonton, Men's Shed Narellan Inc., Menshed Wagga Wagga, Mensheds Bendigo Inc., Mensheds Narrogin Inc., Merredin Community Men's Shed, Merriwa Tourist Welcoming Centre & Men's Shed, Midland Men's Shed Inc., Millicent Men's Shed, Milpara Men's Shed (Korumburra), Milton Ulladulla Men's Shed Inc., Minyip Men's Shed, Mirboo North Men's Shed, Mitcham Community Shed, Moe Life Skills Community Centre, Molong Men's Shed Inc., Monash Men's Shed (Glen Waverley), Monbulk District Men's Shed Inc., Montrose & District Men's Shed, Moonee Valley Men's Shed, Moora Men's Shed Inc., Moorebank Men's Shed Inc., Mooroopna Men's Shed, Mordialloc Men's Shed, Mornington Men's Shed, Mornington Railway Preservation Society Inc., Morpeth Men's Shed Inc.,

Morrison Men's Shed (Mt Evelyn), Mortdale Men's Shed, Mortlake Men's Shed, Morwell Men's Shed, Mosman Men's Shed Inc., Mosman Park Men's Community Shed, Moss Vale Men's Shed, Mossman Men's Shed, Moulamein Menshed and Rice Museum Inc., Mount Barker Men's Shed, Mount Gambier Men's Shed, Mount Gravatt Men's Shed Inc., Mount Pleasant Men's Shed, Mt Beauty and District Men's Shed, Mt Keira Scout Camp Men's Shed (Port Kembla), Muddy Creek Boating & Amateur Fishing Assoc. (Sans Souci), Mudflat Toys (Coorparoo), Mudgee Men's Shed, Mukinbudin 1950's Working Farm Shed, Mulgrave Community Shed, Mullum SEED Men's Shed (Brunswick Meads), Mullumbimby Men's Shed Inc., Mundaring Community Men's Shed, Murgon Men's Shed, Murrabit Men's Shed Inc., Murramarang Men's Shed, Murraylands Community Men's Shed (Murray Bridge), Murrumbateman Men's Shed, Murrurundi Community Men's Shed, Murwillumbah Community Men's Shed, Muswellbrook Men's Shed, Myrtleford Men's Shed Inc., Nagambie Lakes Men's Shed, Nambour Men's Shed, Nambucca Heads Men's Shed, Nambucca Valley Community Men's Shed (Macksville), Nanango Community Men's Shed, Napranum Men's Shed, Naracoorte District Men's Shed Inc., Narembeen Community Shed and Gallery Inc., Narooma Men's Shed, Narrabri Men's Shed Inc., Narrandera Shed for Men, Narromine Men's Shed Inc., Natimuk Men's Shed, Neerim District Community House & Men's Shed Inc., Nelson Men's Shed, Nepean Men's Shed Inc. (Blaxland), Nerang Men's Shed Inc., Newcastle Men's Shed, New Peninsula Men's Shed Mt Martha, Newstead Men's Shed, Newtown Green Men's Workshed Inc. (Windsor Downs), Nhill Men's Shed, Nimmitabel Men's Shed, Noosa Arts Theatre Inc., Noosa Domain Village Shed, Noosa Men's Shed, North Coastal Women's Shed (Clarkson), North Sydney Men's Shed, Northam Men's Shed Inc., Northcliffe Men's Shed, Northcott Men's Shed (Surry Hills), Northern Beaches Community Men's Shed (Manly), Northern Men's Shed Inc. (Cragieburn), Northern Men's Shed Inc. (Wangara), Northern Peninsula Area Menshed (Bamaga), Nowa Nowa Shed, Nowra Men's Shed, Nundah Men's Shed, Nyah District Men's Shed Inc., Nyngan Men's Shed, Nyora Men's Shed, Oakdale Men's Shed Inc., Oaklands & District Men's Shed Inc., Oberon Men's Shed, Ocean Grove & District Men's Shed, Old Bar Men's Shed Inc., Old Hangar Men's Shed (East Grovedale), OMNI Recreation Men's Shed (Tamworth), Operation Flinders Foundation (Port Adelaide), Orange Men's Shed Inc., Orara Historical Machinery Museum Inc., Orbost Men's Shed, Ouyen District Men's Shed Inc., Oxenford Men's Shed Inc., Oxford Community Men's Shed, Palm Beach Men's Shed, Palmerston Men's Shed, Panna Men's Shed (Pannawonica), Para Men's Shed (Paraburdoo), Park Ridge Adventist Community Centre Men's Shed,

Parramatta District Men's Shed Inc. (Pendle), Parramatta Northmead Community Men's Shed, Paynesville Men's Shed, Peak Hill Men's Shed, Pelican Shores Estate Residents Workshop (Leopold), Peninsula Men's Shed - Bethanga Inc., Peninsula North Men's Shed, Peninsula Woodturners Guild Inc., Peninsular Community Men's Shed (Somersby), Penrith Community Men's Shed, Peterborough Men's Shed, Phillip Island R.S.L. Community Men's Shed (Cowes), Pimpama Men's Shed Inc. (Upper Coomera), Pine Rivers Men's Shed Inc. (Petrie), Pines Community Men's Shed (Frankston North), Pittsworth & District Men's Shed Inc., Plantagenet Men's Shed Inc., Playford Men's Shed (Davoren Park), Pooraka Farm Men's Shed, Port Augusta Men's Shed, Port Broughton Community Workshop, Port Cygnet Men's Shed, Port Fairy Men's Shed, Port Lincoln Men's Shed, Port Phillip Men's Shed Assoc. (Albert Park), Port Pirie Men's Shed, Port Sorell Men's Shed, Port Wakefield Men's Shed, Portland Men's Shed Inc. (NSW), Portland Men's Shed Inc. (Vic.), Pottsville and District Men's Shed Inc., Proserpine Nursing Home, Prospect Men's Shed, Pyrmont Ultimo Glebe Men's Shed Incorporated, Quaama Men's Shed, Quambatook Men's Shed, Queanbeyan Men's Shed, Queenscliffe & District Men's Shed, Queenstown Men's Shed Inc., Quirindi Men's Shed, Quorn Men's Shed, RAFT Men's Shed (Rowville), Rainbow Men's Shed, Ravenshoe Men's Shed, Raymond Terrace Men's Shed, Redcliffe Community Men's Shed Inc., Redhead Men's Shed, Redland Bay Men's Shed Inc., RGE Men's Shed Inc. (Gosnells), Riddells Creek Men's Shed, Ridgewood Village Men's Shed Inc., Ridley Road Community Men's Shed (Bridgeman Downs), Ringwood Men's Shed Inc., River City Men's Shed Inc. (Toombul), Riverside Men's Shed (Newstead. Tas.), Riverstone Men's Shed, Rochester Men's Shed, Rockhampton Men's Shed Inc., Rockingham Community Shed for Men Inc., Rocky River Men's Shed (Laura), Roger May Machinery Museum (Pinjarra), Roleystone Men's Community Shed Inc., Roma Community Menshed Inc., Rosebery Men's Shed, Rosedale Men's Shed, Rosefield Men's Shed @ Highgate Park (Fullarton), Rosewood's Men's Shed, Rupanyup and District Men's Shed, Rushworth Community House Men's Shed, Russell Island Men's Shed, Rutherglen Men's Shed, Safety Beach - Dromana Men's Shed Inc., Salamander Men's Shed, Sale Men's Shed, Samford Area Men's Shed Inc., San Remo Community Men's Shed, Sanctuary Point Men's Shed (St Georges Basin), Sandgate & District Men's Shed, Sarina & District Community Men's Shed, Sea Lake Men's Shed, Sebastopol Men's Shed, Sedan Historic Enthusiasts Den Inc., Serpentine Jarrahdale Community Shed, Seymour Men's Shed, Shed West Community Men's Shed Inc. (Kenmore), Shepparton Men's Shed, Shoalhaven Heads Men's Shed, Simpson Men's Shed, Singleton Men's Shed, Snowy River

Men's Shed Inc. (Jindabyne), Social Inclusion & Wellbeing Men's Shed (Croydon), Somerset Community Men's Shed (Wivenhoe Pocket), Somerset Community Shed (Burnie), Sorell Men's Shed, South City Men's Shed (Wagga Wagga) Inc., South Dubbo Veterans & Community Men's Shed, Southern Community Project Group (Adelaide), Southlakes Men's Shed Inc. (Wyee Point), Spring Bay Maritime & Discovery Centre Community Shed (Triabunna), Springbrook Men's Shed, Springvale Multicultural Men's Shed, St Arnaud Community Men's Shed, St George Community Men's Shed Inc. (Qld.), St George Men's Shed (Penshurst, NSW), St Helens Men's Shed, St John's Oxley Community Men's Shed (Sherwood), St Leonards Men's Shed, St Luke's Highton Men's Shed, Stamford Park Men's Shed (Rowville), Stanhope & District Men's Shed, Stanthorpe and District Men's Shed, Station Street Men's Shed (Cannington), Stawell Men's Shed, Stirling Community Men's Shed, Stratford Men's Shed, Stroud & District Men's Shed, Stuarts Point Men's Shed Inc., Subiaco Community Men's Shed Inc., Sunbury Men's Shed, Sunnybank District Community Men's Shed Inc., Sunraysia Men's Shed Inc. (Mildura), Sunshine Valley Men's Shed (West Woombye), Sussex Inlet Men's Shed, Swansea & District Community Men's Shed, SWS Bonnyrigg Men's Shed, T.O.Y.S. Shed (Clarence Park Community Centre (Blackforest), Tablelands Men's Shed Atherton, Tablelands Men's Shed Dimbulah District Inc., Tablelands Men's Shed Mareeba, TAD Disability Services – HUNTER (Adamstown), Tahmoor Uniting Men's Shed, Talbingo Men's Shed Inc., Tamborine Mountain Community Men's Shed Assoc., Tarcutta Men's Shed Inc., Taree Manning River Men's Shed Inc., Tasman Street Men's Shed, TasmanManShed Inc. (Nubeena), Tatura Men's Shed, Tea Gardens - Hawks Nest Men's Shed, Temora Shed 4 Men Inc., Tenterfield Men's Shed, Terang Men's Shed Group Inc., Terrigal Men's Shed Inc., Texas Men's Shed Inc., The Baradine Rusty Club Inc., The Bay Island Men's Shed (Macleay Island), The Booleroo & Districts Men's Shed (Booleroo Centre), The Booringa Blokes Men's Shed Inc. (Mitchell), The Brisbane TRAM Shed (Ferny Hills), The Burra Men's Shed, The Carpenters Workshop (Elanora), The Cowaramup Bull Shed, The Curry Men's Shed (Cloncurry), The Dover Community Workshop, The Entrance Men's Shed, The Forest Community Men's Shed (Belrose), The Green Shed at Gumeracha, The Hills Men's Shed (Castle Hill), The Hub (Brooklyn Park), The Hut Community Shed (Aldgate), The Inglewood Mates Shed Inc., The Kapunda Shed Inc., The Lakeside Men's Shed @ Milang, The Laurels Men's Shed (Bacchus Marsh), The Ltyenties Men Shed (Alice Springs), The Menshed Geraldton Inc., The Mount Morgan Men's Shed Inc., The Mukinbudin 1950's Working Farm Shed, The Nathalia & District Men's

Shed, The Port MacDonnell & District Men's Shed Inc., The Quinty Men's Shed Inc. (Uranquinty), The Red Shed (Woodside), The Rock & Districts Men's Shed Inc., The Shack - San Remo Men's Shed, The SHED (Georgetown, Qld.), The Shed @ Lake Haven, The Shed Coonabarabran, The Shed Online (Hawthorn West), The Shed Veterans & Community Wood Centre Inc. (Prospect Vale), The Tamworth Community Men's Shed, The Tatiara Men's Shed Inc., The Toogoolawah District Men's Shed Inc., The Traditional Tools Group Inc. (Lindfield), The Women's Powder Room Inc. (Forrestfield), The Woodwork and Craft Club Inc. (Currumbin Waters), Thirroul Men's Shed Inc., Thurgoona Men's Shed, Tilligerry Men's Shed Inc., Timboon Men's Shed Inc., Tin Can Bay Community & Men's Shed, Tingate's Men's Shed (Ballan), Tintinara Community Men's Shed, Tocumwal Men's Shed, Tongala Men's Shed, Toodyay Men's Shed, Toolangi Castella Men's Shed, Toongabbie and District Men's Shed Inc., Toowoomba City Men's Shed, Toronto Men's Shed, Torquay Community Men's Shed, Tottenham Men's Shed, Townsville Men's Shed, Trafalgar Men's Shed, Trangie Men's Shed Inc., Traralgon Men's Shed & Woodworking Inc., Traralgon South and District Assoc. Men's Shed, Trundle Men's Shed, Tudor Village Lilydale Men's Shed, Tuggeranong Men's Shed, Tullamarine Men's Shed, Tully and District Men's Shed Inc., Tumbarumba Men's Shed, Tumby Bay Men's Haven, Tumut & District Men's Shed Inc., Tuross Head Men's Shed, Tweed Heads Community Men's Shed, U3A Emerald Men's Shed, Ulladulla Men's Shed, Umina Beach Men's Shed, Umoona Tjutagku Health Service Aboriginal Corp Men's Shed (Coober Pedy), Upper Beaconsfield Men's Shed, Upper Hunter Men's Shed (Scone), Upper Ross PCYC Men's Shed (Rasmussen), Urunga Men's Shed, Venus Bay Tarwin Lower and District Men's Shed, Vermont Men's Shed, Veterans & Community Men's Shed (West Nowra) Inc., Veterans Support Group Men's Shed (Nerang), Victor Harbor Men's Shed, Victoria Park Men's Shed (Kensington), Villa Maria Base Camp Men's Shed (Wantirna), Village Bike Shed (Palm Beach), Vincent Men's Shed Inc. (North Perth), Waikerie Men's Shed, Walan-Budhang-Gibir (Griffith), Walcha Men's Shed Inc., Walgett Men's Shed Inc., Wallaga Lake - Bermagui Men's Shed, Wallamba District & Veterans Men's Shed Inc., Wallis Lake Men's Shed, Wallumbilla Community Men'shed Inc., Walpole Menshed, Wamuran & District Men's Shed, Wangaratta District Men's Shed, Wangi Men's Shed, Waratah-Mayfield Men's Shed, Waroona Community Men's Shed, Warracknabeal Men's Shed, Warradale Men's Shed, Warren Men's Shed, Warrnambool Men's Shed Inc., Warwick Men's Shed Inc., Wauchope Men's Shed, Waverley Community Men's Shed Inc., Waverley Woodworkers Inc., Wedderburn Men's Shed, Wee Waa Men's Shed Inc., Wellington Men's

Shed, Wendouree Men's Shed, Werribee Community Shed, Wesley Melba Men's Shed (Healesville), West Moonah Community Shed, West Winds Men's Shed (Woodbridge), Western Port Men's Shed (Hastings), WHAM Inc. Wingecarribee Health Association for Men Inc. (Bowral), Whitehorse Men's Shed (Box Hill), Whittlesea Men's Shed Inc., Whyalla Men's Shed Inc., William Kibby VC Veterans Shed (Warradale), Williamstown Men's Shed, Willo's Men's Shed Inc. (Willaston), Willoughby Community Men's Shed (Northbridge), Windale Men's Shed & Community Group Inc., Wingate Men's Shed (Ascot Vale), Wingham Men's Shed Inc., Winton Men's Shed, Wisemans Ferry Community Men's Shed, Wodonga Men's Shed, Wollondilly Community Men's Shed, Wongan-Ballidu & District Menshed Inc., Wonthaggi Men's Shed, Woodanilling Men's Shed Inc., Woodend Men's Shed Inc., Woodford and Region Men's Shed Inc. (WARMS), Woodgate Men's Shed Inc., Woodturners Society of Queensland Inc. (Greenslopes), Wyndham Men's Shed, Wynnum-Manly & Districts Men's Shed, Wynyard Community Men's Shed, Wyong Men's Shed, Yackandandah Men's Shed, Yarra Glen & District Men's Shed Inc., Yarra Men's Shed (Collingwood), Yarram Community Learning Centre Men's Shed, Yarrawonga Mulwala Men's Shed, Yass Valley Men's Shed Inc., YB Men's Shed (Yandina), Yea Men's Shed, Yelarbon Men's Shed Inc., Yeoval and District Men's Shed, Yeppoon Men's Shed, Yeronga Uniting Church Men's Shed, Yilgarn Men's Shed (Southern Cross), York Men's Shed.

Ireland: A.R.D. Men's Shed (Galway), Abbeyfeale Men's Shed, Abbeyleix Men's Shed, Allihies Men's Shed, An Bothan Glas na bhFear (Leitir Ceanainn - Letterkenny), An Seid Cumman na bhFear (Galway), An Tobar Men's Shed (Meath), Annascaul Men's Shed, Antrim Men's Shed, Ardara Men's Shed, Ards Peninsula Men's Shed (Down), Arklow Men's Shed, Armagh City Men's Shed, Ashbourne Men's Shed, Athboy Men's Shed, Athy Community Men's Shed, Bagenalstown Men's Shed, Baldoyle & District Men's Shed, Ballina Men's Shed, Ballinamore Men's Shed, Ballinasloe Men's Shed, Ballincollig Men's Shed, Ballinderreen Men's Shed (Kilkolgan), Ballingarry The Commons Men's Shed, Ballinrobe Men's Shed, Ballinskelligs Men's Shed, Ballisodare Men's Shed, Ballybay Men's Shed, Balbriggan Men's Shed, Ballybunion Men's Shed, Ballyduff Men's Shed, Ballyfermot Men's Shed, Ballygar Men's Shed, Ballyhaunis Men's Shed, Ballyheigue Men's Shed, Ballykelly Men's Shed, Ballyleague Men's Shed, Ballymote Men's Shed, Ballyroan Men's Shed, Baltinglass Men's Shed, Bandon Men's Shed, Bantry Men's Shed, Baunogues Men's Shed, Be Safe Be Well Men's Shed (Derry), Belmont Men's Shed, Bishopstown Senior Social Centre Men's Shed, Blanchardstown Men's Shed,

Blarney Men's Shed, Blessington Men's Shed, Borrisokane Men's Shed, Borrisoleigh Men's Shed, Bouncing Back Clubhouse Men's Shed (Dublin), Boyle Men's Shed, Bree Men's Shed, Broomfield Men's Shed, Bruff Men's Shed, Cahir Men's Shed, Cahirciveen Men's Shed, Callan Men's Shed, Carlow Men's Shed, Carndonagh Men's Shed Carn, Carrickmacross Men's Shed, Carrick on Shannon Men's Shed, Carrigaline Men's Shed, Carrigtwohill Men's Shed, Cashel Men's Shed, Castlebar Men's Shed, Castleblayney Men's Shed, Castlecomer Men's Shed, Castlefinn Men's Shed, Castlerea Men's Shed, Causeway Men's Shed, Cavan Town Men's Shed, Celbridge Men's Shed, Charleville Men's Shed, Cherry Orchard Men's Shed, Clane Men's Shed, Clara Men's Shed, Clarecastle Men's Shed, Claremorris Men's Shed, Clasp Men's Shed, Clonakilty Men's Shed, Clondalkin Men's Shed, Clondalkin Traveller Men's Shed, Clones Men's Shed, Clonmel Men's Shed, Cloughjordan Men's Shed, Cobh Men's Shed, Colin Area Men's Shed, Cooley Men's Shed, Corach Men's Shed (Wexford), Crann Go Beatha Men's Shed (Belfast), Croi na Gaillimhe Men's Shed, Cró na bhFear Maighcuilinn, Croom FRC Men's Shed, Cumann na bhFear (Galway), Cumman Men's Shed (Galway), D8 Men's Shed (Dublin), Derry Men's Shed, Donaghmede Men's Shed, Dooradoyle Raheen Men's Shed, Downpatrick Men's Shed, Drogheda Community Men's Shed, Dromore West Men's Shed, Dublin 12 Men's Shed Shedders, Dunboyne Men's Shed, Dundalk Community Men's Shed, Dungarvan Men's Shed, Dun Laoghaire Men's Shed, Dunlavin Men's Shed, Dunleer Men's Shed (Collon), Dunmanway Men's Shed, Dunmore Men's Shed, Dunshauglin Men's Shed, East Down Men's Shed (Downpatrick), East Wall Men's Shed (Dublin), Eastside Men's Shed (Galway), Edenderry Men's Shed, Edworthstown Men's Shed, Ennis Men's Shed, Enniscorthy Men's Shed, Enniscrone Men's Shed, Erris Men's Shed, Fermanagh Men's Shed, Fermoy Men's Shed, Glen, Ballyvolane & Dublin Hill Men's Shed (Blackpool), Glen Neiphin Men's Shed, Glounthaune Men's Shed, Gorey Men's Shed, Gort Men's Shed, Granard Men's Shed Group, Greater Shankill Men's Shed, Greystones Men's Shed, Harryville Men's Shed (Antrim), Headway Irishtown Men's Shed (Dublin), Holywood Men's Shed (Down), Hospital FRC Men's Shed (Limerick), Irish Wheelchair Association Men's Shed (Limerick), Kanturk Men's Shed, KC Men's Shed (Keel & Castlemaine), Kell's Men's Shed, Kenmare Men's Shed, Kilbeggan Men's Shed, Kilcloon Men's Shed, Kilcock Community Men's Shed, Kilcormac Men's Shed, Kilkenny Men's Shed, Kill Men's Shed, Killaloe/Ballina Men's Shed, Killarney Men's Shed, Killeshandra Men's Shed, Killorglin Men's Shed, Killybegs Men's Shed, Kilmacrenan Men's Shed, Kilmessan Men's Shed, Kilmore Men's Shed, Kilmovee Men's Shed, Kilrush Men's Shed, Kilturk Men's

Shed, Kinsale Men's Shed, Kylemore Men's Shed, LBS Men's Shed (Loughlinstown, Ballybrack & Shanganagh), Le Cheile Mallow Men's Shed, Le Cheile Men's Shed (Limerick City), Leighlin Parish Men's Shed, Letterkenny Men's Shed, Lifford/Clonleigh Men's Shed, Limerick City Men's Shed, Listowel Men's Shed, Loughshore Men's Shed (Belfast), Lyreacrompane Men's Shed, Maynooth Men's Shed, Meath Coast Men's Shed, Meenaneary Men's Shed, Meitheal Mara Men's Shed (Cork), Midleton Men's Shed, Millstreet Men's Shed, Mitchelstown Men's Shed, Moate Men's Shed, Mohill Men's Shed, Monaghan Men's Shed, Monsignor McCarthy Men's Shed (Westmeath), Mountmellick Men's Shed, Mountrath Men's Shed, Mountshannon Men's Shed, Moville Men's Shed, Moynalty Men's Shed, Mullaghmeen Men's Shed, Naas Men's Shed, Navan Men's Shed, Nenagh Men's Shed, New Ross Men's Shed, Newbridge Men's Shed, Newmarket & District Men's Shed, Newport Men's Shed, Newtown & Newcastle Men's Shed, North Belfast Community Men's Shed, North Down Community Hub Men's Shed (Bangor), North Leitrim Men's Shed, North Monaghan Men's Shed, Northside FRC Men's Shed (Limerick), Nutgrove & Loreto Men's Shed (Dublin), Omagh Men's Shed, Oranmore Men's Shed, Oughterard Men's Shed, Our Lady of Lourdes Men's Shed (Limerick), Portglenone Community Men's Shed, Portlaoise Community Men's Shed, Ports Community Men's Shed, Priorswood & District Men's Shed, Raphoe Men's Shed, Rathdowney Men's Shed, Ratoath Men's Shed, RCR Connamara Men's Shed, Rochfortbridge Men's Shed, Rosbeg and Portnoo Men's Shed, Roscommon Men's Shed, Roscommon Rural Men's Group, Roscrea Men's Shed, Rosemount Men's Shed, Rosslare Men's Shed, Rush Men's Shed, Sandyford Men's Shed, Shandon Men's Shed, Shannon FRC Men's Shed, Shannow Men's Shed, Sheephaven Men's Shed, Sixmilebridge Men's Shed, Skibbereen Men's Shed, Sligo Men's Shed, Sneem Men's Shed, Solas Men's Shed (Galway), South Armagh Men's Shed, South Tyrone Men's Sheds, Southill Men's Shed, Southside Travellers Men's Shed (Sandyford), St Judes Men's Shed Club (Templeogue), St Mary's Parish Men's Shed (Limerick), St Patricks Craft and Hobby Men's Shed (Limerick), St Josephs Court Men's Shed (Clifden), Steeple Antrim Men's Shed, Strabane & Lifford Men's Shed, Strokestown Men's Shed, Summerhill Men's Shed, SVP Tinahely Men's Shed, Swinford Men's Shed, Swords Men's Shed, Taghmon Men's Shed, Tallaght Men's Shed, Templemore Men's Shed, The Mill FRC Men's Shed (Urlingford). The Mojo Men's Shed (Tallaght), The Southend Shed (Wexford), Thurles Men's Shed, Tintern Men's Shed, Tipperary Men's Shed, Tralee Men's Shed, Tramore Men's Shed, Trim Men's Shed, Tuam Men's Shed, Tubbercurry Men's Shed, Tullacmongan Men's Shed, Tullow Men's Shed, Virginia Men's Shed, Waterford

Men's Shed, West Tallaght Men's Shed, Westport Men's Shed, Wicklow Men's Shed, Williamstown Men's Shed, Tralee Men's Shed, Youghal Men's Shed.

United Kingdom: All Hallows Shed (Ipswich), Andover Men's Shed, *Antrim Men's Shed, Ards Peninsula Men's Shed, (Ballywalter), Armagh City Men's Shed, Ballykelly Men's Shed,* Barrhead Men's Shed (Glasgow), Barrow-in-Furness Men in Sheds, *Be Safe Be Well Men's Shed (Dungiven),* Bede's World's Men's Shed (Jarrow), Bedford Men's Shed, Belfast (Inner) Men's Shed, Belfast (North) Community Men's Shed, Bishop Auckland Cree, Boat Bouys Shed (Gravesend), Bodgers Hut (Whitstable), Brentwood Men's Shed, Bridgend Men's Shed, Bristol Patchway Men's Shed, Brixham Men's Shed, Broadstairs Men's Shed, Buckingham Men's Shed, Camden Town Shed, Carmarthen Men's Shed, Carse Of Gowrie (Longforgan), Clydebank Men's Shed, Collingham Men's Shed, Colwyn Bay Men's Shed, Copnor Men's Shed (Portsmouth), *Crann Go Beatha Men's Shed (Belfast),* Crosshill, Dalbeattie Men's Shed, Dartford Men's Shed, Darwin Court Men's Shed (Southwark), Distington Men in Sheds, *Downpatrick Men's Shed,* Dumfries Men's Shed, Easterhouse Community Men's Shed, Eastleigh Southern Parishes Men's Shed, Eastbourne Men in Sheds, Faringdon Men's Shed, *Fermanagh Men's Shed,* Fizzpop Makerspace (Birmingham), Forfar & District Men's Shed (Angus), Forres Men's Shed, Freehold Community Men's Shed (Muswell Hill), Frome Men's Shed, Futures for Heroes Shed (Margate), Gala Men's Shed (Galashiels), Gerald's Room (Diss), Gosport Men's Shed, Halton Men's Shed, HAMESH (Havant), Hanley Park Men's Shed (Stoke-on-Trent), *Harryville Men's Shed*, Hartford Men in Sheds, Havant Men's Shed, *Holywood Men's Shed,* Horndean Ladies Shed (Waterlooville), Inverness Men's Shed, Inverurie and District Men's Shed, Jed Shed (Jedburgh), Kirby in Ashfield, *Loughshore Men's Shed,* Macmerry Men's Shed Edinburgh, Maidenhead Men's Shed, Maidstone Men's Shed, MakeItWorkshop Southport, Maldon Men's Shed, Manx Shed (Douglas), Market Drayton Men's Shed, Medway Men in Sheds (Gillingham), Men in a Workshop Cockermouth, Men in Sheds Ash (Surrey), Men in Sheds and Gardens Club (Colchester), Men in Sheds Aylesbury, Men in Sheds Bexley, Men in Sheds Blidworth, Men in Sheds Bolton (Breightmet), Men in Sheds Caterham, Men in Sheds Cheltenham & Gloucester, Men in Sheds Chester, Men in Sheds Congleton, Men in Sheds Crewe, Men in Sheds Daybrook, Men in Sheds Ellesmere Port, Men in Sheds Eltham, Men in Sheds Exeter, Men in Sheds High Wycombe, Men in Sheds Kendal, Men in Sheds Leeds, Men in Sheds Macclesfield, Men in Sheds Milton Keynes, Men in Sheds Nottingham City, Men in Sheds Oldham, Men in Sheds Penge, Men in Sheds Tiverton, Men in Sheds Woolwich, Men in Sheds Worksop, Men's Shed at Antrim, Men's Shed

Islington, Men's Shed Poole, Men's Shed Swindon, Men's Shed Merstham, Midlothian Community Men's Shed, Monklands Shed, Moray Men's Shed (Fochabers), MVS Poole, Nailsea Social Shedders, Newham Men's Shed, Newport Men's Shed, Newry & Mourne Men's Shed, Newton Aycliffe Cree, Northern Fells Group - Men's Shed (Caldbeck), *North Belfast Men's Shed,* Norwich Men's Shed, Oban Men's Shed, Old Portsmouth Shed, Pembroke Men's Shed, Percy Hedley Foundation Newcastle, Petworth Men's Shed, Poringland and District Men's Shed, *Portglenone Men's Shed*, Portsmouth Men's Shed, Prestatyn Men's Shed, Preston Tool Shed, Reading - The Silvers Workshop, Remake Scotland Crief, Rhayader Men's Shed, Rhyl Men's Shed, Sansaw Men's Shed (Hadnall), Shed Heaven - Grove Park (Lewisham), Sherwood Shed (Tunbridge Wells), Shettleston Men's Shed, Skills4holme (Holme), So Make It Shed (Southampton), *South Armagh Men's Sheds,* South Shields Men's Shed, *South Tyrone Men's Shed (Coal Island),* Southbourne Men's Shed, Spelthorne Men's Shed (Staines), Stapleford Men's Shed, *Steeple Antrim Men's Shed*, Strathkelvin Men's Sheds (Kirkintilloch), Stratford Upon Avon Men's Shed, Sundial Centre Men's Shed (Toer Hamlets), The Benarty Shed (Crosshill), The Men's Shed – Portland, The Repair Shed (Hemel Hempstead), The Shed Tameside (Dukinfield), The Shed, Melksham, The Tool Shed, Kinghorn, The Tools Shed (Skelmersdale), The Touch Wood Men's Shed (Wincanton) The Wee County Men's Shed (Tillicoultry), Torrington Men's Shed, Ventnor Shed, Waterlooville Men's Shed, Wellingborough Men's Shed, West Belfast Men's Shed, Westhill and District Men's Shed (Aberdeen), Wigan Men's Shed, Worthing Men's Shed, York Men in Sheds.

New Zealand: Aldred / St Albans Community Men's Shed (Christchurch), Alexandra Men's Shed, Amberley Menz Shed (North Christchurch), Ashburton Men's Shed, Bishopdale Men's Shed (Christchurch), Blenheim Menz Shed, Dannevirke Men's Shed, Devonport Clay Store Community Workshop (Auckland), Diamond Harbour Men's Shed, Eastbourne & Bays Men's Shed, Featherston Menz Shed, Halswell Men's Shed, Hamilton Community Men's Shed, Havelock Menz Shed (Marlborough), Henderson Community Men's Shed, Henley Men's Shed Inc. (Masterton), Kaikoura Men's Shed, Kawerau Community Menz Shed, Kerikeri Men's Shed, Levin Menz Shed, Linwood Menz Shed (Christchurch), Lyttelton Men's Shed, Manurewa Collaboration Station (Auckland), Massey Community Men's Shed (Auckland), Matamata Community Men's Shed, McIver's Oxford Community Men's Shed, Men's Shed NaeNae, Men's Shed North Shore (Auckland), Men's Shed Waimea (Nelson), Men's Shed Wanganui Inc., Menz Shed of Kaiapoi, MenzShed Kapiti Inc., Menzshed

Manawatu (Palmerston North), Menzshed Wellington, Motueka Menz Shed, New Brighton Menz Shed, North Taranaki Community Men's Shed (New Plymouth), Oamaru Community Workshops, Pauanui Community Menz Shed, Picton Men's Community Shed, Rangiora Menz Shed, Redcliffs Community Shed (Christchurch), Rolleston Men's Shed, Rotorua Community Menz Shed Trust, Rowley Community Men's Shed, South Dunedin Bloke's Shed, Taieri Bloke's Shed, Tapanui Men's Shed, Tapawera Men's Shed Inc., Taumarunui and Districts Community Menzshed, Taupo Community Men's Shed, Te Awamutu Community Men's Shed, Wainuiomata Menz Shed, Waiuku and District Community Workshop, Wellington City Menzshed, Whakatane Menz Shed, Whangarei Community Men's Shed.

Canada: Nechako Valley Historical Society Menshed, Okanagan Men's Shed, Woodhaven Shed. **Sweden:** Malmo Shed. **Denmark:** Mænds Mødesteder Stevns ('Men's Shed Stevns', Strøby).

APPENDIX 3 ARTICLES ABOUT MEN'S SHEDS, 1995-MARCH 2015

This Appendix (in Table 3b) contains a list of 103 published Men's Shed-related articles in the two decades to December 2014, sorted by year. Table 7 summarises the number of articles published in each year. A detailed analysis of this evidence base is included in Chapter 10. A small number of 2015 publications to March 2015 are included separately below the main table, as are several popular books in the same period about personal men's sheds.

The following key was used to allocate publication the 'Status' of each article, in Table 8, with the number of articles published in the two decades (1995-2014) indicated in brackets.

A   Published journal article (49: 20 were peer reviewed*)
B   Reports, book chapters or thesis (26)
C   Conference papers (13: 3 were peer reviewed*)
D   Evaluation documents (7)
E   Other (8).

The number below each article's Status is the number of times it has been cited on Google Scholar to May 5, 2015. This is a broad indication of the extent to which insights from the article have been incorporated into other articles, sometimes into other fields of study. Recent articles clearly have few or no citations.

The following key was used to allocate the main 'Focus' of each article, with the numbers of articles in the two decades indicated in brackets:

> C: Critical (11); L: Learning (25); D: Disability (12); H: Health (11); I: Indigenous (5); M: Management (5); S: Case Study (17); P: Program Evaluation (5); R: Literature Review (3); D: Data from multi-Shed Survey (1); O: Other (7).

Table 8 Men's Shed Articles by Year of Publication

Years	Articles	Years	Articles
1995	1	2007	13
1996		2008	14
1997		2009	7
1998	1	2010	4
1999		2011	6
2000		2012	13
2001	1	2013	16
2002		2014	19
2003		**Total 1995-2014**	**103**
2004	2		
2005	1	*2015*	*6*
2006	5		

Table 9 List of Men's Shed Articles 1995-2014, Sorted by Year

Authors	Publication Details	Focus, Type, Site	Year	Stat us * #
Earle, L., Earle T. & von Mering, O.	'Sheds and Male Retirement: A Place to go … and come back from', *Australasian 'Leisure for Pleasure' Journal*, 1 (1), 5-19. Reproduced in 1996, in L. Earle, *Successful Ageing in Australian Society*. Adelaide: Recreation for Older Adults Inc., Adelaide, 69-79.	O: Survey & interviews with male retirees, SA.	1995	A
Snashall, R.	'There's a Place for Us', *Community Link*, National Australia Bank, November, Issue 6, 21-23.	S: Shed case study, (Tongala) Victoria.	1998	B

Graves, K.	'Shedding the Light on "Men in Sheds': Report 2001. Bendigo: Community Health Bendigo.	S: Shed case study, (Bendigo) Victoria.	2001	D
Bettany, K.	'Alzheimer's Australia SA Support Backyard Sanctuaries for Men with Dementia', *50's Lifestyle*, 6, 38.	H: Professional experience, SA.	2004	A
O'Hehir, B.	'The "Men's Shed": A Practical Analysis of a Therapeutic Community Intervention Process into Men's Health'.	S: Shed Case study, NSW.	2004	E
Nelson, B.	'The Men's Shed Concept: Mateship and Meaningful Community Contribution', Paper to 3rd Elderly Suicide Prevention Network Conference, Parramatta.	S: Case study, Ashfield Shed, NSW.	2005	C
Dostine, J.	*Brimbank Men's Shed: Evaluation 2006.* Sunshine: UnitingCare Sunshine Mission.	S: Shed evaluation (Brimbank), Victoria.	2006	D
Golding, B.	'Shedding Light on New SpACEs for Older Men in Australia' *Quest* 1, 18-20 & 26.	L: Review Survey, 22 sheds, Australia.	2006	A 5
Golding, B.	'A Profile of Men's Sheds in Australia: Patterns, Purposes Profiles and Experiences of Participants: Some Implications for ACE and VET about Engaging Older Men', Paper to AVETRA Conference, Wollongong, 19-21 April.	D: Empirical, 22 Sheds, 2005 survey, Victoria.	2006	C* 4
Golding, B. & Harvey, J.	*Final Report on a Survey of Men's Sheds Participants in Victoria*, Report to Adult, Community and Further Education Board (plus Appendix) Ballarat: University of Ballarat.	D: Empirical, survey from 22 Sheds, Victoria.	2006	B 3
Hayes, R. & Williamson, M.	*Evidence-based, Best-practice Guidelines for Victorian Men's Sheds*, Report for Office of Senior Victorians, Bundoora: La Trobe University.	D: Review & Shed case studies, Victoria.	2006	B 3
Bruce, N.	'Community Men's Sheds: A New Zealand goal', *Adult and Community Education Newsletter*, December 2007, ACE Aotearoa.	D: Narrative summary of scope for Sheds, New Zealand.	2007	A
Donnelly, T. & van Herk, R.	*Setting up a Men's Shed.* Sydney: Lane Cove Men's Shed.	M: Shed Manual, Australia.	2007	B 3
Golding, B.	'Researching Men's Sheds in Community Contexts in Australia: What does it tell us about Adult Education for Older Men?' Paper to CASAE Adult Education Research Conference, Halifax, Nova Scotia, 6-9 June.	D: Survey & interviews, 24 Sheds, Australia.	2007	A
Golding, B., Brown, M. & Foley, A.	'Old Dogs, New Shed Tricks: An Exploration of Innovative, Workshop-based Learning Practice in Australia', Paper to AVETRA Conference, Melbourne 11-13 April.	L: Empirical. 24 Australian Sheds, survey & interview, 2006.	2007	C*
Golding, B. Brown, M., Foley, A., *et al.*	*Men's Sheds in Australia: Learning through Community Contexts.* Adelaide: NCVER, plus 'Support Document'.	D: Interviews & survey, multiple sites, Australia.	2007	A* 71
Golding, B.,	'The International Potential for Men's Shed-	L: Literature &	2007	A 9

Foley, A. & Brown, M.	based Learning', *Ad-lib: Journal for Continuing Liberal Adult Education*, 34, 9-13.	Shed survey data, 24 Sheds, Australia.		
Golding, B., Foley, A. & Brown, M.	'The Sharp End of the Stick: What Research tells us about Men's sheds in Australian Community Contexts', Paper to 2007 AMSA Conference, Manly, 12-14 September.	C: Interview & survey, 24 Sheds, Australia.	2007	C 4
Golding, B., Foley, A. & Brown. M.	'Shedding Some new Light on Gender: Evidence about Men's Informal Learning Preferences from Australian Men's Sheds in Community Contexts', Paper to SCUTREA Conference, The Queens University, Belfast, 3-5 July.	D: Shed interview & survey, 24 Sheds, Australia.	2007	C 10
Hayes, R. & Williamson, M.	*Men's Sheds: Exploring the Evidence for Best Practice*. Bundoora: La Trobe University.	D: Review & case studies, Victoria.	2007	B 10
Herron, A.	*It Opens up a Whole New World: Older People's Perceptions of the Role of the Creative Arts and Leisure in their Lives*, Master of Arts Thesis. Melbourne: Victoria University.	S: Bricollage, 2 case studies, one Shed.	2007	B
Morgan, M., Hayes, R., Williamson, *et al.*	'Men's Sheds: A Community Approach to Promoting Men's Health and Well-being', *International Journal of Mental Health Promotion*, 9 (3), 50-54.	H: Review, Australia.	2007	A* 18
Slade, J.	*Tales from the Shed: Collected Wit, Wisdom and Tales from the Creswick Men's Friendship Shed*. Creswick: Hepburn Health Services.	S: Shedder Anecdotes, Creswick, Victoria.	2007	E
Vallance, S. & Golding, B.	''They're Funny Bloody Cattle': Encouraging Rural Men to Learn', Paper to ALA Conference, Cairns, 8-10 Nov (published in *Australian Journal of Adult Learning*, 2008, 48 (2), 369-384).	L: Shed Practitioner & researcher narrative.	2007	A (A*)
Brown, M. Golding, B. & Foley, A.	'Out the Back: Men's Sheds and Informal Learning', *Fine Print*, 31 (2), 12-15.	L: Shed survey & interview data from 2006.	2008	A 4
Brown, M., Golding, B. & Foley, A.	'A Long and Winding Road: Autonomous Men's Learning through Participation in Community Sheds across Australia', Paper to SCUTREA Conference, Edinburgh, 2-4 July.	L: Mixed method, 24 Australian Sheds, 2006.	2008	C 2
Cass, Y., Fildes, D. & Marshall, C.	*3 in 1 Mature Men's Project Evaluation Results*, Report for Healthy Cities Illawarra.	P: Evaluation of some NSW Sheds, Mixed Method	2008	D
Foley, A., Golding, B. & Brown, M.	'Let the Men Speak: Health, Community, Friendship and Shed Therapy', Paper to AVETRA Conference, Adelaide, 3-4 April.	C: Interview & survey, 24 Sheds, Australia.	2008	C 2
Golding, B.	'Common Wealth through Community Men's Sheds: Lives and Learning Networks Beyond Work', Commonwealth Forum on Open Learning, London, 14-17 July.	L: Literature, Shed survey & interviews, Australia.	2008	A 1
Golding, B.	'Shedding Time: An Exploration of the Post-retirement Potential of Community Men's Sheds in Australia,' Paper to Australasian Occupational Sciences Symposium, La	O: Empirical, Survey & interviews, 24 Sheds,	2008	A

	Trobe University, 13-14 November.	Australia.		
Golding, B.	'Researching Men's Sheds in Community Contexts in Australia: What does it Suggest about Education for Older Men,' *Journal of Adult and Continuing Education*, 14 (1), 17-33.	L: Shed interviews & survey, 2006, Australia.	2008	A* 7
Golding, B.	'Men, Boys and School: A Shed-based Learning Perspective', Paper to National Boys' Education Conference, Parramatta, 12-14 October.	L: Interview & survey, 2003-7, men, including shedders, Australia.	2008	C
Golding, B. & Foley, A.	'How Men are Worked with: Gender Roles in Men's Informal Learning', Paper to SCUTREA Conference, Edinburgh, 2-4 July.	L: Literature & Shed survey, Australia.	2008	A 8
Golding, B., Foley, A. & Brown. M.	'Shedding School Early: Insights from School and Community Shed Collaboration in Australia,' Paper to AVETRA Conference, Adelaide, 3-4 April.	L: Survey & interview, 24 sheds, Australia.	2008	C* 1
Golding, B., Kimberley, H., Foley, A. *et al.*	'Houses and Sheds in Australia: An Exploration of the Genesis and Growth of Neighbourhood Houses and Men's Sheds in Community Settings', *Australian Journal of Adult Learning*, 48 (2), 237-262.	C: Literature review, Australia.	2008	A* 21
Martin, K., Wicks, A. & Malpage, J.	'Meaningful Occupation at the Berry Men's Shed', *Journal of Occupational Science*, 15 (3), 194-195.	S: Case study, Australia.	2008	A* 6
Misan, G.	*Men's Sheds: A Strategy to Improve Men's Health*, Report to Mensheds Australia: Whyalla: Spencer Gulf Rural Health School.	L: Literature review & consultation, some NSW, Vic & SA Sheds.	2008	B 3
Thomson, M.	'Mark Thomson Talking about Shed Culture'. *Journal of Occupational Science* 15 (3), 190-193.	O: Narrative, Backyard sheds.	2008	A
Ballinger, M. Talbot L. & Verrinder, G.	'More than a Place to do Woodwork: A Case Study of a Community-based Men's Shed', *Journal of Men's Health*, 6 (1), 20-27.	S: Empirical, case study, Australia.	2009	A* 39
DPCD	*Men's Shed Program 2009-10*. Melbourne: Department of Planning and Community Development, Victoria.	M: Guidelines for Shed project funding.	2009	E
Golding, B.	'Older Men's Lifelong Learning: Common Threads/sheds', in J. Field, J., Gallacher, J. & R. Ingram, *Researching transitions in lifelong learning*. London: RoutledgeFalmer, pp. 65-75.	L: Literature, Australia.	2009	B 8
Golding, B.	'Summary of Evidence about the Problematic Role of Mensheds Australia', Ballarat: University of Ballarat.	C: Document review.	2009	E
McMillan, B.	*Community Men's Sheds: A Commentary*, Report for Rowley Resource Centre, Christchurch.	R: Literature review, NZ.	2009	B
Misan, G. & Sergeant, P.	'Men's Sheds: A Strategy to Improve Men's Health', Paper to 10th National Rural Health Conference, Cairns, 17-20 May.	H: Literature and Shed interviews, Australia.	2009	C 17
Sargeant, P.	'Men's Sheds: A Catalyst for Indigenous Men's Health', Paper to National Rural Health Conference, Cairns, 17-20 May.	H: Action research by Mensheds	2009	C 2

		Australia.		
Bruce, N.	'Fresh SHED Insights from Afar: Community Men's Sheds from NZ to Australia, England and Scotland 2009 supported by Winston Churchill Fellowship', Report on Men's Sheds.	D: Review of Sheds from study tour 2009.	2010	E
Fremantle (Project team)	*Men's Shed Health and Wellbeing Project*, Men's Advisory Network & Fremantle Community Men's Shed.	P: Evaluation of Shed-based mental health pilot, WA.	2010	D
Fildes, D., Cass, Y., Wallner, F. *et al.*	'Shedding Light on Men: The Building Healthy Men Project', *Journal of Men's Health*, 7 (3), 233-240.	P: Action research with culturally diverse men.	2010	A* 11
Morgan, N.	'A Room of their Own: Men's Sheds Build Communities of Support and Purpose', *Crosscurrents*, 13 (4), 12-13.	O: Short review, two expert interviews.	2010	A 5
Ormsby, J., Stanley, M. & Jaworski, K.	'Older Men's participation in Community-based Men's Sheds Programmes', *Health and Social Care in the Community*, 18 (6), 607–613.	O: Empirical, interviews, 2 Adelaide Sheds, 2007.	2010	A* 28
Bulman, J. & Hayes, R.	'Mibbinbah and Spirit Healing: Fostering Safe, Friendly Spaces for Indigenous Males in Australia', *International Journal of Men's Health* 10 (1), 6-26.	I: Action research, Australia.	2011	A*
Golding, B.	'Shedding ideas about older men's learning', *Lifelong Learning in Europe*, 2, 119-124.	L: Literature.	2011	A
Golding, B.	'Thinking inside the box: What can we learn from the men's shed movement', *Adults Learning*, 22 (8), 24-27.	L: Literature.	2011	A
Golding, B.	'Older Men's Wellbeing through Community Participation in Australia', *International Journal of Men's Health* 10 (1) pp. 26-44.	H: Empirical, Men's sheds one of 6 Australian organisation types.	2011	A* 13
Golding, B.	'Older Men's Learning through Age-related Community Organisations in Australia', *International Journal of Education and Ageing*, 1 (3), 237-252.	L: Literature.	2011	A*
Golding, B.	'Men's Informal Learning and Wellbeing Beyond the Workplace', in S. Jackson, *Innovations in Lifelong Learning*. London: Routledge, 67-86.	L: Literature (pp.72-3 about men's sheds). Australia.	2011	B
Reynolds, K.	*The Processes of Involvement of Older Male Adults in Men's Sheds Community Programs*, M.A. Thesis, Manitoba: University of Manitoba.	O: Interviews & survey in 'men's spaces', Canada.	2011	B 2
AMSA	*How to Start/Run a Men's Shed*, Windale: Australian Men's Shed Association.	M: Shed Manual, Australia.	2012	E
Beckley, D.	*The Development of the Mosman Park Community Shed.*	S: Case study, timelines & photos.	2012	B
Bevan, M.	'Social Return on Investment: Lane Cove Men's Shed', UnitingCare, Sydney.	S: Empirical, One Shed, 2011 data.	2012	D

Cavanagh, J. McNeil, N., Bartram, T. *et al.*	'An Exploratory Study of the Factors that Promote Indigenous and Non-Indigenous Member's Participation in Australian Men's Sheds', *Journal of Australian Indigenous Issues*, 15 (1), 50-63.	I: Interviews, Indigenous shedders, one Shed, Australia.	2012	A*
Dubbo	*A Shed Load of Stories: From the Dubbo Community Men's Shed*, Dubbo Community Men's Shed, Dubbo.	S: Anecdotes from shedders, Dubbo, NSW.	2012	E
Glover, K. & Misan, G.	'Men Together: Questions of Men's Experience in Sheds', *New Male Studies*, 1 (2), 63-73.	C: Literature.	2012	A
Golding, B.	'Men's Sheds, Community Learning and Public Policy', in M. Bowl *et al.*, *Gender masculinities and lifelong learning*. London: Routledge, 122-133.	L: Literature & Shed data review.	2012	B 1
Healthbox CIC	'Men in Sheds Programme Health Evaluation', Age UK Healthbox.	E: Programme evaluation, UK.	2012	D
La Trobe	*The Australian Men's Shed Association (AMSA) Evaluation*, Report to Department of Health and Ageing. Bundoora: Latrobe University.	P: Evaluation, Mixed method. Survey of 209 Sheds, Australia.	2012	D
McNeil, N., Cavanagh, J., Bartram, T. *et al.*	'Identifying Barriers to Building Organisational Capacity: A Study of an Indigenous Men's Shed', *Health Issues* 109, 17-20.	I: Indigenous Shed, one case study, Australia.	2012	A 1
Milligan, C., Payne, S., Bingley, A. *et al.*	*Evaluation of the Men in Sheds Pilot Program*, Report to Age UK, Lancaster: Lancaster University.	P: Program evaluation, Mixed method, interviews, 3 Sheds, UK.	2012	D
Patton, R., Geary, M. & Watson, J.	'Men's Health in Banyule', *Health Issues*, 109, 21-23.	S: One Shed narrative (Banyule), Victoria.	2012	A
Shann, C.	'Strengthening Men's Health and Wellbeing through Community Sheds', *InPsych*, August 2012.	H: Literature-based, Australia.	2012	A
Carragher, L.	*Men's Sheds in Ireland: Learning through Community Contexts*. Dundalk: Dundalk Institute of Technology.	D: Survey (30 Sheds) & observation, Ireland.	2013	B 3
Cavanagh, J. & Bartram, T.	'Confronting Social Determinants of Aboriginal and Torres Strait Islander Men's Health and Well-being', *Journal of Australian Indigenous Issues*, 16 (3), 51-65.	I: Sheds & Men's Groups.	2013	A*
Cavanagh, J., McNeil, N. & Bartram, T.	'The Australian Men's Sheds Movement: Human Resource Management in a Voluntary Organisation', *The Asia Pacific Journal of Human Resources*, 51 (3), 292-306.	M: Qualitative case study, 3 Sheds, 1 Queensland, 2 Victoria.	2013	A* 4
Cordier, R. & Wilson. N.	'Community-based Men's Sheds: Promoting Male Health, Wellbeing and Social inclusion in an International Context', *Health Promotion International* (on line)	H: Survey to sheds, Australia.	2013	A* 3
Fildes, D., Pember, B., Pitts, L. *et al.*	'The Coniston Men's Shed: More than just a Place to Play with Wood!' Paper to National Men's Health Gathering, Ballarat, 27-29	S: Overview of one Shed, Wollongong,	2013	C

	October, University of Wollongong.	NSW.		
Flood, P. & Blair, S.	*Men's Sheds in Australia: Effects on Physical Health and Mental Well-being*, Ultrafeedback, report to beyondblue, Melbourne, plus Appendices.	D: Quasi-experiment; 17 interviews & survey, Shed & non-Shed men, 2,636 returns, Australia.	2013	B
Milligan, C., Dowrick, C., Payne, S., *et al.*	*Men's Sheds and other Gendered Interventions for Older Men: Improving Health and Wellbeing through Social Activity: A Systematic Review and Scoping of the Evidence Base*. Lancaster: Lancaster University.	L: Comprehensive review of literature.	2013	B
Milligan, C., Payne, S., Bingley, A. *et al.*	*Evaluation of the Men in Sheds Pilot Programme*: Final report to Age UK. Lancaster: Lancaster University.	P: Evaluation of three pilot Sheds, England.	2013	D
Moylan, M., Carey, L., Blackburn, R. *et al.*	'The Men's Shed: Providing Biophysical and Spiritual Support', *Journal of Religious Health*, 221-234.	H: interviews, one Melbourne Shed.	2013	A* 1
Porat, D.	'Redefining a Grassroots indicator of Success Among Community Men's Sheds in Australia: An Exploration, New Community', *A Quarterly Journal*. 11 (4).	C: Observation & interviews, 3 Melbourne Sheds.	2013	A
Reynolds, K., Mackenzie, C. Medved, M. *et al.*	'The Experiences of Older Male Adults throughout their Involvement in a Community Program for Men', *Ageing and Society*, 12, 1-21.	S: Interviews, One Shed, Manitoba, Canada.	2013	A*
Sunderland, J.	*The Taieri Blokes Shed: An Ethnographic Study*, M. Occupational Therapy thesis. Dunedin: Otago Polytechnic.	S: Ethnographic, One Shed.	2013	B
Wicks, A.	'A Transactional Review of Shedding at the Berry Men's Shed' in M. Cutchin & V. Dickie', *Transactional Perspectives on Occupation*. Dordrecht: Springer, 119-132.	S: One shed (Berry) Case study, NSW.	2013	B
Wilson, G.	*Men's Shed Men*, Sun Fly Printing.	D: Men's Shed case studies, including men, photos & art, Victoria.	2013	B
Wilson, N. Cordier, R. & Wilson Whaley, L.	'Older Male Mentors of a Men's Shed Intergenerational Mentoring Program', *Australian Occupational Therapy Journal*.	L: School wood workshop, men & boys, Australia	2013	A* 4
Wilson. N. & Cordier, R.	'A Narrative Review of Men's Sheds Literature: Reducing Social Isolation and Promoting Men's Health and Well-being', *Health and Social Care in the Community*, 21 (5), 451-463.	R: Literature review.	2013	A* 20
Carragher, L., Evoy, J. & Mark, R.	'Men's Learning in Ireland', in B. Golding, R. Mark & A. Foley (Eds.), *Men Learning through Life*. Leicester: NIACE, 148-163.	L: Literature & Shed case studies, Ireland.	2014	B
Cavanagh, J., McNeil, N. & Bartram, T.	'Step inside the Shed', *HR Monthly*, pp. 37-39.	O: Research narrative.	2014	A
Cavanagh, J.,	'The Role of Collaborative Learning on	L: Shed case	2014	A* 1

Southcombe, A. & Bartram, T.	Training and Development Practices within the Australian Men's Shed movement: A Study of Five Men's Sheds', *Journal of Vocational Education and Training*, 66 (3), 365-385.	studies (5), 3 Australian states.		
Cordier, R. & Wilson, N.	'Mentoring at Men's Sheds: An International Survey about a Community Approach to Health and Cell-being,' *Health and Social Care in the Community*, 22 (3), 249-258.	M: Survey, 14 Sheds that do informal mentoring, Australia.	2014	A* 4
Dryden, S.	*A Cross Cultural Study Exploring Structural Factors of Men's Sheds*, Honours Thesis, Paper 2431, Kalamazoo: Western Michigan University.	R: Not sighted. Descriptive, cross-cultural study.	2014	B
Felix, J.	'A Place Worth Exploring', *Manspace*, 82-83.	O: Interview-based article.	2014	A
Ford, S., Scholz, B. & Lu, V.	'Social Shedding: Identification and Health of Men's Shed Users', *Health Psychology*.	H: Not sighted. Survey, 322 shed users, Australia.	2014	A
Golding, B.	'Men's Learning in Later Life: Floating the Idea of *Shedagogy'*, Paper to ESREA Older Learners Network Conference, Valetta, Malta, 22-24 Oct.	C: Literature-based.	2014	A
Golding, B.	'Men's Learning: The Conviviality of Men's Sheds', *Fine Print*, 7-11.	L: Literature-based, International.	2014	A
Golding, B.	'Older Men's Learning and Conviviality', in Schmidt-Hertha, B., Krasovek, S. & Formosa, M. *Learning Across Generations in Europe*. Rotterdam: Sense, 23-34.	C: Literature-based, International.	2014	B
Golding, B.	'Men's Sheds: A New Movement for Change', in Golding, B., Mark, R., & Foley, A. (Eds.) *Men Learning through Life*, Leicester: NIACE, 113-130.	C: Literature, Australia.	2014	B
Golding, B. & Harvey, J.	*Survey of Australian Men's Sheds*, Report to Australian Men's Sheds Association, Tertiary Tracks and Federation University Australia. Ballarat.	D: Empirical, Survey data, 287 Australian Sheds.	2014	B
Golding, B. & McDonald, J.	'Researching Older Men's Self-directed Learning in Australia', Paper to Symposium of Self-Directed Learning, Strasbourg, France, 29-31 0ctober.	C: Literature-based, Shed focus, Australia.	2014	A
Hansji, N., Wilson, N. & Cordier, R.	'Men's Sheds: Enabling Environments for Australian Men Living with and without Long-term Disabilities', *Health and Social Care in the Community*.	H: 12 interviews with shedders with long-term disabilities, Australia.	2014	A*
Mark, R. & Soulsby, J.	'Men's Learning in the UK', in Golding, B., Mark, R., & Foley, A. (Eds.) *Men Learning through Life*. Leicester: NIACE, 131-147.	L: Literature, Includes Sheds, pp.139-41.	2014	B
McGrail, K.	*A Cross-cultural Study Exploring Structural Factors of Men's Sheds*, Honours Thesis, Paper 2441, Kalamazoo: Western Michigan University.	L: Not sighted, USA.	2014	B
Sheehan, P.	*An Exploration into the Popularity of Men's Sheds*, BA (Hons.) Thesis, Waterford	L: Literature & qualitative	2014	B

	Institute of Technology, Waterford.	research, Interviews, one Shed.		
Southcombe, A., Cavanagh, J. & Bartram, T.	'Capacity Building in Indigenous Men's Groups and Sheds across Australia', *Health Promotion International*.	I: Qualitative, 15 men's groups & Sheds, Australia.	2014	A
Volunteer Centre Borders	*Men's Sheds in the Scottish Borders: A Framework for Development. Scotland.*	C: Planning document.	2014	E
Wilson, N., Cordier, R., & Wilkes-Gillan, L.	Men's Sheds and Mentoring Programs: Supporting Teenage Boys' Connection with School. *International Journal of Men's Health*, 13 (2), 92-100.	L: Interviews, 4 teenage boys, Shed, Australia.	2014	A*
	Published Men's Shed-related Articles, 2015 (to March)			
Milligan, C., Payne, S., Bingley, A. *et al.*	'Place and Wellbeing: Shedding Light in Activity Interventions for Older Men', *Ageing and Society*, 35 (1), (published on line Aug 2013).	P: Program evaluation, Mixed method, 3 Sheds, UK.	2015	A*
md consulting	*Learning about Community Capacity Building from the Spread of Men's Sheds in Scotland. Dungarven: md consulting.*	B: Scoping study, 42 Sheds, Scotland.	2015	B
Schroeder, J, Sowden, J. & Watt, J.	*Social Return on Investment: The Westhill and District Men's Shed*, Scotland, Scottish Men's Sheds Association.	S: Case study, one Scottish Men's Shed.	2015	R
Carragher, L. * Golding, B.	'Older Men as Learners: Irish Men's Sheds as an Intervention', *Adult Education Quarterly*, 1-17, On line.	D: Irish empirical research, 30 Men's Sheds, Ireland.	2015	A*
Golding, B. & Carragher, L.	'Community Men's Sheds and Informal Learning: An Exploration of their Gendered Roles', in J. Ostrouch-Kaminska & C. Vieira, *Private World(s): Gender and Informal Learning of Adults*. Rotterdam: Sense Publishers.	C: Australian & Irish empirical research from multiple Men's Sheds.	2015	B
Milligan, C, Neary, D., Payne, S. *et al.*	Older Men and Social Activity: A Scoping Review of Men's Sheds and other Gendered Interventions, *Aging and Society*, 1-29.	R: Critical review of 31 Men's Sheds papers.	2015	A*

KEY: * 'Status' and # Google Scholar citation frequency are defined in the introduction above the table.

Articles about Personal Men's Sheds

Although six popular books produced about backyard men's sheds before 2005 were relatively superficial, they were widely read by and influenced many community Men's Shedders. All were largely pictorial, produced for popular readership, focusing on individual men in New Zealand, the UK and Australia.

- Mark Thomson's paperback books included high quality black and white photographs about Australian men and their individual sheds (*Blokes and Sheds*, 1995; *The Complete Blokes and Sheds: Stories from the Sheds*, 1996; *Makers Breakers and Fixers: More Men and their Sheds*, 2007). They include an accompanying short narrative about each backyard shed and one shedder. None of Thomson's work has covered community men's sheds or aspects of the subsequent community shed movement, in Australia or elsewhere. Mark Thomson provided some useful advice for the current book.
- Jim Hopkins and Julie Riley's *Blokes and Sheds* (1998) was produced in New Zealand in a similar format to that used by Thomson.
- Gordon Thorburn's *Men and Sheds* was produced in the UK in 2002, based on backyard sheds in the UK in a similar format to that used by Thomson.
- Gareth Jones' *Shed Men* was published in the UK in 2004, based on photographs and text of backyard sheds.
- Jasper White published *Man Caves* in 2014, a full colour, pictorial account of personal men's sheds in eastern Australia, with very few words.
- Simon Griffiths produced *Shed* in 2014, featuring full colour photographs and brief words about 40 personal and historic southeastern Australian sheds and one Men's Shed (in Kyneton, Victoria).

There are a number of popular magazines published in Australia, the UK and the US that deal specifically with personal sheds, garages, 'men's dens' and 'man caves', Some of these magazines now regularly include stories or case studies of community Men's Sheds. A good example is the quarterly *Manspace Magazine*, published in Australia.[1]

---

[1] Manspace Magazine, www.manspacemagazine.com.au, Accessed 10 March, 2015.

APPENDIX 4 AUSTRALIAN MEN'S SHED 'HALL OF FAME' RECIPIENTS

In 2013 the Australian Men's Shed Association formally acknowledged the following 'Hall of Fame' recipients 'in honour of their outstanding contributions to the development of Men's Sheds and the Association'[2].

> Ted Donnelly, New South Wales; Professor Barry Golding, Victoria; Bill Johnstone, Fremantle, Western Australia; Frank Doolan (Riverbank Frank), Dubbo, New South Wales; Gary Green, Orbost, Victoria/Tasmania; Graeme Curnow, Queensland; Ivan Armstrong, New South Wales; John Waters, Bridgewater, Tasmania; Lyn Kinder, Brimbank, Victoria; (Late) Len Wallace, Grenfell, New South Wales; Ray Cawthorne, Grenfell, New South Wales; Roger Greenan, Windale, New South Wales; Ron Mitchell, Victoria; Ruth van Herk, Lane Cove, New South Wales; Stuart Holmes, Nambucca, New South Wales.

This honour was specifically bestowed:

> ... on those who have demonstrated a commitment and passion for the men's shed movement, are strong advocates for the shed movement, may have pioneered initiatives for the benefit of their communities and the greater shed movement, may have assisted other sheds to develop by providing advice and support and perhaps played key roles in the development of the State and National Associations.

Ted Donnelly and Barry Golding were acknowledged, in 2011 and 2013 respectively, with the *Ted Donnelly Award*, for their 'Outstanding Contribution to the Shed Movement'.

---

[2] The inaugural AMSA 'Hall of Fame' recipients were announced by the AMSA Board Chairman, Mr Kevin Callinan, at the 5th National Conference in Ballarat, Victoria in 2013.